NORTH CAROLINA
STATE BOARD OF COMMUNITY COLLEGES
LIBRARIES
NASH COMMUNITY COLLEGE

D1112824

THE ENGLISH YEOMAN

The English Yeoman

Under Elizabeth and the
Early Stuarts

BY

MILDRED CAMPBELL

Reprints of Economic Classics
AUGUSTUS M. KELLEY Publishers
New York 1968

© Mildred Campbell 1942, 1960, 1968

This edition published by
AUGUSTUS M. KELLEY,
24 East 22nd Street
New York, New York 10010

Made and printed in Great Britain

PREFACE TO FIRST EDITION

MANY people have helped in many ways in the preparation of this book, making acknowledgment a difficult, albeit a pleasant task. One characteristic of modern American scholarship is the practice which flourishes in many graduate schools whereby scholars learn to be mindful of the work of their fellows and generous in passing on clues or bits of information. More than one nice morsel has come my way because Mary Frear, Elisabeth Kimball, T. C. Caldwell, T. C. Mendenhall, William Willcox, or Hartley Simpson and Wallace Notestein—for at Yale the practice extends to the professorial staff—took the trouble to note a reference to yeomen encountered in their own researches. I am grateful to all of them.

Many people not in the historical field had a hand in helping me search out materials. Two friends who permitted a summer's motoring in England to be turned into an expedition devoted largely to tracking down local manuscript collections gave me a start in that field. Later, upon my return to these, many of the local residents, country vicars, professional men and women, and families long connected with their communities gave generously of their time to put me in touch with materials I should not otherwise have found. I should like to mention them all by name but the list would grow too long. I do wish, however, to express my gratitude to three groups in which many of them are included: the honorary secretaries and their assistants in the local historical societies whose splendid work of collecting and preserving local documents deserves appreciation from every student of history; the local officials, town clerks, and clerks of the peace in county councils, who spared no pains to make available to me the records of parish, town, and shire that were in their custody; and finally, the local librarians, particularly those in a number of county towns through whose efforts the public library is being built into a repository for local manuscripts that is of no mean import. I owe a great deal to the courtesy and helpfulness of each of these groups.

A word of thanks must also go to several individuals for assistance in regard to certain particulars: Mr. Burnet Morris for permission to use the excellent bibliography of Devon materials that he has compiled over a period of years; Mrs. Frances Rose-Troup for the use of the manuscripts in her collection; Mr. and Mrs. L. G. Cruwys for permission to use the Elizabethan manuscripts in the muniment room at Cruwys Morchard; Mr. W. B. Crump, whose able work I have acknowledged elsewhere, for information regarding the seventeenth-century homes of yeomen still standing in the Huddersfield district; Mr. F. A. Bailey for the care he took to identify the yeomen in the Prescott court records which he has since edited; my Sussex friends, Mr. J. Heneage Kelsey and Mrs. Kelsey, for permission to photograph the Marchaunt diary now in their possession; and Mr. Guy Parsloe of the Institute of Historical Research, who has given advice and assistance to so many American scholars in London.

Nor could the work of gathering materials have gone far forward without the facilities of several centers of research. I wish, therefore, to express my thanks to the staff and attendants of the British Museum, particularly to those in the Manuscripts Division, and to the staff and attendants of the Public Record Office for their readiness to help put me in touch with the materials I needed. I wish also to acknowledge the courtesy extended me at the University Library in Cambridge, the John Rylands Library in Manchester, and the National Library of Wales; and by the directors and staff of the Huntington Library in this country. I am particularly indebted to the staff of the Yale University Library for assistance during the early period of my work and on frequent occasions since; and to Miss Fanny Borden and the staff of the Vassar College Library for providing facilities for my work that have made the completion of the manuscript an easier and pleasanter task than it could otherwise have been.

For suggestions and criticisms of the completed manuscript I am deeply grateful to several scholars who gave generously of their time and expert knowledge to that task, though, needless to say, whatever faults still remain are the responsibility of the author alone. Edwin F. Gay kindly consented to read chapters iii, iv, and v, and offered valuable suggestions. My colleagues, Violet Barbour and Louise Fargo Brown, read the entire manuscript and gave helpful criticism from their store of knowledge of the seventeenth century. Elizabeth Parnham Brush of Rockford College, whose insight and critical skill I long ago learned to value, also read the entire manuscript and gave discriminating suggestions regarding both form and content. I owe thanks to Evalyn A. Clark, another colleague, for seeing me through the trying weeks of bibliography making, indexing, etc., often at the cost of interruption to her own work. I am indebted to Charles M. Andrews for helpful suggestions during the early period of my work and for emphasizing the need for such a study in the field of American colonial history. Finally, I owe more than I can easily express to Wallace Notestein, whose ability to make the study of history exciting to graduate students is matched only by his assistance and encouragement to those who later seek themselves to turn historian.

In the exacting task of preparing the manuscript for the press, I have had the aid of Leonard W. Labaree, editor of the Yale Historical Series, whose able assistance, friendly advice, and good stock of patience I wish to acknowledge. Lastly I desire to express my thanks to the faculty and Corporation of Yale University. A part of this study was submitted as a doctoral dissertation in 1932 and it was through subsequent grants of a Sterling Fellowship for the years 1935–37 that the research for it was carried forward in England.

Again in the summer of 1939 I was in England for a final checking of references, working at the Public Record Office until that late August afternoon when by order of His Majesty's Government readers in the Round Room were informed that the doors would not open the next morning. For several days past we had seen great paper-bound bundles being let down from upper-story windows to waiting lorries below, and knew their ominous meaning when a request for Subsidy Rolls and the State Papers brought this response from the attendant, attempting to hide his feelings in a show of gaiety: "Sorry, Miss, they're on 'oliday in the country." A few days later World War II was upon us.

The manuscript for the book was already complete except for revision of form and arrangement. It was the Age of Elizabeth and James I, of the Puritan Migration and Colonial Settlement that had provided its focus, and to relate a story of that period was its purpose. Not until it had some months been laid aside and was brought out for final revision in the summer and fall of 1940 did I think of it in particular in relation to the present. If others see in the story of the yeomen a part of that heritage which proved its mettle in the perilous Battle of Britain, it will be but another piece of evidence of the way in which the past helps to shape the course of a people's behavior. By the same token it may be observed that it is not alone the needs and dangers of the moment that have placed America's sons beside those of Britain in this struggle of "good and lawful men" to protect the rights they hold dear. Theirs is a common heritage. For among those men who three centuries ago went down to the sea in ships, bound for New England, Virginia, and other westward ports, were thousands of English yeomen and the sons of yeomen. They carried little silver in their pockets, but were freighted withal with rich possessions: a love of freedom, a sense of the dignity of the individual, in short, a scale of values that took aeep root and flourished in the New World in a soil that was to its liking.

M. C.

Yonder Hills,
Grandview, Tennessee.
September 5, 1942

PREFACE TO ENGLISH EDITION

When this book was written, two contemporary developments were noted in the Introduction as likely to affect future historical writing in England; namely, "the opening up in recent years of vast collections of historical sources hitherto inaccessible"—a reference to the large collections that were being added to local archives and their greater accessibility—and "the emergence of social history from the plane of the dilettante to that of the trained investigator." It was suggested that on the basis of these developments new centers of interest would likely emerge and old ones be redefined. The forecast was good as far as it went. But if one were then able to sense somewhat the shape of things to come, their extent and specific character were not so easily anticipated. It is now possible again to take stock.

The enlarging and perfecting of local archives has gone on apace. A county such as Wiltshire where even public documents like the Quarter Sessions records were either entirely closed to the student or else hedged about with restrictions that made their use wellnigh prohibitive, has now its trained archivist and a record office with every facility for the researcher. Essex, to take another example, with excellent work on its documents even then underway, has since so increased the number of its records and so augmented every aspect of its work as to become the envy of other local archives and a model for them.

Even more significant in some ways has been the development of new approaches and techniques whereby social history has indeed become the recognized province of the trained investigator. Whether Professor Tawney's reputed advice to scholars "to lay aside their books in favour of their boots" was given in those words or as another version has it, that "it is not more documents but stouter boots" that are wanted, I do not know. But the intent is clear, and that it has been advice well heeded is evident in much of the social and economic history now being written. In the original bibliographical note appended to this book, the work of C. S. and C. S. Orwin was singled out for its fresh approach in attacking the problem of the open fields from the point of view of the practical farmer with emphasis on the physical features of the land, rather than along conventional legal and institutional lines. This method has now become the usual one for dealing with the history of the land, the village, and other aspects of rural life. The boots are indeed being effectively used, not to replace the documents, a thing never intended, but to give them new and fuller meaning.

The historian has, moreover, in recent years formed a closer alliance with experts in other disciplines. He may discover that it is an archaeologist who will prove most helpful to him in a given study. Again, it may be the findings or the techniques of the anthropologist, statistician, philologist or architect that will serve him best. He does not (or should not) forsake his old friends, the theologues, philosophers, poets and playwrights, but a host of new allies have proved their worth.

Studies in Elizabethan and Stuart England, bearing the imprint of these influences, are providing additional materials for a better understanding of the whole social structure and of every group in it. More is now known of the economic depressions and the periods of upswing under which people lived and worked. Population trends and land distribution are being effectively studied. More is known about prices, rents, and wages; and, something though not yet nearly enough, about the mobility of labor. These studies have greatly amplified and enriched many of the materials with which this book deals. On the whole they have strengthened rather than altered its basic arguments and conclusions. Best of all, several studies have been made of yeomen in specific localities. W. G. Hoskins, a great forwarder of the "boots theory" who is teaching a whole generation how to study local history, says of England, that "it may be a small country, but no country in the world has such diversity of soils, climates, natural resources and topography in such small space." It was these very things—soil, resources, climate, and topographical formation—that did so much to make the life of an English yeoman what it was. They affected the way he held his land and how he worked it, the kind of house he lived in, and many of his activities. They were not the only influences that fashioned the pattern of rural society, but they were important ones.

The diversity in local conditions is recognized throughout this study, and again and again local differences are pointed up. But it is only as the yeomen of each shire or area (for sometimes it is topographical features or the given social pattern of a region that count for more than shire boundaries) are studied in the light of their particular surroundings that full account of them can be taken. The very year this book went to press Mr. Hoskins published a study of the Leicestershire yeoman in the sixteenth century; and a few years later, Joan Thirsk, having mastered the vagaries of Fenland farming, turned her attention to the farmer and small landed man of Lincolnshire (see appended bibliography). Each has added rich detail and interpretation concerning the yeomen in these localities. Studies of other localities are bound to do the same. We may by means of them be able to find out more about those yeomen, most elusive of all, who in the competitive life of their day were neither able to advance to a higher status nor even to maintain their place in their own group, but either dropped in the social and economic scale, or in time sought new homes across the sea. Some wholly unlooked-for local differences are likely to crop up, and certainly those already evident will be more fully known and better understood. When such studies are made for every shire or representative area throughout England, a new and better book on the Elizabethan and Stuart yeomen will be written. But these take time. Careful historical work, even that of a single locality, is not produced overnight. It will, therefore, perhaps be useful to have this book in print again.

Mildred Campbell

Vassar College,
Poughkeepsie,
New York,
September, 1959

CONTENTS

THE ENGLISH YEOMAN
UNDER ELIZABETH AND THE EARLY STUARTS

INTRODUCTION

NEWS in 1603 did not travel as fast as it does today. Only those living in London and its environs, within sound of the church bells that rang throughout the early hours of the twenty-fourth of March in that year, knew that their queen was dead. But couriers took horse at once, riding hard in all directions that the news might be reëchoed as speedily as possible from the belfries of every parish church in the land. And as soon as it was known, loyal subjects everywhere laid aside normal activities to commemorate the passing of the old queen and drink a health to her successor.

Later developments were indeed to make the death of Elizabeth and the accession of James Stuart landmarks in English history. But many of the forces making for change were not yet apparent, at least not to many people; and for the most part the accustomed activities that now gave way to the events of the hour were actually little affected by them. Ways of living and thinking are of slow growth. They decline as slowly. The queen was dead. But the age that bears her name did not die with her passing. And the ordinary Englishman, were he knight, gentleman, yeoman, merchant, artisan, country laborer, or wandering vagabond, found life little or no different on the morrow because the crown, Tudor-worn for more than a century, rested now on a Stuart head.

It is not, however, with the ordinary Englishman that most of the historians of the period have dealt. Their attention until recently turned chiefly to princes, parliaments, and ecclesiastics. This fact is not surprising. For it was largely they—kings and queens, princes of the blood, upstart favorites, parliamentary champions, stiff-necked bishops, and no less stiff-necked Puritan divines—whose struggles and decisions fashioned the character of the age in which they lived and set the pattern for the next. It was also they who, quick of tongue and ready with the pen, marked their age as one of great articulateness. Their speeches, debates, and correspondence, produced under the impulsion of stirring times, were so voluminous that the passage of three hundred years and the labors of research students past and present have failed to exhaust them. From the days of Camden and Bacon, Burnet and Clarendon, to our own they have pretty much held the center of the stage.

And indeed if Clio had remained upon Olympus where a Stuart votary placed her, there would probably be little inclination to turn the spotlight elsewhere. But Clio has turned traveler and democrat. And an age that finds her in country hamlets and remote fishing villages, handling the diary of an obscure country vicar or the papers of an unknown sea captain with the care once reserved for royal proclamations and parliamentary enactment, may well expect that new centers of interest will be developed and old ones redefined.

Two circumstances among others are bringing this about: the opening up in recent years of vast collections of historical sources hitherto inaccessible; and the emergence of social history from the plane of the dilettante to that of the trained investigator. No longer does the main stream of events demand the whole attention. The quest turns now and again to the smaller eddies and currents that helped to shape its course. Lesser folk as well as important people get attention. And social and economic conditions which surrounded and often controlled events are receiving their long-merited due.

The social scene may be approached in at least two ways, perhaps more: through a detailed study of a particular community, a single manor or region; or through the study of a single segment of society represented by a class or group that functions as an integral part in the social structure, and bears certain earmarks of political, social, and economic differentiation.

The works of a long list of writers mark the success that has been attained in the histories of particular localities. Studies of the second type have been more slowly undertaken, and for fairly obvious reasons. The task of interpreting any social group or class is beset with problems peculiarly its own. Lines separating one segment of society from another, no matter what the basis for classification, are rarely in any age as sharply drawn in fact as in theory. Overlapping makes fine distinctions difficult. That which really differentiates, moreover, lies often in the realm of intangibles, and is bound up in the intricacies of behavior codes, standards of evaluation, and subtleties of custom and tradition that well-nigh defy detection. Indeed, when one ponders the difficulties that students of contemporary society encounter in their attempts to analyze the strata that represent their own varied social and economic levels, he may well ask what hope there is of interpreting a group that lived three hundred years ago in a social structure considerably different from our own.

The answer, of course, is that the task cannot be carried to full completion. But were this the criterion, valuable historical work in many fields had remained undone. There is so much in the records, inadequate though they are, that has never been exploited, so much of importance which can be discovered that it seems a pity to leave undone that part of the task that can be achieved merely because all of the questions cannot be answered nor the picture be made complete in every detail. It is upon this conviction that the present study has been pursued.

The yeomen of the Elizabethan and early Stuart period owed their existence as a group largely to the economic and social changes of the fourteenth and fifteenth centuries. Pushing ahead under the early Tudors, they had by the time of Elizabeth become an integral and substantial factor in rural society. If they have hitherto been denied the detailed attention of historians, they have at least not been without honorable mention. For there will be few reading these pages who cannot recall the paragraph in their school history books that extolled the yeomen as the backbone of the English nation and deplored their decline. Economic historians have more recently extended that paragraph to a page or two. But beyond this the subject has received little attention. Who the yeomen really were, how they helped to shape or were in turn affected by contemporary developments, and what actually was the pattern of their lives at the time when they were a significant factor in English society, are questions that for the most part remain unanswered.

The difficulty in finding their answers is enhanced by the fact that the yeomen were, in the main, an inarticulate group. They were better judges of sheep and seed corn than of words and fine phrases, and certainly more skilled in the tools of husbandry than the pen. Nor did others trouble to put them on paper. It was an age of prolific writing. But "The Divine Right of Kings" and "The Escape of the Soul from Torment that it may then Glorify God" were the themes of the moment, not the annals of simple countryfolk who talked of the weather and their crops through the week and sat in their pews in the parish church on Sunday.

A few contemporary historians, it is true, did give brief attention to the yeomen in their descriptions of the social structure. Some of these are merely patriotic effusions of little worth. Others were honest attempts to describe society as the writers knew it, and as such they are valuable. A few literary folk, too, character writers and playwrights, seeking to hold the mirror up to nature, dealt with the yeoman among their social types. Fortunately these accounts, and the still more rare diaries, letters, and commonplace books of the yeomen themselves, are supplemented by another and much larger body of material. An early statute of the reign of Henry V declared that henceforth in all legal documents, appeals, writs, indictments, and the like each person's name should be followed by an "addition" descriptive of his "Estate, Degree, or Mystery." It is this usage, generally followed in the age of Elizabeth and the Stuarts, that furnishes the key to most of the history of the yeoman. In wills, deeds, quarter-sessions records, post-mortem inquisitions, the accounts of parish officials, and hundreds of depositions of practically every court in the realm, one meets the people who were styled "yeoman" by their contemporaries.

These documents, some rich in their revelations, others pitifully scant, have through the passage of years found lodgment in many places: in the strong rooms of guildhalls and shire halls; in parish-church chests and vicarage closets; in free libraries and the libraries of local historical societies; and in the muniment rooms of country houses. Some are housed near the spot where they were written; where, indeed, one may take up the telephone directory at the close of the day and find listed among local families the same names that have been met with that day in the manuscripts. Many have found a lodging place in the great national repositories in London, or had until wartime terrors caused them to be whisked away into temporary hiding. But whether read in the cosmopolitan air of Bloomsbury or hard by Chancery Lane and busy Fleet Street or in their original setting, they sooner or later carry the reader to the English countryside.

London, it is true, then as now was the center of national life. But beyond its environs lay the wellsprings that fed the current of that life. Beyond Whitehall and the West Minster, out of sight and hearing of Paul's Walk, Fleet Street, and the Strand, lay the England of shire and country village.

In the north were the great moors and rolling meadows of the border country that stretched southward until they joined the hilly copses and flourishing market towns of the Midlands. Westward were the green slopes of the Cotswold hills, the fertile valleys of the Severn and the Wye, and across the Mendips to the southwest the apple orchards and red-ploughed fields of Devon. Eastward from the Midlands lay the dairy lands of East Anglia and rich Essex farms.

Farther south in Kent there were cherry orchards just as there are now, and hops, a newer crop, kept Kentish farmers busy. The Sussex weald was thinning, but it still furnished magnificent timbers. The downs that stretched across the southern counties were covered with sheepwalks as they are today, and between them small villages furnished centers for the life of the parish.

This was the yeoman's England. It is against this background that he moved and in its light alone that he can be understood. That the picture will not be complete is evident from the beginning. The materials from which it is made are in small pieces and some of the pieces are missing. Much of the color that gave it strength and life has disappeared with the intervening years, but not all. It is still possible, one hopes, to draw the main lines clearly, and perhaps to recapture here and there a little of the original light and shade.

I

FOREBEARS

Although our progenytors and forefathers were at the begynnynge
but plene and sympell men and wemen and of smalle possessyon
. . . yt I do wysshe and exhort you that you sholde not be asshamed
of them . . . for I am sure the gretes oxse was fyrste a lytell calfe.
Consider wythe yourselves what ys wryten in the liij Chapyter of
the profytte Esays which sayithe, Remember of what stones ye
were hewen owt of and of what graves you were dugged owte of.

The Diary and Family Book of Robert Furse, yeoman, 1593

And you, good yeomen, whose limbs were made in England.

Henry V, act III, sc. 1

EVERYONE who has a story to tell would prefer to
begin at the beginning. But it is not always easy to
say what the beginning was, nor when. An attempt
to trace the ancestors of the Elizabethan yeomen to their
remote origins would doubtless bear some fruit, but in the
end it would lead to that baffling point that faces the student of all social origins, where there are no signposts to
point the way beyond.

It is pertinent, however, in a study of the yeomen to look
backward to some extent. Information that pertains to the
immediate ancestors of the group, insofar as it can be
gained, helps to explain the character of the descendants.
And some knowledge of the previous economic and social
developments is practically essential to an understanding
of the position of the yeomen of later generations. It is both
legitimate and necessary to give so much of a backward
look as will take into account these factors.

The earlier form of the word may have been "yonge
men."[1] At any rate, one notes the following differences in

1. The derivation of the word yeoman still remains a matter of doubt.
Interesting speculations were made by Elizabethan "word mongers," but
they could not agree. See William Camden, *Britannia, or a Chorographi-*

the three versions of *Piers Plowman*. In the A text of 1362–63 occur the following lines:

> Emperours and earles and alle maner lordes
> Thorw 3iftes han 3onge men to renne and to ride.[2]

The B text appearing about 1377 uses the word in the same form. But with the appearance of the C text in or about 1393, the final revision of the poem according to Skeat, the word "3emen" has taken the place of the "3onge men" of the former versions.[3]

It is certainly in this meaning, namely as a retainer or attendant or servitor, a person giving not menial but honorable service, that the word occurs again and again in the thirteenth and fourteenth centuries, and hereafter this will be termed its primary usage. It was so used in the Close Rolls, the Patent Rolls, the early Rolls of Parliament, and in the early Statutes, in its Latin equivalents of *valletus* or *valectus*, or in the garbled law-French as *vadlet* or *vallet;*[4] while in such popular literature as the *Canterbury Tales*, the *Tale of Gamelyn*, and *Piers Plowman* it appeared in the various vernacular forms of "3eman," "yoman," and "3onge man."[5]

cal description of the flourishing Kingdomes of England, Scotland and Ireland and the islands adjacent, 1806, cc; Wm. Harrison, *A Description of England*, The New Shakspere Society, 1877, Bk. II, 133; John Cowell, *The Interpreter*, 1637, *YO;* R. Verstegen, *A Restitution of Decayed Intelligence*, 1628, p. 331; Sir Henry Spelman, *Glossarium Archæologicum*, 1664, Pt. II. Nor do modern scholars agree or feel certain about the matter. See W. Skeat, *Etymological Dictionary*, 1901; E. Weekley, *An Etymological Dictionary of Modern English*, 1921; H. Wyld, *Universal Dictionary of the English Language*, 1932; the *New English Dictionary* (Murray *et al.*), 1888; the *Century Dictionary* (Whitney *et al.*), 1911; Felix Liebermann, *Die Gesetze der Angelsachsen*, 1903, I, 620–626.

2. *Piers the Plowman* (Skeat), 1924, I, 82–83. See also the *Tale of Gamelyn* (Skeat), 1884, line 628, and *passim*.

3. *Piers the Plowman*, p. 83.

4. Close Rolls, No. 104, Membrane 3; Charter Rolls, No. 4, Membrane 7; *Rotuli Parliamentorum* (1777), II, 278–281; III, 307, and *passim;* and *Statutes of the Realm* (hereafter cited as *S.R.*), 37 Edward III, c. 9.

5. *The Canterbury Tales* (Manly and Rickert), 1940, III, 101, and *passim; Piers the Plowman*, I, 83; the *Tale of Gamelyn*, line 628, and *passim*.

Sir George Sitwell says that the primary meaning of the word in the fourteenth century was military in nature. It is true that it was often in connection with military life that the yeoman served, but by no means always. "The King's yeoman," and yeomen of other lords, were sent hither and yon on special missions, now to receive or deliver money or gifts, now to carry special messages, now to act as attendants for their lord or his friends.[6] It seems rather to have been that half-military, half-personal type of service characteristic of feudal and semifeudal relationships. The knight's yeoman in Chaucer's "Prologue" has become a familiar picture, and it was the Canon's yeoman who told one of the last of the Canterbury Tales.[7]

With the passing of the days of private warfare and feudal practices this usage of the term became less frequent though it did not entirely disappear. Shakespeare sometimes employed it in this manner, as did other writers of the fifteenth and sixteenth centuries.[8] In connection with this usage also, the term developed a technical meaning, implying a particular type of office or service.[9] Documents dealing with the royal household and the households of great lords speak of the "yeoman of the cellar," the "yeoman of the wardrobe," and the "yeoman of the bedchamber." One encounters items in the State Papers concerning the "yeoman of the spicery" and the "yeoman of the leash." Mu-

6. *Calendar of Patent Rolls, Edward I, 1272–1281,* 1901, p. 92, and *passim; Calendar of Patent Rolls, Edward III, 1348–1350,* 1905, p. 134, and *passim; Calendar of Close Rolls, Edward III, 1327–1330,* 1896, p. 231, and *passim; Calendar of Inquisitions,* 1910, VI, 52.

7. *The Canterbury Tales,* IV, 315–343.

8. "Came there a yeoman that sayd to the duchess . . . the meete is ready," *The Four Sonnes of Aymon* (Copeland), 1554, chap. iv. "Robyn Hood had at his rule and commaundment an hundred tall yeomen," R. Grafton, *Chronicle,* 1809, I, 221.

9. "The lady of the Strachey married the yeoman of the wardrobe," *Twelfth Night,* act II, sc. 5, line 45.

> Host: Master Fang, have you entered the action?
> Fang: It is entered.
> Host: Where's your yeoman? Is't a lusty yeoman?
>   Will a' stand to 't?
> *Henry IV,* pt. I, act II, sc. 1, line 4.

nicipal records tell of the yeoman who carries the mace at public functions. And Unwin deals with the yeoman companies or organizations among the London craft gilds.[10] In like manner a technical meaning survives in our own day in the familiar Yeomen of the Guard in England, and in the less familiar and less important "yeoman of the powder" and "yeoman of the storeroom," offices common to both the British and American navies.

But as early as the beginning of the fifteenth century a second usage of the word had come into vogue. It was now frequently employed to describe rank or status in rural society. In two instances in the more than a score of times that the word appears in the *Canterbury Tales*, there is a suggestion of rank. The miller in the "Reeve's Tale" says that he will have no wife except one well brought up, "To sauen his estaat of Yemanrye."[11] And the summoner in the "Friar's Tale" speaks of a quality of yeomanhood:

> I am a yeman, knowen is ful wyde
> My trouthe wol I holde as in this cas
> For though thow were the devel Sathanas
> My trouthe wol I holde to thee my brother.[12]

But in the main it is not until the fifteenth century that this usage finds its way into common parlance. There is, or so it seems to me, the possibility of a relationship between the second usage and the first. But since it is in its secondary meaning only, as a term denoting status, that the word will be used throughout this book, we may relegate the question of the relationship to the Appendix, and turn now to the background of the group itself, the group to which the term yeoman was being applied by the latter half of the fifteenth century.[13]

10. George Unwin, *Industrial Organization in the Sixteenth and Seventeenth Centuries*, 1904, pp. 51–61, 229–234.

11. *The Canterbury Tales*, III, line 3949.

12. *Ibid.*, lines 1524–1528. Except for these two examples the word is used in the remaining twenty-five times that it occurs in the *Canterbury Tales*, in its primary meaning as servitor or attendant.

13. Appendix I. Miss Nellie Neilson tells me that the word appears

Its background is as chequered as is that of most groups or classes. But the nucleus from which it grew appears pretty clearly to have been the free tenants or freemen of the manor. And yeomen later profited from the traditions claimed as a part of this heritage. Vinogradoff, Pollock and Maitland, and many of their students and successors have made it abundantly clear that there is much yet to be learned regarding the place of the free tenant in feudal society, much indeed that probably never can be learned of his relations with the people above and below him, and particularly of the gradations that existed within his own group. Certain characteristics of his rights and status, however, have been fairly well established and defined by these scholars, as well as by Professors Holdsworth and Lipson and other more recent writers.

In general, it may be said that the free tenant stood below the knight and esquire because of his lack of wealth rather than from any inferiority of birth or blood or legal privilege; for he was free-born and eligible to become a knight if he had the means. In fact, he was expected to assume his knighthood upon arriving at sufficient wealth.[14] On the other hand, he stood above the villein and serf not only by virtue of his wealth and condition but by birth and the privileges of birth, for the serf was base-born.

The free tenant held his land *in feodo*, hence his title was secure. He held for himself and his heirs forever, and not for a certain number of years or at the will of the lord. At his death the land must pass to his heirs, for at that time freehold could not be willed away.

Another factor contributing to the fortunate position of

frequently as a status term in the Plea Rolls of this period, and one can find examples of this usage in many types of literature both official and popular: *The Statutes of the Realm* (hereafter cited as *S.R.*), II, *passim*. Sir J. Fortescue, *The Laws of England*, 1616, pp. 66–67; *The Governance of England*, 1885, p. 151; R. Pecock, *Repressor of Overmuch Blaming of the Clergy*, Rolls Series, XIX, pt. II, 371.

14. *S.R.*, I, *Statutum de militibus, Temp. incert.*, p. 229. In early printed copies this statute is recorded as of the first year of the reign of Edward II.

the free tenant was the protection he enjoyed in the courts of law. If his title were questioned by an encroaching land-lord or trouble of any sort arose he might seek redress at the king's courts, a right denied the base-born man, yet one that did not exclude the free tenant from taking his suits to the hundred court or the manor courts if they better suited his convenience and needs. Free and unfree tenure, king's court and manor court, are terms pretty much outside our present ken, but could we think ourselves into the mentality of the Middle Ages, their importance would loom large.

The free tenants not only got but gave in the society of which they were a part. They contributed to the common wel-fare, and by virtue of this service received a certain recogni-tion. They were the *legales homines*, the "true and lawful men" who were summoned for inquests held to gain infor-mation for the king, or to settle local disputes in their ca-pacity as trial jurors. They as well as their superiors, the archbishops, bishops, earls, barons, and knights, were named in the salutations of royal letters. And as early as the thirteenth and fourteenth centuries subsidies granted to the king were made in the name of the untitled freeholders as well as of knights, barons, and earls.

To what degree all freemen had participated in the choice of the knight of the shire for parliament prior to 1429 is not certain. But the wording of the statute of that year limiting the right of suffrage to the forty-shilling free-holder and those above, is such as to make it seem likely that all of them had participated.[15] The restrictive clause of that act took away the privilege from the freeholder who did not have land of the annual value of forty shillings, but a large number of the group, perhaps the greater part, were still among the enfranchised.

One cannot say exactly what services the free tenant was required to give his lord. The greater the number of mano-rial records examined, the more evident it appears that the duties differed according to locality and period. In the

15. *S.R.*, 8 Henry VI, c. 7.

main, they consisted of occasional boon work and certain payments in kind which were later commuted to money payments. Whatever their nature, these services were usually fixed and certain in contrast with those of the unfree tenant whose time and labor were almost entirely at his lord's disposal.

The free tenant, though bound by certain tenurial duties common to the society of his age, was, in short, his own man, managing his own life as he saw fit and in conformity with the standards recognized for men of his class. The very name "franklin," by which a man of this class was known in the common parlance of the day, emphasizes his free nature and respectable status.[16] It did not always mean prosperity, for there were poor franklins as well as wealthy ones. But it implied a good deal of security and well-being. And the popular literature of the day makes quite clear the position that the free tenants held in the social scale and in the esteem of their neighbors. Piers Plowman says that no one could receive the tonsure as a priest who did not come "Of Franklens and free men."[17] In the story of Jacob and Joseph in the *Cursor Mundi* (*ca.* 1320), Pharaoh, commanding Joseph, calls him a "franckelain," and says of him,

> Now under me es he mast of all
> I give him woning-sted to lend,
> For ever mar, widuten end.[18]

In the *Chronicle of Robert of Brunne* the king is told that he may have as wives for his soldiers,

16. The term *franklin* had largely given way by Elizabeth's time to *yeoman*, though one still meets it now and then. Sir John Ferne, writing in 1586 of the contemporary social structure, speaks of the group below the gentry as "yeomen or franklein," *The Blazon of Gentrie,* 1586, p. 7. And Thomas Overbury in the reign of James I still chose to describe the yeoman under his old title, "franklin," *The Mirror of Character,* 1869, p. 24.

17. *Piers the Plowman* (Skeat), 1924, C text, p. 120.

18. *Cursor Mundi,* 1875, II, 312–313. See also the *Tale of Gamelyn,* line 197, and *passim*.

> Squyers doughtres and franklayns
> To gyve hem to knyghtes and to swayns,
> Other maidens comen of thralls,
> To be maried as them falles.[19]

The *Chronicle of Robert of Gloucester* mentions the "simple franklin,"[20] and the familiar picture of the wealthy franklin in Chaucer's "Prologue" will bear another quoting for the resemblance it holds to the wealthy yeoman of Elizabethan and Stuart days:

> An housholdere and that a greet was he
> Seint Iulyan he was in his contree
> His breed his ale was alweys after oon
> A bettre envyned man was neuere noon
> With oute bake mete was neuere his hous
> Of fissh and flessh and that so plenteuous
> It snewed in his hous of mete and drynke
> Of alle deyntees that men koude thynke
> After the sondry sesons of the yeer
> So chaunged he his mete and his soper.[21]

The ambitious father planning for his son had also a counterpart among many yeoman families of later date whom we shall see sending their sons to Oxford and Cambridge in order to make them gentlemen:

> I haue a sone and by the Trinitee
> I hadde leuere than twenty pound worth lond
> Thogh it right now were fallen in myn hond
> He were a man of swich discrecioun
> As that ye ben fy on possessioun
> But if a man be vertuous with al
> I haue my sone snybbed and yit shal

---

19. *Chronicle of Robert of Brunne,* 1338, Rolls Series, 1887, pt. I, line 6547.

20. *Chronicle of Robert of Gloucester, ca.* 1300, Rolls Series, 1887, LXXXVI, pt. I, 61.

21. "The Prologue," *Canterbury Tales,* III, lines 339–348.

For he to vertu listeth nat entende
But for to pleye at dees and to despende
And lese al that he hath is his vsage
He hath leuere talken with a page
Than to commune with any gentil wight
Wher he myghte lerne gentillesse aright.[22]

It was largely from this group, grown more numerous in the fourteenth and fifteenth centuries as feudal restrictions weakened, that the armies of archers were drawn who brought military prestige and glory to the English on the fields of Crécy and Poitiers and in the Scottish wars.

Whether or not the valor of the English archer has been overestimated in the song and story of succeeding centuries is a matter for speculation and investigation.[23] But there is no doubting the fact that his fame was a matter of popular belief that added much to the prestige of the yeomen of later generations. The truth is that many of the ancestors of the yeomen of Elizabethan and Stuart days were following the plough as bondmen when the armies of British archers went forth to war on the fields of France or crossed the Scottish borders, but this fact did not prevent the group as a whole from sharing the heritage to which some of their number had a valid right. Rarely did a writer of the sixteenth or early half of the seventeenth century mention the yeomen without pointing out that it was their ancestors "who in times past made all France afraid," and that England in the possession of this class with so noble a past was blessed above other nations.[24] After the Civil Wars of the seventeenth century provided the poets and chroniclers with new

22. *Ibid.*, "The Frankeleyn to the Squier," IV, lines 682–694. See below, pp. 36, 39, 270–271.

23. See A. C. Prince, "The Strength of English Armies in the Reign of Edward III," *English Historical Review*, 1931, XLVI, 353–371.

24. See John Coke's comparison of the "good yeomen of England and Wales" with French peasants, *Debate of Heralds*, 1550, p. LI; also Fortescue, *The Governance of England*, pp. 137–140; Thomas Fuller, *The Holy State*, 1642, p. 116; and Thomas Gainsford, *The Glory of England*, 1618, pp. 304, 305.

themes, less was made of the national wars of the earlier period, but at intervals as late as the eighteenth century the deeds of the English yeomen in the Hundred Years' War were still being sung.[25]

Actually, the freemen or free tenants of the earlier period, for all that they were the most talked about later, formed merely the nucleus of the yeoman's ancestors and were by no means his only ones. The history of social classes is not so simple. Especially in periods of stress, when old barriers are breaking down, when social and economic changes make fat purses grow lean and lean ones grow fat, when a husband here chooses a wife there, the problem of analyzing social strata becomes increasingly difficult.

The fourteenth and fifteenth centuries were just such periods. The breakup of the manorial system and the disappearance of villeinage released the latent powers of the lower classes.[26] Not all of the yeomen, or of any class, made progress. Some found the competition too great, and dropped into the new group of hired laborers who held no land but worked for a wage. Their personal freedom was

25. At Cressy and *Poitiers* of old
His Ancestors were bowmen bold;
Where good yew bows and sinews strong
Drew arrows of a cloth-yard long;
For England's glory, strew'd the plain,
With barons, counts and princes slain.

"The Yeoman of Kent," published in full in *A Kentish Garland,* 1881, I, 146–150.

26. Villeinage did not disappear all at once. Examples of it may be found throughout this period, and vestiges remained throughout the sixteenth century; but in many cases it was entirely abolished, and even where it still existed conditions for the villein were improved. See T. W. Page, *The End of Villainage in England,* American Economic Association Publications, 1900, Ser. 3, I, no. 2; E. Lipson, *Economic History of England,* 1932, chap. III; F. W. Davenport, "The Decay of Villeinage in East Anglia," *Transactions* of the Royal Historical Society (cited hereafter as *R.H.S.*), N.S. XIV; Alexander Savine, "Bondmen under the Tudors," *R.H.S.,* XVII; I. S. Leadam, "Villeinage in England," *Political Science Quarterly,* VIII, 653; "The Last Days of Bondage in England," *Law Quarterly Review,* IX, 348. See also examples of late bondage, *Calendar of State Papers, Domestic Series* (cited hereafter as *S.P.D.*), 1603–1610, VIII, May 18; Duchy of Lancaster Manuscripts in the Public Record Office (cited hereafter as *D.L.*), "miscellaneous," 13/20.

now secure, but their economic position was in many cases no better than had been that of the serfs under the old system, if indeed it were as good. Many, however, bettered their position, kept what land they had and added to it. More and more their rents tended to become fixed. Though services were still required, many became less onerous than before.

Two occurrences, the Black Death that raged throughout England in the middle of the fourteenth century and the Peasants' Revolt of 1381, have often been held responsible for these and similar changes. More recent scholars are inclined, however, to the opinion that most of the changes would have come anyway with the natural trend of social and economic developments, and that these two occurrences, particularly the Black Death, accelerated but did not create changing conditions.

Estimates as to the loss of life from that terrible plague that came rather suddenly upon England in 1348 differ greatly, ranging from one fifth to nine tenths of the population.[27] But no one can doubt that there was suffering, and that the poorer classes suffered most of all. Hundreds of them died. At once laborers became scarce. A contemporary chronicler says: "There was such a want of servants in work of all kinds that one would scarcely believe that in times past there had been such a lack."[28]

Scarcity of labor brought a rise in wages. This led to consternation among landowners. The king in a proclamation declared that no man should either demand or pay a higher rate of wages than the old scale presented. Laborers were forbidden to leave their places of labor, and penalties were placed on runaways. Parliament embodied the contents of the king's command in statute form, the famous *Statute of Labourers*.[29] But as frequently happens in times of crisis,

27. Miss Bertha Putnam says that a half is probably fairly near the truth. See her summary of the diverse opinions among scholars who have written on the subject. *The Enforcement of the Statutes of Labourers,* Columbia Studies in History, Economics, and Public Law, XXXII, 1.

28. *Chronicle of Henry of Knighton,* II, Rolls Series, 1889, XCII, 64.

29. *S.R.,* 23 Edward III, c. 1. See also 34 Edward III, cc. 10, 11; 1 Richard II, c. 6; 8 Richard II, c. 2; 12 Richard II, cc. 3–9, for subsequent fourteenth-century acts dealing with laborers.

legislation proved ineffective. Runaways who left one landlord found a welcome and good wages with another whose
crops were suffering for want of care.[30] And within a generation after the outbreak of the plague free labor was re-
placing servile labor to a marked degree.[31] Many landlords
in search of a way out of the difficulty gave up the management of their estates and let their land to tenant farmers for
a fixed rent; others sold a part of their land. In this way the
number of small freeholds increased. The very wealthy
landlord who could survive the crisis had also a good opportunity to increase his holdings, as land was cheap; hence
some enlarged estates appear along with the more numerous
smaller holdings.

The Peasants' Revolt of 1381 is of less concern to the
story of the yeomen for it had little effect on the small landholders or their holdings. Recent historians are also inclined
to give it a less significant place in the disappearance of
villeinage than formerly.[32] The immediate demands of the
peasants were not met, though gradually many of the
changes they had asked for took place. Wages were ad-
justed, villeinage became less common, and on the whole
their condition was greatly improved.

More important, probably, than these two events were
certain economic developments of the early Tudor period,

30. *Chronicle of Henry of Knighton,* II, 64.

31. See tables giving comparative results of examinations made of 126
manors in 1380, E. Lipson, *Economic History,* I, 97–98. See also N. S. B.
Gras, *History of Agriculture,* 1925, pp. 109–115.

32. Stubbs calls the Peasants' Revolt "one of the most portentous phenomena to be found in the whole of our history," *Constitutional History
of England* (3d edition), II, 471. Thorold Rogers, H. de B. Gibbins, and
others of the older historians also make much of it. Some of them, however, including W. Cunningham, *Growth of English Industry,* 1910, I,
396–402, and W. J. Ashley, *Economic Organization of England,* 1914, pp.
49–50, minimize its effects and point out that it has been used by those
who were caught by its dramatic features rather than by the truth of its
real significance. More recently Lipson calls it "only an example on a
larger scale of occurrences which were taking place in many parts of the
country both before and after the insurrection . . . the revolt itself was
but one symptom of a malady which continued to afflict rural society until
villeinage completely disappeared," *Economic History,* I, 110. This is
characteristic of the view held by most of the more modern writers.

which, following hard on the changes of the two preceding centuries, affected vitally the fortunes of the yeomen. The continued rise in prices, the growth of markets, the increased tendency for rents to become fixed, and the growing demand for land all tended toward the increase of their numbers, and helped to shape the pattern of their lives. But as most of these factors continued active throughout the Elizabethan and early Stuart period, they will be treated as a part of the main story. Suffice it to say here that when the last Tudor came to the throne in the mid-sixteenth century those of her subjects who were small landholders faced conditions fraught with both opportunities and dangers wholly unknown to their forefathers. If they could keep clear or improve their titles, increase the production of their land in order to have a surplus for the market, and save enough during fat years to tide them over the lean ones that were sure to come now and then, they had an opportunity for gaining wealth never before known to their class. They could afford to dream dreams of pewter in the cupboard, and maybe silver, of stronger houses and barns, of university careers for their bright sons and good marriage portions for their daughters.

But large landholders as well as small ones were straining every nerve to reap the advantages offered by growing markets and rising prices. They too were eager to get their hands on every possible foot of land, now that money was to be made from it and capital was in demand. The small landholder, therefore, who lacked initiative or foresight, who spent so heavily that he couldn't keep his rents paid, or failed in any way to protect the title to his land, might easily lose out in the game, and in time find himself bereft of his entire possessions. Not his to dream confidently of the future. In the face of such ill luck he would be forced to farm out his services to a more fortunate neighbor or to enter the ranks of the landless wage earners whose numbers increased faster than their wages. Failing employment on the land, or in the near-by towns where work was difficult to secure if a man had not served his apprenticeship, there was nothing left for him but to join the bands of wandering vagrants and beggars who infested the Elizabethan countryside, helping thereby to swell the mounting tide of crime and unemployment.

To see how the yeomen fared and what their lives were like, at a period when the entire agrarian population faced changing conditions that brought both opportunity and danger in their wake, is the task of the succeeding chapters.

II

DEGREE, PRIORITY, AND PLACE

It is better to be the head of the yeomanry than the tail of the gentry.

Old English Proverb

Here comes old Woodcock, the Yeoman of Kent, that's half Farmer and half Gentleman; his horses go to the plow all week, and are put into the coach o' Sunday.

Tunbridge Walks or the Yeoman of Kent, act I, sc. 1

THE will of Robert Upsher, yeoman, of Bures St. Mary, Essex, proved in 1610, deals briefly with the question of funeral arrangements: "I will that I shall have a buriall fitt and decent for my degree." The sentiment conveyed in this statement is one that may be found not only in most of the wills of the period, whatever the rank or degree of their authors, but in every kind of contemporary document, whether the matter in hand were a funeral, a wedding, the investing of an office, or the performance of a public or private duty. For it expresses one of the fundamental tenets of the age, a belief in the doctrine of degree, priority, and place.

The Devonshire squire in a case before the Star Chamber court grumbled because a yeoman had not respected "the great inequalitie and difference . . . in their several degrees and places."[1] A Yorkshire yeoman at the quarter-sessions court declared himself willing to pay his rates only if "assessed equally with his neighbours of his estate and degree."[2] Divines from the pulpit calling "all estates of men to the right path" warned against the evils of desiring to

---

1. Manuscript records of the court of Star Chamber in the reign of James I in the Public Record Office (hereafter cited as St.Ch. 8), 287/9.
2. *West Riding Sessions Records,* Yorkshire Archæological Society Publications (hereafter cited as Y.A.S.), 1915, LIV, 162.

advance beyond the bonds of one's degree.[3] "Linke not in amity with too many men above thy calling" was the advice given merchants in 1616.[4] Kings in proclamations gave out duties to be performed by their subjects "according to their degree and calling."[5] And the very laws of the realm, as hitherto pointed out, declared that men should be described according to their "degree, estate, and mystery." In the tradition of his day Shakespeare gave his *Ulysses* a classical name and placed him on the plains of Troy, but the words that he put in his mouth were those of an Elizabethan Englishman:

> O, when degree is shak'd
> Which is the ladder to all high designs,
> Then enterprise is sick! How could communities
> Degrees in schools, and brotherhoods in cities,
> Peaceful commerce from dividable shores,
> The primogenitye and due of birth,
> Prerogative of age, crowns, sceptres, laurels,
> But by degree, stand in authentic place?
> Take but degree away, untune that string,
> And, hark, what discord follows![6]

It was a principle deep-grounded in the social philosophy of the age and one that played a definite part in fixing the pattern of its thought and action. It is essential, therefore, to understand as accurately as one may the status of the yeomen and their relationship to those above and below them in the social scale.

Sir Edward Coke, John Cowell, and other legal and semilegal writers of the day continued to make the holding

3. Robert Crowley, "The Yeomans Lesson," *Works,* Early English Text Society (hereafter cited as E.E.T.S.), Extra Series, 1872, XV, 64–66.

4. I. B., *The Merchants' Avizo,* 1616, p. 62.

5. Manuscript records of the State Papers Domestic for the reign of Charles I (hereafter cited as S.P. 16; those of the reign of James I will be cited as S.P. 14; and those of Elizabeth as S.P. 12, the system of numbering used in the Public Record Office), XLV, 10, fol. 55.

6. *Troilus and Cressida,* 1866, act I, sc. 3, lines 107–116.

of free land to the annual value of forty shillings the chief basis for yeoman status, a sum, by contemporary reckoning, equivalent to about six pounds in Elizabethan currency. But legal definitions are frequently copied from ancient treatises and make no allowance for the changes that are ever in progress. They often tend to make things appear more fixed and certain than they ever were. Students of history are learning, therefore, to reverse the traditional method of starting with the legal definition and attempting to make the facts fit into it, finding it often wiser to study actual conditions and practices first, and thence to proceed to such definition as will accord with those facts.[7] Definitions thus arrived at are frequently less explicit and watertight than the other kind, but considerably more accurate and more descriptive of things as they actually were.

Certainly one finds that Coke's description of the yeoman as "a freeholder that may dispend forty shillings per annum,"[8] admittedly based upon Lyttleton's *Treatise on Tenures* written a hundred years before, at once runs counter to the evidence of records that deal with yeomen who were living in Coke's day. For these records are full of the accounts of men like John Hewes of Devonshire who was reckoned by his neighbors as a yeoman, and so styled in a court deposition in 1593; yet declared on oath in the same case that his entire living came not from a freehold, but from a copyhold in Branscombe, of the annual value of eight pounds.[9]

That this was not a unique case among Devonshire yeomen appears evident from the statement of Thomas Westcote in 1630. In his description of society in Devonshire, Westcote, himself a member of the gentry, says that some of the yeomen had land in fee simple of their own whereas others held by copy of the court roll.[10]

7. See C. S. Orwin's discussion of this point, "Observations on the Open Fields," *The Economic History Review*, 1938, VIII, 125–135.

8. *The Institutes,* II, 1671, p. 668.

9. The Ellesmere Manuscripts in the Huntington Library (hereafter cited as El. MSS. Hn.), 2123.

10. Thomas Westcote, *A View of Devonshire in 1630,* 1845, pp. 48–50.

Nor can it have been a regional distinction peculiar to Devon or the west. For Thomas Gainsford, who wrote in 1618 of English society as a whole, specifically stated that the yeoman was either "freeholder or coppie-holder."[11] In fact, the definition cannot even be this much restricted. For some men were called "yeoman" who held no lands of their own in either of the above tenures, but leased or rented land for a fixed sum from a large landholder, being thereby "farmers" to their landlords. Westcote included lessees for years or for life among the Devonshire yeomen as did Tristram Risdon, another Devon writer of the same period.[12] Gainsford too is explicit in his reply to the question whether a "farmer" who hired another man's land should be included in the yeoman group. "We were wont," he says, "to interpose this difference between Yeoman and Farmer, that the Yeoman was a landed man, either freeholder or coppieholder." But now, that is by 1618, the farmer "paying a fine or rent and thereby growing rich," has the "denomination" formerly accorded the other two.[13] The oft-quoted speech of Latimer's father furnishes an example of a yeoman of this category: "My father was a yeoman, and had no lands of his own only he had a farm of £2 & £4 by the year . . . and he tilled so much as kept half a dozen men."[14]

William Harrison, whose chapter on social status Sir Thomas Smyth later transferred bodily to his *Commonwealth of England*, offers interesting evidence of the discrepancy between the current legal definition and actual practice. In the first part of his treatise, in the manner of the conventional stylists of his day he defined a yeoman in terms of the current legal formula; namely, as a forty-shilling freeholder, probably a definition he had taken from Lyttleton or Fortescue, as Coke had not yet written. But having got this stereotyped statement out of the way, Har-

11. Thomas Gainsford, *The Glory of England,* 1618, p. 308.

12. Tristram Risdon, *A Survey of the County of Devon, 1630* (hereafter cited as *Survey of Devon*), 1714, p. 10.

13. Gainsford, *Glory of England,* p. 308.

14. Bishop Latimer, *Sermons* (Parker Soc.), 1844, p. 101.

rison proceeded in his own more flexible style to describe the yeomen as he knew them, saying among other things that many of them were "farmers to gentlemen."[15]

I have found only one instance in which the earlier definition appears to have been strictly adhered to. In a suit before the Star Chamber court in the reign of James I, Richard Smith of Hillmorton in Warwickshire is first described as a "yeoman" with certain freehold property in his possession. When later evidence was accepted to prove that he was no freeholder, his status term of "yeoman" was crossed out by a contemporary hand and the term "husbandman" substituted. Likewise in the same case the term "husbandman," applied to another deponent, was changed to "yeoman," apparently after the witness had proved to the satisfaction of his hearers that he had certain freehold properties.[16]

There may be other instances of this kind, and the fact that many yeomen did have freehold and were in many communities synonymous with the small freeholders of the countryside meant often that the two terms were identical. Letters and reports from localities frequently speak of the "good honest yeomen, freeholders of the country." This is particularly true in material of a political nature; for only yeomen who were freeholders held the legal right to the parliamentary vote. But the contemporary evidence is so overwhelmingly against the general usage of the term in so restricted a manner that it is necessary to look for further means of definition.

There is nothing, one may say at the outset, as explicit as the distinction just discarded. Indeed, it is obvious that in its general usage the word yeoman is a descriptive rather than a legal term and that, like most words describing status, it is used loosely in certain instances. Because of this

15. William Harrison, *The Description of England* (Furnivall), Bk. II, 133. Cf. Sir Thomas Smyth, *De Republica Anglorum*, 1906, pp. 42–45. Note Harrison's accusation of Smyth's "borrowing" and his own method of retaliation, *The Description of England*, Bk. II, 176.

16. St.Ch. 8, 40/22.

fact it is felt by some that a study made in terms of status nomenclature had best be avoided; but this view appears to me unwarranted. Words do not continue in popular parlance over a long period of years unless they hold some meaning for the contemporary mind. And when hundreds of Englishmen of Elizabethan and Stuart days in wills, deeds, depositions and court orders, subsidy rolls, parish registers, family accounts, and private as well as official correspondence described themselves or were described by their contemporaries as "yeoman," it is difficult to believe that the term had no significance. It is particularly difficult to believe that an age which based its social structure on the belief that

> The heavens themselves, the planets, and this centre
> Observe degree, priority and place

did not mean something by the terms it used to designate rank and status. It is, of course, only through a study of their usage that one can arrive at that meaning, and in a sense the whole of this book is designed to throw light upon yeoman status as the records revealed it. But certain observations pertinent to the subject will provide foundation material.

First of all, though no particular type of tenure was essential, it is everywhere apparent that the yeomen as a group were occupied primarily with the land and its interests. Hence occupation becomes a partial means of describing their status. To be sure a yeoman might engage in a small trade or business on the side, maintaining meanwhile his agricultural interests.[17] But if in time this trade or business loomed larger than his farming activities, he was no longer styled yeoman but baker, mercer, joiner, or the like, according to his craft. Likewise a youth who grew up in a yeoman household and had not yet settled on an occupation for himself might be known as a yeoman from the status of his family even though he himself had no land. But cer-

17. See below, pp. 156–160.

tainly the term, when used as a means of group classification, applied to those identified with the soil and its interests. The yeomen were then a rural, agricultural group.
But so were the gentry, the knights, and the smaller tenant
farmers. Hence in order to differentiate them from these
groups it is necessary to see where the yeomen stood in relationship to those above and below them in the social scale.

In 1600 William Burre, "labourer," John Snow, "husbandman," and William Browne, "yeoman," were presented at the quarter-sessions court of Hertfordshire for
permitting a brook that bordered on their lands to break its
banks and submerge the highway.[18] In this presentment occur the three terms most commonly used throughout the
Elizabethan and early Stuart period to describe the agricultural groups of the rank below the gentry. It is a classification that occurs over and over in all kinds of records. In
the Worcestershire quarter-sessions papers for 1591–1643
approximately 14,000 names with status identification are
mentioned in the recognizances alone: of this number there
are 1,810 yeomen, 1,303 husbandmen, and 667 laborers.[19]

We need not tarry long with the term laborer. It was generally used to denote the landless wage earner who worked
by the piece, or by the day, week, or year, on the land of
someone else at a wage fixed, and presumably commensurate
with the type of work done. He was free-born and the yeoman's equal before the law, but his status in the social and
economic scale was distinctly lower.

The term husbandman is somewhat more difficult. And as
there has been considerable difference of opinion regarding
its meaning and the position which the husbandmen occupied in relation to the yeomen, it is pertinent to clarify the
point if possible.

18. *Notes and Extracts from the Sessions Rolls, 1581–1698,* Hertford
County Records (hereafter cited as *Hertford Sessions Rolls*), 1905, I, 33.

19. *Calendar of Worcestershire Quarter Sessions Papers, 1591–1643*
(hereafter cited as *Worcestershire Sessions Papers*), Worcestershire Historical Society Publications, 1900, I, xxxv–xxxvi. Now and then the word
"farmer" is used for the group described above as "husbandmen," especially near the end of the seventeenth century.

Mr. Charles Partridge, who noted the frequent use of the term in Bury wills of the period, has explained it as follows: "Husbandman is a term denoting not rank but occupation. . . . Knights, esquires, gentlemen and yeomen were also husbandmen if occupied in agriculture, but were never styled *husbandmen* because of their right to be styled knights, etc. The agriculturist who had no right to be styled Knight or esquire or gentleman, and who, not being a forty-shilling freeholder was not a yeoman, was described as husbandman."[20]

A second view making the term one of rank rather than occupation was presented by Mr. J. C. Atkinson, former editor of the North Riding Record Society: "Among the various other specific names for the divers ranks in society as it existed down to the first half of the seventeenth century, th~ appellation, 'husbandman' still distinguished the man ot the class next below the yeoman."[21]

And still a third view was offered by Sir George Sitwell in 1930: " 'Husbandman' has nothing to do with agriculture, meaning simply householder or head of a family. . . . In Tudor times when 'Husbandman' and 'Yeoman' occur together in the same document, the distinction seems to be one of tenure and husbandmen take precedence, being independent landowners living on their own property."[22]

In support of his theory Sir George quotes the instance of an eldest son of an esquire who was styled husbandman, and cites an entail of 1604 in which some descendants of the ancient house of Okeover were so styled.

As a matter of fact, if the two usages of the word be taken into account, the views of Atkinson and Partridge are not as contradictory as at first appears. From the thirteenth century through the seventeenth the word husbandry was used to denote agriculture and agricultural pursuits.

20. "Calendar of Bury Wills," *Suffolk Institute of Archæology* (hereafter cited as *Suffolk Arch.*), 1909, XIII, 67–68.

21. *North Riding Quarter Sessions Records,* North Riding Record Society, 1885, III, 178. See also J. C. Atkinson's note on the subject in *Notes and Queries,* 6th Series, XII, 363.

22. *The Hurts of Haldworth,* 1930, pp. xlix–l.

Hence a person engaged in the care and cultivation of the land, that is, in husbandry, was rightly called a husbandman, regardless of his rank or degree. Members of the gentry were seldom so styled because, as Mr. Partridge says, they were commonly designated by the term of their rank as gentleman, knight, etc. But they could be described according to occupation and sometimes were, particularly cadet members or branches of landed houses.[23] The only quarrel, therefore, that one has with Partridge's statement is his assumption that the term yeoman as late as the seventeenth century was restricted to the forty-shilling freeholder. His main contention that husbandman was basically a term of occupation is certainly correct; and this, I believe, may be considered the primary and more general usage of the term.[24]

But that the word husbandman did also come, in the roundabout way that words travel, to convey a meaning of rank seems equally certain. And when it was used in this fashion, Atkinson's statement that the husbandman was of the class next below the yeoman has the unquestioned support of contemporary evidence.

If we examine more or less casual evidence first, it will be observed that contemporary writers who habitually thought in terms of rank and degree, whether moving up or down in the social scale, used those terms in their proper sequence. The parliamentary statutes from an early period follow

23. This was probably true of the descendants of the house of Okeover mentioned by Sir George Sitwell. Other instances have been pointed out to me by Mr. John Benson of Salisbury. Westcote says that he was taught that it was a rule of the common law "that where a gentleman is sued by the name of husbandman, he may only say (though he exercise husbandry) that he is a gentleman, and demand judgement of the writ, without saying that he is no husbandman. For though a gentleman profess husbandry he ought to be sued by his more worthy addition." *A View of Devonshire*, p. 58.

24. For material bearing on the derivation of the word "husbandman" and its possible connection with "husband-lands," see *Notes and Queries*, 6th Series, XII, 363; *Archæologia Æleana*, 1894, XVII, 10; Bateson, "A Survey of Long Houghton," *History of Northumbria*, II, 370; *The Statutes of Scotland*, 9 Chas. I, c. 5; and Skeat, *Etymological Dictionary*. Most of this material is suggestive rather than definitive.

this practice. Sovereigns in speeches and proclamations addressed their subjects in the order of their rank. And contemporary historians followed a regular and legitimate sequence in their discussion of the various classes in the social structure. Hence word order is significant in statements dealing with these matters. In his "Caveat" written in 1567, Harman says: "The honourable will abhor them, the worshipfull will reject them, the yeomen will sharply taunt them, the husbandmen utterly defy them, the labouring man bluntly chide them."[25]

John Norden in the reign of James I, moving the opposite direction in the social scale, said of the changing standards of the various groups about him: "The Husbandman will be equal to the Yoman, the Yoman to the Gentleman, the Gentleman to the Squire, the Squire to his Superior, and so the rest."[26]

There seems little doubt here but that husbandman is used to denote the group of men next below the yeomen. In the Gloucestershire muster roll of 1608 which lists the servants of certain noblemen, "gentlemen and yeomen servants" are named in the same brackets, and the "husbandmen servants" are grouped separately below them. In the instances where there were no gentlemen's sons in service, the "yeomen servants" were listed first, and then the "husbandmen" in a separate group below them.[27] Evidence in an Irish Poll Bill for 1661 is very specific:

Every Yeoman or chief Farmer shall pay seven shillings.

Every Husbandman or petty Farmer, three shillings.[28]

English local historians treating of the different ranks and degrees in their shires made the same distinction. Robert Reyce in 1618 discussed first the Suffolk poor at the

25. T. Harman, "A Caveat of warening for common cursetors," *Old Book Collectors Miscellany*, 1871, I, vi.

26. *The Surveyors Dialogue*, 1607, pp. 13–14.

27. *Men and Armour for Gloucestershire in 1608,* 1902, pp. 121, 127–128, and *passim.*

28. Quoted in T. Fosbrooke, *History of Gloucester,* 1819, p. 306.

bottom of the social scale. Then he said: "The Husbandman who followeth in the next place though hee thriveth ordinarily well, yett he laboreth much. . . ." Of the third group he wrote: "In the next rank cometh our yeomanry. . . ." And from there he proceeded upward to the nobility.[29]

These and many similar examples that might be given[30] show that Elizabethan and Stuart writers often used the word husbandman to designate a member of the group below the yeomen. Or, as Uvedale Lambert writing recently of the husbandman in his history of Blechingley parish said: "Above him in the social scale, but with no sharp dividing line, came the yeoman."[31]

I do believe, however, that the word had been more or less accidentally forced into this usage along the lines which Partridge's definition suggests. There seems no reason to doubt his contention that fundamentally the use of the term was an occupational one which came to be applied only to those engaged in husbandry because they had not the right to another cognomen such as knight, gentleman, esquire, or yeoman. Since this group was numerous, including thousands of smaller tenant farmers not in the daily or yearly wage-earning group, and therefore not to be styled laborers, it was inevitable that the word should become identified with them. When that occurred, it came naturally to stand for the status or rank which was theirs in the social and economic scale, and was but seldom used by the other husbandmen who were known by their special status terms.

This explains Westcote's use of the comparative adjective in the following statement. Having dealt with the Devon gentry, he says, "Next to these I place the yeomanry," and after them, "the meaner husbandmen . . ."[32] The husbandmen, it is obvious, were in no sense a different class as that word is used in its more restricted meaning of

29. Robert Reyce, *Breviary of Suffolk,* 1902, p. 56.

30. See below, p. 359 n. for the differences in wealth suggested by the Bedfordshire Subsidy Rolls, 36 Elizabeth.

31. *Blechingley,* 1921, II, 482.

32. Westcote, *View of Devonshire,* p. 50.

blood or birth, but were merely "meaner," of less substance and standing in the community than those who were styled yeomen. We may turn to Sir Thomas Smyth for a final word on how the matter worked. "For amongst the Gentlemen," he said, "they which claime no higher degree, and yet be to be exempted out of the number of the lowest sort thereof, be written Esquires: so amongst the husbandmen, labourers, lowest and rascall sort of the people, such as be exempted out of the number of the rascabilitie of the popular, be called and written *yeomen* as in the degree next unto *Gentlemen.*"[33]

Hence husbandman, though not fundamentally a term of rank, came to be used as such. Since, however, the yeoman's superiority was not of blood or class any more than the esquire was superior to the gentleman in those respects, the terms are frequently found, as are those terms, within the same family. The father in a family may frequently be styled "yeoman" while his sons, working for him it may be, or as tenants to some neighbor, are described merely as "husbandmen." Or an elder brother as heir to his father's lands, and perhaps already assuming the responsibilities of his position in the community, is called yeoman while his younger brothers are described as husbandmen.[34] If through their own efforts or with the aid of gifts of money or lands they came in time to have lands of their own, or rose to be wealthy farmers to gentlemen so that they assumed positions of sufficient "estimation and preheminence" in their communities, they might thereby assume yeoman status. If they continued as small copyholders or tenant farmers of

33. *The Commonwealth of England,* p. 40. See case of Benjamin Taylor in the Devon Quarter Sessions Bundles, 1598; see also *Men and Armour for Gloucestershire,* p. 176.

34. See manuscripts in the Birmingham Public Library (hereafter cited as Birmingham MSS.), k/4, no. 98; St.Ch. 8, 38/14; Manuscripts of the Sussex Archæological Society, The Barbican, Lewes (hereafter cited as Sussex MSS.), H/575; Manuscripts in the Norwich Free Library (hereafter cited as Norwich MSS.), 3/c/2; Calendar of the Essex Quarter Sessions Rolls and Papers at Colchester (hereafter cited as Essex Sessions Records), 49/4.

little substance, they continued to be accounted merely as husbandmen.

This being the case, it is easy to see why the terms were sometimes used loosely; and there are enough instances of overlapping to show that no social cleavage was inherent in their use. But as a group the yeomen in the country community ranked above the husbandmen and were next in position and importance to the gentlemen.

The relation of the yeomen to the gentry also needs some clarification but on different grounds. For while it is easy to accept the fact that there was little if any social cleavage between the yeomanry and the farmer folk of slightly less substance who worked for them and about them, it is frequently thought that a definite gulf existed between the yeomen and the gentry, a gulf made wider because of the "gentle blood" that separated them.

Between wealthy knights or large landed gentlemen and the lesser yeomen of a community there was indeed a gulf, the result of various factors: wealth, lineage, length of settlement in the community, the possession of coat armor, county connections, and the like. But in many country parishes it would take a sharper eye than the average person possessed to determine either from their mode of living or the social intercourse carried on between them any appreciable difference between the well-to-do yeomen and their neighbors of the minor gentry. For if it is true that the doctrine of degree, priority, and place was the accepted tenet of the age, it is equally true that in practice it was not always followed.

A glimpse into the background of the yeomen and the gentry largely dispels the doctrine of "gentle blood" as a basis for distinction between them. For it will be remembered that the group to which the term yeoman came in the fifteenth century to be applied contained the scions of old franklin families, and also the younger sons of knights and their sons, whose blood was as free and "gentle" as that of their neighbors and kinsmen now classed among the gentry.[35] The law of primogeniture frequently assisted in this leveling. As Thomas Fuller said, "An heir is a Phenix in a familie; there can be but one of them at the same time. Hence comes it often to passe, that younger brothers of gentile families live in lowe wayes clouded often amongst the Yeomanry; and yet those under-boughs grow from the same root with the top branches."[36]

It was freely admitted by contemporaries that all "gentlemen" were not "gentlemen of the blood." Francis Markham, describing the "first Round in the Scale of Honor," says that "Gentry or Gentilitie, is taken two waies, that is to say, either by acquisition, or descent."[37] And among those who had acquired gentility there were heirs of old free-tenant families, descendants of copyholders, bondmen, tradesmen, artificers, merchants, and citizens; anyone, in short, who, regardless of heritage, had through the accidents of fortune or by his own efforts succeeded in the course of time in rising to wealth or office sufficient to entitle him to a place among the gentry, "of which sort of gentlemen," it was said, "we have now in England very many."

Contemporary writers frequently went to some pains to point out the means by which those of the lower classes could acquire gentility. William Harrison said in 1577: "There are comprised under the title of Gentry all Ecclesiasticall persons professing religion, all Martial men that have borne office, and have had command in the field; all Students of Arts and Sciences, and by our Englishe custome, all Innes of Court men, professors of the Law; it skilles not what their Fathers were, whether Farmers, Shoomakers, Taylers or Tinkers. . . ."[38] Barnabie Rich in 1609 put it this way:

Gentlemen . . . doo take their beginning in England, after this maner in our times. Who soever studieth the lawes of the

35. See above, pp. 11–16; also Appendix I.
36. *The Holy State,* p. 133.
37. Francis Markham, *The Booke of Honour,* 1625, p. 58.
38. *Description of England,* Bk. II, 129.

realme, who so abideth in the universitie (giving his mind to his booke) or professeth physicke and the liberall sciences, or beside his service in the roome of a capteine in the warres, (or good Counsell given at home, whereby his commonwealth is benefitted) can live without manuell labour, and therto is able and will beare the port, charge, and countenance of a gentleman, he shall (for monie have a cote and armes bestowed upon him by heralds who in the charter of the same doo of custome pretend antiquitie and service, . . .) and thereunto being made so good cheape, be called master, which is the title that men give to esquires and gentlemen.[39]

The desire for arms on the part of the man who was acquiring gentility rested on the fact that coat armor was the recognized mark or badge of the gentry; and by the time of Elizabeth, the College of Heralds had become the established place to apply for this badge.[40] It was the duty of the heralds to make periodic "visitations" throughout the country to check on such rights as were already established and to assist in determining the eligibility of new claimants. Scores of these newly recruited gentlemen came from the yeomanry though many also rose from among the tradespeople.

John Hooker said of the Devonshire yeomen in 1599, "and now of late they have entred into the trade of usurye biyenge of clothes and purchasinge and merchandises clymmynge up daylye to the degree of gentleman and do bringe up theire children accordingly."[41]

"A Yeoman," said Thomas Fuller, "is a Gentleman in

39. *Roome for a Gentleman,* 1609, p. 13.

40. For theories regarding the origin of arms see *The Boke of St. Albans* (fac. ed.), 1881; Wm. Wyrley, *True Use of Armorie,* 1592, pp. 19–21; Sir Wm. Segar, *The Booke of Honor and Armes,* 1590, Bk. V; Sir J. Ferne, *The Blazon of Gentrie;* H. Peacham, *The Compleat Gentleman,* 1622, chap. xiii; and Sir George Sitwell, "The English Gentleman," *The Ancestor,* 1902, I.

41. *Synopsis Chronographical of Devonshire in 1599* (hereafter cited as Hooker, *Synopsis*), reprinted in the *Transactions of the Devonshire Association for the Advancement of Science, Literature and Art* (hereafter cited as *Devon Trans.*), XLVII, 341–342.

Ore whom the next age may see refined."[42] During the age of Elizabeth and the early Stuarts the process of refining went on at a rapid rate. Bishop Latimer, the yeoman's son of Lancashire who rose to prominence and preached before Edward VI, had his counterpart in succeeding generations, as a host of familiar names can testify. Latimer's own field was well represented. Richard Baxter, son of a small Shropshire freeholder, became one of the most enlightened divines of his day. Adam Martindale, a Lancashire yeoman's son, achieved popularity in northern nonconformist communities. Ralph Josselyn, son of an Essex yeoman, took his degree at Cambridge and was the vicar of Earle Colne for forty years.

In other fields and professions it was the same. Sir Isaac Newton was the son of a Lincolnshire yeoman. He was born at Woolsthorpe on the small estate which his grandfather had purchased in 1624. William Harvey was the son of a yeoman of Kent. John Selden, called by Milton "the chief of learned men reputed in this land," was a yeoman's son. His birthplace may still be seen at Salvington in the parish of West Tarring, Sussex. Selden was a member of the Long Parliament and among his fellow parliamentarians sat another yeoman's son, Henry Benson of Yorkshire.[43] The Holles family, famous also in political annals, sprang from yeoman stock in Warwickshire.[44] George Chapman the poet was a Hertford yeoman's son. And it was from another Warwickshire yeoman's family that Shakespeare came.[45] If most of these men were exceptional it was only because of the exceptional nature of their later achievements, not in their having risen from their yeoman status; for scores less distinguished than they among the gentry were offspring of yeoman stock. "I might," said Henry Peacham in 1638, "fill a whole volume if I should reckon up all such great and

42. *The Holy State,* p. 105.
43. Mary Frear, "The Personnel of the Long Parliament," MS. in preparation.
44. A. C. Wood, "The Holles Family," *R.H.S. Trans.,* XIX, 149.
45. See below, p. 160.

eminent personages the cottage has afforded as principall
pillars to the support of our Commonwealth."[46]

The Boutflower Book tells the story of a middle-class
family of the north of England from 1303 to the present.
The records begin with John Bultflour, a freeman but no
freeholder, who held his land of the Bishop of Durham in
the reign of Edward I. As copyholders, the family progressed in substance and importance in their community.
At what time they first acquired freehold land the record
does not state, but of the changes which occurred in the
family's position at the time of Elizabeth and James I, the
author of the recent family history, a descendant of the
house, is very specific. This period, he says, "marks a distinct epoch in the history of the Boutflowers. Henceforth in
the parish registers the heads of the house are 'Mr.' and
'Mrs.' The possession of a fair landed estate, and their connection with the Fenwicks provided them with a county
status. They take to themselves a coat of arms. They form
alliances with well-known families, and are brought into
contact with persons who have a place in history. They begin to understand other arts than that of farming. They
find employment in the professions and services."[47] It would
be difficult to find a better description of what took place in
scores of yeoman families. Records not yet written in narrative form tell the same story.

The reports of the heralds' visitations are notoriously
inaccurate in giving a complete list of the resident gentry
in various counties; there are almost always additional lists
of "disclaimers." But there is, I think, no disposition to
question the right of those who are recorded there to their
place in the list. A comparison of the Lincolnshire visitation
for 1562 and that of 1634 discloses a startling number of
changes in the personnel of the county families in that shire
during the intervening period.[48] The report of 1634 con-

46. *The Truth of Our Times,* 1638, p. 6.
47. D. S. Boutflower, *The Boutflower Book,* 1930, p. 32. Note the development of the occupational surname.
48. *The Visitation of the County of Lincoln, 1562–1564* (Metcalfe),

tains 78 names that are not in the visitation of 1562. Of this number 24 are those of families who came from counties outside Lincolnshire. No attempt has been made to trace their origins. Undoubtedly among them would be found some newly rich families seeking to better their fortunes and to establish themselves where there was land to buy. But of the remaining 44 new families, at least 20, possibly 22, came from yeoman stock.[49]

Perhaps not all sections of England would show so great a turnover as this in the lists of their county families. Various factors, including the large amounts of monastic lands still changing hands and the draining of swamplands, made Lincoln at this time a particularly rich field for the land hungry. But examples of the rise of individual yeoman families all over England show that it was a common occurrence and in no wise restricted to county or region.

In 1614 Spencer Horley, yeoman, bought the site of the manor of Merton and other lands in Warwickshire. Some of these were leased at a good rental during the following years, and in 1634 Spencer Horlye, gentleman, of the same place, either the same man or his son, was engaging in other land transactions.[50] William Clotebooke, yeoman, of Nastend in the county of Gloucester, died in 1626. His son Nathaniel was styled gentleman.[51] Thomas Quenell, yeoman, of Cheddingfold, Surrey, died in 1571. His brother and heir Robert consolidated and added to the family property, leaving it in 1612 to his son Peter who raised the fam-

1881; Visitation of Lincoln, 1634, Copy of MS. of the College of Arms, c/23; *Lincoln Pedigrees* (Maddison), Publications of the Harleian Society, 1902–1906, L, 52, 55.

49. Much of the material for identifying the origin of these families came from A. R. Maddison, *Lincolnshire Wills,* 1888–91, Introduction, and *passim.* The remainder were traced through family documents, chiefly wills in the MSS. of the Free Library and the Probate Registry at Lincoln.

50. The Stowe Manuscripts in the Huntington Library (hereafter cited as Stowe MSS. Hn. to distinguish them from the famous collection in the British Museum that will be cited simply as Stowe MSS.), Uncatalogued Accounts, 1614, 1630, 1634.

51. "The Family of Clutterbuck," *Gloucestershire Notes and Queries* (hereafter cited as *Glouc. N. and Q.*), 1894, V, 557.

ily from its yeoman estate and secured a grant of arms in 1624.[52]

Paul Fletcher, yeoman, of Derbyshire, was in 1638 leasing rich lands from Sir Arthur Ingram for twenty-one years. Before the term of the lease was up the same man, now Paul Fletcher, gentleman, bought the lands he already held by lease.[53] Peter Bartoe, yeoman, of Ottery St. Mary, Devon, died in 1619. One of his grandsons became a physician, another attended Christ's College, Cambridge, and later entered the church, and a niece married into the gentry. The Amories, the Bowdages, and the Northcotes were other yeoman families who entered the ranks of Devon gentry at this time.[54] It is doubtless such as these of whom Hooker was thinking when he said of the yeomen there that "every man is now of an aspiringe mynde and not contented with theire owne estate do like better of anothers."[55] Humphrey Bemond, of Norfolk, in Elizabeth's reign, was described as yeoman, but his son William is styled gentleman.[56] John Bull of the same county was written yeoman in 1593, and gentleman in 1597.[57]

John Baker, yeoman, of Uckfield, Sussex, died in 1597. His son Michael was in 1595 styled gentleman.[58] The Whites,[59] Collinses,[60] Combers, and many other old yeoman families entered the ranks of the Sussex gentry in this pe-

52. T. Cooper, "The Will of Thomas Quenell," *Surrey Archæological Collections* (hereafter cited as *Surrey Arch.*), 1900, XV, 41.

53. Additional Manuscripts in the British Museum (hereafter cited as **Add. MSS.**), 6666, fols. 157–159.

54. Notes on the Bartoe family from the MSS. of Mrs. Frances Rose-Troup, Ottery St. Mary, Devon; "John Damery," *Devon and Cornwall Notes and Queries*, 1919, X, 95; "Tristram Bowdage," *ibid.*, pp. 326–327; Cokayne, *Complete Peerage*, VII, 42. The Northcotes gained a baronetcy in 1641.

55. Hooker, *Synopsis*, p. 341.,

56. Norwich MSS., Rye 53. See also the Leeches of Paston, C. Hoare, *History of an East Anglian Soke*, 1918, p. 355.

57. Add. MSS. 19113. See also John Woodcock, *ibid.*, 19081.

58. *Post Mortem Inquisitions*, Publications of the Sussex Record Society (hereafter cited as Sussex Rec. Soc.), 1912, XIV, 13.

59. R. Rice, "The White Family of Horsham," *Sussex Archæological Collections* (hereafter cited as *Sussex Arch.*), 1886, XXXIV, 128.

60. Add. MSS. 34787.

riod. The formula, happily extant, of the award of arms to the last-named family is interesting because it shows that the king's herald had not even gone through the formality of pretending, as Sir Thomas Smyth says, to have found a title "in perusing and viewing olde Registers where his Ancestors in times past had been recorded to bear the same."[61]

William Comber, yeoman, died in 1561. In June, 1571, John, his son and heir, received the grant of arms. The grounds, according to the award, were simply that the herald had upon investigation among various Sussex gentry been informed that John Comber, "hath long continued in Vertue, & in all his affaires hath so vertuously behaved himself that he hath well deserved, and is worthy to be henceforth admitted, accepted & receaved into the Nombre of other aunciente Gentlemen. . . ."[62] John Comber, in other words, measured up to the standards which that community deemed proper for its gentry, having arrived, as Smyth put it, at the place where he could "bear the post, charge and countenance of a gentleman."[63]

Westcote says that in Devon many yeomen were considered as gentlemen and saluted with the suitable term of "master" because they "were gentlemen's equals by estate,"[64] or had been descended from younger brothers. Hence it would seem that the arms in themselves were at times rather the emblem of the achievement than a prerequisite.[65]

At Burton Lazars in Leicestershire lived William Hartopp, yeoman, member of a family that had been settled in that neighborhood for at least four centuries. In 1596 his son Thomas acquired a grant of family arms and later married Dorothy Cave, a niece of Lord Treasurer Burleigh. A

61. *The Commonwealth of England,* p. 37.
62. "The Combers of Sussex," *Sussex Arch.,* XLIX, 131.
63. *The Commonwealth of England,* p. 37.
64. *View of Devonshire,* p. 50.
65. Though John Shakespeare, the poet's father, did not secure his grant of arms until 1596, he was spoken of as "Master" Shakespeare in various records from the time he held the office of high bailiff in Stratford in 1568, C. Stopes, *Shakespeare's Family,* 1901, p. 54; S. Lee, *Life of Shakespeare,* 1931, p. 12.

daughter Anne married Sir Francis Smith of Lincolnshire, and another son, Edward, became Sir Edward Hartopp.[66]

Whether or not this Sir Edward, in his rise from the estate of yeomanry to knighthood, passed through a stage where he was known as "Master" Hartopp, or Edward Hartopp, gentleman, is not apparent. He probably did. In previous centuries, when knighthood had to do with military service and personal valor, the title had been one of honor. But when kings had more need of money than of soldiers, and land held by knight service came to have no special significance,[67] it lost much of its old dignity. To be sure, in Elizabeth's time it was still held an honor to be dubbed knight as a mark of the queen's esteem. But the lavish use of the custom by the first Stuart who created knights by the hundreds, and his son's efforts on purely mercenary grounds to revive the statute by which all forty-pound landholders[68] must assume their knighthood or pay a fine, still further cheapened the title. For there were now many below the gentry to whom this fine would apply.[69]

There is little to show what would have happened if a yeoman of wealth had appeared at King Charles's coronation and claimed his right to knighthood.[70] It is true that Thomas Gainsford in 1618 spoke of wealthy yeomen of

66. H. Hartopp, "The Hartopp Family of Burton Lazars," *Leicestershire and Rutland Notes and Queries* (hereafter cited as *Leic. and Rut. N. and Q.*), 1893, pp. 209–211.

67. See below, p. 109.

68. In an earlier period the requirement was £20 yearly in land, *S.R.*, I, *Statutum de militibus, Temp. incert.*, p. 229.

69. See p. 218. The statute abolishing the distraint of knighthood in 1660 speaks of many who were so taxed; there is also some intimation that fictitious status terms were invented to enable people to evade the fines, *S.R.*, 16 Car. I, c. 20. Harrison says: "There be manie in England able to despend a knight's living, which never came unto that Countenance, and by theire own consents," *Description of England,* Bk. II, 114.

70. An Elizabethan antiquarian, Mr. Thynne, quotes an instance drawn from an earlier period (for which he gives no date) of a yeoman who, able to spend 100 marks per annum, answered the summons compelling all men worth twenty pounds yearly to take the order of knighthood or be fined. The court, according to the report, was in doubt "how they might put this off," and "at the last he was wayved because he did come the second day." Lansdowne MSS. 254, fol. 64b.

England, "having sometimes their sonnes knighted."[71] And
Philip Gawdy while a young student at Clifford's Inn
(1608) wrote to his brother about the king's recent be-
stowal of knighthoods, deploring the fact that among the
worthy there were also many unworthy "like cockles
amongst good corne." He said: "I have heard your coun-
tryes of Norfolk and Suffolk taxed that there were sheap-
reaves and yomans sonnes knighted."[72] But this was probably hearsay. And it is likely that few if any yeomen gained
their knighthood without first becoming gentlemen, though
among the new-made knights there were certainly many
whose gentility was a recent acquisition.[73]

Class consciousness often weighs heavily on those recently risen in the social scale. Sir Henry Beaumont, in the
reign of James I, brought charges against one Timothy
Saunders for unlawfully pasturing cattle on the common
of one of his manors. In the bill of complaint he designated
the defendant as "Timothye Saunders, yeoman." Whereupon Saunders, answering the charge, protested that Sir
Henry had "by way of Disparagement and Disgrace . . .
caused the addicion of Yooman" to be given him; whereas,
he declared, after dwelling at length on his good descent
and ancient family, "Sir Henry Beaumont well knew . . .
that this Defendante was a gent. before that the said Sir
Henry Beaumont was a Knight."[74]

Some of the defenders of the status quo in society
frowned upon the ambition of the lower classes to move up
in the social scale. Robert Crowley in *The Yeoman's Lesson*,
written in 1550, said:

71. Gainsford, *Glory of England,* pp. 307–309.

72. "Gawdy letters, *temp* Elizabeth and James I," *Historical Manuscripts Commission* (hereafter cited as *H.M.C.*), 7th Report, p. 527b.

73. Barnabie Rich denounced those who purchased knighthood, at-
tributing their action to "a silly humor that loveth admiration." He said,
"We are now so full of Knights that Gentlemen are held in little request."
Roome for a Gentleman, pp. 29–32. See also the work of a contemporary
versemaker who ridiculed the current prodigal practice of conferring
knighthood, quoted in the *Wiltshire Archæological and Natural History
Magazine* (hereafter cited as *Wilts Arch.*), XVIII, 255–256.

74. St.Ch. 8, 26/5.

> For what doste thou; if thou desyr
> To be a lord or gentleman
> Other than heape on thee God's ire
> And Shewe thy selfe no Christian.

He admonished the yeomen to

> Have minde, therefore, thyselfe to holde
> Within the bondes of thy degre
> And then thou mayest ever be bold
> That God thy Lorde wyll prosper thee.[75]

Ancient families of the gentry were often not willing to welcome upstart knights or "gentlemen of the first head" into their ranks. The Earl of Arundel's public taunt to the first Lord Spencer regarding his humble ancestry has become a classic because of the quick-witted Spencer's reply that while his ancestors were tending sheep those of the noble earl were plotting treason.[76] But there were many less famous expressions of disapproval from members of old families who deplored the invasion of their ranks from below. Sir William Vaughan, writing in 1626 of the good old days when society was respectable and everyone content to live within his station, said: "But with us, Joane is as good as my Lady, Citizens wives of late growne Gallants. The Yeoman doth gentilize it. The Gentleman scornes to be behind Nobleman. . . ."[77] And in Sebastian Brant's *Ship of Fools*, first published in English in 1509, appears the following:

> Promote a yeman, make hym a gentyl màn
> And make a Baylyf of a Butchers son
> Make of a Squyer knight, yet wyll they if they can
> Coveyt in their myndes hyer promosyon.[78]

Francis Bacon disapproved the current practice, but on more practical grounds. He felt that the yeomanry should

---

75. *The Voyce of the Last Trumpet*, pp. 64–66.
76. *S.P.D.*, CXXI, 15.
77. Sir William Vaughan, *The Golden Fleece*, 1626, Preface.
78. S. Brant, *Ship of Fools* (Barclay), 1874, I, 187.

be the backbone of the military strength of the nation and feared that "if the gentlemen be too many, the commons will be base." This practice if carried too far might, therefore, bring injury to the state: "Let states that aim at greatness take heed that ther nobility and gentlemen do not multiply too fast."[79] Fear that the process would deplete the yeomanry and lessen its quality is likewise apparent in the opinion of Barnabie Rich who declared that "after the proverb began to grow in custom: That every Jack would be a Gentleman our yeomandry beganne to faint and decay."[80]

The disapproval of some was heightened by economic jealousy. Too much competition by aggressive members of the lower classes lessened the opportunities of younger sons to be well placed in the church, the law, or the army, traditional posts for those whose fathers were not able to settle them on the land. Thomas Wilson, himself a younger son and conscious of it, spoke with feeling when he said in 1600 that it being "now permitted to yeomanrye and merchauntes to set their broode to the studye of comon lawes, that faculty is so pestered, yea many worthy offices and places of high regarde, in that vocation (in olde time left to the support of gentle linage) are now pre-occupated and usurped by ungentle and base stocke." With further disdain he spoke of the sons of well-to-do yeomen who were "not contented with their states of their fathers to be counted yeomen and called John or Robert," but each "must skipp into his velvett breches and silken doublett and, getting to be admitted into some Inn of Court or Chancery, must ever after thinke skorne to be called any other than gentleman."[81]

But many contemporary writers approved the practice and considered rapid gain in numbers among new-made gentlemen a sign "whereby it should appear that vertue

79. *De Augmentis* (Spedding), Bk. VIII, 83.

80. *Roome for a Gentleman,* pp. 29–32.

81. Thomas Wilson, *The State of England, 1600,* Camden Society Publications (hereafter cited as Cam. Soc.), LII, 19.

flourisheth among us."[82] Thomas Fuller made it one of England's chief claims to superiority over other nations, boasting that here the *Temple of Honour* was bolted against none.[83] Sir Thomas Smyth questioned a bit whether or not the process should be allowed to continue in quite such free fashion, but finally decided that it was "not amisse."[84] William Harrison cannily remarked that it was a thing not to be discouraged since the gentlemen "are as subject to the taxes as the yeomen and husband and hence the prince will lose nothing by it." No man, he added shrewdly, "hath hurt by it but himselfe, who peradventure will go in wider buskens than his legs will beare, or as our proverbe saith, nowe and then beare a bigger saile than his boat is able to susteine."[85]

Poets, playwrights, and ballad-mongers, combining their function of entertainer and social critic, lost no opportunity for making the yeoman's acquisition of gentle blood the butt of more or less good-natured ridicule. Exaggerated no doubt their pictures are for effect, but they contain shrewd observations on the existing social order that are borne out by more sober evidence. The widow in Brome's play, *The Northerne Lasse* (1632), exclaimed:

I 'twere a cunning Herald could find better Arms for some of 'hem; though I have heard Sir Paul Squelch protest he was a Gentleman, and might quarter a Coat by his Wives side. Yet I know he was but a Grazier when he left the Countrey; and my Lord his father whisteled to a Teem of Horses (they were his own, indeed). But now he is Right Worshipfull . . .[86]

To claim a coat of arms on the wife's side was not in keeping with the rules of the game. It is likely that heralds sometimes winked at such a claim, but not always. Charles

82. Anon., *The Institution of a Gentleman*, 1586, Bk. IIII.
83. *The Holy State*, p. 106.
84. *The Commonwealth of England*, p. 37.
85. *The Description of England*, Bk. II, 129.
86. Richard Brome, "The Northerne Lasse," *Plays*, 1873, act II, sc. I, p. 23.

Holt of Whitwall in Lancashire, who had married Mary, daughter and co-heir of the Holts of Stubley, was apparently claiming a right to use the Holt coat of arms. But the herald's note of 1613 states that he "could not prove himself to be descended out of the house of Stubley as he pretendeth, for his father and ancestors before were always reputed yeomen untyll this match with Charles and Mary. Since which tyme they usurpe the coat of Holt of Stubley without any right at all, and indede at this daye they have no coat at all and are but yeomen."[87]

Whether there were actually any quack "gentleman-makers" other than those heralds who, according to Harrison and Smyth, were sometimes guilty of quackery in their pretended perusal of old registers for pedigrees, one cannot say. But apparently Brome felt justified in creating one to use in another comedy where he made further sport of the yeoman's acquisition of gentle blood. This play depicts a yeoman who has gone up to London to have himself made a gentleman. He is acknowledged to be "but coarse metal yet," but has that about him which promises to accord well with the estate of gentleman. To a companion, his accomplice in the business, he says:

I have foure hundred poundes sir; and I brought it up to towne on purpose to make myselfe a clear gentleman of it . . . and you told me that you would upon our coming to the City, here bring mee to a knight, that was a Gentlemanmaker . . . and here I am and here's my foure hundred pounds.[88]

Later, he said to the gentleman-maker,

I came to change my Coppy, and write Gentleman; and to goe the nighest way to worke; my acquaintance here tells me, to goe by the Heralds is the farthest way about.[89]

87. *Visitation of Lancashire, 1613,* Chetham Society Publications (hereafter cited as Chet. Soc.), 1871, Ser. I, LXXXII, 90.

88. Richard Brome, "The Sparagras Garden," *Plays,* act II, sc. 3, pp. 140–141.

89. *Ibid.,* p. 142.

He was told that he must be bled until he had rid himself
of all his father's base blood. When he disclosed the fact that
his mother was a gentlewoman, he was permitted to "bleed o'
the one side, the father's side only."

In another play, *Albumazar* (1615), the trick was accomplished by a renowned astrologer. Here the discerning
playwright has his yeoman, Trincalo, say:

> O Ho!
> Now do I smell th' Astrologer's trick; hee'l steep me
> In souldier's bloud, or boyle me in a Cauldron
> Of Barbarous Law French; Or anoint me over
> With supple oile of great mens services;
> For these three means raise Yeomen to the Gentry.[90]

It was indeed by these means, the army, the law, and the
performing of certain services, that yeomen did often rise.
Trincalo's further ambitions were made evident when he
looked with fondness on his old yeoman's coat:

> Ile never part with 't,
> Till I be Shriefe of th' County, and in commission
> Of Peace and Quorum. Then will I get m'a Clarke
> A practiz'd fellow, wiser than my Worship,
> And dominere amongst my fearfull neighbours,
> And feast them bountifully with their own bribes.

The change at last effected, his speech ran thus:

> My veins are fild with newnesse: O for a Chyrurgian
> to ope this arme and view my gentle bloud,
> To try if't run two thousand pounds a yeere.[91]

He now professed himself ready to match his son with a
knight's daughter and to "buy a bouncing Pedigree from a
Welch Herald." In such manner the playwrights mocked
things as they were.

The examples hitherto quoted from the records and those

90. Thomas Tomkis, *Albumazar*, 1615, act II, sc. 2, D 2.
91. *Ibid.*, E, F 3.

in the above plays draw attention only to the advancement
of yeoman families through ambitious sons. A yeoman also
frequently numbered his grandchildren among the gentry
by successfully marrying his daughters into that rank.
Such marriages were a commonplace. Nor was the initiative
always taken by the yeoman. "Decayed knights and gentlemen" thought nothing of retrieving their fortunes by
marrying a wealthy yeoman's heiress; and deeds and other
documents dealing with land conveyances are filled with
references to negotiations over such matches.[92]

The purely business nature of most of these arrangements is well brought out in a case that was tried in the
Court of Requests in 1599.[93] John Chamberlayne, son of a
Berkshire gentleman, was unable from his own resources to
meet the terms of an agreement made with one James Antin
for gaining back some family possessions that his father had
mortgaged. "Being then sole and unmarried," as the record
states, Chamberlayne "determyned by some mariage to
enable himselfe to go through with the bargain." Casting
about for a suitable match, his attention fell upon Anne
Busnell, the niece and heiress of Richard Myllard, a yeoman
of Amport, Southants. Having heard of her uncle's inten-
tions to prefer her in marriage to "some good person," he
immediately entered into communication with Myllard.
These efforts resulted in marriage negotiations whereby
Chamberlayne expected to make good his promise to pay
the necessary £400 cash, and £200 annually for two years
to his creditor. It is a good example of a gentleman's son
seeking to make secure his financial position by marrying
with a bride from a well-to-do yeoman family. There are
many such in the records.

If the bridegroom's family were one of a closely knit cir-

92. Sussex MSS., H. 629, 639; "A Calendar of Norfolk Deeds," *Norfolk
Arch.*, 1898, XIII, 80; St.Ch. 8, 155/2; A Calendar of the deeds, leases,
and other legal documents relating to land conveyance in the Exeter Free
Library (hereafter cited as Exeter Deeds and Documents), 1044; Add.
MSS. 28008, fol. 35.

93. The records of the Court of Requests in the Public Record Office
(hereafter those of Elizabeth's reign will be cited as Req. 2), 190/13.

cle of county families of long standing and connections, there might be resentment over such a match. Families of this type preferred to see their sons choose wives from their own group. Such was the case when Mr. Henry Oxinden chose the seventeen-year-old daughter of James Culling, a wealthy Kentish yeoman, for his bride. The two men had been neighbors and friends. But there was some dissatisfaction with the match among the kin, and had the young squire not loved pretty Catherine Culling for her own sake as well as for her lands and money the match might never have been concluded.[94] But in communities where wealthy yeomen and members of the minor gentry were already fraternizing on the warmest terms, there was no thought of impropriety in a match of this kind. An honorable name was exchanged for a good dowry and the bargain considered a good one on both sides, as dozens of indentures sealing such contracts tend to show.

Frequently a wealthy yeoman's widow was the prize sought after by a knight or gentleman. And young men in the professions were often glad to share their gentility in return for the dower of a yeoman's daughter.[95]

Emphasis upon the ease and rapidity with which members of the yeomanry could advance beyond the station to which they were born must not leave the impression that every wealthy yeoman aspired to enter the ranks of the gentry. The statement that "every Jack would be a Gentleman" contained proverbial truth, but by no means the whole truth. Nor was Thomas Wilson, the disgruntled younger son, correct in thinking that all sons of well-to-do yeomen were discontented with their fathers' estates.

The doctrine of degree, priority, and place, though it set up no actual barrier to the possibility of advance from one status to another, did very definitely put the stamp of approval upon the existence of social gradations. There was

94. *The Oxinden Letters* (Gardiner), 1933, pp. xxii–xxiii.
95. See Req. 2, 196/60; St.Ch. 8, 181/11; "Calendar of Marriage Licences," *Bedfordshire Notes and Queries* (hereafter cited as *Beds N. and Q.*), 1889, II, 72.

no thought even among those who themselves advanced, that the existence of rank and degree was not right and proper. Besides, it is easy always to give more attention to the individuals who push ahead than to the many who either cannot or do not wish to do so. The rise of yeomen into the ranks of the gentry is a distinctive feature of the age of Elizabeth and the Stuarts, and merits the attention given it. But for every one who thus advanced there were many to whom the urge to make their way within their own station in a manner profitable to themselves and creditable to the standards of their group was of far greater concern than any desire to advance beyond it. To add to their lands and make them produce as much as possible, to see their sons well established and their daughters married with good portions, to maintain the family seat in the parish church, and when the end came, to lie beside their fathers in the village churchyard: this was the ambition of most yeomen and concerned them far more than a desire to be addressed as "Master" instead of "Goodman."

There is reason, moreover, to believe that some yeomen, particularly those descended from ancient free-tenant families and settled for many years in the same locality, felt a genuine pride in their station and either were indifferent or actually averse to changing it. Many of those whom we have seen moving into the ranks of the gentry did so naturally through an increase in family possessions, marriage connections, or entrance into the professions. But the conscious "climber" is unpopular in any age or group, and it may well be that the ridicule heaped upon new-made knights and gentlemen caused some yeomen to feel that it was "better to be the head of the yeomanry than the tail of the gentry." Proverbs, in Kent or elsewhere, thrive and endure only because there is a modicum of truth in what they say.[96]

96. Armorial seals are affixed to the deeds and leases of various Sussex yeomen in this period. See especially the Gage Papers in the Sussex MSS. There are also many yeomen on the lists of "disclaimers" sometimes appended to the heralds' visitations.

What percentage of the yeomen of the Elizabethan and Stuart days were descended from ancient free-tenant families it is impossible to say. Probably not the majority of them! For it is estimated that the number of free tenants on the medieval manor was actually quite small. But there were many who had long been settled in the same spot, holding the same land from generation to generation. The Kirklands of Crich, in Derbyshire, according to the record of a tombstone in the parish church, had been settled in that community "above five hundred year." The Gunnes of Cornwall had "from tyme out of mynde byne seised" of their possessions there.[97] The Furses of Devon had been settled on their lands near Tiverton since the fourteenth century.[98] And the Custs of Pinchbeck in Lincoln dated back many generations.[99] Then there were the descendants of the old free-tenant families of Hallamshire, many of whom, Sir George Sitwell says, never chose to write "gentleman" after their names, though they were connected with some of the best of the county families;[100] and the ancient Kentish families of whom Lambard wrote: "A man may find sundry yeomen (although otherwise for wealth comparable with many of the gentle sort) that will not yet for all that change their condition nor desire to be apparelled with the titles of Gentry."[101]

The playwrights also took note of yeomen of this type. Old Strowd of Norfolk, in *The Blind Beggar of Bednal Green*, deplored his son's pretense of being a gentleman, and said to him:

> Come, off with this trash,
> Your bought Gentility, that sits on thee
> Like Peacock's feathers cock't upon a Raven.

97. Req. 2, 209/74.
98. *The Diary and Family Book of Robert Furse* (hereafter cited as *Furse Family Book*), reprinted in part in *Devon Trans.*, XXVI, 168–183.
99. A. Maddison, *Lincolnshire Wills*, p. lvi.
100. *The Hurts of Haldworth*, chap. I.
101. William Lambard, *The Perambulation of Kent*, 1656, pp. 9–10.

With genuine warmth he later declared:

> I am as proud,
> And think myself as gallant in this gray,
> Having my Table furnish't with good Beef,
> Norfolk temes bread, and Country home bred drink,
> As he that goeth in ratling Taffity.
> Let Gentlemen go gallant what care I,
> I was a yeoman born, and so I'll die.[102]

George A'Greene, the valiant yeoman of Wakefield, expressed similar sentiments.[103] And one meets them again in John Carter, the bluff yeoman character of another play, *The Witch of Edmonton*, who replied to the visitor that addressed him as "Master" Carter:

No gentleman I, Master Thorney; spare the Mastership, call me by my name, John Carter. *Master* is a title my father nor his before him, were acquainted with; honest Hertfordshire yeomen; such an one am I; my word and my deed shall be proved one at all times.[104]

There are records to show that these yeomen were not merely the product of the playwright's imagination. James Culling of Kent, owner of extensive lands and able in his will to enumerate cash bequests of £1,600, expressed the wish that his daughter and heiress Catherine should "marry with a Culling."[105] He would have favored her marriage later with Henry Oxinden, a member of the gentry; for he held him in high regard and had named him Catherine's guardian. But he would have been equally pleased had she car-

102. H. Chettle and J. Day, *The Blind Beggar of Bednal Green,* 1902, act II, p. 24. (Though ascribed to Chettle and Day by most authorities, the authorship of this play is in some doubt.) "Temmes" bread seems to have been a loaf made of flour from which the coarser bran had been taken. See Sir W. Ashley, *The Bread of our Forefathers,* 1928, p. 62.

103. Anon., *George A'Greene, The Pinner of Wakefield,* 1911, sc. XIII, lines 1310–1318.

104. T. Dekker, J. Ford, W. Rowley, *The Witch of Edmonton,* 1894, act I, sc. 2.

105. Add. MSS. 28008, fol. 47. See p. 372.

ried out his wish to marry with a yeoman kinsman by the name of Culling.[106]

Adam Eyre of the West Riding of Yorkshire, member of a yeoman family long settled in the north of Derbyshire, had an uncle on his mother's side who was the high sheriff of Derby, and he himself, by rising to be a captain in Cromwell's army, earned the right to be styled gentleman and was sometimes so described in legal documents. But when the time came to dictate his own last will and testament, it was as "Adam Eyre, yeoman" that he chose to describe himself.[107] Nor is "Yeoman John" of whom the Harrow boys have sung for generations a myth. John Lyon, who founded and modestly endowed the institution that through the twists of fortune was destined to become one of England's famous public schools, was a wealthy yeoman who lived in the village of Harrow-on-the-Hill where his farmhouse still stands. When he applied to the queen for the school's charter, the application was made and granted in the name of "John Lyon, yeoman,"[108] and he was so styled on the contemporary brass that may still be seen in Harrow church.

In addition to feeling that their status was an ancient and respectable one, perhaps even above this feeling, there was another reason that kept many well-to-do yeomen content with the class into which they were born. This was the simple fact that in terms of pounds and pence it cost less to be a yeoman. Certain demands were made upon the gentry that came in lower terms to yeomen, or happily not at all. Now thrift, as we shall see, was one of the first lessons learned in a yeoman household and it was largely by the practice of economy that wealthy yeomen had acquired their riches. To many of these a "mastership" scarcely compensated for the costs involved.

It was not that the scale of living between the minor gen-

106. See below, pp. 285, 372.
107. *Diary of Adam Eyre,* reprinted in full in *Yorkshire Diaries,* Surtees Society Publications, 1875, LXV, 353.
108. Harleian Manuscripts in the British Museum (hereafter cited as Harl. MSS.), 2211.

try and the well-to-do yeomen differed so much;[109] but in benevolences and assessment ratings, more was usually demanded of members of the gentry. If an assessment were made by local men, this might not be true. For in that case an attempt was usually made to apportion the amounts on the basis of the wealth possessed and not on the degree or status of the individual. An example in point is the assessment of fines in a forcible entry case that came before the sessions in the North Riding of Yorkshire in 1609. According to the sessions records, three yeomen and one gentleman were fined £3 apiece while five other yeomen were let off with 40 shillings each.[110] But in other cases, particularly where the order originated outside the county and the assessors did not know the ability of individuals, the situation was different. A letter from Queen Elizabeth in 1570 to the sheriff of Wiltshire concerning a royal benevolence requested that money be collected from the people who were "of the qualitie of Esquier or gentleman."[111] Here the yeomen escaped altogether. Another royal order of 1586, for repairing and making beacons in Northampton, divided the expense of the work as follows:[112]

everye Lord within the Countie of Northampton	x *s*
everye knight	vi *s* viii *d*
everye esquire	v *s*
every gentellman	iii *s* iiii *d*
everye other substantiall honest yeoman	ii *s*

Again in Yorkshire in the reign of James I the North Riding Sessions ordered that when jurors who were summoned to appear at the quarter sessions made default, they should be fined, "the gentlemen to 40 s. and yeomen to 30 s. apeece."[113]

109. See below, pp. 218, 239–240.
110. *North Riding Sessions Records,* I, 174.
111. "Queen Elizabeth to Sir John Thynne, Sheriff," *Wilts Arch.,* XIV, 201. See also poll-tax rating, *ibid.,* VII, 2.
112. "The Auncient Order for Beacons," Publications of the Northampton Record Society (hereafter cited as Northants Rec. Soc.), 1926, III, 8.
113. *North Riding Sessions Records,* I, 193.

Economy then in some cases, scorn of a new-bought gentility in others, and with some, indifference to the entire matter, made many yeomen of substance content to remain within the station to which they were born. In matters of office and social precedence they showed deference to their superiors as did every class whether high or low in the social scale. But there was free mingling between groups in country communities and their position was one of respect and well-being. Those of the poorer sort found companionship among the tenant farmers or smaller freeholders of their own economic level, while yeomen of better position were often intimates in the homes of the minor gentry with whom they had both business and social affiliations.

Intermarriages alone made this fact inevitable. Those matches by which a yeoman's daughter raised the status of her children by marrying into the gentry have been mentioned. "Gentility" could not legally be transmitted save through the male line, but the fact that a gentleman's daughter who married a yeoman sacrificed the right of her children to "gentle blood" seems to have been no barrier to this type of match. There were numerous ways in which those children might regain their gentility when they grew up; and if they did not, there were apparently many who felt that it did not matter if lands and good store of sheep and cattle were gained by the exchange.

Henry Peacham writes of a countryman whose wife is "some gentleman's daughter who was matched to him for his wealth."[114] There were many such matches. The two daughters of Edward Stratford, gentleman, of Winchcombe in Gloucestershire, fared no less well than their brothers and sisters in the legacies received from their uncle, an esquire, though both were married to husbands who wrote yeoman after their names.[115] Margaret Townley, described as "sister of the whole blood" to Richard Townley, an esquire of Lancashire, married James Hartley, yeoman, with no indication that the marriage was not satisfactory on

114. *The Truth of Our Times,* pp. 124–125.
115. Stowe MSS. Hn., Uncatalogued Accounts, 1595, 1607.

both sides.[116] Marie Luke, the daughter of Nicholas Luke, Esq., was married to Edward Barnard, a well-to-do Hertford yeoman.[117] Henry Day, yeoman, in 1591 married Alice, daughter of William Harwood, gentleman, he says, "at the request and desier of Mr. Harwood."[118] Alexander Worthington, a yeoman of Adlington, Lancashire, married Margaret, the daughter of Hugh Deconson, gentleman. The bride, a widow, had formerly been the wife of John Adlington, Esq.[119] And when Lawrence Cliffe, of Staffordshire, yeoman, expressed his displeasure because his son had married the daughter of one Lawrence Ashenhurst, "he being a man of very mean estate and quality," it seems likely that it was the poor estate rather than the "quality" of the bride that caused the displeasure; for later the record discloses that her father was a kinsman of Ralph Ashenhurst, gentleman.[120]

The rise from yeoman status was no doubt hastened by these marriages even if gentility could not theoretically be transmitted through the wife. One of the claims made in support of the application of John Shakespeare, the poet's father, for a coat of arms was the fact he had married Nancy Arden,[121] the daughter of Robert Arden of Wilmcote, gentleman.

It was not only by marriages, however, that the border line between the two degrees became less distinct. When one or more members of a yeoman family entered the professions, and thereby became "gentlemen," the result was a great mingling of degrees among members of the same family. There are scores of cases where one son is styled yeoman and his brother gentleman, where a father is a yeoman and his son a gentleman. There were borderline cases in which

116. D.L. 1624, 9/5, no. 6.
117. St.Ch. 8, 199/8. See also *The Index Library*, XXI, 80; and Wills in the Archdeaconry Court in Berkshire in the manuscripts at Somerset House (hereafter cited as Berks Wills), H 307.
118. Req. 2, 196/31.   119. St.Ch. 8, 300/19.
120. *Ibid.*, 98/15.
121. Herald's report on Shakespeare's application, P. Butler, *Materials for the Life of Shakespeare*, 1930, pp. 101–102.

an individual is described as both yeoman and gentleman.
Adam Eyre has already been mentioned as one of this
type.[122] The Essex Sessions Rolls speak of Robert Woode
of Broomfield, "yeoman, otherwise gentleman."[123] It is
small wonder that the servant in the play, upon being asked
who was at the door, answered,

> Men, sir, gentlemen or yeomen, I know not which,
> But the one, sure, they are.[124]

There was general fraternizing among the two groups
in country neighborhoods. Gentlemen were sureties for yeomen, and yeomen for gentlemen.[125] Each borrowed money
freely of the other.[126] Yeomen named gentlemen as executors of their wills; gentlemen did likewise with yeomen.[127]
Humphrey Harryson, gentleman, of Nottingham, left all
of his estate of a thousand pounds to his "neere kinsman,"
John Duckmanton, yeoman, of Derbyshire.[128] Edward
Thomson, yeoman, of Surrey, named his "loveing friende
and neighbour" *Mr.* John Gilpin as guardian to his children.[129] And Thomas Higginbotham, gentleman, of Rush-
ton, Staffordshire, executed an indenture in 1636, naming
"in my stead and place . . . my lovinge frend Cristofer
Phesey of Maney in the county of Warwick, yeoman, my

122. See above, p. 53.

123. Essex Sessions Rolls, 1568. See also Req. 2, 212/74, 219/70; St.Ch.
8, 190/8, 269/11, 303/6, 213/17; The Recusants' Book, El. MSS. 2178.

124. Thomas Middleton, "A Faire Quarrel," in *Works,* 1840, III, act I,
sc. 1.

125. See Recognizances in the records of any quarter sessions court for
this period.

126. Thomas Tate, a Wiltshire yeoman who died in 1620, numbered
among his debtors Sir Francis Seymour, Sir Ferdinand Dudley, Sir
Mathew Carew, Mr. Gray of Enfield, Esq., and others, Manuscripts of
wills in the Prerogative Court of Canterbury at Somerset House (hereafter cited as P.C.C.), 53 Soame. See also manuscripts of the Northampton Records Society (hereafter cited as Northants MSS.), Brudenell,
D 11, 21.

127. P.C.C. 75 Wood; St.Ch. 8, 12/7; *Staffordshire Historical Collections* of the William Salt Archæological Society (hereafter cited as *Staff.
Coll.*), N.S., XXXV, 9.

128. St.Ch. 8, 122/16.   129. P.C.C. 75 Wood.

true and lawfull Atturney . . . to levy and collect all debts and obligations owing to me." He gave him "authoritie to prosecute, arrest, etc. as well as I myselfe might or could doe if I were personally present."[130]

What John Hooker said of the Devonshire yeoman (*ca.* 1599) was true of many in other country communities: "for his fyne beinge ones payed he lyveth as merylie as does his Lande lorde and giveth him selffe for the most parte to such virtue, condicions, and qualities as doth the gentleman."[131] John Furse of Devonshire was a yeoman of this type: "He allwayes mentayned a good house, a good plow good geldynges good tyllage, good rerynge and was a good hussebonde; indede he wolde never be withowte iij copell of good hownds, he wolde surelye keepe companye with the best sorte."[132]

A case in the Court of Requests tells of a Hertford yeoman and his wife who went to live for a year with a gentleman and his wife who were their friends.[133] Another tells of a gentleman living sometimes a fortnight, sometimes by the space of a month or six weeks at the home of a yeoman friend.[134] Members of the minor gentry and yeomen sat together on juries, served together as churchwardens and in other parish offices, and met on terms of good neighborhood in the parish church. Over their mugs of ale at the village tavern the men talked of the price of corn, the need for rain, or the selection of a new constable for the parish, while their wives gossiped of weddings and of wakes, exchanged receipts for "marchpane" and "cowcumber" pickles, or talked of the efficacy of fennel tea for one that had the fevers.

Between the larger landed men in the country and the yeomen there was of course a wider gulf, a gulf based upon differences of wealth, standards of living, education, and social background. Even with these gentlemen of large estate, the personable sons of respected yeoman families were

---

130. Birmingham MSS. 329024.
131. Hooker, *Synopsis,* pp. 341–342.
132. *Furse Family Book,* p. 179.
133. Req. 2, 190/22.   134. *Ibid.,* 205/24.

in great favor as retainers and enjoyed the companionship of the masters whom they served. In an anonymous dialogue written in 1586 the countryman in discourse with his city neighbor says: "Among our Yeomen, you shal finde some, (yea very many) wel brought up, and expert in sundry, seemly and necessary knowledge without which they cannot serve a nobleman or gentleman . . . they can and doe . . . entertaine theire Master with Table Talke, be it his pleasure to speake either of Hawkes, or houndes, fishinge or fowling, sowing or grassinge . . . cheapnesse of grayne or any such matters whereof Gentlemen commonly speake in the Country. . . ."[135] He further shows their position in the household in his reply to the query whether these servants were also supposed to render menial service: "Surely, no, neither is it the manner to offer them any labor of drudgery, for thereof they would take great scorne, being cumly personages, and commonly the sonnes of some honest Yeomen. . . ."[136]

Robert Furse tells how a kinsman, John Furse, though he later married a girl of his own station, had as a youth been a personable lad, and "for his manhode and good quallytes Mr. Shylston hadde hym in serves, and after hym, he served a worthye knight with whom he went to Scotland, and lastly in serves with Henry Curteney Erel of Devon."[137] In this capacity the yeoman's sons were frequently associated with sons of gentlemen, also in the service of the lord.[138]

The Memoirs of Sir John Reresby, written in the later Stuart period, describe the Christmas celebration at Thrybergh, one of the family estates. At this season poor and rich alike enjoyed the hospitality of the great house where sheep were roasted whole, and there were food and drink in great abundance. But it is significant that during the first four days all the lower tenants of the estates were entertained, whereas "the rest of the time some four score gentlemen and yeomen with their wives were invited."[139]

135. *Of Cyvile and Uncyvile Life,* 1586, p. 34.
136. *Ibid.,* p. 38.   137. *Furse Family Book,* p. 176.
138. *Men and Armour for Gloucestershire,* pp. 136, 296.
139. *The Memoirs of Sir John Reresby,* 1875, p. 310.

But though yeomen's sons might go to the great houses to serve, and their fathers on such an occasion as Christmas be invited there with the gentry, their day-to-day association was not with its occupants but with the minor gentry, and others of their own group, or, on occasion, with the townsmen of the near-by towns and villages who were of like substance and standing with themselves.

In larger towns and cities like York, Chester, Ipswich, Southampton, and Plymouth the wealthy merchants and citizens were of substance above the yeomen, and often became landed men themselves or married into the gentry. For not infrequently a decayed county family was glad to see its limited fortune supplemented with that of a wealthy draper, mercer, or other city-bred person of means. With the townsmen of smaller towns, however, and England was largely made up of smaller towns and villages, yeomen fraternized on terms of equality, contracting marriages and carrying on a variety of business relations.[140]

Here, as in the relationship of landholders and citizens of larger means, the yeomen were theoretically accorded a slightly higher rank than that ascribed to tradesmen and artificers: "In Cases and Causes the Law of England hath conceived a better opinion of the Yeomanry that occupy Lands than of Tradesmen, Artificers, or Labourers."[141] It was one of the hangovers from the day when land tenure had been the basis of wealth and the measure of a man's social position. But in the actual life of the countryside the theory counted for little. Well-to-do yeomen matched their daughters with the sons of merchants, clothiers, drapers, or young men of the professions who dwelt in country towns; and lesser yeomen found their wives among the daughters of tailors, weavers, masons, coopers, shoemakers, and other small craftsmen. Often the way for such marriages was

140. Yeomen often owned considerable town property and were frequently elected freemen of the city. See the Bristol Corporation Manuscripts (hereafter cited as Bristol MSS.), burgess books for the period of Elizabeth and James I; and the Barnstaple Manuscripts.

141. Edward Chamberlayne, *The Present State of England,* 1669, p. 442.

paved by members of their own blood-kin who had left the land.[142]

Hence yeoman status viewed in terms of its relationship to other groups in the social structure assumes a fairly definite character. They were a substantial rural middle class whose chief concern was with the land and agricultural interests, a group who lived "in the temperate zone betwixt greatness and want,"[143] serving England, as it was given a "middle people . . . in condition between the gentry and the peasantry" to serve.[144]

Whether their position was that of an upper or lower middle class depended largely on the character of the community in which they lived, their own relative wealth and numbers there, and the number and quality of other residents. If the parish were one in which the large landed gentry were themselves resident and took a leading part in parish matters, the yeomen occupied a less important position. But in parishes where there were few or no resident gentry, the yeomen were the obvious leaders in the community.

A wealthy Londoner in the reign of James I, having made a fortune sufficient for setting up in the country, bought land and moved into Lancashire. Not long afterward he was engaged in a lawsuit with a group of his new neighbors, men whom he describes as having "all the sway and rule of the inhabitants of that place, they being the best in wealthe and abilitye nere thereabouts."[145] The *Reponsio* to his complaint indicates that all of the men so described were yeomen. Other records show a similar situation in other rural communities.[146]

The favorable position of the yeomen under Elizabeth and her immediate successors was pointed out by almost every contemporary who wrote of the social structure of the age. Sir Thomas Smyth called them the "liver-veins of

142. See below, pp. 157–158, 275–278.
143. Fuller, *The Holy State*, p. 106.
144. Bacon, *History of Henry VII* (Spedding), p. 74.
145. St.Ch. 8, 12/10.   146. *Ibid.*, 61/63.

the Commonwealth yielding both good juice and nourishment to all other parts thereof."[147] The Reverend Nathaniel Newbury spoke of them as "the pith and substance of the country."[148] Thomas Fuller declared them to be "an estate of people almost peculiar to England."[149] William Harrison told how "they commonly live wealthily, keep good houses and travailleth to get riches."[150] And Thomas Gainsford in 1618 wrote in the same vein: "You shall find our Yeomen of England a title of estimation in regard of his wealth, antiquity, and maintenance of his familie in continued descent."[151]

In the popular literature of the period the phrases "wealthy yeoman" and "wealthy yeoman's widow" occur too often to be ignored. And local historians who described the people of their own shires appear always to have spoken of the yeomen in favorable terms. Robert Reyce in 1618 pointed to the Suffolk yeomen as the one group who were getting ahead during those "unfaithful times" that were drawing the fortunes of so many downward: "Continuall underliving, saving, and the immunities from the costly charges of these unfaithfull times, do make them so to grow with wealth of this world that whilest many of the better sort, as having passed their uttermost period do suffer an utter declination, these onely doe arise, and doe lay such strong, sure, and deep foundations, that from thence in time are derived many noble and worthy families."[152]

Lambard told the same story regarding the prosperity of the yeomen of Kent.[153] Risdon, Westcote, and Hooker repeated it for the Devonshire yeomen: "After their porcions they are not much inferior with the gentlemen who be their lords."[154] And William Webb, writing in 1621 of the

147. *The Commonwealth of England*, p. 39.
148. Nathaniel Newbury, *The Yeoman's Prerogative*, 1652, Preface.
149. *The Holy State*, p. 119.
150. *Description of England*, Bk. II, 133.
151. *The Glory of England*, p. 307.   152. *Breviary of Suffolk*, p. 58.
153. *Perambulation of Kent*, pp. 8–10.
154. Hooker, *Synopsis*, p. 341; Westcote, *View of Devonshire*, p. 50; Risdon, *Survey of Devon*, p. 10.

improvement in the quality of the houses of the yeomen in Cheshire, said that "though they be but farmers, they live better than many of higher estate in other nations."[155]

These pictures are too rosy in spots. They were written partly by national patriots who wished to glorify England and English society to the detriment of other countries, and partly by local patriots who liked to put the best foot forward in the interest of their own localities. Furthermore, they too often spoke as if the whole bowl of milk were as good as the cream. But even allowing for this exaggeration, their opinions can by no means be discounted entirely. They were written by men who were themselves of the gentry and had no reason for praising to excess the class below them. One notes, moreover, that even national or local pride did not lead them to give equally flattering accounts of the progress of all classes. Certainly it is true that the yeomen impressed their contemporaries not merely as a group that was holding its head above water at a time when the currents were unusually swift, but as one that was living better, and advancing farther and more rapidly, than had its forebears, a group, according to all accounts, distinctly on the make. To evaluate this estimate, to see wherein the picture grows less rosy in the face of facts and figures drawn from the actual records of the lives and activities of yeomen, and when and where they serve merely to throw it into bolder relief, is the task of the succeeding chapters.

155. William Webb, *Description of Cheshire,* published in D. King, *The Vale Royal,* 1656, pp. 19–20.

III

LAND HUNGER

When my money for this ground I gave
I was a yeoman, zo the writings zay,
Now gentleman, I zell the same away:
If gentleman zell land, and yeomen buy,
Zonne Knight, a yeoman let me live and die.

Samuel Rowland, *The Four Knaves,* 1613

For there cannot be an acre of land to be sold
But he will find money to buy it.

Anon., *A Knack to Know A Knave,* 1594

THE story of the English yeomen is essentially a story of the land. It was both center and substance of their lives and their livelihood. Even their social life, in large part, was bound up with seasonal observances whose origins lay deep in ancient rites connected with tillage and the soil.

This is, of course, more or less true of all classes that live upon the land. But by their very position the yeomen bore a relationship to the soil that was in some respects different from that of the other classes about them, unless, indeed, it be the minor gentry, a group on much the same plane as themselves.

The fact that their lands were their own, or directly under their control, bred in them a sense of pride and a personal interest and responsibility, not discernible nor to be expected in the poorer husbandmen or tenant farmers who worked at somebody else's bidding and had often to struggle too hard to make ends meet to derive much pleasure from the lands they labored on. On the other hand, because they shared in the actual care and cultivation of the soil, the yeomen gained a closer and more intimate knowledge of their lands than the large proprietors who were by their social position, public duties, and often the mere extent of their holdings, barred from such intimate contact. Working with his own hands or personally supervising his workmen, a yeoman came to know the individual character of his holdings. He was personally aware if the field called "Little Croft" was out of heart, learned from experience how the "New Close" did better with this crop or that, and knew what labor it would take to bring the "Netherfield" into good heart again.

To understand, therefore, their relationship to their lands and some of the problems it entailed is to go far toward understanding the fundamental interests and concerns of the yeomen. To what extent and by what means were they increasing their acreage? What was the nature of their titles, and what their protection? Finally, by what methods did they force from the land a living for themselves and their families with, happily, a tidy sum left over to provide marriage portions for their daughters or place their sons well? These questions are fundamental in the history of the yeomen.

They are likewise questions that are closely bound up with the course of English agrarian development in the sixteenth and seventeenth centuries, and with the changing character of English land law. Some knowledge, therefore, of the general agrarian situation is essential if one would understand the role the yeomen played in it. For though in its final phase the fortunes of the small landholder were largely determined by his own initiative and industry, the conditions which gave opportunity for the play of those qualities were the result of changes that were in progress in the world about him, changes over which for the most part he exercised no control and of which he was but vaguely conscious.

The age of Elizabeth and the early Stuarts was a period of land hunger. It was not so much that land had grown more important than it had been in the Middle Ages—that could scarcely be possible—but rather that the character of its importance had changed. The dominant place it held

in the earlier period is well known. The Middle Ages operated on a land economy. To a large extent the entire social
structure was based on the system of land tenure. Land provided the measure of a man's social position and often
marked his individual attainments. Gifts of land were the
means whereby men were rewarded for distinguished services, and king and lords bestowed manors on loyal vassals in
gratitude for their assistance in war, or as a mark of affection and esteem. To be the owner of many lands, cared for
by a well-ordered peasantry who rendered labor services,
was one of the badges that divided the privileged classes
from those below them. In these respects land has never
again been so important in Western Europe.

But from the point of view of production the chief purpose of land, at least in the early Middle Ages, had been to
sustain those dependent upon it. There was no particular
reason for increasing the output and little effort was made
to do so. Manors were often self-sufficing or nearly so, and
in many regions there would be poor markets for a surplus,
were one created. War was the principal concern of feudal
lords and their retainers, and those below the status of fighting men had little inducement to labor beyond the point of
feeding themselves and their families and fulfilling their obligations to their lords. Under such conditions land, though
highly important as a measure of social prestige, figured
little as a commercial agent.

But by the advent of Elizabeth tremendous changes had
been wrought, or were in progress, in the agrarian field;
changes so far-reaching in their social and economic implications that they may well be described as *revolutionary*, a
term often applied to them. That is, they may be so described if one keeps in mind the fact that some of the changes
had been long in the making, and that many were not at
once completed. For by no means did the old order change
at once or wholly. There was, still, a certain preëminence accorded the landed classes; and fortunes made in trade and
industry were likely to be spent on land in order that their
owners might set up as country gentlemen and enjoy the

status of a county family. But forms of land tenure largely lost their social significance. And most important of all, the land itself became to a great extent commercialized, assuming thereby a market value far above that of former days.

It was these changes that proved significant to the Elizabethan and Stuart yeomen. The factors that lay behind them were many, only a few of which can be suggested here. They were themselves the result of the cross play of diverse forces, many of which are yet but partly understood. Trade and industry were assuming an importance unknown in the Middle Ages. The increase in town and city populations meant that there were more Englishmen to be fed and clothed than ever before. With larger markets for farm produce there came naturally an increased demand for land upon which to raise it. The rise in prices that began in the early sixteenth century, and for the most part continued through the first half of the seventeenth, wrought enormous changes in the outlook upon agriculture as a source of wealth. Moreover, in this field as in others, the growing tendency toward secularization caused clerical control to give way to lay initiative.

Simultaneous with these developments came the strengthening of the national monarchy with its discouragement of private warfare. Noblemen might still retain a sizable retinue of men for personal and household service, but armed bands of retainers were forbidden by statute, and war as a pastime and profession went out of fashion. Hence knights whose fame had once rested on soldierly prowess, and freemen who made up the famous foot soldiery of former days, now entered upon a more settled life. The ever-increasing number of civic duties that Tudor legislators placed upon their shoulders furnished an outlet for a part of their energies; and sports of the countryside occupied a large share of their attention; but many of them found in the management of their lands both a pastime and a profession. As Thomas Wilson said in 1600, "the gentlemen which were wont to addict themselves to the warres, are nowe for the most part growen to become good husbandes and knowe

[as] well how to improve their lands to the uttermost as the farmer or countryman, so that they take their fermes into their handes as the leases expire, and eyther till themselves, or else lett them out to those who will give most."[1]

It proved an absorbing activity, which, under the growing spirit of rivalry and competition, gave abundant room for the matching of wits and the play of individual initiative. Indeed, many men trained in the competitive life of trade and industry now found opportunity for applying the methods they had learned in the commercial world to ventures of an agrarian nature, to the end that speculation as well as investment for profit became the order of the day.

An increase of individual freedom among the tenantry and a growing need and desire among the landlords for a larger money income were both marked factors in the rising demand for land.[2] And each is significant in the history of the yeomen. It was the increase in free personal status of hundreds who had comparatively recently risen from an estate of villeinage, and the advantage they took of that freedom to move about and improve their condition, that brought many tenants to the position of yeomen. And it was the landlord's desire and need for a greater cash income that furnished the small landholders with a competition so keen that they were either forced out of the game altogether or else, through the struggle, developed sharpened powers and a new aggressiveness that affected both the character and the fortunes of the group.

It was an age fraught with both danger and opportunity. Scheming landlords and land-hungry neighbors were ever ready to take advantage of a man's misfortunes. Though prices in the main went steadily up, there were sometimes fluctuations that came without warning and in uncertain sequence. Other evils added to the insecurity of the times. Uncontrolled epidemics were a constant dread. Loss by fire was common, and insurance of any kind practically un-

1. *State of England, 1600*, p. 18.
2. See N. S. B. Gras, *The Economic and Social History of an English Village*, 1930, p. 95.

known. Either a man must have savings on hand for such
rainy days or else go into debt. But debts required giving
one's lands and other possessions for security, and in case
they could not be promptly met the creditors, often hard-
pressed themselves, felt no scruples about pushing the letter
of the agreement to its fulfillment. It was inevitable under
such circumstances that many who lacked the means to meet
such emergencies, or had not the personal ambition and
initiative to cope with shifting circumstances, should barely
hold their own or else fall hopelessly behind.

But when it is a case of sink or swim, unless the odds are
too great against a man he usually tries to swim. He learns,
moreover, that the same swift-moving currents that carry
one down with the undertow can also, if the waves break
right, buoy one up and bear him far. And despite the uncertain conditions depicted above, more than ever before in
the history of English landholding the little man who had
industry and an abundance of enterprise was getting his
opportunity. Those who could weather the storms found in
the higher prices and better markets opportunities for profit
that urged them on to still greater effort. Gain begets the
desire for more gain. As Lord Ernle has said, medieval husbandmen were content to extract from the soil the food
which they needed for themselves and their families; whereas
"Tudor families despised self-sufficing agriculture; they
aspired to be sellers and not consumers only, to raise from
their lands profits as well as foods."[3] Hence it was that
Elizabethan and Stuart yeomen were sometimes lured,
sometimes driven, to become lively participants in the land
activities that went on about them. It was often the twin
forces of fear and ambition that shaped their course.

A fortunate element for them in the situation lay in the
fact that their hope for gain was not dependent on a large
initial outlay of capital; nor did they have to execute their
work on a large scale in order to produce a profit—a few
extra bushels of grain to sell on the next market day, a few

3. R. E. Prothero (Lord Ernle), *English Farming, Past and Present,*
1922, p. 58.

more sheep and cattle to drive to the fair, and the way prices were going a yeoman could ride home with money in his pocket and plans in his head for the land he would buy when he could add more shillings and pounds to those already in his possession. It was profit in a small way, but nonetheless gratifying on that account.

Many yeomen lived upon lands which their fathers had tilled for generations, and there is evidence of their pride in these ancient heritages. But hundreds of them also occupied lands which they had themselves acquired through their own initiative and industry. In the record that Robert Furse of Devon prepared for his posterity he states that his ancestors were men "of smalle possessyon and hablyte, yt have theye by lytell and lytell . . . so runne ther corse . . . that by these menes we ar com to myche more possessyones, credett and reputasyion than ever anye of them hadde."[4] It is a simple statement of a single Elizabethan yeoman, but it summarizes the story of hundreds.

The very phrase "lately purchased" occurs so often in documents touching the land dealings of yeomen that its significance cannot be ignored. I have met with it as many as twenty or thirty times in the descriptions of the lands of a single man; and to encounter it four, five, six, eight, and ten times in yeoman wills, deeds, post-mortem inquisitions, and the like, is a commonplace. The increase in marketable land that enticed so many yeoman buyers was greatly augmented during the sixteenth and early seventeenth centuries by three developments: the dissolution of the monasteries, the sale of crown lands, and the inclosure and reclamation of lands from forest, waste, and fen.

Probably few yeomen in the earlier years after the dissolution profited by the release of monastic lands; for this property went at first to large landholders as gifts and in payment of services, or was purchased. But large quantities of it came early into the hands of speculators and so on the market, where after division and redivision it was by the

4. *Furse Family Book,* p. 170.

late sixteenth century being brought within reach of the small buyer.

We have noted the rise of Lincolnshire yeoman families through the acquisition of abbey lands in that section. It was so elsewhere, as deeds and other documents touching land conveyance abundantly show. The lands of William Penrice, a Worcestershire yeoman, were described as "lately belonging to the monastery of Bordesley."[5] In 1566 Barnard Luxton, a yeoman of Devonshire, paid £400 for the manor of Abbotsham, "to the late monastery of Hartland belonging."[6] Lands of another Devon yeoman were described as "late parcel of the dissolved priory of Plympton."[7] Deeds of Sussex yeomen tell of lands formerly "a part of Battle Abbey."[8] And dozens of Yorkshire yeomen came in this period to profit from the lands that were formerly in possession of the wealthy religious houses there.[9] Henry VIII effected the dissolution in the interests of the Crown; but in so doing he helped to shape the agrarian developments for a hundred years to come, contributing thereby albeit indirectly, to the growth of the yeoman class.

The second means of stimulating the land market, namely, by the sale of crown lands, was in itself no new one. Kings had often given grants from the royal demesnes and had frequently leased and sold properties, but never before had sales been carried forward on so large a scale. "In their purpose and effects those of the late Tudor and early Stuart period are to be distinguished from those of earlier times. For these transactions were now made with the avowed purpose of raising money, and therefore partake of a more strictly commercial character than formerly."[10]

5. Abstract of Land Grant, Penrice to Penrice, 1550, H. R. Moulton, *Paleography, Genealogy and Topography,* 1930, p. 40.

6. Exeter Deeds and Documents, 702.

7. *Ibid.,* 12084.

8. Sussex MSS. Gage Papers, 21, 23, and *passim.*

9. W. Crump and G. Ghorbal, *History of the Huddersfield Woollen Industry,* 1935, p. 43, and *passim.*

10. G. H. Tupling, *The Economic History of Rossendale,* 1927, p. 131. One report in the Elizabethan State Papers shows that £817,359 was

What was true of traffic in royal lands was true also of inclosures; for inclosing was not a new activity. But again the continued encroachments and inclosures, and especially the opening up of new lands taken in or reclaimed from forest, waste, and swamp, greatly increased the supply of the land market. Tremendous amounts of forest lands were appropriated. At least six royal commissions were appointed to deal with this during the early years of the seventeenth century.[11] The great engineering project for reclaiming the fen country began also under James I. And the business of compounding, leasing, and selling went on until the opening of the Civil Wars. Whole communities were developed on newly inclosed forest lands or lands reclaimed from the waste.[12]

In addition to the increase of buying and selling connected with these new sources of supply a great deal of land already in use was changing hands. John Norden, in 1607, declared that lands "passed from one to another, more in these latter daies than ever before."[13] Sir Edward Montague's report on the state of Northampton in 1614 tells of the breaking up of old land units and ancient estates there.[14] And Sir Simon Degge, writing in 1669 of the great amount of land that had changed hands in Staffordshire in recent generations, remarked that the exchanges had been executed "not so much as of old they were wont to do, by marriage, but by purchase."[15]

Among the land hungry none were more avaricious than the yeomen. Frequently they sought to better their fortunes through the misfortunes of their poorer neighbors, the

gained from the sale of royal lands to assist in the expenses of the Queen's wars, S.P. 12, CCLXXXVII, 59. And another from the State Papers of 1609 states that since the accession of James I, crown lands to the amount of £426,171 19s. 1d. had been sold, S.P. 14, XLVIII, 33.

11. *S.P.D.*, 1603–1610, XII, 81–84; XXIII, 23; XXVIII, 86; XXXII, 59.

12. Tupling, *History of Rossendale,* chaps. II, V.

13. *The Surveyors Dialogue*, Bk. VI.

14. From the MSS. of the Duke of Buccleuch, III, *H.M.C.,* 1926, XLV, 182.

15. Letter of Sir Simon Degge, reprinted in S. Erdeswicke, *Survey of Staffordshire*, 1717.

smaller copyholders and tenant farmers for whom the economic hazards of the times were proving too severe. Mr. Gras says in regard to the yeomen of Crawley in Hampshire during this period: "Land squeezed by economic processes from their neighbours came to be theirs by virtue of purchase from the former holders (often by means of a mortgage) or by fineing for it when it escheated to the lord."[16] It was not a process confined to Hampshire. Yeomen everywhere were profiting in the same manner. It was traffic in small pieces of land, to be sure, but it was because they were small that the man with small capital was able to buy them.

But by no means all of the bargaining of the yeomen was done at the expense of the smallest landholders. William Harrison said of them: "They do come to great welth, in somuch that manie of them are able and doo buie the lands of unthriftie gentlemen."[17] To be sure, Thomas Fuller declared that a yeoman "insults not on the ruines of a decayed gentleman but pities and relieves him."[18] But Fuller was inclined to be an overzealous champion of the yeomen, and evidence from deeds, bonds, leases, and other records touching their land dealings tends rather to support Harrison. They did often *relieve* decayed gentlemen, but not in the way that Fuller meant.

It was a period of shifting fortunes among the great as well as the small. As a result of his investigation into the annual incomes of the gentry and nobility, Thomas Wilson wrote in 1600: "I find great alteracions almost every yeare, so mutable are worldly thinges and worldly mens affaires."[19] Aggressive yeomen were ever ready to take advantage of the situation. Often the land they bought of gentlemen was that which they had formerly held as tenants. A Kentish deed of 1589 states that John Idley, gentleman, of Dover, "released all of his present and future rights in a hundred and twenty-four acres of land, three messuages, orchards, and other appurtenances to John Richards, yeoman, of

16. Gras, *History of an English Village*, p. 112.
17. *Description of England*, Bk. II, 133.
18. *The Holy State*, p. 107.   19. *The State of England*, p. 23.

Goodnestone, who was already in occupation of the lands."[20]
A bond for £600 indicates that the same yeoman had some
years earlier bought more than two hundred acres from another member of the Idley family.[21] A Devonshire deed
shows that Sir Robert Bassett of Heanton Drewgarden and
his heirs sold to John Knight, yeoman, lands, messuages,
and tenements in the parish of Linton that were at the time
of the purchase in the tenure of Knight's father.[22] Instances
like these occur again and again. To buy thus outright the
property which the family had long occupied as tenants was
to secure lands, the needs and possibilities of which were already known to them, a great advantage in the matter of
cultivation.

Estates formerly exchanged, or bought and sold among
the gentry, were now being broken up and sold to smaller
men. In a group of Dorset deeds of the early seventeenth
century, one finds Thomas Dike, a yeoman of Marnhall,
buying lands, partly copyhold and partly demesne, from
the manor of Marnhall. Sir Thomas Barker of Essex and
George Reeves, Esq., of Suffolk were the nominal owners,
but John Tasberghe, Esq., of Norfolk, had also certain
rights in the property. Hence the land acquired by the Dorset yeoman represented the former holdings of an Essex
knight and two East Anglian esquires.[23] The will of Robert
Kirke, yeoman, of Lincoln, 1619, names one baronet, two
knights, one esquire, and one gentleman among those from
whom he has at various times bought lands.[24] And there is
scarcely a set of documents of any size touching the land
activities of the yeomen that does not contain some, usually
many, examples of this kind.

Buying and selling were particularly active in the south
and east where the agrarian situation came earliest under
commercial influences. One frequently finds it possible in

20. *Kent Records,* Kent Archæological Society Publications, 1922, VII,
12.
21. *Ibid.*   22. *Devon Trans.,* XXXVIII, 249.
23. "Dorset Deeds," *Somerset and Dorset Notes and Queries,* 1905, IX,
169.
24. P.C.C. 54 Soame.

collections of documents touching land conveyance to follow a single estate or a piece of land as it was bought and sold through a period of years. Not only do such records reveal the rapidity with which land changed hands and shifted from one class to another but they show as well the rise in land values.

An example is the manor of Plumpton near Lewes, which was granted to the Carews by Henry VIII. In 1555 the Mascalls, a family of Sussex gentry, paid Sir Francis Carew £400 for the demesne of the manor. In 1596 the same estate, consisting of approximately seven hundred acres of land with the manor house, hop garden, fish pond, and the like, was leased to Phillip Bennett of Wyston, yeoman, for a yearly rent of £150. This sum, it will be noted, was more than a third of the purchase price of forty years before. A small parcel of copyhold land belonging to the above manor shows the trend even more clearly. This land, known as "Wales," consisted of about thirty acres and a strip of downland. In 1555 it was in the occupation of one Richard Freeman, husbandman. In 1559 it was converted into a freehold by the same tenant, to be held henceforth for an annual rent of ten shillings, and a ten-shilling "relief." In 1570 Freeman died, and the land "late enfranchised and made free" passed to his widow and later to his son Thomas. This Thomas, though earlier styled husbandman as his father before him had been, was by 1599 styled yeoman. He sold the land that year to John Rowe, gentleman, for £165. During the next twenty years "Wales" changed hands twice, being sold first to another gentleman, and then to an esquire. In 1619 it was sold to John Thetcher, yeoman, for £340; and in 1655 Thetcher's son resold it for £437 10s., a price higher than had been paid for the entire demesne of the manor in 1555 with its seven hundred acres of land.[25]

The increase in the value of land was not everywhere so striking, nor did it occur everywhere without fluctuations. In the west country, for instance, and other regions where

25. Sussex MSS. A 48, 55, 62, 64, 68, 79, 95, 103, 183. See also C 269, 271, 274, and *passim* for rise in land prices.

the clothing industry was of great importance, the land market suffered repercussions brought on by contemporary industrial dislocations. The reduced export of cloth, aided perhaps by other factors, led to intervals of economic depression, at which times land came down in price in predominantly grazing sections.[26] But the needs of an expanding population served for the most part to keep the price of grain high; and competition, especially in districts near to markets, kept land prices soaring.[27] Yeomen in their eagerness for larger acreages were willing, and apparently able, to pay high prices.

In 1576 Hugh Cornford, a yeoman of East Malling, and his son Robert bought lands from Francis Challoner, Esq., and his son in Lynfield, Sussex, for £563 6s. 8d.[28] In 1588 John Fawkener, a yeoman of Waldron, Sussex, bought the manor of Waldron from Anthony Browne, Viscount Montague, for £500.[29] In 1605 William Relfe, a yeoman of Penshurst, paid £1,225 to Sir John Ashburnham for lands and the next year bought more from the same knight for £540.[30] In 1610 Robert Pettet, a wealthy yeoman of Buckstead, Sussex, paid £1,100 to an Essex man for houses and lands.[31] In 1616 Nicholas Durrant, another Buckstead yeoman, paid £1,100 for lands he bought from Christopher Warneet.[32] Lands thus bought were kept, or soon sold again, according to what step promised the most gain. In 1588 John Akehurst, a yeoman of Sussex, bought lands of Sir Robert Sydney for £100 which he sold only nine years later to a wealthy Kentish yeoman for £240, a tremendous gain for so short a period.[33] Yeomen, it is apparent, bargained at each

26. T. C. Caldwell, "Devonshire from the Accession of Queen Elizabeth until the Civil Wars," MS. in Yale Library (hereafter cited as Caldwell, Devonshire), pp. 50–51.

27. F. J. Fisher, "The Development of the London Food Market, 1540–1640," *The Economic History Review*, 1935, I, 46–57.

28. Sussex MSS. F 201.

29. Add. Charters in the British Museum (hereafter cited as Add. Ch.), 30890.

30. Sussex MSS., Ashburnham, 411, 412.

31. *Ibid.*, PN, 11.

32. *Ibid.*, LM, 25, 31, 32, 34.   33. *Ibid.*, P, 15, 20.

other's expense as well as at the expense of their landlords and poorer neighbors. One contemporary writer pointed out that aggressive tenants "by reason of this greedinesse and spleene one against the other in hyring and buying land" were "more theire owne enemies than is either the Surveyor or the Landlord."[34] Certainly they bought wherever and from whom they could.

The foregoing examples have pointed particularly to the high prices of land in the southern counties and the wealth of the yeomen there. The upswing in the prices of farm produce brought about by London's growing needs created excellent markets for them. The wealth of the Kentish yeomen was proverbial. A familiar rhyme of the countryside indicates the reputation they enjoyed:

> A Knight of Wales,
> A gentleman of Cales,
> A laird of the North Countree;
> A yeoman of Kent
> Sitting on his penny rent
> Can buy them out all three.[35]

According to a popular ballad of the period, a yeoman suitor who could say "I have house and lands in Kent" was thought to have his love suit well begun.[36]

But yeomen elsewhere were also buying and selling, at what were for their group high prices, especially in East Anglia and the Midlands which like the southern counties were within reach of markets, but also farther afield. Thomas Jacob, a Suffolk yeoman, in 1610 purchased lands for which he paid £2,001.[37] John Sleach, an Essex yeoman,

34. R. Churton, *An Olde Thrifte Newly Revived,* etc., 1612, pp. 12–13. There is some doubt concerning the authorship of this work. See Prothero, *English Farming,* p. 424.

35. *A Kentish Garland,* I, 139. For special opportunities offered Kentish farmers, see Fisher, "The Development of the London Food Market, 1540–1640," *E.H.R.,* 1935, I, 46–47.

36. "The Wooing Song of a Yeoman of Kent," *Kentish Garland,* pp. 143–144.

37. Add. MSS. 19081, fol. 52.

in the same year sold lands for £1,100.[38] John Fletcher, yeoman, of Derbyshire, paid £2,100 for the manor and lands that his father had leased a few years before from Sir Arthur Ingram.[39] William Scarlett, a yeoman of Hogstow, Shropshire, was said to have paid £2,000 for the lands that he owned there.[40] And a bond of £1,160 was made out in 1658 to Thomas Davies, a Gloucestershire yeoman, in connection with a land transaction recently made.[41]

These sums represent the land dealings of wealthy yeomen. They show the top range in which the able members of the group could buy and sell. But those who bought within a smaller range were nonetheless eagerly adding to their holdings. An examination of slightly more than 4,000 deeds and other documents describing the land transactions of yeomen in the period from 1570 to 1640 shows the purchase of lands in sums ranging from 9 pence paid for a single rood of ground to £2,100 laid out upon a sizable estate. Often such documents do not make clear the full purchase price, but 3,103 of the above number which definitely stipulated the sum involved in the sale yielded the following information:

1,152 or about 37 per cent were for purchases amounting to less than £50.

675 or about 22 per cent were for purchases between £50 and £100.

573 or about 19 per cent were for purchases between £100 and £200.

441 or about 14 per cent were for purchases between £200 and £500.

262 or about 8 per cent were for purchases above £500.[42]

38. Sussex MSS. PN 11.   39. Add. MSS. 6666, fols. 157–158.
40. St.Ch. 8, 263/3.

41. "Gloucestershire Deeds," *Glouc. N. and Q.*, VI, 8.

42. The deeds and calendars of deeds from which these figures were taken represent land dealings of yeomen in twenty-seven counties and were taken from various local collections of deeds (see Bibliography). Thousands of deeds for this period are now in the process of being calendared by archivists, local scholars, and others, and it will be possible as this work proceeds to make much more use of them for studies of this

These represent only a sample of the thousands of transactions which took place and another set of documents might show quite different proportions, but they are suggestive of the price range within which the yeomen operated.

The activity in the land market was by no means limited to buying and selling. Leasing, to some extent practiced since the Middle Ages, now became more popular than ever and was the means whereby many yeomen gained the use of lands they did not own. Since high rents could be demanded, a landlord often found it to his advantage upon the termination of tenures to lease his land rather than to renew the tenure.

A long-term lease was usually accompanied by a relatively large money payment commensurate with a purchase price and a correspondingly low, or merely nominal, rent. Occasionally leases were made for an extravagantly long term of years: John Scott, a Sussex yeoman, leased certain lands of Edward Apsley, Esq., for a term of 10,000 years.[43] The lease of a Norfolk yeoman in 1613 named a term of 5,000 years.[44] And certain leases which John Norden found on the manor of Kingswood in Wiltshire were for terms of 1,000 and 2,000 years.[45] Leases of this type could be let and sublet before their expiration, and many of them were let many times over.

In fact, the original long lease was almost tantamount to a purchase and was practically so regarded. It was the short lease for high rent, whether of land let for the first time or sublet again and again, which offered the greatest opportunity for profit and speculation and drew down upon the heads of the "leasemongers" the ire of contemporary writers.

As early as 1550 Thomas Lever in a sermon at St. Paul's deplored the activity of the speculator who dealt in leases as

kind. Even where they do not give the exact amounts of the sale price, they are frequently valuable for the minute descriptions of lands, land measurements, and the like.

43. Sussex MSS. E 182.   44. Norwich MSS. Filby 5370, 4 F 1.
45. Add. MSS. 6027, fol. 140.

a commodity to be bought and sold at will. He complained that by this practice the tenants were made to pay so much and landlords received so little "that neither of them is wel able to keep house."[46] Robert Crowley gave a gruesome account of the leasemonger who fell ill and dreamed that he was to be sent to Hell for his sharp practices.[47]

That rents on leases, particularly short ones, ran high was certainly true; but apparently they were no higher than land-hungry buyers were willing to pay. And prosperous yeomen were among the readiest customers for those who had land to let. John Taylor, the Water Poet, whose shrewd comments on the contemporary social scene are worth noting, said of the yeoman:

> For if a Gentleman have Land to let;
> He'l have it, at what price so 'ere 'tis set,
> And bids and overbids, and will give more
> Than any man could make of it before.[48]

Documents touching their land dealings lend a good deal of weight to Taylor's words; for yeomen were everywhere leasing lands and often at high rents. A Suffolk yeoman leased lands of Sir Simonds D'Ewes for twenty-one years at a rent of £92 per annum.[49] A Bucks yeoman in 1626 leased the site of the manor of Denham Deerham for twenty-three and a half years at a rent of £22 for the first two years and £50 for each succeeding year.[50] John Muffit, yeoman, of Long Stanton, Cambridgeshire, leased a manor house and lands from Sir Christopher Hatton of Northants for one year at £40.[51]

Frequently the lease was merely the steppingstone to a purchase. Robert Phillips, a Lincolnshire yeoman, in 1583 leased the manor of Wishington for seventeen years for a

46. Thomas Lever, *Sermons* (Arber), 1870, p. 128.
47. "Of Leasemongars," *Works,* pp. 40–41.
48. "The Country Yeoman," *The Works of John Taylor, the Water Poet to 1630,* 1630, p. 12.
49. Add. MSS. 19081, fol. 52.
50. London Corporation Manuscripts, Report 41, fol. 40b.
51. Northampton MSS. FH 3565.

payment of £45 and a yearly rent of £8 8s. 2d. In 1585, when his lease had yet presumably fifteen more years to run, Phillips bought the manor and additional lands for £1,006 10s. By 1603 he had advanced sufficiently in wealth and position to be described as Robert Phillips, gentleman.[52]

In 1627 Henry Chatfield, a Sussex yeoman, leased 66 acres of land from Sir William Gormy for a term of twenty-one years. In 1641, seven years before the termination of the lease, Barnard Chatfield, his son and heir, bought the whole for £480.[53]

A set of 67 leases in the Gage Papers in Sussex for the period 1570–1649 shows 18 gentlemen (including knights and esquires), 12 tradespeople, 3 husbandmen, and 30 yeomen among the lessees. The annual rents ranged from a sixpence which an innholder paid for one rood of land, to £240 paid by one of the yeomen for his lands, the acreage of which is not given. Yeomen gave five of the six highest rents paid, each running above a hundred pounds a year.[54] Those with money to invest often also leased town property, houses and lots, shops, and small business sites.[55]

Nor were the yeomen always in the role of the lessee. Many of them were of sufficient substance to lease to others, often on a small, sometimes on a surprisingly large scale. Thomas Longe, a Dorset yeoman, in 1664 leased a farm and water mill for twenty-seven years to a gentleman for £754 and a yearly rent of 80s.[56] A Somerset yeoman leased half of the parsonage of Glaston that was in his tenure to a mercer for £400.[57] In 1582 John Latham, a yeoman of Bucks, leased a mansion house and two hundred acres of land to George Ball, gentleman, for ten years, for £100, and a rent of £50 per year.[58] Nathaniel Fuller, a yeoman of Bredfield, Suffolk, purchased a small estate in 1644 for

52. Add. Ch. 32819.   53. Sussex MSS. S 32, 34.
54. *Ibid.*, The Gage Papers, 1570–1649.
55. Barnstaple MSS. 19, 49, 62, 99, and *passim;* Bristol Corp. MSS., Burgess Books.
56. Manuscript Calendar of Dorset Deeds in the Dorchester Library, 2717.
57. Req. 2, 196/25.   58. *Ibid.*, 210/77.

£350, and shortly afterward leased it for an annual rent of £20.[59] William Honiwell, a Devonshire yeoman, listed in his diary for February, 1605, nineteen parcels of land that he had leased for a period of five years. The rents he would receive ranged from 2s. to £9 per piece, and amounted to a total of £48 1s. 6d. per annum.[60]

Whether the trend under Elizabeth and the early Stuarts was toward shorter or longer leases is a question that demands further investigation. Such evidence as I have examined tends to show great lack of uniformity in the prevailing practices, based chiefly on regional differences, with a general tendency, more marked in some places than others, toward a shorter term. Reginald Lennard says that during the first half of the seventeenth century there was a turn toward leases for term of years rather than for lives, and in the earlier part of the period a rather less-marked tendency toward a shorter term of years. He suggests thirty-one years as a term in common use.[61] The change from lives to a term of years was certainly being made in many places; but twenty-one years rather than thirty-one was the standard in certain regions, with many for even shorter terms. An examination of 144 Sussex leases made between 1560 and 1650, in which yeomen figured as one or more of the contracting parties, shows the following proportion of short term leases.[62]

Leases under 21 years	55
Leases for 21 years	64
Leases above 21 and below 99 years	10
Leases for 99 years or longer	15

These were all leases of private lands. The particulars of 103 leases of royal lands in Kent and Sussex for the period

59. Add. MSS. 19086.

60. William Honiwell, "The Diary of a Devonshire Yeoman," reprinted in serial form in *The Western Times,* Exeter, October, November, 1832 (hereafter cited as *The Honiwell Diary*).

61. Reginald Lennard, *Rural Northamptonshire Under the Commonwealth,* Oxford Studies in Social and Legal History (hereafter cited as Lennard, *Rural Northamptonshire*), 1916, V, 32.

62. Sussex MSS., Gage, Ashburnham, and other family collections.

of Elizabeth and James I show the same tendency, 84 of the 103 being for a term of twenty-one years.[63]

But farther west the situation was quite different. Here out of 240 leases of private lands in which yeomen were involved in the counties of Devon, Cornwall, Dorset, and Somerset during the same period, the figures are as follows:[64]

Leases under 21 years	3
Leases for 21 years	23
Leases above 21 and below 99 years	26
Leases for 99 years or longer	188

Two hundred one royal leases from the same counties in the time of Elizabeth, with Gloucester substituted for Dorset, show the same preponderance for terms of three lives or ninety-nine years though a smaller percentage:[65]

Leases under 21 years	0
Leases for 21 years	69
Leases above 21 and under 99 years	24
Leases for 99 years or longer	108

These figures are in general accord with Mr. Tupling's statement that long leases were popular in the Rossendale region in Lancashire.[66] I have seen no particulars of the leases of private lands farther north except occasional ones of the border yeomen, but of 79 royal leases for Cumberland and Westmoreland, 54 were for twenty-one years and 25 for a longer term.[67] The shorter term for royal leases in the north and west when compared with leases given for private lands is not surprising. Under Elizabeth, and especially under the first two Stuarts, royal agents were everywhere laboring to push the advantage of the Crown.[68] And

63. Royal leases in the manuscripts of the Court of Exchequer (all Exchequer MSS. hereafter cited as E.) in the P.R.O., 310, 25/144, 15/60.
64. These were gathered from various local collections in the west country, but chiefly from the Exeter Deeds and Documents.
65. E. 310, 14/54, 11/29, 10/19, 23/125.
66. Tupling, *History of Rossendale,* p. 89.
67. E. 310, 10/21–23, 25/146.   68. See above, pp. 71–72.

their familiarity with the profits gained by shorter leases in other regions would lead them to press the change on royal manors elsewhere. Even so, it is observed that they did not attempt, or were not able, to depart wholly from the custom of the locality. It appears quite clear that high rents and short leases were more characteristic of the regions near to London and its markets where the changes that occurred in the commercial world were first felt in the agrarian; whereas farther west and in the more conservative north long leases were still customary, or but slowly giving way.[69]

Examples have been given of the high rents that yeomen were paying and collecting. Only the ancient rents of freeholds or copyholds in inheritance[70] remained unchanged. Wherever renewed tenures or leases went into effect, rents showed an unprecedented rise.

Richard Norton of Kent stated in a deposition of 1608 that at the time he had first occupied land in the parish of Ivechurch, it had rented for 7s. 6d. to 10s. the acre, but that now it was being let for 20s. the acre and thereabouts.[71] Arable land in Norfolk and Suffolk increased from 1s. 8d. per acre in the last decade of the sixteenth century to 10s. the acre in 1640–50; pasture rose from 4s. 6d. to 12s. in the same period; and meadow from 4s. 6d. in 1590–1600 to 11s. 8d. in 1630–40.[72] Essex land that rented in 1566 for slightly more than 2s. per acre was by 1651 bringing slightly more than 9s. per acre.[73]

Certain lands in Warwick brought rents amounting to £2 8s. 6d. in 1556. By 1613 the same lands had advanced to

69. The situation in East Anglia appears to have been rather unusual and points to an earlier practice of very short leases, growing somewhat longer during the period in question, but remaining still in the short-lease group as compared with those of the west. See D. Kemp, "Social and Economic History," *Victoria History of Suffolk,* pp. 661–664; and J. Spratt, Agrarian Conditions in Norfolk and Suffolk, 1600–1650, a MS. thesis of the University of London in the Library of the Institute of Historical Research, p. 212.

70. See below, pp. 114–116, 121.   71. St.Ch. 8, 308/33.

72. Spratt, Agrarian Conditions in Norfolk and Suffolk, p. 216.

73. T. Lennard, "Some Essex Manors and Farms," *The Essex Review,* 1906, XV, 131. See also Add. MSS. 23150, fol. 6a.

£8 11s. 0d.; and by 1648 they were renting for £25. Better lands in the same place, that brought £8 in 1556, had advanced to £24 by 1613 and to £66 13s. 4d. in 1648.[74] Evidence from Yorkshire shows the same advance in process there.[75]

So steady was the rise in rents that men who dealt in land grew heady with the thought of the possibilities the future held. They appear to have believed that the advance would continue on and on. A statement in the State Papers for 1610 concerning certain royal manors in Northamptonshire gives a total of £771 13s. 4d. as the rents of the grounds as "they were heretofore letten." The total sum showing "how they are now letten" was £861 16s. 8d. And the improvement that might "be made hereafter when the prices of wool rise againe" was set at £980 6s. 8d.[76] Even a temporary setback had not destroyed the confidence in the future outlook. A description in 1637 of 252 acres in Leicestershire states that the lands were under lease for nine years at a rent of 8s. per acre for the first five years of the term and 12s. per acre for the remaining four years. And "by that time that the lease be out," says the writer, "it is very like to be worth 16s. an acre for it is very like to be good lands and lie well."[77]

Inclosing was mentioned above as one of the means of developing the activity of the land market. The place of the yeomen in the inclosure movement is well worth noting, the more so because it has frequently been obscured by the attention paid the large landlords who have usually figured as the villains in the inclosure story, or as its heroes if one happened to approve of inclosures.

Inclosing found both protagonists and enemies among the popular writers of the day:[78] men who believed that it

74. S. Copland, *Agriculture Ancient and Modern,* 1866, p. 27.

75. See table of new rents versus old rents in the complaint of the tenants of Whitby *vs.* Sir John Yorke, *Select Cases from the Court of Requests,* Selden Soc., XII, 200.

76. S.P. 14, LVII, 37.   77. S.P. 16, CCCXCI, 91.

78. See Walter Blith, *The English Improver Improved,* 1649; Robert Child, "The Large Letter," in Hartlib's *Legacie,* 1651; R. Churton, *An*

would "make every sort of people happier,"[79] and those who held it to be an evil practice, and often blamed it, as Mr. Gay has said, "for ills not its own progeny."[80] There seems, however, to have been no tendency even among the enemies of inclosing to deny the fact that it enhanced the worth of the ground. Comparisons were continually being made between the value of inclosed and uninclosed lands, either in terms of rentals and sale prices or of productivity. The most conservative estimates held that an acre of inclosed land was worth one-and-a-half acres that were uninclosed. Some writers placed the estimate much higher.[81] Fines at 4s. the acre on uninclosed land on a manor were set at 13s. 4d. the acre for inclosed land on the same manor.[82] This being true and the tenor of the age what it was, it was inevitable that inclosing should continue.[83] Statutes, if and when enforced, might succeed in checking or partially checking the evils that sometimes accompanied it, but inclosure provided the means of fulfilling too many needs and desires to be easily set aside.

Olde Thrifte Newly Revived, 1612, II, 38–39; Adam Moore, *Bread for the Poor,* 1653; Gabriel Plattes, *Practical Husbandry Improv'd,* 1640; Robert Powell, *Depopulation Arraigned,* 1636; Arthur Standish, *The Commons Complaint,* 1611; Sylvanus Taylor, *The Common Good: or the Improvement of Commons, Forests and Chases by Inclosure,* 1652; Francis Trigge, *Humble Petition of Two Sisters: the Church and the Commonwealth,* 1604; J. W., *Systema Agriculturæ,* 1675, p. 12.

79. Moore, *Bread for the Poor,* Preface.

80. Edwin F. Gay, "The Midland Revolt of 1607," *R.H.S. Trans.,* N.S., XVIII, 237. Often the pulling down of inclosures was merely a way of satisfying personal grudges and paying off neighborhood scores. See St.Ch. 8, 242/1, 12/7, 67/4, 40/9, 204/19. Frequently the wives and women servants of those who were offended by an inclosure engaged in its removal as the law was likely to be less severe with them. A Cheshire yeoman in 1638, vexed by an inclosure, said to his servant, "Kathereine, cannot thou and Peter Saint's daughters goe and pull down yonder fence?" To which request the servant replied: "Master, will you beare mee out?" Chester Sessions Rolls in the MSS. of Chester Castle, 1638, File 4, no. 4.

81. See Norden, *The Surveyors Dialogue,* Bk. III; *Best's Farming Book,* Surtees Society Publications, XXXIII, 130; Egerton MSS. in the British Museum (hereafter cited as Eg. MSS.), 3007, fol. 41; Add. MSS. 38444, fols. 5–6; G. Plattes, *Practical Husbandry Improved,* p. 18.

82. Req. 2, 186/102.

83. See Hubert Hall, "The Romance of Marshland Farming," *The Contemporary Review,* June, 1933.

Fortunately the labors of modern scholars on the subject of inclosures have furnished us with a corrected perspective of many aspects of the movement. Mr. Gay, Mr. Leadam, Mr. Gonner, Miss Leonard, and others who have attacked the problem, though differing on some points, agree on many. Because of their work we no longer regard the inclosure movement as a historical calamity whereby all great landlords became the potential enemies of all tenants whose holdings they attempted to divest of the plough and convert to the sheepfold. Nor is inclosure regarded as a phenomenon which ceased at the end of the sixteenth century and began again at the beginning of the eighteenth. It appears rather as a natural and gradual development, now more and now less active, with a growing tendency toward inclosures for better production rather than wholly for pasturage. It is obvious, moreover, that inclosures were of two kinds: those which took in open fields already under cultivation, and those which inclosed the heretofore unutilized lands of forest, waste, and fen.

The methods as well as the nature of inclosing are also better understood than formerly. And the picture of the large incloser bringing hundreds of acres under his control at the expense of unwilling tenants must at least be partially modified. Scores of voluntary inclosures were brought about by agreement between landlord and tenants, first one and then the other taking the initiative. The work of the piecemeal incloser is moreover much better known: the person who bargained with his landlord or his neighbors for a bit of the common, or took it without bargaining; encroached a little on the edge of the waste or forest; or moved his pales a few feet to take in a narrow strip from the king's highway. Knights and gentlemen were not above this land nibbling, but it was a method eminently suited to the needs and ways of smaller men, already accustomed to augment their holdings in piecemeal fashion. The yeomen, suited by position, temperament, and ambition to carry on this kind of inclosing were probably the most numerous of all piecemeal inclosers.

Land in some counties was already pretty well inclosed when the Elizabethan period opened,[84] but throughout the sixteenth and seventeenth centuries the process continued in greater or less degree practically everywhere in England. As a matter of fact, in the examination of documents touching the land dealings of Elizabethan and early Stuart yeomen, I have encountered instances of inclosing and encroaching in all but four of the English shires. I should be surprised if further perusal of the records of those counties did not also produce examples there.[85]

In cases where the landlord is accused of inclosing without the consent of the tenants, the yeomen were among those objecting to the inclosures as were also knights and gentlemen who were tenants.[86] But in scores of instances the yeomen were themselves the inclosers and encroachers. Francis Trigge, boasting in 1604 of England's good fortune in possessing a yeoman class, said that "Gentlemen which are Inclosers, overthrowing the Yeomanrie doe blotte out the ancient glory of England."[87] But had he examined the presentments of the quarter-sessions courts in almost any county where inclosing activities were general, or followed the records of inclosure cases in the higher courts, he would have found the yeoman as active at inclosing and encroaching as the best of them.

A complaint made in the reign of James I against inclosures in Warwick and Northamptonshire charged specifically that it was "knights, esquires, gentlemen and yeomen" who were doing an injustice to their small neighbors by their inclosing activity.[88] A contemporary ballad on the subject stated that

84. E. C. K. Gonner, *Common Lands and Inclosure,* 1912, Bk. II, p. 179.

85. Rutland, Cumberland, Westmoreland, and Shropshire are the counties for which I happen to have seen no evidence of encroaching or inclosing. Mr. Gay says that Rutland came within the sixteenth-century inclosing activities, but that the other three counties were outside the general area of those activities.

86. St.Ch. 8, 184/6, 293/12; Req. 2, 209/74.

87. *The Humble Petition of the Two Sisters,* reprinted in *Ballads from Manuscripts* (Ballad Society), 1868, I, 35.

88. St.Ch. 8, 15/12, 15/21.

> There be many rich men
> Both Yeomen and Gentry
> Who for theire owne private gaine
> Hurt a whole country.[89]

That the yeomen inclosed for their own private gain is indeed true, but that the harm resulting from their activity was so widespread that it hurt the whole country is in many cases not borne out by the evidence.

Scores of examples exist of inclosures by agreement that were to the benefit of all concerned. In the township of Cowpen in Northumberland where the open-field system of husbandry of the "run-rig" type existed and the queen's demesne was "strinkled rig by rig together with the freeholders' lands," there was an agreement made in 1619 for a general inclosure. It was arranged that the ten occupants of the land, one knight, one esquire, three gentlemen, and five yeomen should draw up the articles of agreement. They declared the purpose of the undertaking to be the prevention of waste and spoil on the lands and the "improving and husbanding thereof." They were to have "semblable proportion and allotment," according to their holdings from each of the two fields into which the whole was divided, care to be taken that the apportioning be done so that "some have not all the best ground and the other the worst." The results show that the five yeomen fared well. The knight, Sir Ralph Delavale, received the largest portion, 594 acres of pasture and arable, and 11 acres of meadow. The next largest allotment of 192 acres of arable and pasture and 23 acres of meadow went to John Preston, one of the yeomen. Three other yeomen and one of the gentlemen received equal acreages of slightly more than 93 acres of arable and pasture, and 11 acres of meadow each; and the remaining two gentlemen and one yeoman received somewhat lesser portions.[90]

89. J. Ashton, *Humour, Wit and Satire in the Seventeenth Century,* 1883, pp. 247–248.

90. "Thornton and Croft Papers," reprinted in *History of Northumberland,* 1909, IX, 325–327.

The situation leading to the agreement for the inclosures
made on the manor of Loughton in Bucks is well described
by John Farnell, a yeoman whose lands were among those
inclosed. Testifying in a case that came before the Court of
Star Chamber in 1619, Farnell says that Loughton was a
place that consisted wholly of husbandry in tillage but
lacked sufficient pasture and meadow for furnishing food
for the draught horses and dairy cattle that the tenants
owned. This he suggests had caused no great hardship in
earlier days when the price of hay and grass was not so high,
but for some forty years now prices for these products had
risen so high in the neighboring districts from which the
Loughton farmers bought that they could no longer afford
to buy outside for their stock. Whereupon "for the generall
good and benefitt of the whole Towne and of all the inhabitants," it was agreed by both landlord and tenants that hereafter it should be lawful for any of the tenants to inclose for
his own use a piece of ground "to be taken at the outside of
the feild or els adjoining to the towne there, of his owne, or
as he could agree with his neighbours." Once since that time
an absentee tenant had objected to the agreement and taken
the matter to Chancery, but because it could be shown that
the inclosures were "for the publique and common good of
the whole towne, they were adjudged and ordered to remaine," and inclosing had been going on ever since.

The issue in the above case, in which Farnell the yeoman
was the plaintiff, was not against inclosing as such, but
against the methods and the distribution of the commons
and waste. Complaints were made by some of the tenants
that Farnell and others among the larger holders were not
living up to the intent of the agreement that the inclosing
should be done in such a way as to benefit "the pettie freeholders as well as the greater ones."[91] Their complaints were
probably valid, and there were no doubt many troubles of

91. St.Ch. 8, 141/16. See also interesting examples of inclosures by
agreement, Add. MSS. 5701, fols. 133–138; P. Williams, *Horstead and
Stanninghall*, 1937, p. 84. There are scores of examples of such inclosures,
differing in detail, but similar in principle.

a similar nature to iron out. But under just such circumstances did inclosing go on apace. Indentures of sale and exchange frequently set forth the conditions under which further inclosing might take place, evidence of the acceptance of the growing trend in that direction.

Sometimes one finds a yeoman inclosing on a fairly large scale. William Burton of Warwickshire is an example. There was competition among the inclosers in that county in the reign of James I, and it is significant that we learn of Burton's activities through a libel case in which he was charged with an attempt to discredit certain other inclosers in the community. It was natural that the witnesses brought to testify against him should lose no time in pointing out that Burton himself was "a man that of late did not only himself make a great inclosure of tillable feilds and converted two hundred acres of arable to pasture and Decaied two tenements in Ladbrooke . . . and hath depopulated parte of that Towne but alsoe was a principal instrument of the Decaye of fifteene or sixteene Houses of Husbandry and soe manie ploughs in the same towne."[92]

But usually the yeomen were among the land nibblers who were relatively free from opprobrium among their contemporaries, and for the most part among later writers. The fact also that the small inclosures were usually for benefits of tillage rather than conversion to pasture helped the men who made them to escape much of the abuse heaped upon those who assisted in the process of depopulation.

A survey of the inclosure situation in various counties, chiefly in the Midlands, in 1630, is significant. Grain was scarce and high that year and it was desirable to find out if lands needed for corn had been inclosed for grazing. A number of the reports, notably those from Derby, Notts, and Huntingdon, indicate that many of the inclosures in those counties were from one to eight acres apiece. They also show that few of the small inclosers were gentlemen, but mostly yeomen and husbandmen.[93] A report from Leicestershire

92. St.Ch. 8, 61/35.
93. S.P. 16, CLXXXVI, 6 (1); CLXXXIX, 94; CXCII, 93–94.

listed certain large and harmful inclosures that had been made there. They likewise mentioned certain others. But since the latter were of lands either still continued in tillage or areas so small that they were not held productive of the evils which the investigation had set out to rectify, it was not thought necessary, the report states, to mark them down for condemnation.[94]

Again and again, in the inclosing and encroaching activities of the yeomen, one notes the growing tendency of the individual to infringe upon "ancient common rights." It is apparent that efforts in this direction usually went unchallenged, if the taking in of a few roods off the waste or common made little difference to anyone. But if it were done on a large scale or at the evident expense of someone who was able or cared to make an issue of the matter either on his own behalf or that of the community, the right of the incloser was challenged through legal action. A suit brought against George Lydgould, a Middlesex yeoman, in the reign of James I is a case in point.

The customs of the manor of Greenford, where Lydgould was a tenant, permitted inclosure upon agreement between lord and tenants. But Lydgould had, it appears, inclosed an acre and a half without consulting anyone. When brought to task about the matter, he contended that the customs of the manor gave a tenant who held uninclosed lands there the right to inclose any part of his own lands if he were willing, in turn, to forfeit his rights of common in the remainder of the fields. Had the acre and a half which he inclosed been on the edge of the field, it may be that Lydgould's act would have gone unchallenged regardless of its validity. Things like that were happening. But it was in the middle of one of the open fields and during that part of the year when the land was under cultivation Lydgould would, in going to and from his field with his stock, wagons, and the like, be a hindrance to others whose lands he had to cross. He was therefore charged with infringing upon the common interest.[95] Sometimes the change between inclosure and champion was

94. S.P. 16, CLXXXIV, 7.   95. St.Ch. 8, 197/14.

accompanied by a transitional stage in which a man inclosed land for his own use but permitted it still to be used for common pasturage after reaping time.

Matthew Fordham, an Essex yeoman, in 1566 inclosed about thirty acres described as a "great part of the common" at Stanway.[96] John Lewis, a yeoman of Monmouthshire, in the reign of James I was charged with inclosing three- or fourscore acres from the waste in which all the inhabitants claimed rights of common.[97] Thomas Crawley, a Hertfordshire yeoman, was charged with "severing and taking in with a pale a common pond that had been for time out of mind in King's Walden."[98]

No encroachments of which the yeomen were guilty appear more often than those in which a bit of land was taken from a road or "common way." These infringements were usually not of sufficient importance to merit the expense of legal action in one of the larger courts, though they are often mentioned there as a minor charge along with others. But the records of the quarter sessions are filled with them.

William Sorell, a yeoman of Great Saling in Essex, was presented in 1572 because he had "hanged upp three gates in the Queenes highwaye."[99] George Sampson, a Sussex yeoman, was presented "for setting up and maynteyning of a gate acrosse the King's highway,"[100] and Christopher Greene, yeoman, of Yorkshire, for "ploughing up the King's highway."[101] William Boreham, a Hertford yeoman, was presented "for inclosing with poles and pales a well lying on the highway."[102] Instances like these are numerous and no other class figures as often among the offenders as the yeomen.

The fact that they kept on appearing in the records at

96. Essex Sessions Rolls, 1566.
97. St.Ch. 8, 10/18; see also 187/13, 275/2.
98. *Hertford Sessions Records*, I, 62.
99. Essex Sessions Rolls, 1572, 40/20.
100. Indictment book in the manuscripts of the *Sussex Sessions Records* at the Shire Hall, Lewes (hereafter cited as Sussex Indictment Book), I, 1632.
101. *West Riding Sessions Records*, Y.A.S., 1915, LIV, 190.
102. *Hertford Sessions Records*, I, 62.

intervals through the years is, however, in itself proof that this type of infringement continued. The inclosers and encroachers probably felt that they had a gambler's chance of escaping censure entirely. And even if the courts did exact a penalty, it might not prevent them from ultimately obtaining the lands they had taken in. Sometimes, to be sure, the culprit was ordered by the court to remove the inclosure. Sometimes he had, in addition, to pay a small fine. But often, by paying a small sum to the individual who claimed harm from the act, or to the common stock if it were common rights that had been infringed upon, or by promising restitution in some other way, he satisfied the order of the court but was left in possession of the land he had taken in.

Moreover, as Mr. J. C. Atkinson has suggested in the case of Yorkshire, it seems likely that many of these tracks or ways found on the waste or through the open fields, and from long use regarded as highways, were in reality little more than short cuts or deviations for convenience from a deeply worn cart or wagon track; hence their obliteration was necessary if local inclosing were to be to any purpose. The inclosers were probably alive to this situation and hoped to make good their acts under favor of the growing trend toward improved agriculture.[103] That a good many of the "common ways" which figured in the presentments against inclosures were either temporary or minor roadways is brought out in the evidence of the records. John Gaylor, a yeoman of Brawhinge of Hertfordshire, who had inclosed about six acres, his own land apparently, in a certain field, was charged with stopping up a certain "way and common passage" which the Brawhinge inhabitants had long used. But later details of the presentment make it clear that the passage in question had only been available for use during that part of the year when the field was not sown with grain, and hence was at best but a temporary roadway.[104] John Fillwood, a yeoman of Rushden in the

---

103. *North Riding Sessions Records,* IV, 35.
104. *Hertford Sessions Records,* I, 7.

same county, was likewise charged with setting up a hedge and ditch around land that was his own freehold, thus denying the people of the parish "free passage" and common of pasture for their cattle on two certain pieces of land "whenever it was lying uncultivated and unsown."[105]

These examples are of special interest because they show how deeply intrenched was the habit of thinking in terms of common rights; and at the same time how this method of thought and action was now being challenged by the spirit of private initiative that an age of competition was teaching its landholding as well as its industrial classes.

Of course there were limits past which one could not go, and if a man's greed led him actually to take over the land of a highway of importance and permanent usefulness and need, he might expect trouble. Christopher Greene, a yeoman of Seacroft in Yorkshire, had the audacity to plough up the king's highway between the important market towns of Leeds and York in 1639 and to "enclose the same with ditches, so that the King's subjects could not go thereon with horses, carts, or carriages without great danger." His action was held a grievous annoyance to his neighbors and a bad example to others. He was therefore indicted upon presentment to the sessions in 1640, and later, upon confession of guilt, paid the sheriff five shillings, though it is perhaps suggestive that he made no move to restore the highway. This, however, was too great a detriment to the public good to be overlooked. Hence a second order was issued which said that Greene should "laye open the said King's high waye before 1 Maye next upon paine of fortye pounds."[106] Forty pounds was a large fine for a yeoman to pay and probably more than the land was worth. No further mention of the case is made in succeeding records and it is likely that Greene complied with the order.

Often inclosures were made from land hitherto unused. A description of the lands of Henry Munday, a Wiltshire

105. *Ibid.,* p. 1.
106. *West Riding Sessions Records,* pp. 190, 206.

yeoman who died in 1630, mentions "eleven acres of land enclosed from out of the marsh."[107] Among the lands of Thomas Greene, a yeoman of Westmarden, Sussex, was a parcel of ground "lately taken out of the coppes or wood."[108] Far from being frowned upon, inclosures like these were often welcomed especially by the lords of the forests, waste, or swamp; for through them they could realize rents on lands that hitherto brought little or no income.

The development of the entire district of Rossendale in Lancashire was on lands inclosed from the royal forests. The expansion of the community began shortly after the disafforestation order of Henry VII, and, according to Mr. Tupling's account of the district, inclosing here so increased the numbers of little proprietors that by the beginning of the seventeenth century large holders in the district were in the minority. Indeed, he says that "the emergence and persistence of the small holder is the most significant fact in the development of that region, in the late sixteenth and early seventeenth century."[109]

But whether they took from forest and fen, or ditched and fenced in their own holdings in the open fields, or encroached upon a neighbor's rights or those of the community, the yeomen were everywhere active and important agents in the inclosure movement. Through "divers little particles" here and "sundry little encroachments" there, they were rounding out boundaries, adding coveted acres, and improving the holdings already in their possession.

Their hunger for more land was matched only by their reluctance to part with any that was already in their possession unless they could do so at great profit to themselves. Hence they often accepted with poor grace that part of the Elizabethan poor legislation which demanded that four acres of land be laid to every cottage or dwelling built for a laborer.[110] Prosperous yeomen frequently found it neces-

107. *Wiltshire Post Mortem Inquisitions* (hereafter cited as Wilts P.M.I.), *The Index Library,* XXIII, 5.
108. Sussex MSS., WH 231.
109. Tupling, *History of Rossendale,* pp. 97, 161.
110. *S.R.,* 31 Elizabeth, c. 7.

sary to erect such houses for their smaller tenants and laborers; but many of them complied grudgingly with the above demand, if one can judge from the number of presentments at the quarter-sessions courts of those who refused to grant the necessary four acres to the cottage.

John Graie, yeoman of Sandon in Hertfordshire, was presented in 1612 for having erected a cottage for one Stephen Chamberlain, "without assigning four acres of his own freehold land to be occupied by the tenant of the said cottage."[111] Thomas Justice, a yeoman, and Alexander Justice, a tailor, both of Sutton in Lancashire, were presented for a like offense.[112] Charles Hudson, yeoman of Blockley in Worcestershire, was indicted at the Worcester sessions in 1631 for converting a sheep house into a cottage for one John Shirley without giving him the stipulated four acres.[113] These examples could be multiplied over and over. And again, as in the case of the piecemeal inclosures, the yeomen are the class most often presented for the offense. Whether the gentry with their larger estates and a certain reputation for largess to maintain would not stoop to the niggardliness of denying a cottager four acres of ground, or whether they were of such influence in the county as to make it either politic or useless to present them to the sessions, it is difficult to say; possibly both were true.[114]

Even for the landholder who was able to keep his hands on all of his lands and to add to them by purchase, lease, or inclosure, there often still remained a major problem, that

111. *Hertford Sessions Records,* I, 39.

112. *Lancashire Quarter Sessions Records,* Chet. Soc., 1917, Ser. II, LXXVII, 65.

113. *Worcestershire Sessions Papers,* I, Pt. II, 481.

114. There was a way of getting around this law that the yeomen frequently took advantage of. If a poor man were homeless, he might petition the sessions to grant him a license to build on whatever land they chose to select for him; but a license granted for such a request did not carry with it the obligation of a grant of four acres to accompany the house site. There was probably a good deal of conniving between employers and workmen which resulted in the latter petitioning for such licenses. Some of the sessions records contain a great many licenses of this type. See especially the Somerset sessions records in the manuscripts at the Shire Hall, Taunton.

of consolidation. Practically the only large amounts of adjacent lands under one holder in the Middle Ages had been the lord's demesne, though even this was not always in a compact area, being sometimes scattered in strips among the tenants. Where the ancient demesne had consisted of compact areas, Elizabethan and Stuart yeomen counted themselves successful, as indeed they were, if they could secure parts of it when large estates were being sold. And lands newly inclosed from forest and swamp which had never been divided into strips according to the old open-field practice were in compact areas. But even in these two most favorable circumstances the yeomen were hampered in that they rarely had enough capital to purchase large amounts of land at one time, but were forced to buy piece-meal when and where they could.

Most of the land, moreover, whether bought in large or small amounts by great or small buyers, consisted of the old customary holdings which often yet lay in their original form. Even on lands long inclosed the process of consolidation seems to have been slow, though practically everywhere it was going on, here to a less, there to a greater degree. The result was that lands of individual farmers were usually far from uniform in appearance. Mr. Gras says in his study of a Hampshire village that from the sixteenth century on "the old simplicity of virgates in South Crawley and far-thinglands in North Crawley was passing. And in its stead had come the ceaseless change in size and ownership of holdings."[115] The same conditions existed elsewhere.[116] It is true that there were places like the manor of Hooton Pagnell in Yorkshire where the process seems scarcely to have begun and where "lands" still held their ancient uniformity of strips and parcels.[117] But places of this kind grew fewer

115. N. S. B. Gras, *History of an English Village*, p. 99.

116. Note Mr. Tawney's contrast of the fairly uniform size of thirteenth-century holdings with the lack of uniformity in the sixteenth century, *The Agrarian Problem in the Sixteenth Century*, 1912, pp. 61–62. See also T. Caldwell, Devonshire, for evidence of the same trend.

117. A. Ruston and D. Witney, *Hooton Pagnell, The Agricultural Evolution of a Yorkshire Village*, 1934, p. 187.

and fewer and deeds, leases, inquisitions, and other documents which give detailed descriptions of holdings show that change in size as well as ownership was the order of the day. One is tempted to say that there is nothing typical about the lands of the yeomen of the period in respect to their form unless, indeed, it be their diversity.

Even in a single locality there was the greatest possible variety in form, placement, and size of holdings. Here consolidation was well advanced, there scarcely begun. The eight acres and one rood of land sold by William Colvill, a Sussex yeoman in 1620, lay in seven "lands" varying from three roods to three acres in size.[118] Another yeoman near by leased lands of which eleven pieces comprised a total of fourteen acres, whereas an additional twelve "parcels" contained a total of fifty-two acres.[119] Hugh Corneforde and his son, on the other hand, both yeomen of the same region, possessed more than three hundred acres of land, a great portion of which seems to have lain contiguously and not to have been divided into small holdings.[120]

Yeomen in East Anglia were buying up the small holdings that had earlier been characteristic there. The lands of Richard Younge of Thornham in Norfolk were divided into twenty-one parcels, only three of which contained more than three and a fraction acres each. Only six of the twenty-one were inherited lands. The remaining fifteen parcels which Younge himself had purchased had fewer than two acres each. It is significant that most of these had been bought from different owners.[121] John Childerston of Mildenhall, Suffolk, speaks in his will of 1615 of "11½ acres of coppiehold lying in 13 several pieces."[122] On the other hand another Suffolk yeoman of the same period purchased over four hundred acres of demesne land from the manor of Aldeburgh, much of which lay in a compact area.[123]

118. Sussex MSS., WG 380.   119. *Ibid.,* S 34.
120. *Ibid.,* Ashburnham 233, 461; Gage 16, No. 12; Misc. B 174.
121. St.Ch. 8, 311/17.   122. P.C.C., 11 Rudd.
123. Add. MSS. 19099. Many pieces of land on Norfolk manors were not in strips, but in compact blocks, P. Williams, *Horstead and Stanning-*

In counties where there was yet much uninclosed land, holdings were often still dispersed in the open fields. A description of fifteen acres belonging to a Cambridgeshire yeoman with its mention of "sellions," roods, and half-roods in different fields; and its talk of "furlongs" makes one realize how long medieval land divisions and land terms lingered in certain communities.[124]

It is often difficult to tell from contemporary descriptions whether or not an individual's land lay in a compact area; for even after consolidation occurred, the "lands" continued in many cases to hold their old identity and to be labeled individually. This was no doubt partly the result of habit and had no particular significance; but often separate holdings were governed by differing conditions of tenure, which made it necessary that each retain its identity even though it no longer had the appearance of a particular "land."[125]

The desire for consolidation acted as a stimulant to buying and selling, but another way of getting scattered lands together that proved popular with the yeomen, and no doubt with all landholders, was by exchange. If A had land next to B's land in two or more fields or within the strips of a single field, it might be to the advantage of both to exchange. If they both had lands bordering on the holdings of C, then the latter might find it to his favor to exchange other lands with A and B in return for such of their lands as bordered on his own. Scores of extant indentures in which the terms of such exchanges are set down testify to the prevalence of this means of consolidation. A case in Chancery tells of an exchange effected by Nicholas Jackson, a Northamptonshire yeoman, "for the better accomodation of some of his other lands."[126] John Thorpe, yeoman, and

hall, p. 84. This appears to have been true also in at least parts of Kent, *Victoria County History, Kent,* III, 321.

124. *The East Anglian,* Ser. II, XIII, 293–294.

125. See the demands of tenure, below, chap. IV.

126. Records of the Chancery court (hereafter cited as C.) in the manuscripts of the P.R.O. 21, G. 2/1.

Daniel Harbye, Esq., of Evedon in Lincolnshire in 1602 exchanged lands, "for theire better husbandeinge of theire severall inheritance." By the bargain Thorpe was to have "soe muche lande layde togeither in two plottes within the feildes of Evedon as he had lands dispersed in all the feilds of Evedon." In addition, he was to have, in exchange for his rights of common in the fields and wastes, one parcel of inclosed land.[127]

John Chattock and John Knight, both yeomen of Warwick, exchanged one-half acre for one-half acre on an even deal. One piece was in a common field, the other in a lately inclosed one; but in relation to their other lands, the trade was to the advantage of both.[128] The same was true in the exchange between a yeoman and a gentleman in Norfolk of five acres and a rood each, a part of which was copyhold and a part freehold.[129] An indenture of exchange between Robert Yack, a Northamptonshire yeoman, and John Isham, Esq., in 1576 states that Isham gave nineteen pieces from his lands in exchange for forty-five pieces from those of Yack. Several additional bits, a half-acre here and a rood there, were exchanged between the two men.[130] A yeoman of Durham in the reign of James I says of lands recently exchanged that they had been "so obscure and dispersed and intermixt" among his neighbors, and had led to so many controversies and suits at court over the various property rights, that "the consent of all was willingly given to effect the change."[131] The right of tenants on a given manor to exchange lands with each other without paying a fine to the lord for the exchange of title was sometimes written into the customs of the manor.[132]

127. Req. 2, 185/2.
128. Birmingham MSS., Warwick, 19934. See also the *Hypomnema,* or Commonplace Book of Simon Rider, 1566–1618, in the manuscripts of the William Salt Library at Stafford (hereafter cited as Rider Commonplace Book), 1573, fol. 10.
129. Norwich MSS., Filby 5375.
130. Northants MSS., Isham Papers, 1576.
131. St.Ch. 8, 302/18.
132. See customs of the manor of South Teign, 1607, Exeter MSS.

The amount of land included in a yeoman's total acreage differed, of course, according to his ability and the nature of the land. It is not always easy to discover exact acreages. There are thousands of extant deeds and other indentures describing the lands that yeomen bought and sold, but often they speak merely of "lands" or "parcels" without giving any precise information regarding the size of the area included. Even when terms of land measurement are used they differ so much in meaning from locality to locality that accurate computation is extremely difficult, or wholly impossible. The statute acre was established as early as the reign of Edward I;[133] but other measurements continued to be used, some with general, some with distinctly local meanings. Lands were described in terms of *selions, laynes, oxgangs, yardlands, virgates,* and other terms, the same term frequently carrying different meanings. The editor of John Rowe's description of certain Sussex manors in the early seventeenth century points out the difficulties there: "The virgate or yardland seems the usual name for a holding but it varies in area from 208 to 10 acres and has lost all meaning as a measure."[134] Even when the term acre is used, one cannot be sure that it is a statute acre that is meant unless the record so stipulates.[135]

It is, however, possible in the course of examining a great many documents touching the lands and land activities of yeomen to arrive at some idea of the size of their estates. I venture to say that from twenty-five to two hundred acres in regions chiefly arable, advancing to five or six hundred acres held by well-to-do members of the group in grazing regions, is a range that would include most of their estates.

133. *S.R.,* 5 Edw. I, 31 Edw. II, and 24 Henry VIII.
134. W. H. Godfrey, *The Book of John Rowe,* Sussex Rec. Soc., XXXIV, 1929, xii–xiii. See also I. B., *An English Expositor,* 1616, for variations of the meaning of "yardland."
135. The Cornish acre contained 207 statute acres, *The Book of John Rowe,* p. xiii. A Welsh acre was estimated the equivalent of two English acres. An acre of coppice was measured differently from an acre of unwooded land, *Dictionarium Rusticum,* p. 313. See also Sloane MSS. 3815, fol. 96a.

Whatever the size of their holdings, their efforts for increasing and improving them place the yeomen clearly alongside their neighbors of larger means who sought to put farming on a profit basis. That all should not succeed equally in this determination was natural. Professor Gras has rightly described it as an age that brought "opportunity for the capable, loss for the incapable,"[136] or perhaps for the unfortunate. The stories of those who failed in the struggle, as is always the case, are harder to find than are the success stories. We know there were failures, men like Ferne's ploughman who could say: "I am an honest man's sonne as the best of them were. But vortune hath left me a beggar, and yet my vather (was) a good yeoman and lived many a winters season in good reputation and kept a homely house among his neighbours, and brought up his children cleanly so long as our old lease and Landlord dured, but soothly since they ended, and that a marchant of the good towne of Middlesex had dwelt among us awhile, then vare well all our thrift."[137] Those who thus suffered from the harshness of landlords or through other financial difficulties[138] would in time drop from their yeoman status to the position of landless or semilandless men.

Most of the stories of those who not only maintained their inheritances but increased them are also unwritten in narrative form. But they are to be had for the looking in the records of the land dealings of the yeomen; in their leases and deeds of bargain and sale, their bonds and mortgages, exchange indentures and inclosure agreements, and in the records of the courts through which the scheming methods of the unscrupulous and overambitious among them are brought to light.

And the story they tell is, one finds, not that of hand-to-mouth tillers of the soil, a contented peasantry that reaped

136. *The Economic and Social History of an English Village,* p. 99.

137. J. Ferne, *The Blazon of Gentrie,* p. 21.

138. See family of Richard Warde, a Norfolk yeoman, who prospered under Elizabeth and declined as a result of financial losses in the early seventeenth century, P. Williams, *Horstead and Stanninghall,* p. 95.

and sowed as the seasons fell and took no thought for the morrow. Rather is it that of a group of ambitious, aggressive, small capitalists, aware that they had not enough surplus to take great risks, mindful that the gain is often as much in the saving as in the spending, but determined to take advantage of every opportunity, whatever its origin, for increasing their profits. These were the English yeomen of the late sixteenth and early seventeenth centuries.

IV

COPYHOLD AND FREEHOLD

And this I say by the waye, if the ground that you deale withall, be not your owne inheritance, procure unto yourselfe some certeyne tenure therein leaste another man reape the fruit of your traveyle and charge.

Reynold Scot, *A Perfite Platform of a Hoppe Garden,* 1578

And for my wit, to deal truly with you, I had rather hold it in Copy of good tenure than by the title of an idle braine to keepe a fooles head in Freehold.

Nicholas Breton, *The Courtier and the Countryman,* 1618

WHEN a man buys land today he expects upon full payment of the purchase price and a proper recording of the deed of sale to enter into free and absolute ownership of his property. And except in rare cases, where the shreds of some former irregularity have left a legal flaw in the title, he assumes that as long as he pays the taxes levied by the state upon all landholders, he may do as he likes with his own. Such, at least in general, is the *fee simple* nature of modern freehold.[1]

It was not as easy as that for the landholders of Elizabethan and Stuart days. Land tenure, it is true, had made great strides toward freeing itself from the numerous obligations and encumbrances of medieval practices, a process that was to continue through many years. But despite all gains, it was yet a far cry from the tenurial controls of Elizabeth's time to the free and untrammeled state of land ownership today. And questions of tenure were often the

1. Mention should perhaps be made of the modern building restrictions, zoning ordinances, and the like that flourish among us. But these apply chiefly to urban property, and though the prospect of a greater planned economy may lay limitations on future farmers that tend to some extent to control the uses they make of their land, the picture among rural freeholds is at present substantially that stated above.

determining factor in shaping the fortunes of the yeomen. They and hundreds of their fellows learned from experience the vagaries of tenurial practices which we must now in retrospect attempt to understand; for though shorn of its former social significance, tenure had by the sixteenth century a practical significance far greater than that of earlier days.

Even the villein or serf on the medieval manor who could not get away from his land had at least the assurance that his land could not get away from him. "Evidences" of his right to his property were not always being sought out and inquired into. He lived meagerly, but with a certain security on the acres that his fathers had tilled; for neither his neighbors nor his landlord were trying to get them away from him. The case was different with the small landholders of the Elizabethan and Stuart period. Scheming landlords and ambitious neighbors with sharp-witted lawyers at their elbows left a man no peace, and showed no scruples whatever in bringing the title of one's property into question. John Norden, advising a would-be purchaser of land in 1607, said: "I take it that the Title is first to be duly considered, and then the drawing of the Evidences, for in these daies there goe more words to a bargaine of ten-pound land a yeare, than in former times were used in the grant of an Earldome."[2]

Tenants grew accustomed to the visits of land agents who came to question them concerning their property, their rights and titles therein, and often to sound them out on the possibility of making alterations in existing tenurial relationships. Countryfolk, naturally more or less averse to intrusion, did not always welcome these visits, as the reports of land agents clearly show.[3] But if they did not, and if the yeomen and other small landholders were often puzzled by the disputes over customs and titles and the talk of compounding and surveying that went on about them, they came nevertheless, because of such talk, to have a new con-

2. *The Surveyors Dialogue,* Bk. VI.
3. S.P. 14, XXXVII, 107; Lansd. MSS. 119, fol. 117b.

sciousness of the value of their land and of the necessity of guarding their hold upon it.

The written "evidences" of their titles in the form of deeds, leases, bonds, and other indentures became their most cherished possessions. It was the "chest that holds my evidences," often described as "the iron-bound chest," the "chest with the foure lockes," the "stronge chist," or the "greate chiste," which stood in the master's bedroom and was the strongest the house afforded. If its contents were ever molested by theft or fire, as court records indicate they sometimes were, the goodman was in a bad way indeed; for the present practice of recording deeds in public repositories had not yet developed. Conscious of the importance of such information Robert Furse, a Devonshire yeoman, set down in his diary a minute description of all of the family's possessions and the rights by which they were held. He urged his heirs to continue the practice, saying, "it will be to thos that shall come after you . . . gret quyettenes, perfyt knowledge, and a trewe menes to understond all there evydenses and tyteles."[4] Not many yeomen took this much precaution; but there were few among them who did not know by observation or experience how troublesome, even tragic, it might be if such proof were missing when it was needed.

Land law in the late sixteenth and early seventeenth centuries rested yet on the framework of medieval tenures and sought to operate on precedent; but new usages that crept in with changing conditions subjected it to a great deal of stretching. The feudal system proper had broken down, but the manorial system in large part remained. It is true that some of its older practices, admittedly outworn, had disappeared entirely, and many more were in the process of modification. But others lived sturdily on to bless or curse the people who were enmeshed in them.

Since these changes came to different parts of England at different times as agrarian life was drawn, now here, now

4. *Furse Family Book,* p. 170.

there, into the current of commercialization, tenurial practices were by no means uniform. For that matter, they never had been! In the frequent disputes that arose concerning them, therefore, it was often hard to determine exactly what the law was on given points. This uncertainty led to a multiplicity of land suits, the long records of which still exist in staggering bulk and numbers, providing a storehouse of information on the practices with which they dealt. Such suits gave plenty of business to scheming lawyers, but often proved a harassing matter to the yeomen and other landholders involved in them.

Courts, theoretically at least, still recognized the medieval structure of tenure and continued to discuss it in traditional terminology. When Sir Edward Coke came to rewrite Lyttleton's famous treatise on *Tenures*, he allowed the general classification to stand pretty much as it was. And Lyttleton, writing in the fifteenth century, had held to much of Bracton's work of the thirteenth. But again it is necessary to check legal forms against actual practices.

The five tenures around which the major part of land law had developed were knight service, socage, copyhold, frankalmoin, and sergeanty. As sergeanty had practically disappeared by the Elizabethan period,[5] and frankalmoin had only to do with ecclesiastics, they need not concern us here. Of the remaining three, knight service was destined to be abolished in 1660 while some of the yeomen whom we shall meet in this chapter were yet alive. Copyhold died a harder death and a slower one, not becoming wholly obsolete until the passage of the land acts of 1922–26. Socage, proving itself more adaptable to changing conditions, became the pattern for modern land ownership. But under Elizabeth and the first two Stuarts all three flourished side by side; and though the small landholders held less frequently by knight service than by the other two tenures, it was not unusual to find them holding lands that were subject to all three forms. It is necessary, therefore, to recall

5. Holdsworth, *History of English Law,* III, pp. 46–51; see E. Kimball, *Serjeanty Tenure in Medieval England,* 1936.

briefly the basic features of these tenures if one is to understand the problems with which the yeomen were so often confronted.

Knight service, or "knight's service" as it was earlier written, was originally a military tenure requiring that the tenant furnish a stipulated number of mounted men to serve in the king's wars. A knight's fee (fief) was the accepted measure of land that could presumably maintain a knight and his horse. Later, military service of this kind gave way before a tax or *scutage*, a money payment that enabled the king to hire his own soldiers whenever and for as long a time as he needed them.[6] By the sixteenth century, however, with the king preferring grants of subsidies from his parliaments, scutage had fallen into disuse and knight service was merely a method of holding land.

Even as a tenure, knight service had undergone a good many changes since medieval days. The annual rent required as one of the "incidents" of the tenure was now usually a small one, often merely nominal. *Homage*, an integral part of feudal practice, though frequently still recited in charters, was completely ignored or given with little ceremony. *Fealty* in the days when lords no longer depended on their tenants as their fighting men had lost most of its meaning; and though sovereigns sometimes devised means of exacting gifts from their subjects, *aids*, a traditional part of this obligation had practically disappeared. *Suit at court* was still demanded where the manor courts functioned, but these too had in many places fallen into disuse, or met but seldom, now that the spheres for private jurisdiction had narrowed.

Only two, therefore, of the earlier incidents common to knight service continued to be of much import: the *relief*,

6. Pollock and Maitland say that scutage was a special tax levied by the king with the consent of the tenants and that they had no alternative, *The History of English Law,* I, 276. Miss H. Chew holds that the tenants *in capite* could commute military service by paying scutage, "Scutage Under Edward I," *The English Historical Review,* XXXVII, 322–336. See also Sydney K. Mitchell, *Studies in Taxation Under John and Henry III,* 1914, p. 64, and *passim.*

and the right of *wardship and marriage*, particularly that of wardship. Since the relief, that is, the fine paid by the heir for admission to his lands at the time of their descent, was common to the other two tenures, it will be discussed later. We may say a word here of the way in which wardship might and frequently did work an inconvenience and hardship on the yeomen who held land by knight service. Under the right of wardship, the minor heir of a tenant became *ipso facto* the ward of his lord who, as guardian, preserved the right to collect the revenues of the land and to use them to his own profit throughout the heir's minority. This practice in its inception had been a useful one. And in the days when the young ward, either heir or heiress, went to live in the home of the lord, receiving the same nurture afforded his own children, it had gone unquestioned. But tenurial relations were now far less personal. And with the growing demand for land and profits, a wardship had come to be regarded almost wholly as a remunerative thing. Wardships were bought and sold as commodities.

Often the landlord was far removed in person from the lands which he held. This was of course particularly true in the case of royal domains, and tenants grew skillful in concealing and ignoring wardship rights. To offset this evasion a special Court of Wards and Liveries was established in the early Tudor period for the purpose of pressing wardship claims and collecting revenues therefrom, particularly when the Crown was due to reap the benefits. This court carried on a brisk business, and concealments, either real or the creation of clever officers of the Crown, could cause trouble years after they had or were alleged to have taken place.

The suit involving Thomas Caroles, a Herefordshire yeoman in the reign of James I, is a case in point. Charges brought against Caroles in the early years of the reign stated that a part of the lands bequeathed him thirty years before by an uncle had been held by knight service, and that during his minority this fact had been concealed so that the Queen had been cheated of her wardship dues. If the charges could be proved, it meant that Caroles, the yeoman, now an adult, must make repayment to the Crown of all the money that had gone by default through the years, a sum, he claimed, that would result in his utter ruin. The jury returned against Caroles in the lower courts. He then declared that the King's Escheator had counterfeited the jury's verdict and himself brought the case to the Star Chamber.[7] Unfortunately the verdicts of this court have not come down to us, but regardless of its merits or demerits, the case shows how troublesome knight-service tenure might prove to be, even when the victim was in no way responsible for the situation brought upon him.

A slightly different angle of the way in which wardship sometimes operated is shown in the case of Richard Whittle, a yeoman of Lancashire, who fell heir to lands of his grandfather that were held by knight service of one James Anderton, Esq. Whittle was but three years old when his grandfather died, so Anderton entered the premises and, except for the amount allowed for the boy's maintenance and several small parcels of land in which his mother and aunt had an interest, enjoyed the full benefits of the income for almost twenty years. But according to the law governing wardships, if a man held by knight service of the king, and also of another lord, the Crown had priority rights over the wardship.

This stipulation was to bring Whittle difficulties. Several years after he became of age and had the full income from his lands, one Leonard Houghton, a gentleman of Yorkshire, declared to the king's officers that at the time of the death of Whittle's grandfather the legacy to the boy had included a small piece of land, one eighteenth of an acre, that was held by knight service of the Crown. Young Richard, he therefore claimed, should have been the ward of the Crown rather than of Anderton, all through his minority. Since the Crown had thus been cheated, it should now collect what it had lost through Anderton's years of

7. St.Ch. 8, 90/2.

gain. A commission was directed to investigate, and a jury upheld the charges; so a case was opened in the Court of Wards and Liveries to recover the money due the Crown. Whittle, the yeoman, declared that he had already paid his wardship dues to Anderton, and that he would now be completely ruined if compelled to pay them again to the Crown. He furthermore declared that the jury supporting the charges had been packed, and brought a countersuit in the Court of Star Chamber in the hope of gaining a verdict there.[8] Again there is no record of the final decision. But cases like these make abundantly clear the reasons for the unpopularity of knight service so frequently expressed in contemporary writings.[9]

Mr. Plucknett says that this tenure came to be only a "troublesome but lucrative anachronism."[10] Needless to say it was more troublesome than lucrative to most of the yeomen who came in touch with it; though now and then one encounters a yeoman like Walter Dillon of Holbeten, Devon, who, in 1571, bought the wardship rights of Andrew Cholwych, a child of seven years, from John Fortescue, Esq., expecting apparently to make a good thing out of it.[11] But as time went on, knight service, though a free tenure, grew more and more unpopular with all classes. In 1621 a bill was presented in Parliament for its abolition. This bill failed, and it was not until 1645 that the Long Parliament passed a resolution for its abandonment. The resolution was put into statute form in 1656, and was one of the reform acts upheld by the Restoration Parliament in 1660.[12] But prior to its abolition it was an active tenure which often brought inconvenience and loss to those whose land was subject to its annoyances. It is true that the problems pertaining to knight service did not affect the yeomen to the same degree as did those of the other two tenures in which they held, because a smaller number of them had land

8. *Ibid.*, 293/4.
9. See also Req. 2, 181/12; and S.P. 14, CXIX, 41–42.
10. J. F. T. Plucknett, *History of the Common Law,* 1929, p. 333.
11. Exeter Deeds and Doc., 1963.   12. *S.R.,* 12 Car. II, c. 24.

in this tenure; but the *post-mortem inquisitions* which listed yearly the lands of deceased tenants of the Crown, show a fair representation of yeomen among those holding by knight service, and court cases like the above indicate that they did not always escape its evils.[13]

The second of the free tenures, and the one by which hundreds of yeomen held all or a part of their land, was socage. "Free and common socage," as it was generally termed, had in the Middle Ages been reserved for those freemen who were unable to equip and maintain themselves as mounted men. Knight service with its emphasis on military obligations was in this earlier period considered the more honorable tenure, and "smelleth not of the plough like socage," as Cowell explained.[14] But knights of the Tudor and Stuart period were more interested in lands than they were in wars. Besides, knight-service tenure had long since ceased to have a military connection or even to be a badge of social distinction.

Socage, therefore, was now considered by all landholders, large and small, the best available tenure. Being a free tenure, it had all of the advantages of knight service without the right of wardship that had brought that tenure into disrepute. What the steward of certain Sussex manors said of the tenants there could probably have been said of all landholders: "They had rather hold of *meane* Lordes by socage tenure, than of Kinge in Capite, the rather because the Escheators and ffeodaryes of these times have Argus eyes peircinge into all conveyances."[15] When Sir Richard Pawlett in 1604 claimed the right of wardship over John Lee, the son of a deceased Hampshire yeoman, it was of great import to the fortunes of the latter that his counsel could

13. As in the case of the subsidy rolls, the yearly evaluation of lands listed in the *P.M.I.* records is far below their actual value; hence the records are of little use for that purpose. They are sometimes useful for the descriptions they give of lands; but the acreages given are often as deceptive as the value put upon them.

14. Cowell, "Chivalrie," *The Interpreter.*

15. *The Book of John Rowe*, p. 137.

produce "evidences" to show that his lands were held in socage and not by knight service.[16]

Never so heavily encumbered as the *unfree* tenures, socage had tended with the passage of time to lose even those incidents that had once been connected with it. If not actually lost they became largely ineffectual. The annual rent still common to most lands held in socage was, for instance, in many cases exceedingly small, or merely nominal. Indeed, those yeomen whose socage lands were a part of manors already disintegrated possessed what more nearly approximated the full rights of present-day land ownership than anything then existent. This was particularly true if these lands had been a part of the ancient demesne. Even on manors where considerable organization existed, the socage lands were in some cases remarkably free from restraints. So much so that Mr. Tawney says of the sixteenth century: "It would seem by our period, at any rate in the south of England that the connection of the freeholders with the manor was a matter of form and sentiment rather than substance."[17] This was especially true if the tenant were not himself an occupant of the manor in which his land lay. As John Norden said in 1607: "When Freeholders dwell out of the mannors whereof they hold and pay unto their Lords but a small acknowledgement as a rose, a pepper corne, a jyllyflower, or some such trifle, or are to do some service at times, whereof in many yeares has been no use . . . they have not been looked for neither have their suites been continued for a long time insomuch as they and their Tenures have growne out of memorie, and their services out of use."[18]

Certainly there were many cases where the socage tenants escaped most or all of the old manorial obligations. The lands of Robert Shepherd, yeoman, of Donnington, in Lincolnshire were said to be held "in free and common socage and not in chief or by Knight's service," with apparently no "incidents" at all attached.[19] Many socage lands were

16. St.Ch. 8, 204/13; see also 199/8.
17. *Agrarian Problem in the Sixteenth Century,* p. 30.
18. *The Surveyors Dialogue,* Bk. III.   19. P.M.I., C. 142, 731/150.

like those of William Andrewes, a Wiltshire yeoman, held
"by fealty only,"[20] which for all practical purposes meant
no obligation at all. The lands of John Hengeston, yeoman,
of South Mylton, Devonshire, carried the annual rent of
"one nutt mygge."[21] Thomas Fountayne, a yeoman of
Bucks, held his socage lands "by suit of court, and the annual rent of 14 pence."[22] Giles Haynes, a yeoman of Framp-
ton-on-Severn, Gloucestershire, held "in free socage by
fealty, suit at court every 3 weeks, and by the yearly rent of
4s. 7d., 1 pound of pepper, and 1 pound of cummin."[23] Free
lands in a certain Sussex manor carried the rent of "two
brode arrowe heades," another demanded a "race of gin-
ger," and another "one red rose."[24] These requirements may
have been a nuisance, if or when enforced, but certainly
they entailed little or no hardship.

One can, however, go too far in assuming that all socage
tenure had come to be so unencumbered. Custom dies hard,
and there were still many places, as deeds and other land
documents show, where freeholders' lands were yet definitely a part of the manorial organization, and commanded
numerous, if often petty, obligations.

The relief or fine exacted of a tenant when he came into
his inheritance was an incident of freehold tenure frequently guarded jealously by landlords long after other
rights had been relinquished. It was often a nuisance, sometimes more than that. The freeholders of the Almondbury
manor in Yorkshire, according to a survey made in 1584,
paid double their annual rent as a relief upon inheriting
their lands,[25] while those of the manor of South Teign in
Devon, according to the customs reviewed in 1607, paid one
year's rent.[26] These are the amounts most commonly exacted and examples of both are to be found in the customs

20. *Wiltshire P.M.I.,* pp. 339–340.
21. Exeter Deeds and Doc., 1198.   22. P.M.I., C. 142, 782/127.
23. *Glouc. P.M.I.,* 1625–42, *The Index Library,* 1893, XXI, 81.
24. *The Book of John Rowe,* p. 51.
25. Manuscripts in the Collection of the Yorkshire Archæology Society
at Leeds, 205.
26. Customs of the Manor of South Teign, Exeter MSS.

of many manors, and in land suits where the payment of the relief is a moot point. When the freehold rent was nominal or amounted to only a few pence as in some of the above examples, the relief caused little inconvenience. But to men with small cash incomes, whose freehold rents amounted to sums of five to thirty or more shillings a year as was sometimes the case, it was no small item.[27]

The customs of certain manors, moreover, required that the relief be paid upon alienation of freehold lands as well as at the time of inheritance. Tenants fretted under these hangovers of an age when there was not as much buying and selling as in their own day, and tried to free themselves from them as opportunity afforded. An interesting case in point came before the Chancery in 1619. Sir Richard Buller, lord of the manor of Tratford in Cornwall, brought suit against John Hawkey, a neighboring yeoman, contending that it was the custom of his manor that every free tenant pay a relief upon alienation as well as upon inheritance. Buller accused Hawkey of contracting with one of his tenants for free land and making secret conveyances whereby the lord was cheated of his "relief." Hawkey declared that he did not know the land he bought was held of the manor of Tratford. He also raised the question whether the "customs" actually did require a fine upon alienation.[28] If cases of this kind tend to show that incidents of socage tenure still furnished cause for annoyance and possible loss, they likewise show the attempts of the tenants to challenge and escape them.

Another of the incidents of socage still active on some manors was the *heriot*. This privilege which gave the lord upon the death of a tenant the right to seize his best beast, or sometimes more than one, was designated in the customs of many manors only in the case of copyholders; but it is not in the least unusual to find it also an incident of freehold. Here also, because of the uncertainty in many instances re-

27. Socage rents as high as this are frequently quoted for lands of yeomen listed in the *P.M.I.* for this period.

28. C. 3, 302/12.

garding the exact nature of the customs, there was fertile soil for disputes. And disputes there were. In some cases it was the lord's right to the heriot that was questioned, in others the nature of that right. Might a lord, for instance, have a heriot for each of the lands the deceased tenant held of him, or would one heriot suffice for all his holdings? Certain manors like those of Braunton in Devon were very specific on this point. But one heriot was to be given for all holdings in any one manor there.[29] But the matter was often not so well defined; and where there was doubt, trouble brewed.

A Hampshire yeoman by the name of Lee, who died in the reign of James I, held five pieces of socage lands in a manor in Hants. Upon his death his landlord claimed five heriots, and sent his servant to select three horses and two kine from Lee's stock. Lee's heir was a minor, but his mother brought suit against the lord. Certain witnesses among the tenants declared that the lord was permitted to take one heriot unless the tenant had indentures to show that he had been relieved of that obligation, but that he could not take more than one. The counsel for Lee contended that since his client had by indenture commuted for a rent that was stated to include all former services and demands, he should be free from the payment of any heriot, at the most he should be required to pay only one. Again the verdict of the case is not extant, but it shows that landlords were loath to give up their tenurial benefits even in the case of socage tenants, and also that tenants were challenging the lord's traditional rights all along the way.

Despite the encumbrances of socage tenure still persisting in particular manors, the yeomen who held all or a part of their lands in this fashion knew that they were fortunate. Chief among its advantages was that of providing a secure title which commanded the full protection of the law. Among socage tenants there was no fear of eviction, the current bugaboo of everyone whose title was not secure. As John Norden had his prospective land purchaser say: "It is

29. "Customs of the Manors of Braunton," *Devon Trans.*, XX, 275.

a quietnesse to a man's minde to dwell upon his owne, and to know his heir certaine."[30] Socage lands could also be freely sold, leased, or exchanged, and at death, devised at will. These were privileges coveted by all landholders, but usually not available to those who did not hold in a free tenure.[31]

But by no means all, or even a large percentage of English land was freehold; nor as we have seen were all yeomen freeholders. It was the copyholders, said William Harrison, by whom "the greatest part of the realm doth stand and is maintained."[32] His contemporary, Sir Edward Coke, agreed with him,[33] as did many other writers; and modern scholars have found no reason to disagree. Mr. Tawney's figures from 118 manors located in several regions show that 19.5 per cent of the tenants were freeholders as against 61.1 per cent who were customary tenants.[34] A study of 11 manors in East Anglia from 1600 to 1650 shows only one ninth of the land held by freeholders who did not also hold in some other tenure, while one third was held by those who were customary tenants only.[35] On 23 Sussex manors for the period of Elizabeth and James I, there were 539 copyholders and 321 freeholders.[36]

Since manorial records do not usually give the status of the tenants except in terms of their tenure, it is impossible to tell what percentage of yeomen fall in either of these groups. But from wills, deeds, leases, and other documents touching their land dealings it is obvious that they held their lands in diverse tenures. In sections where freehold was plentiful, they sometimes had most or all of their land in

30. *The Surveyors Dialogue,* Bk. VI.

31. Until the passage of the Wills Act in 1540, it was required that freeholds pass to the heir only and if there were no heir to the next in line. See contemporary arguments giving benefits of socage tenure, Titus MSS. in the British Museum, 5, fol. 276a.

32. *Description of England,* Bk. II, 242.

33. *An Abridgement of the Reports of Sir Edward Coke* (hereafter cited as Coke, *Reports*), 1793, III, fol. 86.

34. R. Tawney, *Agrarian Problem in the Sixteenth Century,* p. 25.

35. Spratt, *Agrarian Conditions in Norfolk and Suffolk,* p. 108.

36. *The Book of John Rowe, passim.*

free tenure. In the manor of Hoo in Sussex, for instance, there were 77 freeholders and no copyholders.[37]

But different tenures were often intermingled or adjacent. One might hold both free land and copyhold in the same manor, or free land in one manor and copyhold in another.

Nicholas Flagg, a yeoman of Suffolk, had both freehold and copyhold lands scattered over four manors.[38] Edward Atwood, a Warwick yeoman, had certain freehold lands of his own and a future share in his father's copyhold lands.[39] Robert Holborough of Suffolk speaks in his will of his lease land, free land, and copyhold.[40] Robert Yardley, a Hertford yeoman, described his lands as "lease grund" and "free grund."[41] These cases are in no way unique. In his study of East Anglian manors, Mr. Spratt estimated that of the 12,788 acres of land in question 7,231 acres were in the possession of tenants who had lands in both tenures.[42] On nineteen out of the twenty-three Sussex manors mentioned above there were both freeholders and copyholders.[43] A study made of certain manors in Devonshire shows the situation to have been the same there.[44] And it was true of individual manors elsewhere in many places.

But there were regions where copyhold dominated or was exclusive, and here there were many yeomen who had no free lands at all. At least thirty-eight out of the eighty-four tenants on the manor of Prescott in Lancashire in 1619 were yeomen, but all of their land was copyhold, for there were no freeholders on that manor.[45] Farther north in the Rossendale district where many yeomen were at this time adding to their possessions the land was likewise all copy-

37. *Ibid.*, p. 225.   38. P.C.C., 11 Rudd.
39. C. (Depositions), Car.'I, A. 1/20.
40. P.C.C., 62 Pile.   41. *Ibid.,* 2 Welden.
42. Spratt, *Agrarian Conditions in Norfolk and Suffolk,* pp. 113–114.
43. *The Book of John Rowe, passim.*
44. Caldwell, Devonshire, pp. 54–58.
45. Mr. F. A. Bailey determined the status of the tenants on this manor from his analysis of the manorial records. See his edition of the *Prescott Records 1447–1600,* Lanc. and Ches. Rec. Soc., 1937, LXXXIX, 62.

hold. The aggressive yeomen of Crawley, in Hampshire, described by Mr. Gras, were "free men in person but they were not freeholders."[46] It is necessary, therefore, in order to understand many of the tenurial problems that confronted the yeomen, to pay attention at least to the basic characteristics of copyhold.

It was a tenure beset with difficulties, and at the same time one that was struggling with considerable success to free itself from those difficulties: this is the chief conclusion that a study of copyhold practices brings one to. Hundreds of yeomen were affected by its encumbrances, and hundreds were involved in the struggle to lessen the onus of them. Their land suits appear in the records of all the courts which dealt with these matters, and an appalling number of these have to do with their copyholds.

There seems little reason to question the traditional theory that copyhold grew out of the villeinage tenure of the Middle Ages. But it is necessary to keep in mind the fact that unfree status had practically passed away by the Elizabethan period;[47] hence unfree tenure, though often burdensome, carried no social taint; and gentlemen, knights, and great lords, as well as yeomen and lesser husbandmen, held copyhold lands.

Manorial records and other contemporary documents use the terms tenants-at-will, customary tenants, and copyholders with great looseness. But in general it seems correct to consider customary tenure the more inclusive term, meaning thereby, as Mr. Tawney says, "all holders of lands which pass by surrender and admission in the court of the manor, and which are subject to the custom of the manor as evidenced by the records of the court."[48] Those customary tenants who held by written indenture with the specific terms of their tenure defined "by copy of the court roll" were called copyholders. By the Elizabethan period the tenure was largely specified in this form.

46. N. S. B. Gras, *History of an English Village,* p. 112.
47. See above, p. 16 n.
48. R. Tawney, *Agrarian Problem in the Sixteenth Century,* p. 47.

The question of chief importance to the yeomen who were copyholders was the nature of their copyholds, that is, whether they represented estates in inheritance, or for a term of years or lives. A "copyhold in inheritance" was next to a freehold the best tenure one could have from the point of view of security. The courts upheld this title and no man could be evicted from his copyhold in inheritance which at his death passed to his heirs.

If, on the other hand, a tenant held a copyhold for a certain term of years, or for his lifetime, or "for lives," meaning usually the lifetime of himself, his wife, and heir, the estate was bound to terminate at intervals. At its termination it was necessary, if the tenant wished to continue his tenure or have it continued in his family, to seek a renewal of his term. This was the point from which many copyhold difficulties issued; for here the landlord was obviously at an advantage. The terms of the renewal might be made so high that the tenant would be unable to meet them, or he might be unable to get the lands again at all except by lease for a short term at a much higher rent than he had ever paid before.

Second only in importance to the nature of the copyhold estate was the nature of the payments that accompanied it; whether or not the fines and rents were fixed and certain or arbitrary, and subject to change at the will of the lord. A copyhold in inheritance which had fixed rents and fines certain was practically as good as a freehold; for the payments defined in an earlier age were small and could not be increased.

But if these payments were uncertain the story was different. The lord could claim, certainly not without some justice, that the increased value of land justified the increase of rents or fines. And because of the abounding greed for land, there seemed always to be buyers and lessors ready to take it at the new terms however high they were; so that the former tenant had either to succumb to them also, or to give up his tenancy entirely.

Traditionally, jurisdiction in cases involving copyhold

rested with the manor court. But these courts had often by now disappeared entirely. In one case involving a copyholder's rights it was stated that there had been no court held on the manor in question for thirty years.[49] Even on manors where courts were held, and there still were many such, their activities were largely restricted to small matters of manorial import like the keeping up of repairs, cleaning streets, scouring ditches, and the like. Where points of tenure were in dispute copyholders had now gained for themselves a hearing in the courts of equity and the common law, where yearly the amount of litigation appeared to increase.

The history of copyhold has not yet been written nor can it be written until these multitudinous court records, and the thousands of extant manorial records yet unused, have been examined and their findings tabulated. For the history of copyhold will have to be the sum total of the history of manorial practices with all the diversity which that implies. It will be also the story of the struggle born of that diversity and directed toward the breaking away from tenurial fetters.

Many copyhold disputes, as was true in a lesser degree of disputes over freeholds, centered on the interpretation of manorial customs. Theoretically it was impossible to create a custom. No practice was a proper custom that had not been recognized *time out of mind to which the memory of no man is to the contrary*. But throughout the years changing conditions had brought new practices, which, if observed until they could be held traditional in character, were apparently regarded as customs. As John Norden, an experienced man in manorial matters, said: "You cannot make any newe custome, although all the Tennants consent willingly thereto, yet if such . . . were made and continued without any contradiction of posterities, *time* might create a new custome, by prescription."[50] In such a situation there were

49. John Godbolt, *Reports of Cases arising in severall courts of Record in the raignes of Q. Elizabeth, K. James and the late King Charles* (hereafter cited as Godbolt, *Reports*), 1653, p. 2.

50. *The Surveyors Dialogue*, Bk. II.

obviously many debatable customs. But it was the authority of the customs that courts of law recognized and depended on in their treatment of most copyhold disputes. Hence it was necessary to have them as specifically known as possible, and under Elizabeth, James I, and Charles I many new manorial surveys were made "for the utter abolishing of all future doubts and questions concerning the usages and customs."[51]

Such surveys were sometimes made by experienced surveyors like Norden, and sometimes by the steward of the manor, if he had been long enough in the post to be considered expert on the question of accepted manorial practices. The task was never an easy one. It depended on whatever written evidence could be found, and beyond that on the testimonies of the tenants, usually the oldest men among them. The memories of these witnesses were often confused, as well as prejudiced by their own interests or those of their heirs, so that there was frequently wide disagreement among them. As John Rowe said when he attempted to make such a survey of a Sussex manor: "Its customs I find so variable, as that I can not certainlye resolve myselfe thereof, much lesse satisfye others." Of another manor he said: "I find their estates to be intangled with the like difficultyes fitter for the reverend judges of this Kingdome upon mature deliberacon then for mine insufficiency to determine."[52] Sometimes it did fall to the lot of the reverend judges themselves to determine when a custom was or was not "reasonable," or whether it "existed" or not.[53] Sometimes lands of two or more manors were intermixed and thence were gov-

51. Add. MSS. 5701, fols. 138–143; see also new customary drawn up for manor of Crondal, 1567, "to put an end to uncertainties." F. Baigent, *The Crondal Records,* 1891.

52. *The Book of John Rowe,* p. 93. Rowe had been steward for twenty-five years of the manors of Lord Abergavenny in the barony of Lewes when he was asked in 1622 to make the survey there.

53. John March, *Reports on cases coming before the Court of King's Bench and the Court of Common Pleas in the years 1639 to 1642* (hereafter cited as March, *Reports*), 1675, p. 28. See also the account of a decree in Chancery fixing the customs of the manor of Ingleton: Ruston and Witney, *Hooton Pagnell,* pp. 318–320.

erned by different customs, a condition which but added to the confusion.[54] Because of it, however, manorial rolls in which customs were recorded assumed a new importance.[55]

It was this situation and various elements growing out of it which so profoundly affected the interests and fortunes of hundreds of yeomen. Some were placed on the defensive, some on the offensive, by the changing conditions which challenged old practices. For it was now the landlord, now the tenant, who took the initiative and sought with the aid of cunning lawyers to take advantage of whatever uncertainty the occasion offered, and to outwit tradition if opportunity arose.

The case of John Davis, yeoman, of Somerset, provides a good example of one of the many kinds of disputes that grew out of copyhold tenure. Davis had a cottage and sixteen acres of land in the manor of Abbotsleigh of which George Norton, Esq., was lord. He held other lands, said to be of better value, of Sir Arthur Cappell on another manor. The yeoman wished to make his home on the latter holdings because there was a better house there. But the customs of the manor of Abbotsleigh required that a copyholder must dwell on the land held of that manor unless he had a license from his lord to do otherwise. Davis says that he applied for such a license, offering to pay the required fee, but that it was refused him; whereupon he appears to have moved without leave to the other property. He was first presented to the manor court of Abbotsleigh for this infringement. The court found him guilty and fined him. Davis apparently ignored the order of the court which thereupon repeated the fine, and increased it. This made Davis angry and the quarrel continued, reaching a new development when Norton charged his tenant with having broken another custom of the manor of Abbotsleigh by becoming involved in a suit at

54. Norden said in 1617, when attempting to make a survey of the manor of Blewbery in Berkshire, that its bounds could not be distinguished "for that there are other manors within and intermixted with the same." Add. MSS. 6027, fol. 14a; see also *Agrarian Conditions in Norfolk and Suffolk*, pp. 18–21.

55. S.P. 14, CXLIII, 113.

common law with one of his fellow tenants. Norton held that the customs forbade any copyholder's suing another tenant in a court outside the manor without the lord's permission, upon pain of forfeiture of his lands.

Davis challenged this custom and the steward of the manor, acting for Norton, attempted through the manorial jury to carry out an inquiry, there being no written statement of the customs. The jury, doubtless mindful of future implications, declared that there was no such custom "active," and the case was carried to the Star Chamber. It offers an interesting illustration of a landlord's attempts to hold on to his fast-slipping powers of private jurisdiction and of a tenant's efforts to improve his situation by defying a custom, the authenticity of which was debatable.[56]

Questions of surrender and descent were also often hedged about with difficulties growing out of peculiarities of customs. Edward Atwood, a Warwickshire yeoman, became involved in a Chancery suit in the reign of Charles I concerning his copyhold inheritance. Atwood was a younger son, whereas the customs of the manor of Aston Cantlod to which the lands belonged held that the homage of the manor court must always recognize the superior right of the heir to copyholds in inheritance. Atwood tells how his father, having planned to leave his freehold properties to his eldest son and heir, wished him, the second son, to have the copyhold land. But because of the peculiarity of the customs, he could not be sure of his title until the eldest son had signified in formal agreement his willingness to have the copyhold settled upon his brother.[57]

The transference of a copyhold to a new occupant, whether through descent or purchase, usually followed a more or less routine procedure: the land was surrendered into the hands of the lord, who upon the payment of the fine or relief regranted it to the new tenant. The transaction was normally carried out by the steward of the manor acting in behalf of the lord and in the presence of several of the ten-

56. St.Ch. 8, 116/6.   57. C. (Depositions), Car. I, A. 1/20.

ants; but this practice was not uniform and peculiarities of customs could on occasion assume a troublesome importance. A copyhold dispute in the reign of James I, involving Simon Bensted, a Hampshire yeoman, hinged upon such a detail. The question was whether the surrender by descent of copyhold land on the manor of Hambldon, where Bensted's lands were, had to be made in the presence of the steward in open court, or whether it might be made out of court in the presence of one of the tithing men and two other copyhold tenants.[58] One gathers from the depositions of witnesses in such cases that details of this kind had through the years received but casual attention until the scramble to get land at any cost now raised them to a position of importance. They became significant technicalities on which the decision of an important land suit might rest. Clever lawyers could help a man to much gain, or else do him out of his entire possessions on the interpretation given a single relatively unimportant technicality.

The multitude of obligations incident to copyhold tenure, and formerly accepted as a part of the existing scheme of things, was often now also the target for challenge and dispute as personal initiative marshaled its forces against traditional prohibitions that stood in the way of its advance. But many of them were yet taken for granted and were in general operation.

The heriot, already mentioned as an incident sometimes present in socage tenure, was practically an accepted feature of copyhold. Its demands might differ slightly, but the right of the lord to seize one or more beasts, the best or the second best as the custom stipulated, at each tenant's death and sometimes upon alienation, was unquestioned. Almost always this demand was limited to livestock. But the customs of the manor of Sonning, in Berks and Oxon, held that in the absence of "cattle," which term was used to include horses, sheep, and kine, "the best goods" of the tenant should be taken as a heriot.[59] Indeed, a gentleman from Col-

58. St.Ch. 8, 65/20.   59. Lansd. MSS. 105, fol. 9.

chester told me recently that until the passing of the land acts of 1926 abolishing copyholds, a man of his acquaintance, the lord of an Essex manor where copyhold still prevailed, appeared regularly upon the death of one of his tenants to claim the best horse or the best cow as a heriot. If this were true of so recent a time, one can the more easily understand the reluctance of the landlords of the Elizabethan and Stuart period, not yet so far distant from the days of strict feudal services, to give up their privileges.

Regulations regarding the timber growing on copyholds were many and important. Large forests still covered certain sections of England but there was already talk of the scarcity of wood. In general it was held that no copyholder should have to buy housebote, ploughbote, and firebote.[60] Likewise the rights of "topping and lopping" were generally allowed if the tree was in no way injured thereby. Since particulars regarding timber rights were usually governed according to the local supply,[61] they differed rather widely. One finds John and Thomas Bull, yeomen, of Sutton Hosy (Long Sutton) in Somerset, involved in a suit in 1611 defending or overstepping—it is hard to determine which— their copyhold rights of lopping and topping against James Arnewood, gentleman, the lord of the manor.[62] There are many similar cases. If a lord felled more timber than he should, to the prejudice of the rights of the customary tenants, the latter were awarded right of action in the courts.[63]

Rights of common were one of the few incidents of copyhold that worked often to the advantage of the tenant. Usually the tenant was allowed rights of common for his stock in woods, waste, and meadow and on open arable between harvest and sowing time, the extent of the privilege being ordinarily determined by the amount of the land he held and the rent paid. This was a matter of special importance to

60. Aaron Rathbone, *The Surveyor,* 1616; Lansd. MSS. 105, fol. 9; G. Plattes, *Practical Husbandry Improved,* p. 11.

61. Eg. MSS. 2223, fols. 1–13; St.Ch. 8, 287/4; W. Copinger, *Manors of Suffolk,* 1905, IV, 240–241; Lansd. MSS. 105.

62. St.Ch. 8, 39/17.   63. *The Book of John Rowe,* p. 81.

the sheep farmer whose animals needed a wide range for pasturage. For this right the owner of a small flock had advantages that he could not possibly enjoy if dependent on his own lands for pasturage. But as land became more valuable and inclosures increased, the rights of common were continually encroached upon, which, together with the problem of overstocking the common, resulted in many difficulties among copyholders.[64]

The property rights of the wife of a copyholder at her husband's death raised a question that was answered differently on different manors, though the common-law practice, active probably from the fifteenth century, of fixing the widow's dower at a third of the land of which the husband had been seised for an estate in inheritance,[65] was now generally accepted on many manors. The will of William Midgley, a yeoman of Brigley, Yorkshire (1612), speaks of a third part of his possessions as his wife's "reasonable parte," according "to the custome of the province wherein I dwell."[66] Certain customs set down specific details affecting the manner of payment and the like; not infrequently the widow could retain her estate only if she did not marry again.[67]

By the Elizabethan period a man could bequeath his copyhold land as he chose unless limitations were named in the indentures covering specific pieces of land, or there were particulars in the customs of the manors forbidding it. On certain manors, the custom of "Borough English" prevailed. This required that the copyholder's land must go to

64. Richard Brownlow and John Goldsborough, *Reports of cases in law arising in the Courts of the realm* (hereafter cited as Brownlow and Goldsborough, *Reports*), 1650–52, p. 232; Add. MSS. 5705, fol. 134 ff.; D. L. Special Com. 44/901; Northants MSS. FH. 410.

65. Holdsworth, *History of English Law,* III, 193.

66. "Yorkshire Wills," *The Bradford Historical and Antiquary Society Publications* (hereafter cited as *Bradford Antiquary*), Local Record Series, I, 20–21.

67. C. (Depositions), Car. I, A. 1/25. For special regulations, see "Customs of the Manors of Braunton," *Devon Trans.,* XX; William Blount, *Ancient Tenures,* 1679, pp. 144, 481; W. A. Copinger, *Manors of Suffolk,* 1905, V; St.Ch. 8, 287/4.

his youngest rather than his eldest son as was the case in the common-law usage. Mr. Copinger has estimated that as many as eighty manors in Suffolk were governed by this custom. Unless special provision were made for its interpretation,[68] Borough English could and often did carry with it germs of trouble.

A yeoman living in St. Byrd's parish in Monmouthshire in the reign of James I was in danger of losing outright his lands held in Borough English, because the failure of direct issue in the three preceding generations brought the validity of his title into question.[69] Trouble also arose among the heirs of Lancelot Hartshorne, a Yorkshire yeoman who held of the manor of Skidby where the custom of Borough English prevailed. In addition to the provision that the property should go to the youngest son, the customs of this manor stipulated that lands held in this tenure should descend to a daughter if there were no son. Hartshorne was married twice, having a daughter by the first marriage and a son by the second. At his death the land went to his son. But when the latter died, a dispute arose as to whether the land should then revert to the daughter of the first marriage or go to the next in descent from the son.[70]

Suit at court, if a manor court were still held, was one of the incidents of copyhold as of freehold, though more troublesome in the former than in the latter case. For as a rule freeholders were required to attend the court but once or twice a year, whereas copyholders were expected to be present every three or four weeks. The number of amercements for nonattendance in manorial court rolls attests the unpopularity of this obligation though it was a nuisance rather than an actual hardship, and furnished less cause for dispute than many of them.

As land activities became more commercialized, the right to lease their lands freely was a privilege greatly desired by copyholders. Earlier it had been held that a tenant could

68. See specific regulations in Customs of Barony of Lewes, Add. MSS. 5705, fol. 105 ff.

69. St.Ch. 8, 118/15.   70. *Ibid.*, 285/4.

not lease his copyhold for longer than a year and a day
without securing a license from his lord for which he paid a
fee. Contemporary treatises on manorial law upheld this
principle,[71] and the customs of certain manors specified it.
But by hook or crook copyholders were striving for, and in
many places gaining, more liberal regulations. Simon
Rider, yeoman, says that on the manor in Staffordshire,
where he held lands, the copyholders might lease their lands
for three years, and so "from three years to three years" for
a term of twenty-one years, apparently the common term of
leases in that section.[72] Tenants on some manors were trying to read into the customs the right to lease without license, and the matter frequently became a point of dispute
in land suits.[73]

Practically all of the above incidents of copyhold were
present wherever the tenure existed, with perhaps certain
local variations in practice. In addition, many others purely
local in character were called into existence by the nature of
local conditions. Mining rights, in regions where mining
was done, were of great importance to tenants. It appears
generally to have been accepted that a freeholder had the
right to dig coal on his lands, but not a copyholder. As it
was said of one copyholder in 1608, "he feared to seeke or
gette coale on his customary lands, but if it had byn his
freehold lands he would have sought for coals."[74] But certain manors had special mining rights set down in their customs, just as others had special fishing rights, salt-making
rights and the like, in regions where those industries flourished.

Regulations controlling copyhold tenure provide an al-

71. The Order of Keeping a Court Leet or Court Baron, "English
MSS." in the John Rylands Library, 54; Harl. MSS. 6714.

72. Rider Commonplace Book, p. 43.

73. See especially Req. 2, 177/33; 186/102. In the latter case, dated
1574, the tenants who testify, of whom the majority are yeomen, declare
that it is only within the last two or three years that the lord has claimed
the right to a fine for copyhold leases. They say that leasing has always
been a privilege of the copyholders there.

74. E. (Depositions), Lyttleton vs. Law, 5 Jac. I, Hil. 17.

most inexhaustible subject for investigation. We have carried it far enough here to arrive at two conclusions: first, that the yeomen who held their lands in this tenure were often subject to inconvenience, uncertainty, and sometimes actual loss; and secondly, that those who were thus annoyed or brought to grief did not accept their lot with resignation or bow meekly to the existing order, but everywhere were attempting, now with greater, now with less success, to lessen those inconveniences and dangers.

The question whether in general the copyholders of Elizabethan and early Stuart days occupied a favorable or unfavorable position has been a subject of controversy from Sir Edward Coke's day to our own. Coke gave a rosy picture of their advance, describing the happy position they had reached by the reign of James I. In an utterance that has become a classic in the history of copyhold, he said: "But now copyholders stand upon a sure Ground, now they weigh not their Lord's displeasure, they shake not at every sudden blast of wind, they eat, drink, and sleep securely, (only having a special care of the main Chance *viz*) to perform carefully what Duties and Services soever their Tenure doth exact, and Custom doth require: Then let the Lord frown, the Copyholder cares not knowing himself safe, and not within any danger. . . . Time has indeed dealt very favourably with copyholders in diverse respects."[75]

Fitzherbert, writing somewhat earlier it is true, gave a less favorable picture,[76] and Aaron Rathbone, an Elizabethan surveyor, admitted that in certain of its more important aspects the question was debatable.[77]

Among modern writers there is equal diversity of opinion. Leadam's picture is almost as rosy as that of Coke.[78] Ashley disagrees.[79] Sir William Holdsworth, who empha-

75. *The Compleat Copyholder*, p. 31.
76. Fitzherbert, *Surveyinge*, 1539, chap. XIII.
77. *The Surveyor*, 1616, p. 189.
78. I. S. Leadam, "The Inquisition of 1517: Inclosures and Evictions," *R.H.S. Trans.*, VI, 167–314.
79. Sir Wm. Ashley, *Economic History*, I, Pt. II, pp. 274–282.

sizes the tremendous importance of the copyhold question to the peace and prosperity of the sixteenth century, is inclined to think Coke justified in his basic conclusion. He says that "the strong government of the Tudors, acting through the Council, Parliament, and all the courts new and old, did much to remedy the grievances of the copyholder."[80]

Thus far, as Tupling points out in his brief but admirable survey of the question, there are not sufficient data for settling it.[81] But certainly some of the seeming contradictions among those who have discussed the matter rest upon differences of approach and emphasis rather than upon fundamental divergences, a fact not perhaps sufficiently recognized.

One needs, for instance, in respect to the right of the copyholder's protection before the law—an important point in the arguments of all those who talk of his advance —to distinguish between his legal right to this protection and his ability to take advantage of that right. It is also important to know to what extent he might expect fair treatment in the courts if he went to them. Again, in regard to the uncertainty of fines and their increase, an issue greatly stressed by those who picture the sorry plight of the copyholder, it is not only necessary to point out the evils of uncertain fines but equally imperative that one consider how far such uncertainty and increase were counterbalanced by the increase in prices that the copyholder received for his produce. It makes a difference, furthermore, whether one is thinking in terms of security of title, or from the point of view of required services, obligations, and the like. Again, it is important to note the fact that the economic position of the copyholder had a distinct bearing on the magnitude of his tenurial problems, and that copyholders cannot, therefore, be considered as one group in a discussion of this subject. Finally, is one to look from the thirteenth century forward or from the twentieth century backward when con-

80. *History of English Law,* III, p. 211.
81. *History of Rossendale,* pp. 127–155.

sidering the favorable or unfavorable position of the Elizabethan copyholder? The vantage point makes a good deal
of difference in what one sees.

As a problem in its own right, of which the above questions are all a part, this matter lies beyond the scope of the
present study, and any final settlement of it is dependent
upon far more data than is now available. But a few observations on the above points insofar as they affect the yeomen are pertinent.

In regard to legal protection, the copyholder's right to
bring his case into every court of the realm that dealt with
land matters, both the courts of equity and the common
law, appears by the time of Elizabeth to have been definitely
established. The records of scores of cases in the Star Chamber Court, the Court of Requests, and Chancery; and the
reports of cases before the Court of King's Bench show how
frequently copyhold rights were made the subject of suits
in these courts, now the landlord, now a tenant or group of
tenants, appearing as the plaintiffs.

But to what extent this right could be taken advantage
of by the copyholders of all classes is obviously a different
matter. A Northamptonshire man in 1617 declared the Star
Chamber Court a "wonderful court of charges and expenses," stating that he had spent ten pounds in court fees
during the first term of a suit now pending, and that it
would cost him at least a hundred marks more before it was
over.[82] A statement in the records of a case before the Court
of Requests in 1594 enumerated the costs of a suit in that
court at £4 9s. 2d., a sum which included fifteen small fees.[83]
This of course included only the court costs and none of the
traveling expenses or incidentals often connected with carrying a case to the higher courts. Fees differed. But it is obvious that even the Court of Requests, earlier known as the
poor man's court, was closed to hundreds of poor men unless
they were able to band together to pay the costs of a suit. A
poor copyholder as an individual, one is forced to think, had

82. St.Ch. 8, 65/11.   83. Req. 2, 196/65.

little opportunity to take advantage of the redress legally open to him. That the yeomen were able and did secure the services of all of the above courts, the records amply testify. In the total of 8,173 cases which went before the Star Chamber Court in the reign of James I, yeomen appeared among the principals, that is, as plaintiff or defendant or both, in 2,112 cases. Not all of these were land suits; but of 1,099 land suits, scores of which had to do with disputes growing out of copyhold tenure, 566, or slightly more than half of them, show a yeoman as the plaintiff, the person who instituted the suit.[84]

To what extent the courts dealt fairly with their suitors, regardless of their wealth and position, it is of course impossible to say. Doubtless there has been no age in which the dispensing of justice has not been to some extent affected by influence and position. Certainly there is no indication that the age in question was without guilt in this regard. On the other hand, though the verdicts in the Star Chamber cases and in many others are not extant, it seems scarcely likely that yeomen would have continued year after year to institute land suits if the landlord always got the better of it. Certainly they sought the courts continually with their copyhold problems, sometimes for protection and sometimes, as above examples show, in the hope of pushing an economic advantage.

What the proportion of uncertain fines was and to what extent landlords were absorbing copyhold estates into their own domains by raising fines so high that the tenants could not pay them are questions for which much more data are needed.

Mr. Tawney's table for 142 manors based upon his own and Mr. Savine's figures shows that 53 had fines certain, whereas on 93 the fines were uncertain and on the one remaining they were partly certain, partly uncertain.[85] There appears to have been absolutely no uniformity even in

84. Compiled from the typescript Index of Star Chamber cases in the reign of James I, in the Public Record Office.

85. *Agrarian Problem in the Sixteenth Century*, p. 300.

manors in the same region or belonging to the same lord. A survey of 1608 of the royal manor of Walburton in Sussex declared the fines there arbitrable, and assessed at the king's pleasure, as was also true of the manor of Preston. But for the royal manor of St. Leonard in the same county they were certain.[86]

Mr. Tupling makes it clear that the copyhold tenants of Rossendale had no alternative but to accept the king's terms for the composition of their fines, and they were high terms.[87] And an order made in connection with a project for getting money from the copyholders on the royal manors in the north in the first decade of the reign of James I states that if any refused to comply with the plan for increased rents and fines in exchange for the discharge of services and confirmation of their customs, the royal agents should seek to find their tenure defective and threaten them with the conversion of their copyholds to leaseholds.[88]

But the evidence is not all in this direction. Though Mr. Spratt in his study of the agricultural situation in East Anglia from 1600 to 1650 found that forty-six out of eighty manors in Suffolk and Norfolk in that period had uncertain fines, he saw no evidence that they were being raised to exorbitant rates.[89] Mr. T. Caldwell in his study of Devon under Elizabeth and the early Stuarts, where the customary tenants of many manors far outnumbered the freeholders, likewise states that he could find no evidence that the landlords were gaining large tracts or driving tenants out.[90]

Individual court records, moreover, frequently bear witness to the copyholder's success against the lord's efforts to raise his fine. A dispute in the Court of Requests over the copyhold lands held by a Dorset yeoman on the manor of Yetmenster Upbery is an example. The tenant, one Willis,

86. Add. MSS. 5705, fols. 134, 135.
87. *History of Rossendale,* pp. 148–160.
88. S.P. 14, XL, 38. (A paper written during the period of Lord Salisbury's treasuryship, 1608–12.)
89. *Agrarian Conditions in Norfolk and Suffolk,* pp. 115–117.
90. Caldwell, Devonshire, p. 58.

had died some years previously and the lands had passed to his widow. Now at her death they would, upon the payment of the admittance fine, be granted to their son who as heir to the deceased tenant had the first right to be the next occupant. Apparently the land was desirable and the lord was offered a higher fine by a new applicant than he had previously received. Whereupon, he held to the custom of permitting priority rights to the heir, but demanded of him as a fine the same amount that the other suitor had offered. Willis refused to pay it upon the ground that it was not a "reasonable" fine, and protested the lord's action. According to the customs of the manor, the matter was turned over to the reeve and some of the tenants who were chosen to make an "indifferent" decision. They judged the sum requested by the landlord too high and fixed what they considered a "reasonable" fine. Their decision stood and upon the basis of it Willis was admitted to his land.[91]

William Barler in his *Concordance* on manorial practices says that "Lords of manors for theire owne quyetnes are forewarned to beware how they deale hardelie with copieholders."[92] And Barnabie Googe in his revision of Heresbach in 1577 says of the letting of land that the lord does best not to deal with a tenant "so straightly in every poynt as by lawe he might," for if he does, more harm than good will come from it. Wise landlords knew, he says, that old tenants are best for "they will better use the land because of their familiarity with it."[93] John Norden espoused the cause of the landlord when he said that there was "little cause why Tennants should so much grudge as some of them do." If they say their rents are raised, said Norden, "or complaine of the greatness of their fines, let them enter into consideration how they vent their commodities: and they shall finde as good inequality of the prices of things now and in times past, as is betweene rents and fines now and in times

91. Req. 2, 191/50.
92. *Concordance of all written lawes concerning Lords of Manors, Theire Free Tenants, and Copieholders,* Manorial Society reprint, 1911.
93. *Four Books of Husbandry, englished by Barnabie Googe,* 1577, p. 47.

past!"[94] Earlier he had declared that as far as he could perceive "an observing and painfull husband liveth fareth and thriveth as well upon his Farme of Rackrent as many doe that are called Freeholders or that have Leases of great value in small rent."[95] Norden may have been biased in favor of the landlord class which he served but he does not always spare it; and his practical labors as a surveyor of many estates had given him opportunity to observe matters of this kind. That the uncertainties connected with copyhold tenure created much inconvenience, and often led to loss among small copyholders, in particular, was certainly true. But to attribute all of their losses to their tenure would be to leave out of account the many other hazards of the time. Nor can one ignore the fact that hundreds of copyholders were succeeding in spite of their tenure. Corn ripened and sheep fattened on copyhold acres as well as upon freeholds.

In 1608 it was said of the lands on the manor of Harthurst in Sussex that "all Sales of Copiehold lands have been at as high a price as freehold lands."[96] Certainly gentlemen and yeomen were not deterred from buying land because it was copyhold. Either, one must suppose, they believed that they could improve the tenure, or else they felt that with all of its hindrances there was still enough profit to be made from it to offset the burdens the tenure imposed. Sir John Saville, speaking in the House of Commons in 1626, told how the copyholder "languisheth" and was decayed, having to bear "3 parts out of 4 in the Subsidy books."[97] This statement of the unequal burden of the subsidies is certainly justified.[98] But it must be remembered that one did not get in the subsidy book at all who was not of the economic standing of a yeoman or a reasonably well-to-do husbandman.

And in spite of the fact that the copyholders of the Rossendale district, where there was no freehold, had under

94. *The Surveyors Dialogue,* Bk. III.
95. *Ibid.,* Bk. II.   96. S.P. 14, XL, 21.
97. Sir J. Whitelocke, Parl. Diary, 25 Feb. 25/26.
98. See below, pp. 358–359.

Elizabeth no alternative but to compound with the Crown on high terms for their fines, it is significant that the progress and advancement of the small holders in that region are reckoned by Mr. Tupling as the dominant development there in the sixteenth and early seventeenth centuries.[99] Mr. Gras likewise tells the same story of the yeomen of Crawley though the land there did not become freehold until the nineteenth century.[100]

It is interesting, moreover, to note that the initiative for enfranchisement often came from the landlord as well as from the tenant. The Stuart kings as well as private landlords sought this means of raising money.[101] One even finds in the report of one of the royal agents who was sent to treat with a group of the king's copyholders on the matter, that one of the objections the tenants made to the proposed plan was that they had no reason to wish enfranchisement.[102] To support this contention, they pointed out that as copyholders they were not forced to sit upon juries, an irksome duty demanded of freeholders, nor to fill offices for which they got no pay. As copyholders, moreover, they had all of their land transactions recorded in the court roll, hence they need not fear secret mortgages or fraudulent "evidences." The reliefs demanded of freeholders, they said, were often as large as the fine the copyholder paid, so there would be little gain in that regard. They would, moreover, lose their right of common and other customary privileges.[103] As a

99. *History of Rossendale,* pp. 91–92.

100. *History of an English Village,* pp. 95–98.

101. See Sir Henry Nevill's plans for compounding with copyholders on Essex and Sussex manors. Caesar Papers, Add. MSS. 497, fol. 342. For accounts of royal compositions, see S.P. 14, LXI, 66; LVIII, 57, 75; LIX, 43; XLIII, 113; XLV, 70, 71; CXIX, 41–42; CLIV, 11; CCIII, 11. At the beginning of the reign of James I it appears that a plan was on foot for enfranchising all of the king's copyholds and customary lands, but this was later given up as impracticable, S.P. 14, IV, 31.

102. S.P. 14, LIX, 44.

103. See also the petition of the two copyholders on the Queen's manor in Somersham in Hunts who desired to be allowed to purchase the freedom of their copyholds and still keep the rights of common they had enjoyed as copyholders. El. MSS. Hn. 764.

matter of fact a full reading of the report makes one suspect that the chief purpose of these arguments was to try to make the king reduce his composition price rather than a reluctance to forsake copyhold. But it does show that not all of the elements of copyhold were held unfavorable, and certainly there was not a desire to change it at any cost. It is significant that a letter, written in 1610 to the commissioners who were to treat with royal tenants regarding the conversion of their copyholds to socage tenure, instructed them how to proceed in case the tenants "shall rather desire to continue coppieholders still."[104]

With these facts in mind, it seems more and more evident that in any consideration of the copyholder's position a distinction must be made between the many small copyholders who held little or no land beyond that which afforded their living and perhaps a slight profit, and those of the substance and position of the yeomen or above, who were in possession of larger estates.

It was the small copyholder with his eggs all in one basket who was the sufferer. It was he who, without credit or savings, had no alternative when faced with an increased fine or rents beyond his capacity to pay, but to forfeit his lands. Whereas, a yeoman, or man of greater substance, though he might suffer inconvenience and even some loss, could probably find a way out. Often it was not his whole possessions that were affected; for men with fair amounts of land often held on several manors subject to varying obligations. Even on the same manor, as we have seen, they frequently held lands in different tenures.[105] Even when all of a yeoman's lands were copyhold, they had usually been acquired at different times, for that was the way their estates were built up; hence their fines, even if uncertain, rarely came due at the same time.

The yeoman, therefore, was not only often able to survive trouble but could frequently fight his way through it to greater gains. At the termination of a tenure for which the

104. S.P. 14, LXI, 65.   105. See above, p. 119.

rent was uncertain he had several alternatives. If he considered the new rent high but thought the chance for future profit great enough to overbalance the temporary loss, he paid the higher rent rather than see the land go to someone else. If the price seemed exorbitant, a temporary refusal, which he could afford to give because his whole livelihood did not depend on that one property, might bring the landlord to better terms. If, moreover, he had on hand some savings or was of sufficient position to command credit, he might offer the lord a sufficiently attractive composition fee to purchase the future right of fines and rents certain, or even enfranchisement, thereby removing the necessity of being faced again with the same problem, at least for that particular land. He was, in other words, not only able to meet the difficulty even if the cost were dear, but often able to turn it to his future advancement, a course denied the smaller copyholder who stood to lose his all, even the roof over his head, if he met with a stroke of ill luck or pressure from above.

Yeomen whose own lands were involved often became the spokesmen for smaller tenants in the face of such pressure. The records of a Star Chamber suit in which the copyhold lands of James Bond, a Hereford yeoman, were threatened with forfeiture, furnish an interesting example. According to the account, the Lord Treasurer in 1610 requested the high steward of the manor of Ledbury, where Bond held land, to choose some of the ablest copyhold tenants on the manor to compound with the King's agent for making their fines certain. Ambrose Elton, Esq., and Edward Skynner, gentleman, were chosen, and through them arrangements were made for all of the copyholders to pay at the rate of one year's value of the land for their "heritable" lands, and one-and-a-half year's value for all that were "not heritable," and so at every death and alienation, in return for having their fines made certain.

There is no indication that this composition price was unwelcome or considered exorbitant. Apparently a survey had recently been made of every man's tenement and its estimated yearly value. But according to Bond, Mr. Elton and Mr. Skynner, hoping to lighten the burden of the composition for themselves and their friends and kinsmen, ordered a new survey to be made. By an unfair connivance they planned, Bond declares, to have the authors of the survey underestimate the yearly value of their own copyholds and those of some of their relatives and friends and to overvalue those of the poorer copyholders. Hence a copyhold belonging to Elton's mother, declared in the earlier survey to be worth a yearly value of £30, was now put at £11, and others accordingly; whereas those of poorer copyholders were greatly overvalued. Furthermore, although the first plan for the composition had called for a payment in eighths, the first of which had been collected at Easter by Elton and Skynner, a new letter purporting to be from the Lord Treasurer now called for the remaining seven eighths to be paid by Michaelmas. This was a blow to the poorer copyholders who had no savings upon which to draw. Some had to sell their cattle and others to borrow money on interest which they could little afford in order to meet the payments. Bond, the yeoman, as one of the copyholders affected, believing the last demand to have been framed by Elton and Skynner rather than by the Lord Treasurer, protested the move on behalf of the tenants. It was, he says, the anger of Elton and Skynner at his discovery of their fraud that led to their suit against him in the Star Chamber.[106]

Another yeoman, Peter Lane, a tenant on the manor of Etall in Northumberland, brought a suit to the Star Chamber in 1602 in defense of the rights of the copyholders of that manor.[107] There are many cases like these which show the yeomen as leaders of the peasantry in resisting pressure

106. St.Ch. 8, 70/2. There is no way to judge the merits of the story. It was introduced into the defendant's *responsio* as evidence to support his side in the pending forfeiture suit. It is doubtless colored somewhat in Bond's favor, and Bond may himself have lost in the long run for his boldness. But apparently he thought his cause a good one, and there is no reason to suppose that the account does not offer a fair sample of the tactics employed against the smaller and more ignorant copyholders.

107. St.Ch. 5, L 8/4.

from above. It is not to be supposed that it was his altruism that placed the yeoman in this role. He was as quick to take advantage of a fellow tenant as of a landlord. But if, as frequently happened, he could identify his own cause with the ills of all or the majority of the tenants, playing thereby the role of the champion of the oppressed, he was in a much better way to gain the ear of the court than if he presented his own case alone.

In respect to the various services and obligations incident to copyhold, time was indeed dealing kindly with those who held by this tenure. And here again the yeomen, possessing greater bargaining ability than the smaller copyholders, were active participants in effecting the change. The commutation of rents and services had begun by the late thirteenth century. The movement continued steadily and was still in progress when Elizabeth came to the throne. Interesting examples of rents in kind can be found as late as the mid-seventeenth century,[108] perhaps later; but for the most part by that time they survived only on the occasional manor. Services and "works" also, where still in existence, came continually under the hammer, and through legal challenge or by peaceful bargaining were fast disappearing. On the manor of Plumpton in Sussex the tenants in 1555 could still choose between the new method of paying rent and the old. Lawrence Snelling, a yeoman who held one-half yardland there, had his choice of working three days for his rent or paying ninepence. With other tenants it was the same in proportion to their holdings.[109] Where this option did not exist, services were constantly being

108. Thomas Grovener, a yeoman of Hunts, paid his annual rent to Henry Williams, Esq., with "fifteen bushels of good wheat," Add. Ch. 39, 268. John Page, a Sussex yeoman, in addition to paying a sum of money gave also for the rent of his lease, "eleven quarters of goode sweete wheat well wynied with heaps to every quarter," and eleven quarters of "good sweet barley with heaps likewise," Sussex MSS., Gage, Box 8, No. 13. In 1655 a Devon yeoman's rent included one harvest day's labor, one fat capon, and "a grinding of corn spent upon the premises," Exeter Deeds and Doc. 2809. See also Add. Rolls, 39,446.

109. Sussex MSS., A 19.

challenged and usually composition of some kind was offered for their removal.

In 1602 there were still "bond villaine services" on the manor of Etall in Northumberland, which required that the tenants "carry the dung out of the master's house and yard, lead his cowes before their own, carry his cole and turffes, plow his land, and wead and pull up his wifes hempe and lynt all without recompence and wages."[110] But the request for their removal was set forth with vigor in the court struggle led by Peter Lane, yeoman, on behalf of the copyhold tenants of the manor, and it is almost certain that some of them had already fallen into disuse.

John Wilkinson, a yeoman of Risholme in Lancashire, who owed labor services to Oswald Mosley of Ancoates, secured a written agreement in 1616 whereby in return for an annual payment of ten shillings he was discharged "of all workes or services of plowinge, harrowinge, shearinge, leading of corne and turves" that had been formerly required.[111]

Simon Rider, yeoman, of Staffordshire, upon being asked by the steward of a manor of which he held whether his lands were "heriotable," replied that they were not, and produced two deeds to show that he had at an earlier time bargained with his lord for the discharge of the heriot.[112]

Richard Didefolde, a Sussex yeoman, held a hundred acres of copyhold land of Anthony Kemp, Esq., in the reign of James I. Tenant and landlord, it seems, were continually in dispute over timber rights, fines, lease rights, and other copyhold obligations under which the ambitious Didefolde was chafing. Finally, "as well for the clear taking away of such doubts as have already been moved and stirred as for avoyding others," they reached an agreement which was sealed by indenture and recorded in the court roll. By paying a larger yearly rent Didefolde secured the following privileges for himself and his heirs: the assurance of fines

110. St.Ch. 5. L 8/4.
111. "Notes on Mosley Family," Chetham Soc., N.S. XLVII, pt. IV, 28.
112. Rider Commonplace Book, p. 5.

made certain; a fixed statement regarding the heriot to be paid on death, surrender, or alienation; the privilege of leasing or letting his lands for a term of years up to twenty-one without license or composition; the right to cut timber without interference; and a written promise that he and his heirs should be forever discharged of all fines or services other than those set down in the indenture.[113]

Thus it was that the yeomen, through their personal initiative and their determination to better their lot, were little by little freeing their copyhold lands from onerous obligations. To what extent this tendency took the form of outright conversion of copyholds to freeholds, it is difficult to say. Individual instances of enfranchisement are by no means unusual. In 1583 Thomas Anger, a Norfolk yeoman, bargained with his lord for the conversion of his copyhold to socage. Another yeoman of the same place did likewise in 1598.[114] John Pollard and his son-in-law, yeomen of Sussex, paid the Earl of Dorset and Sir Edward Sackville £52 10*s.* for the enfranchisement of their copyhold lands in 1618.[115] A note made upon a survey of lands in Moore Hundred in Chester in 1628 states that the tenants were copyholders "but have each of them lately bought out ther owne lands to hold in fee farme in free and common socage."[116] John Rowe in 1622 writes that in the hundred of Barcombe, Sussex, there were "some copieholdes infranchised within these sixty yeares."[117] And Anthony Woodward, a Derbyshire yeoman, in return for a certain sum paid the lords of the manor of Matlock in 1640 secured the enfranchisement of his lands.[118] Enough examples of this type occur to show that the process was not an unusual one.[119] But on the whole

113. Sussex MSS., E 181. See the account of labor services that still existed on the manor of *Southese cum Hayton* in Sussex, 1622, *The Book of John Rowe,* pp. 222–223.

114. *Norfolk Arch.,* XIII, 60, 66.

115. Sussex MSS., Gage, Box 41, No. 10; see also Box 6, Nos. 33, 36, 37.

116. Harl. MSS. 2010, fol. 6.

117. *The Book of John Rowe,* p. 136.

118. Salt Charters from the MSS. of the Wm. Salt Library, No. 871.

119. At the time of his purchase of the manor of Manydown in Hampshire, 1649, Mr. William Wither made this statement to his tenants: "I

they are rather less frequent than one would expect. The aim in most cases seems to have been to secure an improved copyhold rather than an outright conversion to freehold. Whether this was because private landlords, in particular, wished to keep a vestige of their ancient authority over manorial lands, or because tenants felt that there was so little difference between freehold and an improved estate in copyhold that they preferred not to pay the high composition cost for enfranchisement, it is difficult to say.

The landlord who offered enfranchisement on the largest scale was the king. Being an absentee landlord, it may be that he felt less reluctance in seeing the symbols of the lord's prerogatives disappear. More likely it was because the first Stuart kings were willing to resort to almost any means to supplement the royal income. At any rate enfranchisement was the bait which their agents were ordered to dangle in front of the eyes of tenants on many of the royal estates.[120] Sometimes it was effective. Sometimes, however, the demands of the purchase price were too exorbitant to tempt even those who were eager for the change. But whether by improvement of titles or outright enfranchisement, certainly many copyholders were gaining a greater security and freedom of title during the very period when many of the smallest among them were forced wholly off of their holdings.

Aside from the major tenures with which this chapter has dealt, there were also various forms of customary tenure peculiar to individual manors, like the "forest tenure" and the "bord tenure" on the manor of Bosham in Sussex;[121] the "more tenure" and "less tenure" of the manor of Iwerne in

doe promise and agree that in case any of the said coppyholders shall desire to infranchise their respective Coppyholds by purchasinge the inheritance thereof after their respective lives mentioned in their respective Coppies, That they, . . . making knowne their said desire unto me and likewise bringinge in their moneys respectively due . . . shall infranchise their respective coppyholds as aforesaid at the like rates and prises which according to the Survey, I shall paye for the same." *The Manor of Manydown,* Hampshire Rec. Soc. 1895, X, 176–177.

120. Add. MSS., 5701, fols. 122–132.

121. *Ibid.*

Dorset;[122] the "five-acre tenure," "old Barton tenure," and "new Barton tenure" of the manor of Ottery St. Mary in Devon;[123] the "inter-tenure" and "foreign-tenure" of the manor of Duddleswelling in Sussex;[124] and the "bond-land tenure" and "overland tenure" of the manors of Taunton and Taunton Deane, in Somerset.[125] But while often important to the yeomen who held lands on those particular manors, the numbers which they affected were appreciably small. There were, however, two forms of regional tenure that affected a considerable number of yeomen and created problems sufficiently significant to merit attention.

The first of these was the "gavelkind" tenure in Kent. Reference has already been made to the traditional well-being of the Kentish yeomen. They were, it was said,

> All blessed with health, and as for wealth
> By fortune's kind embraces
> A Yeoman gray shall oft outweigh
> A Knight in other Places.[126]

Wills, deeds, leases, and other documents touching the land dealings of Kentish yeomen go far toward substantiating that boast. According to various contemporary writers and also to later ones, no small part of this prosperity was due to the system of gavelkind tenure that flourished among them. Lambard, writing in 1577, says of the yeomen: "Neither be they here so much bounden to the Gentry by Copyhold or customary tenures, as the inhabitants of the Western countries of the realm be, nor at all indangered by the feeble hold of tenant right as the common people of the northern parts be: for Copyhold tenure is rare in Kent, and Tenant right not heard of at all: but in place of these the custome of Gavelkind prevailing everywhere, in manner everyone is a Freeholder, and hath some part of his own to

122. Harl. MSS. 71, fol. 35b.
123. *Devon Trans.*, LXVI, pp. 211–233.
124. Add MSS. 5704, fol. 137.   125. Eg. MSS. 2223, fols. 1–13.
126. *A Kentish Garland*, p. 143. Cf. Wm. Lambard, *Perambulation of Kent*, 1826, p. 8.

live upon. And in this their estate, they please themselves and joy exceedingly."[127]

Gavelkind was in effect a kind of socage tenure with certain differentiations.[128] One of its peculiarities had to do with descent. Whereas the common law recognized the eldest son as the preferred heir, lands held in gavelkind must, at the death of the owner, be divided equally among all of the sons, and if there were no sons, among the daughters. This was a practice likewise recognized in the customs of certain manors outside of Kent,[129] just as Borough English on some manors required that the youngest child be recognized as the heir. Chief among the other distinguishing features of gavelkind were those having to do with the age at which an heir could sell land, certain rights of husbands and wives, and the security of title to an heir whose father was a felon under death sentence, a security denied by the common law.[130]

On the whole the tenure is spoken of by both Kentish men and outsiders in extremely favorable terms; and inasmuch as its natural result was in the direction of many small estates rather than the building up of large ones, it was conducive to a numerous yeomanry in that county, and to a large amount of freehold, although it is not true as was sometimes claimed that all Kentish land was freehold. Nor was gavelkind wholly a safeguard against tenurial difficulties, as court records frequently show.[131] But in the main it appears to have merited the reputation it enjoyed.

A second type of regional tenure to which some attention must be paid is that which flourished in the border counties under the name of "tenant-right." Tenant-right was in

127. *Perambulation of Kent,* p. 9.
128. For discussions of gavelkind tenure, see S.P. 14, XLV, 94; *Perambulation of Kent,* p. 9 ff.; C. Elton, *Tenures of Kent,* 1867, p. 10; N. Neilson, "Custom and the Common Law in Kent," *Harvard Law Review,* XXXVIII, 482–498; C. Sandys, *Consuetudines Kanciae,* 1851.
129. *Calendar of Border Papers,* 1596, II, 268.
130. *Perambulation of Kent,* p. 9.
131. See the dispute among descendants of the Taylor family, of old Kentish yeoman stock, concerning the custom of descent in gavelkind, St.Ch. 8, 51/14. See also Req. 2, 191/63.

character a kind of cross between customary tenure and knight service in its ancient form, with features drawn from both.

As Kentish men prided themselves on their traditional position in the vanguard of English armies[132] and enjoyed a reputation for bravery and the freedom of their estate, so the men of the north claimed a certain preëminence as the guardians of the borders, and took pride in maintaining the record for prowess established by their forefathers. Some held that the feudal manors of the border counties were the outgrowths of free communities that had been in existence before the Conquest, and that the tenants there had always been of a more free and honorable estate than those on lands in the south.[133]

Whatever the truth of that claim, one of the duties long required of the tenants on the border had been to equip themselves with horse and armor for border service. The customs of manors there enumerated this duty among their required services, and throughout the reign of Elizabeth it is set down as an obligation in the leases of lands on royal manors. Whether consciously or otherwise, therefore, this military service had become identified with the right of the tenants to their lands, and was held to be one of the chief features of the tenure known as tenant-right.[134]

That the full and exact nature of tenant-right had never been clearly defined seems evident from the records of certain cases that came into the Elizabethan courts. In a case in the Court of Requests in 1587 concerning the lands of James Davisson, a yeoman, who held, as he claimed, by tenant-right some witnesses declared that the tenure amounted almost to freehold and that time out of mind the custom had been that land so held should descend to the male heirs.

132. Camden, *Britannia,* 1806, I, 307. In addition to Camden's statement, several earlier authors are quoted.

133. *Transactions of the Cumberland and Westmoreland Antiquarian Society,* 1926, Series II, XXVI, 319.

134. S.P., Border Papers, XXXI, fol. 171; see royal leases in northern counties, E. 310.

Others, however, contended that lands held by tenant-right were held during the lord's will and pleasure only.[135] The inability of the witnesses on either side to clarify the matter, and their confusion, arising apparently from their own uncertainty rather than from a desire for evasion, makes one suspect that the tenure had never been specifically defined in their own minds. Anciently, this would have mattered little. But now that the land was coveted by both landlord and tenant, it was of moment to both.

The Crown was jealous to preserve the military protection which tenant-right provided for the borders. Hence in such disputes as the above between landlords and tenants where there was a threat of eviction, royal authority was unreservedly placed on the side of the tenants. In 1571, in fact, an act was passed in Parliament confirming the tenants of Cumberland in their lands that were held by tenant-right. It set the entrance fine for such lands at the sum of six years' rent, but charged that beyond that nothing except the ancient customary rents should be demanded. Arbitrary fines were declared detrimental to the state which depended upon these tenants for its defense.[136]

Then came the death of Elizabeth in 1603, and the union of the two thrones which removed the need for border service. The new situation led to a complete *volte face* on the part of the Crown. The new king, in dire need of money, determined to press the very claim that the Crown had heretofore denounced, namely, that the border tenants were tenants at will of the Crown, who should now, in return for their release from border service, have their lands regranted on new terms which included a rent double the customary rent, with fines made certain at double the improved rent.[137]

This move resulted in the keenest opposition among the tenants. Lawsuits came thick and fast. The objections were so pronounced that the Crown finally shifted its position, and in return for a composition fee of £2,700 confirmed the

135. Req. 2, 198/15.   136. *S.P.D. Eliz. Addenda*, XX, 28.
137. S.P. 14, XL, 38.

estates of the tenants on all of the royal manors as copyholds in inheritance to be held by the ancient rents.[138]

In the meantime, however, lords of private manors, who had accepted the king's previous invitation to follow his example, were in hot water with their tenants; and suits continued to be carried to the courts.[139] The king finally became annoyed with the struggle and in July, 1620, issued a proclamation which stated that, since the union of the two kingdoms, the memory of tenant-right instead of being kept green ought to be "damned to a perpetual oblivion."[140] Lands formerly held by this tenure should be let by indenture only, which meant in effect that they should become leaseholds. The proclamation further ordered that judges suppress all cases based upon tenant-right claims. But the tenants were obdurate and a long and bitter struggle ensued.

Not all the details are known, and the story is too long to be told in full, but one phase of it will bear repeating for the light it throws on the character of the tenurial struggle, and particularly for the lively picture it shows of a group of north-country yeomen helping to lead their fellow tenants in a spirited struggle against encroaching landlords. They were tenants on the barony of Kendal in Westmoreland. There had obviously been much talk and some activity among them prior to a meeting that was held in the Stavely churchyard on a midwinter afternoon in 1621. But we may well begin the story there. It was some six months after the king's proclamation had been issued.

It is somewhat difficult to say exactly how many were at the Stavely meeting, but there appear to have been eight ringleaders: six yeomen, the vicar, and a member of the local gentry. A document or resolution, later dubbed a libel, a product of the vicar's pen but endorsed by all of the leaders, was read aloud at the meeting. It bore the title: *Reasons*

---

138. Act of Confirmation, reprinted in J. Nicolson and R. Burn, *History of Cumberland and Northumberland*, 1778, I, 51–52.

139. See interesting case, St.Ch. 8, 161/16.

140. S.P. 14, CLXXXVII, 84.

*of all the Commoners of Westmoreland to uphold their cus-
tom of tenant-right.* It did not mince words, but spoke elo-
quently of Janus' axe which "had a sharp edge when it
looked toward the poor tenants, cutting up the tree by the
root, but when it looked toward the landlord was so blunt
as it was not able to cut down the Boughs and Branches but
they must stand without foundation." After the reading it
appears that several copies of the document were passed
around while the more active ones worked up support for it
among those who were present.

A little more than a fortnight later, in the same neighborhood, another meeting was called by the constables, osten-
sibly to effect a levy for the repair of Paynsone bridge, but
actually for the purpose of holding another discussion of
the tenant-right question. Thomas Kilmer, one of the yeomen present, said that "upon discourse one neighbour with
another in the markett," they had decided to meet to see
what course could be taken toward making their titles more
secure. As with the first meeting, the details of what occurred are somewhat confused in later reports; but it seems
rather clear that the libel, or part of it, was again read, and
that a collection was taken to defray the expenses of sending a messenger to London with a petition to the king and
Parliament. If there were objections made to the king's
proclamation at either of these meetings, the fact was later
denied by the tenants. Wishing to avoid the appearance of
disobedience to the royal command, they decided to base
their case on the claim that their lands had always been estates of inheritance, and not upon the claim of tenant-right
grounded in border service. They requested, moreover,
merely that they have as fair a settlement as the king had
granted the Crown tenants in his confirmation. On paper,
at least, and in all formal statements, they made repeated
declarations of loyalty and vehemently denied any spirit of
rebellion. This was held to be good policy. Privately and
informally no such attitude of decorum prevailed. Feeling
ran high. The lords declared the tenants to be tenants at
will, and the tenants objected that the lords were trying to

cheat them out of their lands, intending, as they said, "to pull the skins over their ears and bray their bones in a mortar." Jasper Garnett, formerly a Lancashire schoolmaster, now a resident of Kendal, wrote an appropriate play that was performed at Kendal castle in 1621.

One of the scenes showed an ingeniously constructed *hell* placed a little to the side and below stage wherein ravens were supposedly feeding on poor sheep. Henry Ward and Thomas Duckett, two of the tenants, in their characters of clown or fool inquired of a boy who stood looking into this hell what he saw there. The boy replied that he "did see Landlords and puritanes and Sheriffs bailiffs and other sorts of people," whereupon the one clown said to the other:

Ravens quotha, no, thou art farr by the square, its false landlords makes all that croakinge there, and those sheepe wee poore men, whose right these by their skill, would take awaie, and make us tenants at will, and when our ancient liberties are gone theile puke and poole, & peele us to the bare bone.

When called later to testify in court, Garnett tried to save himself by declaring that he had not meant any hurt or disgrace to the landlords of Westmoreland in particular, but that he merely meant the shoe to fit where it would, that it was "for all in general."

The suit that was brought against the tenants stretched the quarrel over several years; for cases in court, then as now, moved slowly. Final settlement was not made until after the death of James I. The decision, when given, was in favor of the tenants. Their estates were declared to be copyholds in inheritance and plans were put under way for making their fines certain as they desired. The determined little group who had gathered their neighbors together in the Stavely churchyard had labored to good advantage.[141]

The tenants did not always win in such cases. A suit that was fought out in the Court of Chancery in 1618, also in-

141. The above account is taken from the voluminous records of the case in the Star Chamber Court before which it finally came, St.Ch. 8, 34/4.

volving the lands of yeomen, went against the copyholders, who were forced to change their copyholds for twenty-one-year leases at double the former rent.[142] On the whole, however, they appear to have waged a successful struggle over a period of many years.

As late as 1676 Sir Roger North writes that it was still going on in Cumberland. He complained that the people had formed a sort of conspiracy to undermine the estates of the gentry "by pretending a tenant-right" which was "a customary estate not unlike our copyhold."[143] He declared that in the courts the verdict was always sure to be in favor of the tenants, because, whatever the merits of the case, the juries were wont to uphold their side. Country juries almost to a man, as we shall discover, were drawn from the yeoman class.[144] North says that finally the gentry, "finding that all was going, resolved to put a stop to it by serving on the common juries."[145] His testimony is biased in favor of his class and it is doubtful if they suffered as much as he said. But the entire struggle exemplifies the importance of tenurial problems, as it also indicates the leadership of the yeomen in the struggle of tenants to improve and secure their titles to their lands.

In addition to the problems that arose from forms of tenure and the obligations attached to them, land matters were still further complicated by the fact that each tenure recognized also certain "estates or conditions" that defined a man's particular "interest" in his land. Was it held in *fee simple, fee tail,* or *fee tail male?* What were the exact rights belonging to a tenancy for life or lives? What were the rules governing *reversions* and *remainders,* those "estates in expectancy" whereby a man sought to have a hand in determining who would hold his property generations hence? If these "interests" permitted a certain amount of flexibility, they likewise led to complexity in land ownership. Re-

142. See S.P. 16, CCCCXXXVIII, 1; Nicolson and Burn, *History of Cumberland and Northumberland,* pp. 56–59.

143. R. North, *Lives of the Norths,* 1890, I, 180–181.

144. See below, p. 340.   145. *Lives of the Norths,* I, 181.

versions and remainders were bought and sold again and
again, providing manifold perplexities. Robert Crowley
said, as early as 1550,

> And one thyng there is that hurteth
>   moste of all;
> Reversions of farmes are bought
>   long ere they fall
> Reversions of farmes
>   are bought on ech syde;
> And the old tenant must pay well
>   if he wyll abyd.[146]

The adoption of the *Statute of Uses* in the reign of
Henry VIII,[147] which gave legal sanction to a practice already surreptitiously carried on whereby a landholder
might sell or bequeath property to someone while retaining
the "use" of it himself or might grant that "use" to someone else, furnished ground for new and complex relationships.[148] The lease also, though it was neither a proper tenure nor an estate or condition of tenure, came to stand for
an "interest" in the land that merited the protection of the
common law.[149] Most of these developments in the long run
brought additional freedom and power to the landholder,
but they had both good and bad effects since the variety of
"interests" which might be held in a piece of ground[150] often
resulted, as a contemporary said, in "unremediable intangle-
ments," arising from an "intermixture of Interest of sev-

146. "Of Forestallars," *Works,* pp. 33–34.
147. S.R., 27 Henry VIII, c. 10.
148. Holdsworth, *History of English Law,* IV, 449–473.
149. Holdsworth, *An Historical Introduction to the Land Law,* 1927,
pp. 71–73. The action by which such protection was secured was a personal
action and the *interest* it entailed was held to be "personal" not "real"
property.
150. For illustrations of the above "interests" and of certain "estates
and conditions" that defined a man's "interest" in lands, in documents
dealing with the land activities of yeomen, see P.C.C. 68 Wood, 70 Skynner; Req. 2, 206/43, 207/70, 207/79, 210/132, 221/13; St.Ch. 8, 43/4; Salt
MSS. 1019; Birmingham MSS., Worcester 430216; Deed of Thomas
Moore, 1616, in the MSS. of Tullie House at Carlisle.

erall persons in the same Common, in the same Close, nay sometimes in the same Acre."[151]

There were probably few yeomen who escaped entirely the problems of title and tenure. But theirs was the struggle to labor for the improvement of their estates in order that they might pass them on less encumbered to their children. How many fell by the wayside in the struggle and lost their yeoman status entirely, it is impossible to say. Certainly there were some.

But far better than their lesser neighbors, the yeomen were able to cope with the wealthy merchants turned land-lords, or the lords of ancient lineage who, like themselves, sought to satisfy their ambitions on the land. We have in this and the preceding chapter seen something of their ef-forts to increase their acreages, and to improve their titles. We are now ready to consider the purpose for which these efforts were made: the cultivation of the land and the prof-its to be gained therefrom.

151. C. Dymock, *A Discoverie for Division or setting out of Land as to the Best Form,* 1653, p. 3. (Sometimes attributed to Hartlib.)

V

EARNING A LIVING—AND A PROFIT

The husbandman's pride and his wit, are verie neere alike, yet they will calculate of dearth and plenty, and will prognosticate today, of corne, cattell, butter, cheese, and such other, what price they will beare for a yeere or two to come.

Barnabie Rich, *Faults and Nothing Else But Faults,* 1606

Good farm and well stored, good housing and dry,
Good corn and good dairy, good market and nigh:
Good shepherd, good tillman, good Jack and good Jill,
Make husband and huswife their coffers to fill.

T. Tusser, *Five Hundred Points of Good Husbandry,* 1557

QUESTIONS of purchase and tenure were of paramount importance to the yeomen only because they contributed to the increase and security of their means of production. Their ultimate concern was how to make use of the lands thus acquired and protected in such a way as to assure the maximum results in produce and profit. What price cattle went per stone last market day and how to make the "Netherfield" produce a greater yield of wheat or barley were the matters of chiefest concern in their day-to-day thinking and planning.

It is true that not all yeomen restricted their economic concerns to agriculture. The semiagricultural and non-agricultural activities of some members of the group contributed no small part to their economic advance. And a word should be said concerning these activities.

Not infrequently one finds yeomen exercising a craft or carrying on a small business on the side. Sometimes the head of the household set his own hands to such an enterprise. Frequently it was carried on under his supervision by another member of the household, or an outsider hired to do the work. In other instances an additional business was purely an investment in the form of a shop, mill, or tavern which could be leased to the management of another for a good rent.

John Smyth, a yeoman of Laverton in Somerset, operated a gristmill, having in addition to the profits he made from grinding his neighbors' corn the right to the fish that were in the millpond.[1] Francis Jenks, a Shropshire yeoman, had two "water corne mills" and four fulling mills.[2] Edmund Buckley of Yorkshire also owned an interest in a "fullers mill."[3] In 1573 Robert Burton, another Yorkshire yeoman, erected "divers horse mills, wynd mills and Quernes" near Pontefract.[4] William Rogers, a Surrey yeoman, and his wife, had an inn, "The Red Lion," at Kingston-on-the-Thames which they leased for a rent of eight pounds a year.[5] Thomas Ford, yeoman, of Dorset, another innholder, owned "The George" in Sherborne which he bought from a Somerset gentleman.[6] Henry Relfe, a yeoman of Sussex, owned two shops that had a good frontage on the market place in Mayfield.[7] Simon Rider of Staffordshire speaks frequently of his "smithie."[8] Examples of this kind appear over and over in wills and in other records touching the business dealings of yeomen.

By these means enterprising members of the group sought to turn an extra penny into the family purse, adding thereby to the present profit and future security of themselves or some member of their family. The shop, or inn, or interest in a business, was frequently the means of providing for younger sons when all or most of the land went to the eldest, or of adding to the marriage portions of daughters whose fathers were reluctant to divide their lands for that purpose. Christopher Merritt, a Gloucestershire yeoman who died in 1625, bequeathed most of his lands to his eldest son Richard. "The Crown," an inn which was likewise

1. Somerset Sessions Rolls, 1613, 17.   2. P.C.C., Pile 55.
3. *Wills and Inventories,* II, Lanc. and Ches. Hist. Soc., XXVIII, 50.
4. D.L. 4, 16 Eliz. 31.   5. Rylands MSS., Ry. Ch. 1211.
6. Exeter Deeds and Documents, 34.   7. Sussex MSS., WH 245.
8. Rider Commonplace Book, p. 56, and *passim.*

the family dwelling, passed with other properties to his wife, already no doubt accustomed to its management. And a shop adjoining the inn was left to a second son provided he follow the art or trade of a mercer.[9] It is the sort of arrangement one comes upon, with variations, many times.

The keeping of alehouses and ordinaries was frequent among the less well-to-do yeomen. Keepers of these houses had to secure licenses from local justices in return for which they bound themselves not to keep open on the Sabbath, not to permit unlawful games, not to harbor wanderers and vagrants, nor in any way to infringe upon the regulations which established and maintained local respectability. Failure to secure such a license made the alehouse keeper liable to presentment at the quarter-sessions court. The long lists of those to whom licenses were granted and the presentments of those who were operating without them show that many yeomen were engaged in this manner, though they are usually somewhat outnumbered by the husbandmen similarly engaged.[10]

These alehouse licenses were easy to secure unless the community were overrun already with such places, for the work required no particular training or experience. But the yeoman who wished to exercise a craft or trade along with his farming often encountered difficulties. By the statute of 1563 it became illegal to engage in any "art mystery or manuall occupation" without having first served an apprenticeship of a stipulated term of years.[11] Hence a yeoman who attempted to carry on such work as an adjunct to his farming, without having served the apprenticeship term, acted illegally and was liable to presentment at the sessions court for so doing. This practice was particularly resented when it meant competing with someone who had put in the necessary years of training. The sessions records are filled

9. Gloucestershire, *P.M.I., The Index Library*, IX, 8.

10. In Devon there were few yeomen among the alehouse keepers, but a great many were applying for licenses to bake and brew. See Sessions Bundles, 1605.

11. *S.R.* 5 Eliz. c. 4.

with presentments of yeomen who set up as grocers, bakers, tailors, linen drapers, mercers, and the like without the proper apprenticeship.

The fact that there were many more presentments some years than others suggests that the statute was poorly adhered to in normal times, but more rigidly enforced during years of stress when farmers felt the need of turning their hands to something beside their farms, and harassed craftsmen were more unwilling than usual to have their domains encroached upon. In 1631–32, for instance, an unusually large number of the yeomen of Norfolk were presented for exercising trades without licenses, presumably trades for which, without special training, they could not lawfully procure licenses.[12] This year was an especially bad one for farmers.[13] Wet weather had almost ruined the crops and there was not enough work on the farm to supply the normal labor. Farmers and their sons were discouraged and sought to turn their hands to other things. But the craftsmen and wool workers of Norfolk were in a bad way too. The East Anglian cloth trade was still suffering from the depression into which it had fallen in the early 'twenties, and high grain prices brought suffering to the unemployed of the towns. Hence yeomen who were setting up in crafts for which they had not served the proper apprenticeship were presented to the sessions.[14]

When the economic situation was not acute, it appears that no such strict account was taken. If a community had not already an oversupply of persons exercising a given craft or trade, there was probably no objection to an enterprising farmer serving in that capacity if he were skillful enough to turn his hand to it. Certainly many yeomen supplemented their incomes in this way. If in time one found it expedient to turn to the new occupation and leave the land entirely, he would then cease to be called yeoman but would be styled according to his occupation. But as long as he car-

12. Norfolk Sessions Rolls, 1631–32.   13. See below, pp. 187–188.
14. See also Add. MSS. 34399, fol. 220b; *Staffordshire Sessions Records,* III, 60–61.

ried on in both fields, he was frequently known by both terms. Hence Henry Taylor of Warwickshire, who figures in a Star Chamber case in the reign of James I, is sometimes styled yeoman, sometimes innholder, and once as victualler.[15] Some of the yeomen living on the Prescott manor in Lancashire at the same period were styled tanner, painter, tailor, and the like, as well as yeoman.[16] Many yeomen of Shropshire were among those listed as maltsters there. William Pamfret of Newport Pagnell in Bucks, who is styled yeoman, was said also to have exercised "the trade of a pettie chapman."[17] And John Shakespeare, the poet's father, is in some documents styled yeoman[18] and elsewhere described as glover, butcher, and whittawer.[19]

Yeomen likewise participated in the new or improved industries now flourishing in many English localities. It was natural that the farmers up and down the countryside should look with interest on these enterprises. Those of the poorer sort found extra labor here when the crops were poor, or after they had been harvested, while well-to-do yeomen sought in such industries opportunities for investment that forwarded their advance to the position of small capitalists.

Numerous Cheshire yeomen around Middlewich, Nantwich, and Northwich possessed an interest in the saltworks that flourished there. A Star Chamber case tells of a Devonshire yeoman who was also a "stavemaker," furnishing thousands of staves for beer and cider barrels used in the shipping of those beverages from western ports.[20] A Sussex yeoman in 1608 owned a house "for the making of glass."[21] Edmund Dirricke, a Somerset yeoman, was a dealer and workmaster in the Mendip lead mines,[22] where other yeomen

15. St.Ch. 8, 279/19.

16. Unpublished letter of F. A. Bailey concerning Prescott manor records.

17. S.P. 16, CCCLXI, 1.

18. Deeds in the MSS. at Shakespeare's Birthplace, Stratford.

19. C. Williams, *A Short Life of Shakespeare with the Sources,* 1933, pp. 10–11; also Unwin, *Economic Essays,* p. 319.

20. St.Ch. 8, 242/22.   21. *Ibid.,* 179/7.

22. *Ibid.,* 116/13.

were also engaged. Philip Jule, a yeoman of **Devonshire,** had control of certain tinworks near Plympton,[23] and other Devon and Cornwall yeomen were connected with the tinworks.[24] Yeomen in Lancashire and Yorkshire dug alum. In Buckinghamshire they operated paper mills. And in Northamptonshire they opened stone and slate quarries and from their tan yards helped to supply leather for an increased market for leather goods.[25]

But it was the coal, iron, and clothing industries that gave farmers and small gentry their greatest opportunities. The northern counties of Durham, Northumberland, and Cumberland were major coal-producing sections in the sixteenth and seventeenth centuries, but the Midlands were not far behind and some coal was mined in the Forest of Dean and in Somerset and Devon.[26] The move toward a greater organization in the mining industry was already evident in Elizabeth's time as the widening of activities led to a demand for greater technical improvements and a division of labor. Conditions differed greatly, though. And one finds the yeomen connected with the industry in various capacities as the particular developments of their localities gave opportunity for their varied abilities. Henry Walmsley of Headlesdan, Lancashire, speaks in court in 1623 of matters pertaining to his "coleryies."[27] Nicholas Wadsworth, another Lancashire yeoman of wealth and enterprise, tells of leasing coal rights. A copyholder on one of the manors where Wadsworth's lease was operative claimed that £300 worth of coal had been taken from one pit on his holdings.[28] The history of Lancashire's coal industry was obviously already in the making.

Another court record shows Michael Hall, yeoman, and John Halworth, merchant, leasing coal rights from several gentlemen of Durham.[29] In 1615 two colliers in the Mendip district induced two yeomen who held lands on the manor of

23. Exeter Deeds and Documents, 1343.
24. St.Ch. 8, 55/28, 272/21.   25. Unwin, *Economic Essays*, p. 324.
26. See J. Nef, *Rise of the British Coal Industry*, I, pt. 1.
27. D.L. 9/5, Affidavits and Petitions, 1623.
28. St.Ch. 8, 310/33.   29. *Ibid.*, 163/18.

Midsomer Norton, Somerset, to become their partners in a
"coal work" there.[30] Hercules Horler, a yeoman of Stratton-
on-the-Fosse, was also active in several coal works in the
Mendip district. He and his partner, an esquire, owned a
mine together, an eighth part of which they granted another yeoman in the neighborhood on condition that he work
the pits continuously for their benefit.[31] Hence as laborers,
as managers of a small pit or two of their own, as partners
with other yeomen or gentlemen, or as "overmen" or "bank-
men"[32] in the employ of larger owners, yeomen were identifying themselves with the development of England's coal.
Some of them gained and rose with the industry. Some
gained temporarily only to lose later as the industry moved
into the hands of men with larger capital.

The Exchequer records tell the story of the valiant but
losing fight of John Preston and other yeomen in a Northumberland neighborhood in their attempt to defend the
mineral rights on their freeholds against a large investor.
Preston had freehold and leasehold lands worth £60 per
annum, "salt panns" that yielded £20 a year, and a mill
that brought him an additional yearly income of £10. He
had apparently also been making a good thing of the coal
on his lands, as had his neighbors. There was a traditional
claim there that the landlord had no mining rights on freeholds except as the freeholders were willing to compound
for them. But in this case, and there were almost certainly
others like it, the queen, for it was a royal manor, and Peter
Delaval, the wealthy investor whose money she needed, appear to have been getting the best of it.[33] The details of the
settlement are not available, but it appears that the freeholders had to be content with the composition offered
them.[34] Many, however, who became identified with the industry profited by its development.

30. C. Proc. Sec. I, B. 20/72.

31. Case cited in Nef, *Rise of the British Coal Industry,* p. 423.

32. See explanation of these terms, *ibid.,* pp. 418–421.

33. E. 134, 39 Eliz., Hil. 11. See also E. Decrees and Orders, Series I,
XX, 40 Eliz.

34. See also E. Depositions, 41 Eliz. Easter.

The iron industry in Sussex was perhaps at its best during the Elizabethan period. Its decline began soon afterward, but many furnaces were active throughout the early seventeenth century. And it was the yeomen along with the lesser gentry and skilled tradesmen who saw to the actual management of most of the iron business.[35] Ponds still standing in patches of woodland on Sussex estates mark the sites of the ancient ironworks that dotted the holdings of the landed folk. The leases, deeds, and other documents concerned with the land dealings of Sussex yeomen give ample testimony of their participation in these activities.

John Fawkner and John French, two Sussex yeomen, leased ironworks from Sir Edward Gage and his son in 1567, with permission to take from 600 to 1,000 loads of ore. They promised that after digging they would fill up the pits so that the land might later be used for tillage or at least for pasture.[36] In 1581 Michael Martin, a yeoman of Cattesfeld, leased from William Waters, gentleman, his newly erected iron forge and "Iyerneworke," and certain pieces of ground, for ten years at a yearly rent of £32 6s. 8d.[37] In 1601 William Cheeseman, a yeoman of Rotherfield, promised to pay £10 a year for the lease of a forge from John Middleton, gentleman, of Horsham, for a period of three years. As a part of the agreement Cheeseman promised to deliver to Middleton at least 190 tons of "good and merchantable sowes of iron" if the latter would pay the carriage costs and £3 3s. 4d. per ton for the iron. It was said that from £2,000 to £5,000 worth of iron passed between them during the three-year period.[38] Almost every farm of any size had its forge where farmers worked when not employed in the fields. They operated smithies and produced nails, locks and keys, and agricultural implements.[39] It was through iron that the Fowles, the Fullers, and the Frenches,

35. See E. Straker, *Wealden Iron,* 1937, chaps. vii–viii.
36. Sussex MSS., Gage, Box 13, No. 97. See also Box 13, No. 45.
37. Sussex MSS., Ashburnham, 298.
38. Req. 2, 186/35. See also Sussex MSS., Phillips Col. 24.
39. S. Smiles, *Industrial Biographies,* 1863, p. 47.

all old yeoman families in Sussex, won the wealth and position which enabled them to acquire coats of arms and a place among the county families.[40]

Sussex was the principal county for iron but there were mines and furnaces elsewhere. It was said of Humphrey Lowe, a yeoman who lived in Shropshire in the reign of James I, that he laid out his whole estate and also went in debt in order to procure a mine and furnace "for the making of iron sowe metal." From Lord Dudley he leased other ironworks for the making of "sowe iron" and "barre iron," paying £200 yearly for his lease and hiring twenty colliers and woodcutters to cut wood for charcoal to keep the furnace going.[41]

The third large industry which attracted many yeomen was the clothing business. From the poorer sort, who in their own homes wove a few more bolts of cloth than were needed for family consumption, to those who became promoters and clothiers on a small scale the industry that had flourished in England for two centuries offered means of advancement. The yeomen clothiers of the Huddersfield district in Yorkshire in the early seventeenth century provide an excellent example of the way in which agricultural and industrial activities were combined.[42] Christopher Hall of Poidfield near Marley, described as both "yeoman" and "clothier," died in 1615. His total personal estate was valued at £220. Of this amount £112 represented the stock of cloth and wool on hand. He was apparently not only weaving kerseys but finishing them. In his wool chamber were 36 stones of "fleece woole," 14 stones "in dighted wefte woole," and "26 keirsaye peecies." In the "lowme chamber" were "3 paire of lowmes and geare belonging to them." Among his finishing tools were "walker shears, papers, and tighting towles, . . . one prasse and a stange." He had altogether £8 worth of clothing tools.[43]

40. *Victoria County History, Sussex,* II, 1907, p. 247.

41. St.Ch. 8, 202/3. See also 292/12.

42. W. Crump, *The Yeoman Clothier of the Seventeenth Century,* 1932, *passim.*

43. *Ibid.,* pp. 13–14.

In other instances no attempt was made at finishing in the home, but some spinning and weaving were carried on under almost every farmer's roof in that part of Yorkshire. Many yeomen in the uplands of Lancashire divided their time between farming and cloth making.[44] Scores of wills and inventories of Lincoln yeomen tell the same story. And it was the same wherever the wool industry had a foothold. In Lincoln, Bedford, and elsewhere bolts of linen as well as woolen are listed in yeoman inventories. Henry Boulton of Lincoln, who died in 1632, had on hand in his home at the time of his death 80 yards of "linen cloth," 40 yards of "course new linen cloth," 50 yards of "new cloth," 16 yards of "linsey woolsy," and 14 yards of "woolen cloth."[45]

Of Devonshire, another center of the wool industry, John Hooker wrote in 1599: "Wheresoever any man doth travell you shall fynde at the hall dore as they do name the fore dore of the house . . . the wiffe, theire children and theire servants at the turne spynninge or at theire cardes carding."[46] Many farmers had a room or rooms fitted up in their homes as a "shoppe" where home industry might flourish. Jasper Jessop, a Kentish yeoman whose will was proved in 1617, spoke of such rooms in his house, and bequeathed to his second son "all my loomes, implements and tacking belonging to the trade of weaving."[47] And such was often true with the yeomen clothiers of Yorkshire.[48] Others with money to invest went into the business on a larger scale and became promoters and managers. Their ventures were not always successful; for the woolen trade went through several serious slumps in the late sixteenth and early seventeenth centuries. But it remained a means of wealth to many. The Northcotes of Devon, an old yeoman family, became comfortably rich by the woolen trade, gaining a baronetcy in 1641.[49] The Selwyns, another family of ancient yeoman stock in Devon who proved their right to arms in the reign

44. Tupling, *History of Rossendale*, p. 168.
45. Inventories and wills at the Lincoln Probate Registery, By 15.
46. Hooker, *Synopsis*, p. 346.   47. P.C.C., 10 Welden.
48. W. Crump, *The Yeoman Clothier, passim.*
49. Cokayne, *Complete Peerage*, VII, 42.

of James I, rose as clothiers;[50] and Richard Hilton of West Leigh, Lancashire, is described as a "wealthy yeoman and fustian manufacturer."[51]

The English potteries were chiefly a development of the eighteenth century, but already under Elizabeth and the early Stuarts members of the Adams family and others of ancient yeoman stock in Staffordshire were describing themselves as both "yeoman" and "potter," and were so styled by their contemporaries.[52] Some farmers who advanced in wealth and position through industrial activities left the land and came in time to be identified wholly with the industry; or with extra money to invest in larger estates, they moved from the ranks of the yeomanry into the gentry. But many upon whom fortune smiled less lavishly continued as yeomen, combining their agricultural activities with whatever outside pursuits proved feasible and profitable.

For the group as a whole, however, agriculture was the chief occupation. For many it was their sole occupational interest, and absorbing and demanding enough they found it. Tristram Risdon said of the yeoman in Devon: "His chief Travels be in matters of Husbandry, whether it be by Grazing, buying and selling or cattle,[53] or Tillage."[54] And this was as true elsewhere.

In order to treat with any degree of understanding the farming interests of the Elizabethan and Stuart yeomen, it is necessary to take some account of the diversity of physical conditions, particularly of soil and climate, that characterize the English countryside; for it was these differences that very largely determined the character of farming practices.

One may for general purposes speak of the section east of an imaginary line drawn from Berwick-on-Tweed to

50. W. Bazeley, "Matson in Tudor and Early Stuart Times," *Bristol and Glouc. Arch.*, XLVI, 341–342.

51. *Lanc. and Ches. Hist. Soc.*, Ser. I, III–IV, 190.

52. P. Adams, *A History of the Adams Family of North Staffordshire*, 1914.

53. All farm stock, including sheep, were termed "cattle."

54. *Survey of Devonshire*, p. 6.

Dorset as predominantly arable acreage, and that west of the same as predominantly suited to grazing.[55] But there were many deviations from the rule. And from the days of Camden, Speed, John Norden, and the host of those who wrote on husbandry in the Elizabethan and Stuart period,[56] to the writers of our own time who deal with the subject in the light of more scientific knowledge,[57] the great variety of soils existing within notably small areas has been a matter for comment.

Many counties like Derby, Lancashire, Yorkshire, Lincoln, Hampshire, Surrey, the East Anglian shires, and others contained a variety of both fertile and unfertile ground.[58] In High Suffolk, for instance, toward the east there was chiefly pasture with only enough tillage to satisfy the farmers' own needs. The middle part of the shire, on the other hand, was given over chiefly to tillage, whereas in the western part the soil was so poor that the farmer could get results only when his husbandry had passed through "a long tedious course with much expense."[59] And Suffolk was not unique.

But whatever the differences, contemporary writers held the opinion, confirmed by their successors, that an attempt to make the care and use of the soil coincide with its quality was essential to successful farming. "It is the office of every good Husbandman before he puts his plough into the earth truly to consider the nature of his grounds and which is of which quallities and temper."[60] Again Gervase Markham wrote: "It is to be understood that Husbandry doth vary

55. G. E. Fussell, "Farming Methods in the Early Stuart Period," *Journal of Modern History* (hereafter cited as Fussell, "Farming Methods," *J.M.H.*), VII, 1935.

56. See below, pp. 168, 412.

57. C. Brooks, "Historical Climatology of England and Wales," *Journal of the Royal Meteorological Society*, LIV; Sir E. John Russell, *The Farm and the Nation*, 1933; Lord Ernle, *Farming Past and Present*, chap. XXXIII; Fussell, "Farming Methods," *J.M.H.*; *Great Britain, Essays in Regional Geography* (Ogilvie), 1928.

58. Norden, *The Surveyors Dialogue*, p. 230.

59. Reyce, *Breviary of Suffolk*, p. 30.

60. G. Markham, *Farewell to Husbandry*, 1653, p. 118.

according to the nature and climate of countries . . . So must the skilful husbandman alter his seasons, labours, and instruments."[61]

Markham was only one of many to give such advice. Husbandry, a favorite theme of classical authors, received renewed attention among the Elizabethans and their successors. Fitzherbert's *Boke of Husbondrye*, an early Tudor publication; the doggerel rhyming instructions of Thomas Tusser who could tell other people how to farm better than he could do it himself; and the work of Barnabie Googe, largely rewritten from a treatise of the German, Conrad Heresbach, were among the earliest of these writings. They were followed by a veritable flood of literature on the subject that appeared in the late sixteenth and continued throughout the seventeenth century. Thomas Hill, Leonard Mascall, Reynold Scot, Gervase Markham, Sir Hugh Platt, Gabriel Plattes, William Lawson, Sir Richard Weston, Samuel Hartlib, and Walter Blith are a few of the authors whose works were most popular.[62] Often they copied from each other, or from foreign writers like Estienne, Liebault,[63] Heresbach,[64] and Dubravius.[65]

Many of their notions appear quaint if not actually ridiculous in the light of modern agricultural knowledge; but despite this, their books contain much practical information. And because they frequently described the state of affairs they wished to improve, they provide a picture of contemporary conditions which we should be sorry to be without.

To what extent were the ideas of these writers known, or followed, by the yeomen or by anybody else? According to

61. *The Boke of Surveyeng and Improvements,* 1623, Bk. I.
62. A number of the works of these men are listed in the Bibliography.
63. C. Estienne and J. Liebault, *L'Agriculture et Maison Rustique,* 1586; also C. Estienne, *Prœdium Rusticum,* 1554.
64. Heresbach's *Rei Rusticae libri quatuor* was published in Cologne in 1570. *The Foure Bookes of Husbandrie,* "newely Englished and increased by B[arnabie] G[ooge], Esquire," was first published in London in 1577; after that year it went through various editions.
65. J. Dubravius, *A New Booke of Good Husbandry,* "translated into English at the speciall request of George Churchey," 1599.

the authors themselves, the landed group of whatever class was too much under the thumb of tradition to achieve great advancement. Conscious of their own role as "innovators" and "lovers of ingenuity," these writers on husbandry derided both yeomen and gentry for prejudice against "new projections." Many farmers were so fixed in their resolutions, said Walter Blith, that "no issues or events whatsoever shall change them" and if their neighbor "hath as much corne of one Acre as they of two upon the same land, or if another plow the same land with two horses and one man as well as he, and have as good corne, if he hath been used with four horses and two men, yet so will he continue."[66] Norden wrote in the same vein: "They only shape their courses as their fathers did; never putting in practice any new device," but remaining in "a plodding kind of course."[67]

The charge is a recurrent one among agricultural reformers of whatever age. James Donaldson, an "improver" of the eighteenth century, says that the farmers he approached replied to him: "Away with your fool Notions; there are too many Bees in your Bonnet-case. We will satisfie ourselves with such Measures as our Fathers have followed hitherto."[68] And, in places, the same refrain is echoed in our own day.

But whether their advice were followed or not, proof that the books were read lies in the fact that all of the best-known works of the above writers went through many editions in the first half-century or more following their publication. The profit motive and the new business spirit in agriculture described in foregoing chapters released new energies and created a desire for improvement. It was a trend that suffered a temporary check from the Civil Wars and the social and political changes of the late Stuart period,[69] but one that developed with renewed vigor in the next century.

The gentry, however, not the yeomanry, were the chief

66. *The English Improver, Improv'd*, 1652, Preface.
67. *The Surveyors Dialogue*, p. 210.
68. Quoted in Lord Ernle, *English Farming*, p. 134.
69. *Ibid.*, pp. 104–105.

readers of the books on husbandry though the authors made
a bid for the latter's patronage, promising that which was
"Of Great Profite both for Gentlemen and Yomen."[70] The
yeomen were but poor readers at best,[71] and besides they
were not the type to take kindly to learning to farm out of
a book. They were like the farmers of the next century, of
whom Richard Bradley, Oxford professor of botany, said:
"They will ask me whether I can hold a plough, for in that
they think the whole mystery of husbandry consists."[72] I
have as yet found no mention of a book on husbandry in
such meager libraries as the yeomen possessed. But if they
left the academic study of the subject to the gentry, it is
not true that they remained indifferent to what the gentlemen learned either from that source or otherwise; for despite the charges of the writers on husbandry, there were
many among them who were watching their profits with
great care and were as eager as their landlords to learn how
to increase their yields.

One could, of course, press the point of their determination for improvement too far, both as regards gentry and
yeomen. Conditions of farming differed greatly in various
districts; and it is likely that the general level was nowhere
high compared with later standards. But certainly the story
which the contemporary records tell is one of an accelerated
interest and activity in agriculture; and ambitious yeomen
were among those who participated in it. It was a time, as
Mr. Fussell says, "when an ingenious husbandman would
break away from the traditional practice when he was so
inclined."[73]

And there is a good deal of evidence to show that at least
a degree of skill in husbandry was becoming a matter of
pride among the yeomen. A farmer gained or lost in the
estimation of his neighbors according to the skill he dis-

70. Dubravius, *A New Booke of Good Husbandry*, title page.

71. See below, p. 268.

72. R. Bradley, *Complete Body of Husbandry*, 1727; quoted in Lord
Ernle, *English Farming*, p. 134.

73. "Farming Methods," *J.M.H.*, p. 140.

played in caring for his land and making it produce. In 1597 Nicholas Horne, a London grocer of some wealth, gave over his trade and moved to the country. He leased a manor in Essex from one Robert Lee, a yeoman. After some time the venture failed and Horne sustained heavy losses. The ex-grocer had his own explanations for his failure, but Lee, who claimed to have farmed the land successfully before Horne took it over, blamed the latter's ill-success on his lack of farming skill. He says Horne had not been on the place two years before the fences and inclosures were broken down, the timber wasted and carried away, and the land spent. His ability and skill in farming, says Lee, "was all together unfytt and insufficient."[74]

Chancery depositions of 1639 regarding property held by Nicholas Jackson, a Northamptonshire yeoman, say that the lands were "very much out of heart" when Jackson took them over some years previously; but because of his good husbandry they later became much improved. One witness estimated that the land had improved from 5s. to 6s. 8d. per acre under Jackson's care, and another that the estate as a whole had been raised in value from £400 to £600 or £700.[75] Edward Biddle, a Hampshire yeoman who leased lands from a neighbor, was compelled to promise that he would "husbandly fallow and manure the premises each tillage season."[76] This promise was exacted in scores of leases.

There was an increasing appreciation of the fact that good soil must be cared for if it were to last and likewise that naturally poor soil could be greatly bettered by care and nourishment. More importance was placed on the use of manure. New fertilizers were tried out, and those anciently used revived, or their use increased. Devonshire was the shire most often referred to as a shining example of the way in which a naturally somewhat barren county could become one of the most productive through care and treatment of

74. Req. 2, 224/67.
75. C. (Depositions), G 2/1, 1639, Co. Northants.
76. Harl. MSS., 1579, fol. 3.

its soil. The husbandry "innovators" begged less industrious and less wideawake sections to follow Devon's example.

Camden described the land in Devon as "leane and barren which notwithstanding yeeldeth fruit to the husbandman plenteously, so that he be skilfull in husbandry, and both can take paines, and be able withal to defray the cost."[77] Adam Moore says that the farmers of Devon spared "neither charge nor toile" to improve their lands.[78] And Devon men themselves were loud in praise of what their countrymen had accomplished. Thomas Westcote admitted that the soil was not by nature fruitful, but "requireth and expecteth some help by the labours and manuarance of the husbandmen."[79] John Hooker, writing in 1599, declared that the change that had been wrought in Devon in recent times by improved husbandry was nothing short of a "marvelose metamorphoses." It had been done, he declared, wholly by the industry of the Devon farmer who "accordinge to the nature of his grownde . . . useth these helpes as be most fytt for the same."[80] Risdon also said of the Devon yeomen that "they are found nowhere more industrious and skilful in suiting every soil with Improvement answerable to its quality." He is confident that anyone who "observeth the Charge and Paines of Devonshire men employed this way in sterile Grounds for the preparation of their tillage . . . cannot but confess that in Industry, they surpass all others."[81]

Other western men had a good reputation as farmers, particularly those of Somerset, of whom Norden said, "they take extraordanary paines, in soyling, plowing, and dressing their lands."[82] But elsewhere, too, people were learning that poor soil could be improved. Markham says that anyone who took the trouble to ride into the barren parts of

77. *Britannia*, 1610, p. 199.
78. A. Moore, *Bread for the Poor*, p. 17.
79. Westcote, *View of Devonshire*, pp. 55–56.
80. Hooker, *Synopsis*, pp. 343–344.
81. Risdon, *Survey of Devonshire*, p. 7.
82. Norden, *The Surveyors Dialogue*, pp. 231–232.

Devon and Cornwall, the mountainous parts of Wales, the "hard parts" of Middlesex and Derbyshire, or into the "cold parts" of Northumberland, Cumberland, Westmoreland, Lancashire, or Cheshire would find that where sufficient industry was being used, the results everywhere justified the pains.[83]

Such improvement no doubt appeared greater to the men of that day than it would to this age of scientific advancement. But allowing for the difference of standards, the enthusiasm of the "innovators," and the pride of the local historians, there is yet enough evidence in the records that touch upon the land activities of actual farmers to show that many of them were aroused to searching for new ways and means of bettering their output in order to increase their profits. And the textbook writers who tend to leave all of the agricultural improvements to the days of Jethro Tull and Thomas Townshend err as greatly as do those who imply that English industry was stagnant until Kay, Hargraves, Arkwright, and their fellow inventors revolutionized it. English farmers began to take a marked interest in improving their yields as soon as prices and markets made it worth their while to do so.

The Devon men claimed that a part, at least, of their success in improving the soil was due to a method known as "denshiring," thought by some to be a corruption of the word "Devonshiring," a practice that was held in great esteem there. It was described by Risdon as "paring the Grain of the Ground with Mattocks into turfs, then drying and loughing these Turfs into Burrows, and so burning them, and spreading their Ashes on the Ground."[84] Farmers of other counties adopted the practice, and it was used far beyond the boundaries of Devon.

Lime, long known, was now used in greater and greater quantities as a fertilizer. Westcote says in 1630 that of all fertilizers it was one of the most popular.[85] William Honi-

83. G. Markham, *A Way to Get Wealth,* 1628, Bk. II, chap. xxii.
84. *Survey of Devonshire,* p. 7.   85. *View of Devonshire,* pp. 55–56.

well, a Devon yeoman, wrote in his diary in 1598 of getting seven hogsheads of it.[86] Robert Loder bought it yearly for his Berkshire farm.[87] And Adam Eyre's Yorkshire diary contains frequent mention of lime being spread over the fields.[88]

Another highly prized fertilizer was marl. The enriching value of this earthy substance found at various depths under the soil was known as early as the Middle Ages. Fitzherbert recommended it highly in the early sixteenth century, and now with the growing interest in ways and means for increasing yields its use became widespread.

Adam Martindale tells of the confidence that his father, a Lancashire yeoman, had in marl as a fertilizer. He "put himself out of money and into some present debt by marling two closes called the Sheepcroft at vast charges." Soon afterward, having lost money through a neighboring gentleman for whom he had furnished bond, the elder Martindale was forced to lease his "precious new-marled ground" for seven years to make good the payment. But the marling was so effective that when Martindale, who had other good corn land and some means, "made a good shift to weare out these years," he found the land still rich when it came back to him.[89] Fitzherbert declared that marl was better than dung, muck, or lime, and that it would last twenty years if well done. Licenses were granted for the digging of marl on the Rotherfield manor in Sussex in the early seventeenth century where many loads were taken out each year.[90] Some yeomen in Kent had marl on their own lands.[91] A report made to the Privy Council from Dorset in 1631, complaining of the excessive charges to which the farmers there had put themselves for the improvement of their lands with marl

86. *The Honiwell Diary,* April, 1598.
87. *Robert Loder's Farm Accounts 1610–1620* (hereafter cited as *Loder's Farm Journal*), Cam. Soc. 3d Series, LIII, *passim.*
88. *Diary of Adam Eyre,* pp. 95, 96, and *passim.*
89. *Life of Adam Martindale,* Chet. Soc., Series I, IV, 2–3.
90. Rotherfield Court Rolls, quoted in C. Pullein, *Rotherfield,* p. 277.
91. P.C.C., 60 Cobham.

and lime, stated that in so doing "great quantities of corne
have of late yeares been gotten out of barren ground."[92]

When marl or lime was not plentiful, efforts were made
to make use of whatever materials were at hand that were
thought to be effective as fertilizers. Norden says that on
the coast of Cornwall a certain kind of seaweed and sea sand
were spread over the soil for its enrichment. Pebbles and
stones from the shore were burned and spread on the land
in Sussex, Kent, and Suffolk. Refuse from the streets of
London and the city ash heaps was spread over Middlesex
farms. Dredges from the river were used in Hants; and
fields in Bucks, Herts, and Middlesex were also enriched by
the "moore earth" from the river.[93] Plot tells how chippings
of stones were used near Banbury, and "Taylers shreds"
near Watlington.[94] And Robert Loder speaks of purchasing both "black ashes" and malt dust for fertilizer to supplement the supply of animal manure produced on his
Berkshire farm.[95]

The latter was the fertilizer most commonly used by all
farmers, and that which received the highest praise from the
writers on husbandry no matter what other soil restoratives
they might advocate. Robert Loder's *Farm Journal* gives
an excellent picture of the interest of a small independent
farmer in the possibilities of soil improvement from ma-
nures. Not only did Loder keep a close watch to see what improvements the lands treated with manure showed over
those that had no such care, but he noted also the efficacy of
the different kinds of manure used, and of the relative effect upon grasslands and arable. By 1621, for instance,
after several years of experimenting, he was convinced that
sheep dung was especially good for his grasslands. Of the
cow dung he was not so sure: "Wherefore it were good for
me to observe & marke the next yeare how the sayd cow

92. S.P. 16, CCIII, 60; see also 105.
93. Norden, *The Surveyors Dialogue*, pp. 227–230.
94. R. Plot, *Natural History of Oxfordshire*, 1676, pp. 244–245.
95. *Loder's Farm Journal*, p. xviii.

dounge prospereth, which if it answer not ye charge, then
it were good to lay it upon my lande,"[96] meaning his arable.
In one field he tried a mixture of cow and horse dung "being
the first that I ever dounged soe." He also used sheep dung
and pigeon dung, and experimented with other fertilizers.

The "black ashes," perhaps wood, peat ash, or soot,
bought in the neighboring village at a cost of 2s. 6d. to 2s.
8d. a load and applied by measure of eight loads per acre,
he believed after trial to be worth while: "And therefore I
take it to be a very good course to buy as much as may be
had, in our own towne, or elsewhere."[97] One of the marked
characteristics revealed in Loder's journal is his disposition to try things out, and consciously to weigh results so
that he might know what practices proved profitable and
what showed themselves impracticable. He is an excellent
example of the ambitious farmer who was eager to make the
most of growing markets and rising prices.

Methods of cultivation depended partly on the soil and
partly on local practices. An Elizabethan statute speaks
of carrying on tillage "according to the nature of the Soyle
and course of Husbandrie used in that parte of the Country."[98] And the Hampshire yeoman who promised in a lease
to fallow and manure his lands "according to the course of
husbandry of this country [county]"[99] merely followed a
common stipulation set down in many leases in different regions.

H. L. Gray was one of the first to point out the fallacy of
supposing that the three-field system with an orthodox rotation was in use everywhere.[100] It is likely that an increased
number of local studies will point out even more variety
than he suggests. Mr. Fussell, whose valuable work is adding much to our knowledge of early agriculture, concludes
that the farmer of the Stuart period was under no more
compulsion to grow wheat in one field and barley in the

96. *Ibid.*, p. 169.   97. *Ibid.*, pp. xix, xx, 157.
98. *S.R.*, 39 Eliz. c. 2.   99. Harl. MSS. 1579, fol. 3.
100. H. L. Gray, *English Field Systems*, 1915, *passim*.

other on all of the strips that he farmed in the open fields than is the modern continental peasant in regions where strip cultivation is still carried on. In the latter case the individual occupier does not feel bound to grow the same crop as his neighbor even though different crops are interspersed in fields undivided by fences.[101] Certainly farmers like Robert Loder felt no compulsion other than the practical logic of their own experimentation. The drawback to our knowledge is that while there is sufficient evidence to show that there was a variety of methods used, with many references to "the course of husbandry followed in this county," there is little in any of the records to show exactly what that course of husbandry was. One can glean enough, however, from local historians and estate accounts to suggest certain of the regional variations.

In Staffordshire, at least by the latter half of the Stuart period and probably earlier, where the heath was inclosed for tillage, the land was cropped for five years in the following order: barley, rye, peas, and oats for two years. It was then thrown open to grazing again. On other lands there, taken off the waste where the gorse was dug up and the land treated with marl, from seven to eight crops were taken before it was turned back to grazing.[102] The Shuttleworth accounts indicate a long rotation consisting of rye, wheat, barley, peas, lupines, vetches, or other pulse, and then wheat again, on their lands in Lancashire. It was said that the land would remain in good heart for sixteen years with this rotation.[103] The anonymous author of a seventeenth-century treatise on husbandry says that parts of Essex and most of Cambridgeshire practiced a rotation by which a year of fallow was followed by wheat or rye or barley, then oats, and peas, and then fallow again. At Wentworth, in the Ely region, where the writer appears to have been connected

101. Fussell, "Farming Methods," *J.M.H.*, p. 5.
102. Plot, *Natural History of Staffordshire*, pp. 343–344.
103. The house and farm accounts of the Shuttleworths of Sawthorpe Hall . . . Lancashire (John Harband), Chet. Soc. 1856, XLI, 414.

with an estate, he also describes "5 cropp land" and "2 cropp land."[104] In some parts of Oxfordshire a four-course rotation was followed, but the three-course system was also used. In Lincoln the two-field system was in general use. In the middle parts of Suffolk two crops and sometimes only one were thought to be as much as should be taken before fallowing again, though some farmers took more.[105]

And wherever we are fortunate enough to have the accounts of individual farmers, their story bears out the fact of considerable freedom, diversity, and experiment. Robert Loder's accounts, and particularly his own revealing commentaries upon them, give fairly specific information in this regard.[106] Loder farmed about 150 acres of land on the north side of the Berkshire downs. It lay in open fields in a two-part division, the East Field and the West Field. Sometimes he repeated a wheat crop on the same lands after only one fallow year; sometimes a longer interval elapsed before wheat went in again; or barley might follow the fallow instead of a second wheat crop. Some lands in the West Field that were sown with wheat in 1613 lay fallow in 1614, bore a crop of pulse in 1615, were fallow again in 1616, and put to wheat again in 1617. But other lands in the same field were treated differently. In general, Loder's favorite rotation appears to have been wheat, fallow, wheat or barley, and fallow, with sometimes a catch crop of peas, beans, or vetches, sown on some of the strips between the two cereal crops.[107]

Farmers' calendars, husbandry books, and such personal records as are available indicate a fairly uniform method in preparing the ground for the seed and its cultivation. It was

104. Sloane MSS. 3815.

105. Fussell, "Farming Methods," *J.M.H.*, pp. 13–19.

106. George Elmdon, who farmed in Norfolk under Elizabeth, is another example of the individual who is trying various farming methods. See Gray, *English Field Systems,* pp. 440–441.

107. I have used Mr. Fussell's estimate of Loder's acreage. His expert knowledge of agriculture, both past and present, has also been of great assistance in the interpretation of Loder's record. See his Introduction in *Loder's Farm Journal.*

customary for cornlands, both for winter and spring crops, to have three ploughings or "stirrings" that came approximately in the spring, summer, and autumn. Four ploughings were recommended for some soils. Previous to the planting, the ground was harrowed. Barley and oats were sown in the spring, as were also wheat and vetches. As soon as harvest was over in the autumn, the winter grain, either wheat or rye, was sown, and preparation went forward to prepare the land that would be used for the spring crops.

These four main cereal crops were all merchantable. Peas, vetches, and other pulse were used chiefly for forage, and to some extent for building up the soil. Wheat required the best ground but it also brought the highest prices, and with the increased use of white bread there was an added incentive to increase the wheat acreage. Loder was clearly doing that on his Berkshire farm. When in 1615 he came to cast up accounts and to ponder over his failures and successes, he concluded as follows: "Soe that it is undoubtedly my best course to sow more wheat & less barly yearly, for the proffite is greater as aforesayd."[108] It was a decision that he frequently acted upon thereafter; for except for an occasional year, his wheat acreage appears to have increased steadily. His yields fluctuated according to the weather, the care he was able to give the ground, perhaps the quality of the seed, and other factors. But if his figures are at all accurate, the period covered by his journal, 1612–21, shows a yield that was high for his day, varying from the lowest return of 13.7 bushels per acre in 1613 to slightly more than 35 bushels per acre in 1619 and 1620, with the ratio of the yield to the seed varying from 5.5:1 in 1613 to 14.6:1 in 1620. It is clear that Loder himself felt that he was doing well. In 1614, when he made 13 bushels of grain to each bushel of seed sown, he called it "a most marvellous yeld," and closed his accounts with this note: "The Lorde my God be praysed and magnified & glorified therefore. Amen, amen." Loder had reason to be proud; for his highest re-

108. *Loder's Farm Journal*, p. 109.

turns are as high as those of the national average in England today. This was not true of the barley yield which ran consistently below what would be the average crop today.[109]

Next to wheat, barley required the richest soil. Rye, it was thought, would grow almost anywhere if the ground be "well tempered and loose." The Midlands were perhaps the nation's chief granary, but not the only one. Farmers in Lancashire grew wheat and barley as well as oats. Parts of Yorkshire, Lincoln, and Durham were good grain sections, and there were grainfields in the valleys of the border counties where the "statesmen" searched for seed corn of a hardy variety that would suit their rigorous climate. Oats did particularly well there, being almost the sole grain raised in some northern localities. An abundance of grain was raised in parts of East Anglia, and some was grown in all of the southern counties.[110]

Though grain, along with pulse and vetches, formed the staple crops, hemp and flax were grown in moderate quantities in certain sections. We hear of yeomen in Worcestershire and Staffordshire who had flax fields.[111] Flax wheels and bolts of homespun linen are mentioned in the inventories of Lincoln and Bedfordshire yeomen. And the presentments of flax growers of Nottinghamshire for washing their flax in the streams, contrary to statute regulation, point to its growth there.[112] Hemp was grown in Kent and in other parts near London, but neither of these crops achieved the popularity Elizabethan legislators coveted for them.[113]

Hops put money into the pockets of yeomen in some districts, notably Suffolk and Kent. The traditional date of their arrival in England is 1524. A popular couplet had it that

109. *Ibid.*, pp. xvii–xviii, 74.
110. This paragraph is based on the works of various writers on husbandry, and the grain reports in the State Papers, 1588 to 1642. See W. Ashley, *The Bread of Our Forefathers*, 1928, for map showing the rye-growing districts in England.
111. St.Ch. 8, 35/5, 12/7.   112. *S.R.*, 33 Henry VIII, c. 17.
113. S.P. 16, CLXXX, 90; S.P. 12, CCLXXXII, 42.

Hops, reformations, bays and beer
Came into England all in one year.

Whether that was correct or not, it is certain that hop cultivation increased steadily throughout the Elizabethan and
Stuart period. According to Reginald Scot who wrote a
book on hop culture, they did best where the ground was
dry, and "riche, mellow, and gentle."[114] Parts of the west
Midlands proved well suited to their culture. Yeomen in
Warwick in the reign of James I were inclosing lands for
hops,[115] and they were being raised in parts of Worcestershire and Hertford. The number of taverns and alehouses
throughout the country is a sufficient explanation of the
popularity this crop enjoyed. There was apparently always
a good market for it.

Barnabie Googe, and later Sir Richard Weston and
others, advocated the raising of turnips on a large scale for
the livestock and for soil enrichment. But little heed was
paid them by their own generation. What turnips there
were grew chiefly in kitchen gardens, and another hundred
years passed before they had an important place in English
agriculture.[116]

But a word should be said of the fruit that was raised; for
most farmers had some fruit for home use, and in some localities there was a surplus for the markets. Tradition had
it that there had been little fruit in England until the time
of Henry VIII.[117] This seems unlikely, but whatever the
date of its introduction, fruit trees were common throughout England by the late sixteenth century, and many yeomen added a neat surplus to the family income by the cherries, damsons, pears, and apples that they carried to market.

John Shermenden, yeoman of Surrey, in a statement of
the tithes he owed the vicar in 1637, mentioned the apples,

114. *A Perfite Platforme of a Hoppe Garden,* 1578, p. 2.
115. St.Ch. 8, 80/15.
116. Lord Ernle, *English Farming,* pp. 100, 107–108, 135.
117. "N.F.," *The Fruiterer's Secrets,* 1604.

pears, strawberries, raspberries, gooseberries, cherries, damsons, and other plums, "apricocks," peaches, and quinces that were in his garden and orchards.[118] No farmer in the north and perhaps by no means all in the south could have named so great a variety. But some fruits could be grown almost everywhere. Then as now cherries were abundant in Kent, and to some extent in other southern counties near the London market. Apples flourished in parts of Sussex and Surrey, but did best in Devon and the west Midland counties of Hereford, Worcestershire, and Gloucestershire. And pears of fine quality were grown in Worcestershire.[119] As in the case of other produce, those farmers living near the larger cities, particularly those near London, had the best markets for their fruits, too perishable to send far. Mr. Fisher says that "it was in the early seventeenth century that the orchards of Kent and the hop-grounds of Kent, Essex, Suffolk, Sussex and Surrey became really prosperous." That they were called into being principally to serve the London market seems scarcely open to doubt.[120]

The necessary equipment which the Elizabethan farmer used in his work was simple, and chiefly of home construction. The plough was the chief article of "husbandly furniture." Ploughs were made wholly of wood with the exception of the share, which was of iron. Although all were built on the same general principles, there were modifications in design and weight to meet the needs of different soils: "One sort of Plough will not serve in all places, therefore it is necessary to have diverse manner of Ploughs."[121] In parts of Somerset where the land was "tough," a broad, thin share-beam was held desirable. On the other hand the stiff clays of Huntingdon, Bedford, Cambridge, and certain other parts took large and heavy ploughs and harrows. A proper

118. Examinations in the records of the Court of Delegates, P.R.O., 3/2.
119. Practically all of the writers on husbandry dealt with orchards and their care. See the following: W. Lawson, *A New Orchard and Garden*, 1626. "N.F.," *The Fruiterer's Secrets*, 1604. L. Mascall, *A Book of the Art and Maner how to plant and graffe all sorts of trees*, etc., 1572.
120. "The Development of the London Food Market," *E.H.R.*, I, 53.
121. See W. Lawson, *The Epitome of the Art of Husbandry*.

implement for mixed soils like those in Northants, Hertfordshire, most of Kent, Essex, and Berkshire was thought
to be one of middle weight and size, while the light sandy
grounds of East Anglia, parts of Lincoln, Hants, and Surrey responded best to smaller, lighter implements.[122]

The same motive which led to a desire for soil improvement made men interested in improved farming implements, and considerable experimentation was being carried
forward. Jethro Tull had his forerunners.[123] How many
yeomen were abreast of the times in this regard it is difficult
to say, but at least some were themselves experimenting with
new or improved models. Of the two innovations in plough
construction that Samuel Hartlib mentioned in the *Legacie*,
one was the work of "an ingenious yeoman of Kent" who
"hath two ploughs fastened together very finely, by which
he plougheth two furrows at once, one under another and so
stirreth up the land 12 or 14 inches deep which in deep land
is good."[124] A Star Chamber deposition in the reign of
James I tells of a yeoman who planned to make "a strange
new plow" for use on a piece of ground that was hard and
had lain unsown, "the better to break it up and increase his
profit."[125]

Many harrows still had wooden teeth, but those with iron
teeth were also in use. The former were thought more desirable for "light grounds" and clay grounds.[126] Along with
the plough and harrow, the cradle for cutting and the flail
for cleaning the grain comprised the farmer's most important equipment and together with the wain or wagon used
in hauling were the chief articles of his "farm gear." In addition, and according to his needs and ability, he had a variety of small tools and implements: the saw, axe, adze,
mattock, pitchfork, and the like, all of which are mentioned

122. L. Mascall, *The Government of Cattell*, 1627, pp. 297–298.

123. Patents were taken out for new types of ploughs in 1623, 1627, and
1634; for a draining machine in 1628, and for instruments of mechanical
sowing in 1634 and 1639. See Lord Ernle, *English Farming*, p. 104.

124. Samuel Hartlib, *Legacie*, 1655, p. 6.

125. St.Ch. 8, 213/7.

126. G. Markham, *Cheap and Good Husbandry*, 1614, chap. VI.

in scores of yeoman inventories as a part of the equipment of outhouse and barn.[127]

Thus far we have spoken of the crops the yeomen raised and their methods and means of cultivation. It is equally important to know how they disposed of their farm produce; for in the long run, as with the farmers today, the ultimate success or failure of their efforts depended largely upon the markets. Price fixing and market regulation occupied a large place in the activities of Tudor and Stuart legislators. Their interest in the question grew partly from their attempts to maintain a nice balance between foreign and domestic trade and partly from their efforts to take care of the country's poor. The story is too long to recount here, but a few details from it are necessary for the bearing they have on the fortunes of the yeomen.

There had been attempts to regulate markets and control the exportation of grain from the fourteenth century on. But it became increasingly evident under Elizabeth that it was necessary to keep England's corn at home if her growing population were to be fed; that is, except when an unusually good corn yield created a surplus.

Since neither the grain yield nor the state of poverty was the same in all sections, Parliament passed an act in 1570 providing that the Lord President and Council of the North, the Lord President and Council of Wales, and the justices of the Assize within their respective jurisdictions should annually, with the aid of the chief inhabitants in their localities, fix market prices and regulations. This statute further provided that grain might be exported to foreign parts upon a payment of twelve pence per quarter for wheat with other grains in proportion.[128]

In 1593 another act forbade the exportation of grain en-

127. See below, p. 238.
128. *S.R.,* 13 Eliz., c. 13. Henry Best, writing in 1642, says that barley was usually about eight shillings higher than oats, and rye about seven shillings higher than barley, with wheat varying in value over rye according to its quality. *Best's Farming Book,* Sur. Soc., XXXIII, 99. But these proportions varied somewhat with time and place. See grain reports S.P. 14, XL, CXXX, CXXXVIII, CXLII, and those for the year 1631.

tirely if wheat were in excess of 20s. per quarter with other grains in proportion. If below that price, the duty was increased 2s. for wheat over the duty named in the former act, with that of other grains raised in proportion.[129] But prices were going up so steadily that by the early years of the seventeenth century the price in any normal year was above 20s. Hence upon the demand for revised legislation a new act of 1604 permitted exportation when wheat did not exceed 26s. 8d., and other grains accordingly.[130] In 1623 the deadline was set at 32s.;[131] and by 1660 exportation was allowed whenever prices at the port of embarkation did not exceed 40s. per quarter for wheat, with other grains accordingly.[132]

These acts are in themselves eloquent testimony of the rise in grain prices throughout the period they cover. The evidence they give is borne out by contemporary accounts of all kinds; and Sir William Beveridge and his colleagues are putting the story into tabulated form.[133] Wheat sold in 1650 for more than three times what it brought in 1570. For the most part the rise was gradual and fairly consistent though occasionally several bumper crops in succession, or sometimes improper distribution, led to overstocked markets and a sharp fall in prices. The years 1582–84, 1591–92, 1603–4, and 1619–20 were like that, with wheat sometimes going eight or ten shillings per quarter below what it had been the preceding year.[134] Wealthy yeomen with savings or credit to tide them over these years did not face acute suffering, but the poorer among them, like the poorer husbandman who depended upon current profits only for his rents and other expenses, were placed in a sorry plight by these sudden fluctuations.

But sharp turns upward were equally frequent. A lighter yield, faulty distribution, or famine abroad that brought

---

129. *S.R.*, 35 Eliz., c. 7.   130. *Ibid.*, 1 Jac., c. 25.
131. *Ibid.*, 21 Jac., c. 28.   132. *Ibid.*, 12 Car. II, c. 4.

133. *Prices and Wages in England from the twelfth to the nineteenth century,* 1939, Vol. I; also MSS. of The Beveridge Committee.

134. See quotations of prices of grains in different counties in the grain reports, S.P. 14, XL, CXXX, CXXXI, CXXXVIII, CXLII, CXLIII.

greater demand on English grain, could send prices sky-rocketing. In 1620, for instance, a year of low prices, wheat sold at slightly more than 22s. the quarter. By the next year it had risen to 35s., and before the 1622 season closed, had jumped to 45s. and in some places slightly higher.[135]

Sudden upward soarings like these brought great suffering to the poor who had to buy grain, and to thickly populated centers.[136] On the whole, however, the yeomen profited by them. To be sure, they did not wholly escape the ills of the times. Years of dearth left them with little surplus to sell. Moreover, the farmers found that when the prices of grain rose, other prices rose accordingly. The iron for their ploughshares, the salt for their stock, and other things which they were forced to procure from the outside became dear,[137] to say nothing of the increased rents that some of them were forced to meet. Furthermore, the yeomen in the grazing and dairying section who did not raise enough food for their stock suffered from having to buy at high prices.[138] But despite these factors in the situation, the greater part of the evidence points to the fact that the yeomen profited more than they suffered by the turn of affairs.

The reasons for this are not far to seek. Rarely, if ever, did it happen that the yeomen did not have enough food to supply their own households, and wool with which to keep themselves in warm clothes. Hence the rise in the prices of these staples affected their expense outlay to a much less degree than it augmented their incomes which were based al-

---

135. *Ibid.*

136. Bucks, secure in its grain fields, reported at the close of the 1622 season that there was no need to limit the amount of grain sold at the markets there, S.P. 14, CXLII, 44. Northumberland, on the other hand, had such a scarcity in grain that year that the poor had neither corn to make bread with, nor money with which to buy it. Their remoteness from markets made it difficult for others to serve them, and their sorry plight was increased by a dearth in meat supplies because there had been only rotted fodder that winter to feed their cattle and sheep. *Ibid.*, CXXXI, 29. All urban centers were badly off. Bury St. Edmunds and other populous Suffolk towns as late as February, 1623, were still reporting their fear that they would not have enough grain to last until the next harvest. *Ibid.*, CXXXVII, 33; CXLII, 14.

137. S.P. 16, CCIII, 59, 63.   138. *Ibid.*, XLII, 14.

most wholly upon the sale of grain, wool, and livestock. Fortunate in this respect above the urban classes and the rural
poor who could not provide their own maintenance, they
were also, because of their simple standard of living, spared
much of the burden of increased costs that fell upon the
gentry who found that clothes, house furnishings, and other
articles procured from the outside were rising steadily in
price. It was this situation which caused Robert Reyce of
Suffolk to speak in 1618 of the yeomen, who were "painfull" in industry and ambition, and at the same time free
"from the costly charge of these unfaithfull times" as the
only class in the country which was rising in wealth.[139]

Under the circumstances it was a great temptation to
those farmers who did not have to sell their grain to meet immediate needs to hoard it during cheap years until prices
were better. This practice was known as "engrossing," and
together with "forestalling," the buying or contracting for
any produce before it reached the market, and "regrating,"
whereby produce was bought at the market and resold elsewhere at a higher price, comprised the chief evils against
which market regulations were leveled.

These offenses had been the subject of legislation long
before the Tudor period.[140] But it was the dear years, the
high prices, and subsequent hard times for an increased
number of poor in the reigns of Elizabeth and the early
Stuarts that were responsible for a flood of new measures
relating to market offenses, and more careful observance of
those already in existence.

The year 1630–31 may be taken as an example. It was a
dear year all over England. Prices soared and the poor suffered. As early as May, 1630, the King issued a proclamation forbidding the exportation of all grain whatsoever,
since "by reason of late unseasonable weather . . . the
hopefulness of the next ensuing harvest is much indangered." In June another royal proclamation informed the

139. *Breviary of Suffolk*, p. 58.
140. As early as the reign of Henry III, forestalling was forbidden. See
also *S.R.* 5 and 6 Edward VI, c. 14.

country that the dearth continued to be widespread, and warned corn growers against hoarding, forestalling, and engrossing.[141] In addition, the Privy Council that year revised and reissued the *Book of Orders* which had previously been published on similar occasions under Elizabeth and James. This book contained the most minute directions regarding market and price regulations, and called for the strictest surveillance to be exercised. It was sent to the J.P.'s of every county in England.[142]

Preachers went into their pulpits that year to denounce those who placed their own private gain before the public good. They flayed without mercy the hoarders and hucksters who "pinched the guts of the poore to fill and extend their own purses, taking advantage by the dearth of corne to make it more deare." "He that with holdeth corne, the people will curse him: But blessing shall be upon the head of him that selleth it," was the text that one pulpiteer read to his congregation from the Book of Proverbs. The justices were begged to "drawe forthe the poor imprisoned graine out of Private Barnes" and give it the freedom of the market.[143]

Probably no one was more in need of this kind of preaching than the yeomen. To be sure Thomas Fuller, whose pride in the yeoman class made him loath to admit their shortcomings, declared that it was not covetousness that made them hoard their grain in dear years, but rather foresightedness and a provident nature which led them to keep reserve supplies on hand for times of need, in order that they might act as "the Josephs of the country who kept the poor from starving."[144] Now charity was not lacking among the yeomen as we shall see,[145] but neither were they the kind

141. *Proclamation, Prohibiting the exportation of Corne*, 1630.

142. See *Proclamation for preventing the dearth of Corne and Victual*, S.P. 16, XLV, 10.

143. C. Fitz-Geffrie, *The Curse of Corne horders with the Blessing of Seasonable selling, being three sermons preached before the sessions in Cornwall*, 1631, pp. 1–2.

144. Fuller, *The Holy State*, p. 107.   145. See below, pp. 380–382.

to turn a deaf ear when business opportunities knocked at the door. And the examples in sessions records and other documents of yeomen who were guilty of market offenses are sufficiently numerous to make one suspect that Fuller's interpretation in this instance is more sympathetic than accurate.

William Abbye, a yeoman of Bedfordshire, was taken to task because he had "by way of forestalling and ingrossing" brought into the open market 500 quarters of wheat, 1,000 quarters of barley, and 500 quarters of peas, and other grain besides, with the intent to sell again.[146] Thomas Regnell, yeoman, of Hunts, was presented at the sessions in 1618 for "ingrossing upon the ground," 20 acres of wheat, 20 acres of rye, 40 acres of barley, 20 acres of peas, beans, and vetches, and 20 acres of oats.[147] William Hichcokes, a Staffordshire yeoman, was presented in 1586 for being "a Common ingrosser of Corne in Dyvers markets," having three or four ricks of his own in store.[148] In the Middlesex sessions of 1621 a true bill was brought against William Agreenehill, a yeoman of Harrow, who "ingrossed and bought ten quarters of wheat . . . with the intention of selling the same."[149] Charges were brought against Nicholas King, a Hertfordshire yeoman, in 1626, for engrossing corn at Langley. And the minutes of the Nottingham sessions for various years in the reigns of James I and Charles I are filled with charges as are those of Norfolk and Essex.[150] In Lincoln in 1631 Christopher Hart, gentleman, and William Hall, yeoman, were imprisoned for three days and then bound over with sureties for not obeying the in-

146. St.Ch. 8, 78/20.

147. Hunts Sessions Papers, Add. MSS. 34399, fol. 220b.

148. *Staffordshire Sessions Rolls,* I, 117.

149. *Sessions Rolls,* Middlesex County Records (hereafter cited as Middlesex Sessions Rolls), 1886, I, 108.

150. *Hertford Sessions Rolls,* I, 61; Nottingham Sessions Rolls in the MSS. at the Shire Hall, Nottingham (hereafter cited as Notts Sessions Records); see especially those for 17 Chas. I; Norfolk Sessions Rolls, see especially constables' accounts for 1630–31; Essex Sessions Rolls, see especially those of 1576, and 1630–33.

structions against engrossing that were set down in the new
Order Book.[151] It is doubtful if such stringent measures
were taken except in times of acute need. But people were
starving in England in 1631.

Evidence of the above type, and scores of similar examples might be given, leads one to suspect that John Taylor,
the Water Poet, was a better judge of many yeomen in this
respect than Thomas Fuller. Taylor declared that the yeoman welcomed years of dearth for the profit he could make
from them and that in years of plenty he would

> hoard up corne with many a bitter ban
> From widowes, Orphanes and the lab'ring man.[152]

Of course the yeomen were not the only culprits. Gentlemen, and especially maltsters, were often among the guilty
ones; but certainly transgression among the yeomen was
widespread. There was a good deal of chafing at the amount
of government direction and surveillance in these matters,
and arguments and examples were not wanting among those
who held that the regulations aggravated the very causes
they were designed to alleviate.[153] Some declared that the
government's program was not practical.[154] Others, that
too much blame for soaring prices was placed on hoarders
and forestallers, when in reality they were the natural result
of occasional years of scarcity brought on by the "hand of
God" and therefore not to be questioned.[155] On the whole,
however, there was perhaps less grumbling than might be
expected, and when one realizes that it was the yeomen and
gentry, in their capacity as shire and parish officials, upon
whose shoulders fell the task of putting into effect regulations that were in many cases not beneficial to themselves
and their group, it is perhaps surprising that they gave as

151. S.P. 16, CLXXXIX, 58.   152. Taylor, *Works,* 1630, p. 12.
153. S.P. 16, CCIII, 48. See also CLXXXIX, 39; CLXXXIV, 61; Sessions Records, I, 28. Order Book, Hants.
154. S.P. 14, CXII, 91.
155. S.P. 16, CCIII, 98; see also 48, 78, and 89; CLXXVI, 57;
CLXXXIV, 16.

much coöperation as they did. Certainly in years of dearth or other crises the sessions records show a much stricter account being taken of market offenses than in normal years.

It was within the power of the justices to modify the market regulations in certain respects if the common good were thereby served.[156] They might, for instance, grant licenses to men to buy in the markets and sell again in remote parts, at a small profit, to customers who had no accessible markets. Men who were granted this legal right to peddle their wares were called "badgers" and a good many farmers among the poorer yeomen and husbandmen secured such licenses to sell. Sometimes the magistrates of a town or community where there was a dearth of corn in the local markets petitioned justices to permit badgers to come to them.[157]

The need for badgers is but one of many factors to suggest what so often proves to be the case in the annals of economic history, namely, that the lack of proper distribution was one of the chief causes of the current economic disturbances. In October, 1628, the Sussex farmers with a bountiful harvest left over from the year before, for which they could get but 20s. a quarter for wheat and 12s. for barley, begged that the regulations on exportation be lowered.[158] Only two months later in the same year reports from northern shires stated that grain was very scarce there, with wheat selling for 80s. the quarter and rye for 60s.; whereupon they protested against the southern counties being allowed to export until they could be supplied.[159] Likewise, in Norwich in 1630 justices reported that they could not get enough corn to feed their poor, though they heard that other parts of Norfolk had an abundance and were exporting it.[160]

The question of distribution was closely allied to that of

156. Order Book, Hants Sessions Records, I, 28.
157. "Petition of Mayor and Magistrates of Bath, 1608," *Wilt. Arch. and Nat. Hist.*, XVIII, 156.
158. S.P. 16, CXVIII, 19.   159. *Ibid.*, CXXXII, 17.
160. *Ibid.*, CLXXXVI, 26.

transportation and it was largely transportation facilities
which determined the position of markets. Coastwise and
river transportation proved the surest outlets for traffic in
grain.[161] Roadways were of course used, especially to local
markets, but road carriage was expensive for long distances
and even local markets were often almost inaccessible because of the condition of the roads at certain seasons of the
year.[162] It was no accident that led Robert Loder to increase
his wheat acreage. Other farmers, situated as he was, could
with assurance do likewise. For the Midlands, parts of
Worcester and Hereford, parts of Yorkshire, sections of
East Anglia, and most of the south had fairly easy access
to river or ocean transportation.[163]

Contemporaries were quick to attribute the wealth of the
Kentish yeomen and others near to London or the sea to the
fact that they were close to excellent markets. In fact, in
the home counties and those near by, the farmers were saved
the trouble of seeking the best markets because the best markets were seeking them. In 1595 the deputy lieutenants for
Hertfordshire wrote the Privy Council that whereas it had
been customary for men called "loaders" to buy up the
grain and carry it to London, "now the bakers and brewers,
not content to receive those commodities from the loaders,
come down and greedily buy great quantities of grain, and
offer such high prices as to do great hurt."[164] This may
have upset local markets, but it redounded to the wealth of
the farmers who had grain to sell.

There are many evidences of the wealth of the yeomen in

161. See T. Willan, *River Navigation in England, 1600–1750*, 1936; and
his *English Coasting Trade, 1600–1750*, 1938.

162. The J.P.'s in Essex reported in January, 1630, that the roads were
so bad that instead of bringing their corn to the country markets as they
were supposed to do, the farmers were sending it by water to London,
S.P. 16, CLXXXII, 67. The reports from the far northern shires in years
of dearth repeatedly gave their remoteness from markets as the reason
why they could not easily be served when their own supply was low.

163. Fussell, "Farming Methods," *J.M.H.*, p. 10. For increased demands
of the London market not only on the home counties but farther afield, see
F. J. Fisher, "The Development of the London Food Market," *E.H.R.*, I,
46–57.

164. *S.P.D.*, CCLIV, 10.

the region surrounding London.[165] Norden, speaking in 1592 of the opportunities enjoyed by those farmers who lived in Middlesex or its borders, said: "Another sort of husbandmen or yomen rather ther are, and that not a few in this shire, who wade in the weedes of gentlemen; theis only oversee their husbandrye, and give direction unto to their servantes, seldome, or not at all settinge their hand unto the plough, who havinge great feedinges for cattle, and good breede for younge, often use Smythfelde and other lyke places with fatt cattle, wher also they store themselves with leane. And thus they often exchaunge not without great gayne, whereby and by their daylye increase at home they commonly become very riche."[166]

But it was not merely the growth of London but the development of current commercial and industrial activities everywhere that increased the demand for the farmer's produce and was often the instrument that determined the course of his husbandry. Expeditions for trade and exploration and especially the development of colonial ventures opened new markets to Devon farmers and others of the western counties within reach of the ports of Plymouth and Bristol. John Hooker, writing in 1599, said that although the Devon yeomen had always had sufficient to satisfy themselves, they were now "also hable and do daylye furnishe no small nombre of shippes which from tyme to time do harborew theym selffes in the havens and creeks of that countrie, with beefes, barrows and porkes but also wth byskett and beere and sider, beanes, and peasons" for outgoing voyages, "whether it be at new founde lande for fishinge or the Ilandes and countries for merchandyse."[167] It was charged in Cornwall in 1630, where grain was double its normal price, that the increase was due to engrossing and

165. See below, pp. 204 n., 217–218, 233–235.

166. "The meanes most usuall how the people of Middlesex doe live." This section which was omitted from Norden's *Description of Middlesex* published in 1593 is reprinted from the Harl. MSS., 570, in the Introduction of Norden's *Historical and Chorographical Description of the County of Essex,* Camden Soc., 1840, p. xii.

167. Hooker, *Synopsis,* p. 343.

forestalling among Devon farmers in order that Devon promoters might be assured of provisions for a projected voyage to "Newfound Land," though it was said by some of them to be poor business, since the fish taken on the voyage would be sold elsewhere, thereby depriving local people of an opportunity to share in the profits of the voyage.[168] These particular charges may have been exaggerated, for corn prices rose everywhere that year; but they are suggestive of the way in which the repercussions of commercial activity were felt in agrarian circles.

A letter written by "the yeomen and farmers of East Kent" to their justices in 1619, and forwarded by them to the Privy Council, offers another interesting example of the growing consciousness of the interdependence of agriculture and commerce. The letter stated that the land in eastern Kent, being mostly arable, produced more grain than could be disposed of locally. Hence it was customary for farmers to sell to certain buyers in the near-by port towns who "adventured the same to London and other places in the realm as occasion served . . . to the increase of trade and the betterment of everybody." But of late years the "portsmen" had been forced to refuse their grain because their right to pass wheat from port to port was challenged. The result, according to the Kentish farmers, was a decay in the trade and shipping of the port towns for which "we also feele the smart thereof." The local justices approved the farmers' request that the restrictions against the "portsmen" be raised and likewise protested to the councillors against permitting importation of grain when there was a time of plenty and cheapness at home.[169]

Many other examples might be given to show that the yeomen were alive to the importance of securing the best possible markets. They sought not only the best place but the best time for disposing of their products. Unless forced by government request to sell between Michaelmas and Candlemas in order to forestall the evil effects of a dearth, or otherwise pressed to do so in order to meet autumn rents,

168. S.P. 16, CLXXV, 35 (3).   169. S.P. 14, CXII, 12..

pay servants' wages, or to have on hand money for holiday provisions,[170] they were likely to hold their grain over for awhile. All barns were full just after harvest and prices were lowest then. The best prices of the year could be expected from late May to early September.[171]

Yeomen likewise kept their ears open for news of better markets outside their own immediate localities. The J.P.'s of Leicestershire in one instance protested that they could not enforce the market regulations with any degree of success because the farmers were selling in other counties where they could get higher prices.[172] The enterprising ones among them learned also to know what markets were best for certain things and what affected the prices in various localities. Farmers in eastern Yorkshire, for instance, had learned that if Tuesdays and Fridays were calm days, their oats would go well in the Beverley markets; for on such days the Lincolnshire men came over to Hull and bought of the Beverley oatmeal vendors to carry back to Brigg and other markets. They discovered also that there was little activity at the Beverley market before eleven in the morning, whereas the market at Malton was quickest between nine and ten since there were many badgers there from a distance who wished to buy early in order to get home before dark.[173] Fine points like these meant much to men whose profits were measured in terms of a few more shillings here, and a few more pence there. And their awareness of such matters is in itself evidence of the extent to which farming had progressed beyond the subsistence level of earlier days.

Not only did they seek better markets for themselves but they frequently played the role of middleman for the smaller farmers of their communities, acting in the capacity of either purchasing or distributing agent as opportunity afforded.

An interesting record in the Court of Requests for 1567 shows Thomas Cooper and Robert Ward, two Yorkshire

---

170. G. Markham, *The English Husbandman*, Pt. I, p. 31.
171. *Ibid.*, p. 32.   172. S.P. 16, CLXXVI, 56.
173. *Best's Farming Book*, pp. 100–101.

yeomen, engaged in buying up grain in Lincolnshire to transport to York, presumably for sale to the maltsters there. Richard Read, a Lincolnshire gentleman, was partner to the enterprise in that county. He agreed to purchase the grain, 120 quarters of barley, from small growers in Lincoln. Cooper and Ward in turn agreed to purchase it from him for the sum of £96 with the intent of selling again in Yorkshire. It was part of the agreement that Read should by Candlemas deliver the grain to Stallingborough, a small landing place on an estuary of the Humber about five miles from Grimsby, and that the two yeomen should see to its transportation from there to York. Hence on the Wednesday after Candlemas Ward and Cooper brought their boats to anchor at the landing, and some twenty or more small farmers, of whom Read had purchased from 2 to 7 quarters of barley each, appeared with the grain. But upon seeing it Ward and Cooper declared it to be grain of an inferior quality and charged Read with holding back his best grade at Barrow five miles away. They declared they would take only 90 quarters of the Stallingborough consignment. Read was disgruntled but, "be cause I love no brablynge," agreed to have them put in at Barrow for the remaining 30 quarters. Ill-feeling was by this time aroused and a quarrel ensued over the payment of the money. Read declared that the two yeomen had been unfaithful to their bargain, and they in turn swore "by Cockes bones" that he had tried to beggar all the county of York with his unfair dealings.[174] What the merits of the case were it is hard to say, but it furnishes interesting evidence of the way in which agrarian interests were being steadily commercialized and shows the yeoman in the role of small capitalist as well as producer, a role that he not infrequently played.

We have spoken chiefly thus far of tillage and the growing and marketing of grain; and rightly so. For not only did many yeomen look to this as the sole source of their profits, but practically all of them engaged in the growing of some food crops, at least enough for their own mainte-

174. Req. 2, 186/107.

nance. There were, however, many yeomen whose chief means of profit was in animal husbandry. These farmers who lived in the great grazing sections of the west and north, or managed dairy farms in East Anglia, or watched their flocks grow fat on the lush grass of Romney Marsh or the less lush, but more extensive, pasturage of the Downs were by no means indifferent to the grain situation and to grain prices. They might be forced to buy extra food to see their stock through the winter. But it was the wool market, and the prices of sheep, cattle, and dairy products upon which their gains and losses chiefly depended. Their search of *Almanacks* and *Prognostications*, therefore, was not for hints on the proper time for sowing and reaping, for hop picking and fruit picking, but rather for portents pertaining to lambing time and sheep-shearing time, and to the proper cures for the various animal ailments with which they must contend.

In an earlier period English wool was sent largely to the continental markets. But by the time of Elizabeth wool manufacturing was well established in the west as well as in the north and east of England. Wealth flowed out from these centers. It led to an advance in towns and villages, and furnished a means whereby middle and lower classes often rose in the social scale. If clothiers must have wool, then farmers must raise sheep. And the fortunes of hundreds of yeoman families were closely linked with the wool industry.

The story of this industry was by no means one of uninterrupted progress. Indeed, near the close of Elizabeth's reign and throughout that of James I wool was often an exception in a scale of constantly rising prices, and there was acute suffering in some regions. Prohibitions in foreign markets,[175] overproduction, and the relatively inferior quality of a good deal of English wool are among the factors responsible for this situation.[176] But in spite of it, and perhaps because the ills it produced were often regional in nature, sheep continued to be raised in large numbers and in

175. "Lieutenancy book of Essex," *The Essex Review*, XVII, 203.
176. Lord Ernle, *English Farming*, 1927, p. 81.

the predominantly grazing sections were the mainstay of husbandry.

Travelers from abroad were impressed with the number of sheep they saw grazing on the hillsides and meadows of the English countryside.[177] As Mr. Fussell says, "the sheep was ubiquitous" in England, being no less an integral part of the open arable-field system where it grazed upon the fallows a part of the year, and upon the stubble and head-lands and balks during another part, than of the predominantly grazing areas.[178]

Each shire or district had its favorite breeds according to the suitability of the animals to their environment. The smaller short-wool breeds were found best for the moors and glens of the north. Their wool produced a coarse, cheap cloth, but it was this cloth that clothed England's poorer classes, and mills in Yorkshire and thereabouts were able to use all of the local supply.[179]

Large sheep that grew the longest wool were raised in Lincoln and Leicestershire, in Romney Marsh, in Devon, and the Cotswolds. Michael Drayton in his *Poly-Olbion* singles out the Cotswold sheep for special mention:

No browne, nor sullyed black the face or legs doth streak
Like those of *Moreland*, *Cank* or of the *Cambrian* hills
That lightly laden are: but *Cotswold* wisely fills
Her with the whitest kind: whose browes so woolly be,
As men in her faire sheepe no emptiness should see.
The Staple deepe and thick, through, to the very graine,
Most strongly keepeth out the violentest raine:
A body long and large, the buttocks equall broad;
As fit to undergoe the full and weightie load,
And of the fleecie face, the flank doth nothing lack
But every-where is stord; the belly as the back.[180]

177. "Travels of Rathgeb," reprinted in Harrison's *Description of England,* Appendix II, p. lxxxiii; "Hentzner's Travels," *ibid.,* p. lxxxiv.
178. Fussell, "Farming Methods," *J.M.H.,* p. 136.
179. H. Heaton, *Yorkshire Woollen and Worsted Industries,* 1920, pp. 113, 145, 328.
180. M. Drayton, *Poly-Olbion,* 1933, pp. 297–298.

The question of pasturage was of course a vital one for the sheep grower and regulations governing the rights of common were of importance. In some places the holder of every tenement was given pasturage for six sheep on the common; and for as many additional ones as there were acres in his holdings.[181] Some such arrangement whereby the number of sheep on the common was in proportion to the sheep owner's holdings on the manor was the normal practice. Sometimes there were complaints that the commons were so overstocked that the sheep were underfed. Rights of common on the lands of William Henfield, a Sussex yeoman, included feeding for 289 sheep on the downs, and two nights' fold weekly from the flocks pastured on the downs.[182] Details governing rights of common were usually set down carefully in leases and deeds of land conveyance. Sheep could themselves be leased. Richard Hunt, a Wiltshire yeoman, let 400 sheep, wethers and ewes, to Sir William Kellwaye for five years "for ten weights of good well tried wool per annum." At the end of the five years Kellwaye was to return the sheep in as good condition as he had received them or else pay Hunt seventy pounds.[183]

If a farmer were stocking his lands for the first time or even if he were adding to his flock, his chief problem was to find the best animals he could get of a breed suited to his locality. Much less attention was paid to breeding than is the case today, but farmers were not unaware of its importance. According to Henry Best of Yorkshire, a member of the minor gentry who knew the sheep business from both observation and experience, "the most experienced sheepmen endeavour by all meanes possible to get into a good stocke." It was better bargaining, he said, to pay ten shillings "for an ewe that is well quartered, and of a good staple, with an handsome straight lamb att her heeles than

181. D.L., 44/901.
182. Sussex MSS., Knole 15. See Northants MSS., F.H. 412, for agreement between lord and tenants for reducing number of beasts each was allowed to have on the common.
183. Req. 2, 218/57.

to give 5s. for an ewe that is of a shorte runtish kind with a shorte grasse belly'd lambe following her."[184]

If a purchase were in view the farmer visited one or more near-by fairs or markets in order to have as wide a choice as possible. When the Yorkshire yeoman, Adam Eyre, set out to restock his lands after his return from the army in 1647, he planned to buy sheep at the Tideswell fair in October. He wanted a hardy variety, for the animals that he bought would be put on the moors. The day before it was time to start to the fair, Adam learned that Thomas Eyre, a kinsman, was on the way there with sheep to sell; so he rode out to meet him and to have a look at his sheep. After inspecting them he offered his cousin seven shillings apiece for a hundred ewes. But either Thomas Eyre hoped to get a better price at the fair, or else hesitated to sell outside the market limits, for he refused the offer and the two men went on to the fair together. Once there, however, Thomas apparently found no better price and Adam no better sheep; so they sealed the bargain for 101 ewes at the price Adam earlier offered. In addition, he bought five rams from another dealer.

Whenever a farmer purchased sheep, he must as soon as possible see that they were properly marked. They would run with the sheep of other owners on the common, or the moor, and if they were lost or stolen the mark served as the owner's identification. Adam Eyre marked the sheep he bought at Tideswell fair a few days after he got them home. In addition to his own animals he was wintering some sheep for his father-in-law and several of the neighbors. Each of these was marked also. Fresh redle was used for the marking and Eyre's own sheep were branded with an H, for Haverhead, the name of his farmstead.[185]

In the west country the marking or branding of sheep was called "signing." The sessions papers of Devon for 1631 recount the story of a yeoman who had one of his sheep stolen. His son went with the constable to search the house

184. *Best's Farming Book*, p. 6.   185. *Diary of Adam Eyre*, p. 113.

of a suspect. They found a part of the sheep already in the pot cooking, but its identity was established because the lad recognized his father's "signinge" on some of the wool they found hidden about the house.[186] Sheep not marked were often stolen and marked with another's symbol, or sometimes the symbol was altered so as to resemble that of another.

Even though sheep could forage for their own food, they required considerable attention. The constant dread of sheep owners was a liver ailment known as the rot that attacked their animals particularly after wet seasons, often causing them to die by the score. A Berkshire yeoman in 1586 bought 100 sheep for £20 only to have them all die with the rot a month after the purchase.[187] Robert Loder relates his disheartening experience of having 400 of his sheep suffer with the rot in one winter. By January at least 80 had died, and he daily expected the loss of more.[188] The disease in its early stages was not easy to detect and farmers sometimes tried to get the stricken animals off their hands at another's expense.[189] Those who depended on their sheep for a main source of their income were indeed in a sad plight when disease attacked their flocks. Contemporary medical and household books contain many cures for sheep ailments. Henry Best advocated treating the lambs with melted tallow all over their bodies as a preventive measure against the general ills that were likely to attack them during their first year.[190] Accidents as well as disease took their toll. Adam Eyre went often to the moor to see if all was well with his sheep. One day he found a ewe with her leg broken, the next day a tup suffered a like accident. Again he found one of his ewes dead. They took constant watching.[191]

Lambing time, usually March or late February, kept the sheep farmer and his helpers busy, particularly if the sea-

---

186. Devon Quarter Sessions Bundles, 1631.
187. Req. 2, 186/138.   188. *Loder's Farm Journal*, p. 69.
189. St.Ch. 268/24; *Loder's Farm Journal*, p. 69.
190. *Best's Farming Book*, pp. 29–30.
191. *Diary of Adam Eyre*, pp. 112–117.

son were cold and wet. The lambs frequently required careful nursing to get them through the first weeks. Just prior to shearing time, that is from the first to the middle of June, the sheep which were to be sheared were washed, a difficult operation. From a day to a fortnight after the washing, the shearing or "clipping" was done, and there was wisdom in the old proverb:

> The man that is about to clippe his sheepe
> Must pray for two faire days and one faire week.

One day was needed for the wool to dry after the washing. The shearing occupied another day, and it was well if the animals could have a week of fair weather for becoming hardened. After the shearing the wool from each sheep was rolled separately and the "tithe skins" set aside for the parson.[192] All bits of wool left about were gathered up at the close of each day and saved for the poor who came abegging at the end of shearing time. The workmen who washed the sheep were served at the noon hour with something to eat. On Henry Best's estate in Yorkshire they were given a hot drink of boiled milk, ale, and crumbed white loaf, flavored with a dash of nutmeg. The clippers, or shearers, got a groat's worth of ale, bread and cheese, and sometimes cheese cake, at noon. In the evening they were all served a huge dinner.[193]

The fluctuations in sheep prices in the last decades of the sixteenth century and the early years of the seventeenth have already been noted. The accounts of the Durham parish books from 1584 to 1623 illustrate something of their instability. In the first decade, 1584–94, the price of sheep in this region practically doubled, rising from 4.83s. to 8s. per stone. The next seven years witnessed a drop of 2s. to 3s. But again from 1602 to 1608 prices rose as high as 10.39s. per stone. In 1612 there was another drop to 5.93s. From 1616 to 1618 there was another gain to slightly above

192. See Henry Best's lively description of the selection of the tithe wool. *Best's Farming Book,* pp. 24–25.

193. *Ibid.,* pp. 17–23.

10*s.* and again a moderate decrease in the next five years.[194]
A situation like this made it necessary for sheep growers to
watch the markets carefully in order to be able to sell at the
most advantageous time. There was, of course, considerable
variation in prices, according to the breed of the animals
and the quality of the wool.[195]

But if the business of sheep raising was somewhat pre-
carious, perhaps it was no more so than tillage; and even
when wool prices tended to be low, there were yet many ways
in which the sheep proved an asset to the owner. Grain provided the farmer with food; sheep gave him both food and
clothing. Grain took richness out of the soil; sheep enriched
the fields they ran on. Fewer laborers were necessary for
sheep than for tillage. If the following rhymed boast of
Leonard Mascall somewhat exaggerates the value of sheep,
it is at the same time suggestive of the esteem in which they
were held by the contemporary writers on husbandry:

> These Cattle sheep among the rest,
> Is counted for man one of the best,
> No harmful beast, no hurt at all,
> His fleece of wool doth cloath us all,
> Which keeps us all from extream cold;
> His flesh doth feed both young and old;
> His tallow makes the candles white,
> To burn and serve us day and night
> His skin doth pleasure divers waies,
> To write, to wear, at all assaies;
> His guts; thereof we make wheel-strings;
> They use his bones for other things;
> His horns some shepheards will not loose,
> Because therewith they patch their shoes;

194. From the figures compiled by the Beveridge Committee on Price
History, in preparation for publication.

195. See following references for prices of sheep and wool in various
localities between 1570 and 1649; *Diary of Adam Eyre, passim; Diary of
William Honiwell, passim;* Stowe Accts. Hn. 1612–1624; Bedford County
MSS., Inventories for 1619; Essex Sessions Rolls, 45/60; Req. 2, 185/38,
218/57; St.Ch. 8, 145/14, 268/24.

His dung is chief I understand,
To help and dung the Plowmans land ;
Therefore the sheepe among the rest,
He is for man a worthy beast.[196]

Even in regions where tillage predominated practically every farmer owned some sheep. One notes that a "ewe lamb," a "gimmer sheep,"[197] "one of the best sheep," or "a sheep of the second best" are listed among the personal bequests in scores of yeoman wills, being particularly favored as gifts for godchildren, grandchildren, and women kindred.

The yeomen who were numerous among the buyers at the sheep sales in certain Leicestershire markets from 1612 to 1624 were buying from 100 to 200 sheep and lambs at a time; but oftenest their purchases were from 4 or 5 to 20 or 30 animals apiece.[198] In predominantly grazing sections their flocks were larger. It was stated in a description of a Wiltshire manor that every copyholder on the manor had from 80 to 200 sheep on the common.[199] John Dobbs, a Northamptonshire yeoman, in 1557, bought 1,000 sheep, 500 ewes, and 500 lambs for which he paid £420. But not many yeomen would have as much money as that to spend on one purchase.[200]

While sheep were raised in larger numbers than any other livestock, almost every yeoman had enough cattle, horses, and pigs for his own needs, with now and then extra ones for the market. In some places, moreover, like the dairy sections of Cheshire, parts of Shropshire, eastern Suffolk, and southwest Norfolk, cattle raising was more important than sheep raising.[201] Herefordshire cattle also brought top

196. L. Mascall, *The Government of Cattell,* 1662, p. 196.
197. A young ewe between the first and second shearing was called a "gimmer."
198. Stowe Accts. Hn. 1612–19.
199. *Wiltshire Arch. Soc.,* XXXII, 310.
200. Req. 2, 198/32.
201. S.P. 16, CXCIII, 27; Reyce, *Breviary of Suffolk,* p. 39. For the widening area served by the London market for meat and dairy products see F. Fisher, "Development of the London Food Market," *E.H.R.,* pp. 48–51.

prices at the markets, and those of some parts of Lancashire and Durham were classed among the best. Cattle required more food during the winter than sheep, but like sheep, they brought profit in a variety of ways. They were valued for milk and dairy products, for beef at market, for hides, and for the enrichment they gave to the land. And they could be used as draught animals.

The problem of the grazier or dairyman of the Tudor and Stuart periods was predominantly one of feed.[202] Since the period of concentrates and roots had not yet arrived, the farmer could keep through the winter only so many beasts as his supply of grass, hay, and straw would take care of. Pasture conservation, therefore, became a prime question with the stock and dairy farmer; and he was forced to work out a careful use of his grasslands in order to make the most of them, and of his corn stubble after harvest was over. Open grazing for the sheep during certain months of the year; a later curtailing of this in order to provide ready pasture for cows at calving time and summer feed for yearlings and working oxen; and a careful apportioning of garnered hay and straw to see animals through the winter, particularly the last two lean months before the return of the spring pasture: these were the matters that kept stock growers busy. The practice of "convertible husbandry," whereby lands were used for tillage for a year or a certain number of years and then returned to pasture for a time, was increasing throughout this period. It appears to have been at least partially successful as a means of controlling the food supply and at the same time improving the land.[203]

Yeomen rarely kept more horses than their actual needs required, sometimes not more than one. They rarely owned a carriage but traveled on horseback, carrying their wives, when there was occasion for them to go abroad together, on a pillion seat behind. Horses as well as cattle were used as draught animals; but again the expense of feeding them

---

202. Fussell, "Farming Methods," *J.M.H.*, p. 20.

203. *Ibid.*, pp. 129–132. See also J. Stewart and G. Fussell, "The Alternate Husbandry," *Journal of the Ministry of Agriculture,* 1929, XXXVI, 214–221.

through the winter was an item to be reckoned with and a
farmer cut down his costs in this respect as much as possible.

If the horse and cattle sales recorded at the Shrewsbury
fairs can be taken as an index, the prices of these animals,
except for occasional years, followed the general upward
trend throughout the Elizabethan and early Stuart period.
Horses in 1560 sold there for an average of slightly above
30s. By 1580 they were around 40s. From 1590 to 1610
the range was between 40s. and 50s.; by 1620 about 54s.;
and from 1630 to 1638 between 77s. and 83s. During the
decade of the Civil Wars it went still higher, at one point
reaching 102s.; but by 1660 there was a marked drop back
to the range of 1620–30, or around 68s.[204] Top prices
throughout this period were, of course, a good deal higher,
and bottom prices a good deal lower than the above figures.
As one would expect, there is a wide range to allow for the
difference in quality of the animals. The Shrewsbury market was one of the most important in the west and buyers
came from all over central and western England. Of the 652
buyers from 1607 to 1628 for whom an occupational or
status term is given, 35 were gentlemen, esquires, and
knights, 94 husbandmen, 117 tradesmen and craftsmen,
and 406 yeomen.[205] No doubt many of the yeomen there
were acting as agents or buyers for gentlemen, but many
were buying in their own right.

Pigs and poultry comprised the remaining livestock that
ran about the farmyards of the yeomen. Swine flourished
particularly in Sussex and other regions where oak forests
were still numerous enough to furnish mast for them, and in
counties where orchards provided an abundance of waste
fruits; but some were raised everywhere. Probably neither
pigs nor poultry were looked upon as a major source of in-

204. These averages, mostly yet unpublished, were worked out by Sir
William Beveridge and his associates for the series on international price
history and are in the MSS. of that committee.

205. Horse and Cattle Sales, 1607–27, in the Municipal MSS. of the
Town Hall of Shrewsbury.

come, though farmers who lived near towns or markets never thought it amiss to have an extra pig or a few "pullen" ready for market day. In fact, they followed the natural course of supplying as nearly as they could anything for which they would have a sale. In his description of Middlesex in 1592, Norden shows how the farmers and their wives there turned everything possible to account: "And theis commonlye are so furnished with kyne that the wife or twice or thrice a weeke conveyeth to London mylke, butter, cheese, apples, peares, frumentye, hens, chyckens, egges, baken, and a thousand other country drugges, which good huswifes can frame and find to gette a pennye."[206] Conies were raised both for home consumption and the market. The keeping of bees was a hobby with many gentlemen farmers and yeomen also frequently had a few stands of bees.[207] Honey was a favorite ingredient in cookery and medical receipts. The Devon records contain many instances of yeomen buying or selling butts of bees, and a Cornish yeoman in a Star Chamber case referred to the payment of eight gallons of honey as his tithe to the prebendary.[208]

Whether the farmer's chief source of profit came from tillage or stock, or a combination of both, it is clear that his was a busy life. The Kentish parson who advised the yeomen that theirs was "no easie, no slight, no lazy employment,"[209] told them nothing that they did not already know. Their first task was to make ends meet; but they were not satisfied with that. Profits as well as subsistence were the goal of the Tudor and Stuart yeomen. And profits in a competitive age like theirs depended on constant care, watchfulness, and industry. Even when not engaged in an actual

206. Norden, *Description of Middlesex,* reprinted in *Description of Essex,* p. xii.

207. There were many treatises written on beekeeping: see Thomas Hill, *The Merveilous governmente . . . of the Bees,* 1568; E. Southeme, *A Treatise concerning the right use and ordering of Bees,* 1593; C. Butler, *Feminine Monarchie,* 1609; J. Levett, *Orderinge of Bees,* 1634.

208. St.Ch. 8, 258/29.

209. Nathaniel Newbury, *The Yeoman's Prerogative,* 1652, p. 12.

task about the place, the head of the house felt obliged to keep an eye on every part of his estate. "The best dung is the master's foot" was an oft-quoted proverb that had grown out of experience. And Thomas Westcote wrote proudly of the Devon yeoman that "his own eye fattens his flock."[210] Entries like the following that appear frequently on the pages of Adam Eyre's diary probably describe the kind of thing most yeomen did.[211]

Walked in the fields before and after dinner.

.   .   .   .   .

Walked in the fields to-day.

.   .   .   .   .

Walked in the fields after supper.

His description of a single day's activity gives a good idea of the variety of tasks that confronted a man who was his own bailiff, mechanic, buyer, and errand boy, and likewise workman on his own farm. Describing a day's work in March, 1648, Eyre states that the first thing in the morning he "sett Geo. Bray on harrowing in the New field." Then he started Edward Marsden to walling a gap in the Croft head. Then he remembered that there were some rake-heads that had to be repaired at the smithy. This involved a trip to the village where he stopped long enough at the ordinary for a drink which cost sixpence, and to buy a cheese from a woman. Then he went home, but was soon off again to get from his neighbor, Reginald Rich, some materials needed for repairing the pigsty. These things seen to, he says he remained "with the work-fokes, hewing wood in the Croft head til night."[212] Other days differed only according to the season's duties unless an interruption came to demand his time for some work of the parish where he was an official, as were most yeomen from time to time.[213]

210. Westcote, *View of Devonshire*, p. 50.
211. *Diary of Adam Eyre, passim.*
212. *Ibid.*, p. 103.   213. See below, chap. IX.

There was no season that did not bring its special labors, and farming calendars, almanacs, diaries, and common-place books give us a pretty clear idea of the way in which the farm work was distributed over the year.

In January and February lands had to be ploughed, har-rowed, and spread with manure. These were also the months for setting trees and hedges, for pruning fruit trees and lopping timber. March and April saw spring activities at full tide. The land for wheat and rye had at that time to be "stirred" again, and the spring sowing done. Vetches were sown as well as the cereal crops of oats and barley. Now also, and in early May, gardens were planted; hop vines were trailed to their poles in hop-growing districts; ditches were scoured; and coppices cleaned. May was also weaning time for the sheep farmers, and a month when sheep had to be watched closely for the rot, especially if it were a wet season. In June, as we have seen, the sheep were washed and sheared. This was also an accepted time for liming, marling, and manuring the fields and for the summer ploughing. July was haymaking time; and if, when it was over, there came a brief midsummer lull before the grain harvest be-gan, it was used by the provident farmer for bringing in coals or getting the winter's wood or turf supply.

Harvest time began in August, and often continued into September. Like planting time, it was one of the busiest seasons of the year. Extra help must be hired, and men rose early and worked late. So did the women, for there were extra mouths to feed. But a quickened tempo in farm life was welcome and the extra labor was carried on with spirit. Harvest was no sooner over than it was time for the rye to be sown; and a little later, often after some of the threshing was done, wheat was planted. Then came a round of other autumn duties: cider and perry were made in the regions where apples and pears grew; trees and hedges were pruned, and rosebushes and bulbous roots planted. The fall planting was finished by November, but a dozen tasks must be done before the winter set in. It was slaughter time for the animals that furnished the winter's supply of meat.

Straw must be laid on moist places to rot for dung to enrich next year's fields. Stock that could not stand the rigors of the out of doors must be housed for the winter. Strawberry and asparagus beds had to be covered.

Autumn was also the time when the larger fairs were held. Fair time was a gala time but a busy one for farmers who sought this opportunity to compare their animals with those of other owners, and to buy, sell, and barter with a sharp eye, replenishing their own needs and getting rid of surplus stock and farm produce.

Plough land was prepared for beans in early December and further preparations for winter were made. The Christmas season brought a few days of respite, with feasting and merriment, when only the farm animals were taken care of and necessary chores done. But almost before the echoes of the Christmas celebration had died away, January had come again with the ploughing and harrowing and spreading of manure; and the topping and lopping of trees. Thus the circle began again and time wove in and out the pattern of a farmer's life.

Whatever the season, the weather was ever a subject of importance, as it must always be to men who make their living from the soil. Heavy winds or a few weeks of rain at a crucial time could mean the difference between well-filled granaries and empty ones, between "sweet" and moldy corn, and between sound animals and diseased ones. Richard Hilton, a wealthy Lancashire yeoman, was away from home in the early autumn of 1662. His servant, aware that the master's mind would be on how things were at home, wrote this rather gloomy report: "I shall gett the wheat to Weysleigh so sonne as dry, but we have continuall wett weather. The lord cease itt, for itt treatens sore."[214] An entry in Adam Eyre's diary tells how the wind blew down some of his shocks of grain. It is perhaps significant that he made no comment except to say that he set them up again.[215] Experi-

214. *Lanc. and Ches. Hist. Soc.,* IV, 190.
215. *Diary of Adam Eyre,* p. 110.

ence had taught him, as it taught other farmers, that the elements were not to be questioned, but accepted and out-witted whenever a man could. Farmers learned that it was cheaper to hire extra men and have a short harvest time than to lengthen the process because of few laborers and risk the onslaught of wet weather.[216] Those who could read scanned their almanacs eagerly and told their neighbors what portents and prognostications they found there.

The profits which a farmer had to show for his pains by the end of the year depended not only upon prices and such imponderables as the weather, but partly also upon his own skill in keeping expenses down to the lowest possible mini-mum. Fortunately not much that was needed for the upkeep of his lands or the business of farming had to be procured from the outside: salt for his stock perhaps, and iron for ploughshares and harrow teeth where they were made of iron; lime, marl, or other fertilizer if the manure produced on the farm were not sufficient for fertilizer; and possibly seed corn to improve next year's yield. Other expenses that had regularly to go on the debit side of his accounts were rents, if any of his lands carried rents; his tithe, paid either in money or in kind; his share in the local poor rate and per-haps in other local levies; and his tax to the king if he were of sufficient substance, as most yeomen were, to be listed in the subsidy book. One other item, that of the hired labor, completes the list of the normal expenses that a farmer had to reckon with as he set about to count up his year's gains, though of course there were continually repairs of building, thatching, and the like, that demanded considerable time and labor and often at least a small outlay of money.

The expense of hired laborers depended much on the farmer's individual needs and especially upon the number of his own household whose service was at his disposal. A yeoman of smaller substance who had several sons to help in the fields, and a daughter or two to assist with the house-work and the dairy, would perhaps require no extra help at

216. Treatise on Husbandry, Sloane MSS. 3815, fol. 72.

all except at harvest time or other busy seasons. The more well-to-do yeoman, however, often had several servants, both men and women, beside extra laborers hired by the day as occasion required. John Wynniat, a Gloucestershire yeoman, in 1608 had eight men servants.[217] Few yeomen needed or could afford to keep as many as this, though one frequently finds in yeoman wills and other documents mention of three, four, or five servants. Mr. Tawney reckons from the Gloucester muster roll that the yeomen of that shire had an average of 1.1 men servants each.[218] There is no source available to show how many women were employed by the same families.

Whether the farmer hired his help by the year, the day, or the piece, the amount of the wage to be paid was more or less outside his control; for wages were prescribed by law, the rate being fixed by the justices of each shire and subject to change from time to time as current conditions demanded. What bargaining went on between master and servant below the prescribed figure it is difficult to say, though there must have been some; for Henry Best tells of the master and his prospective servant going aside to "treat for wages";[219] and Robert Loder apparently bargained with his workmen over the pay they should receive.[220] It is of interest to note that the law called for a maximum, not a minimum wage; the employer should not pay "above" the amount prescribed. The thought of any bargaining that would pull the wages below the figures set down in the official schedule is not a happy one to contemplate; for the figures they disclose are pitiably low, even when one allows for the differences in currency values between that age and our own. Some increase was made in wages paid to servants by the year, particularly to men servants, in the course of the period in question; but neither they nor the day laborers enjoyed a rise in earnings in any degree proportionate with

217. *Men and Armour in Gloucestershire*, p. 59.
218. R. Tawney, "An Occupational Census of the Seventeenth Century," *Eng. Econ. Rev.*, October, 1934.
219. *Best's Farming Book, passim.*
220. *Loder's Farm Journal, passim.*

the rise of prices in both the agrarian and the industrial fields.

The wage schedules differed somewhat from locality to locality, in accord with differing conditions. Those prescribed for servants by the year in the counties of Devon, Dorset, Essex, Hertford, Kent, Rutland, Suffolk, and Yorkshire, at intervals between 1592 to 1635, indicate that yeomen who hired a bailiff or manservant of the best sort paid him from 33s. 4d. (East Riding of Yorkshire, 1593) to 80s. (Dorset, 1635). A woman servant of the best sort, able to take charge of malting, brewing, and baking, could be had for 13s. (East Riding, Yorkshire, 1593) to 40s. (Suffolk, 1630).[221]

The average yeoman would not employ either the highest-paid manservant nor the highest-paid woman servant. He was his own bailiff in husbandry, and the goodwife as a rule managed her own brewing and baking. But wealthy yeomen who had larger establishments to maintain, and other servants to look after, could, and sometimes did, afford a servant of this skill. In the Yorkshire schedule the chief servant is specifically stated to be an "overman," of the kind hired by "a gentleman or rich yeoman that does not labor himself but putteth his whole charge to his servants"; and the chief woman servant as one who is hired by "a gentleman or rich yeoman whose wife doth not take the pains and charge upon her."

But the servants most often employed by the yeomen were those of "the second best sort" and the "third best sort," or the "plain laborer in husbandry," as the latter was sometimes called. The wage for a manservant of the second best ranged from 26s. 8d. (York) to 60s. 10d. (Essex); and of "the third sort," from 16s. 8d. (Essex) to 46s. 8d. (Dorset). Wages for women of the "second best sort" were from 13s. 4d. to 30s. Only one schedule, that of Rutland, named a third classification for women servants. There in 1610, a woman servant to do "out work and drudgery" received 16s., not quite as low as the Yorkshire schedule

221. See Appendix III for table of these wages.

named for a woman servant of the second best. The wages named above were those paid when apparel was furnished. Without apparel, they ran from 3s. to 10s. higher for the servant in each degree. The highest wages registered in the schedules for the above counties were those of Dorset in 1635 and Suffolk in 1630; and the lowest those of the East Riding of Yorkshire in 1593. These were somewhat lower than those of Herts in the preceding year, 1592, and considerably lower than those of Devon in 1594.

Since servants hired by the year lived in the farmer's own household, on fairly intimate and familiar terms with his family, their honesty and general personal desirability were important factors for consideration. Whether or not he "bee a gentle and quiet fellow," whether he "bee addicted to keeping company or noe," and if a woman, whether she "be a good milker" and not of "a sluggish and sleepie disposition," were questions which prospective masters asked concerning the servants they sought to hire.[222]

In addition to the servants hired by the year, yeomen frequently had apprentices "in husbandry" living with them. This might be from choice or as a means of meeting their obligation to the orphaned or charity children of the parish. These young servants received no wage beyond their board unless perhaps a small sum or a suit of clothes at the end of their term of apprenticeship.

But for help in the fields, the practice of hiring servants in husbandry by the year was steadily giving way to the employment of day laborers. An extra mouth to feed had not mattered in the earlier days when there was no market for surplus food. But it was different now that prices were steadily rising; and farmers found it to their advantage to manage with as few servants as possible by the year, hiring extra help only when it was needed.[223] The wages of these men and women, whether by the day or by the piece, were

222. See the interesting description of the way in which the servants and masters met to make agreement with each other for service each autumn in Yorkshire, *Best's Farming Book*, pp. 132–136.

223. See Lord Ernle, *English Farming*, pp. 86–87.

also fixed by the justices, and even by the relative price scale of their own day were pitiably small.

Ordinary laborers could be had from spring until Michaelmas for three to six pence a day with their meat and drink included, or from seven to twelve pence without. From Michaelmas to Lady Day or Easter, the scale was even lower: two to four pence a day with meat and drink, or six to eight pence without, the variations depending largely on the locality. Wage schedules recognized minute differences in particular kinds of work. Hence a man who cut grass earned slightly more than one who reaped wheat, and a woman doing either work received about half as much as a man. A person cutting barley earned more than one who cut oats. Threshing and cleaning grain were usually paid by the quarter. A man threshing wheat or rye received from twelve to twenty-four pence per quarter, whereas the wage for cleaning and threshing barley ran from six to ten pence, and still different sums were set for threshers of oats and peas.[224] Robert Loder, following the wage scale set by the Berkshire justices, often argued with himself whether he did better to hire workmen by the day or by the piece. He appears to have favored the latter practice, though he did not always act on it.

Presentments at the sessions against employers who did not pay wages according to the official schedules are to be found, but they are not numerous. Thomas Wawne, a yeoman of the North Riding of Yorkshire, was presented for "giving wages to Rymer his servant exceeding the rate sett down by the justices."[225] Apparently other employers did not wish to compete. Years of dearth when farmers had less work for them to do brought great suffering to the day laborers.[226] The Lindsay Session Rolls for 1631 are filled with petitions from poor laborers who were unable to collect the

224. See schedules of wages: Devon Sessions Records, 1594; Dorset Sessions Records, 10 Chas. I; Essex Sessions Papers, 1612, *Archæologia*, XI, 201–202; Suffolk wage rates in the MSS. of Cambridge University, Add. XXII, 76.
225. *North Riding Sessions Records*, I, 105, 127.
226. See S.P. 14, CXL, 10.

wages due them. The sums named in their petitions are pathetically small, usually not more than a few pence.[227] Certainly the plight of this class was a sorry one, and it is not surprising that many of them gave up entirely the struggle for independence and joined the hordes of beggars and vagabonds that became a "festering sore" to the Commonwealth.

As the above pages show, the price which a yeoman had to pay for his hired labor was not an exorbitant one, though it was an item of consequence to him. What profits he had left after this and all other expenditures were deducted from his yearly earnings were variable, depending on the individual himself, the quality and extent of his lands, his nearness to markets, and the indeterminate factors of weather, prices, and the like. One wishes that more farmers had kept accounts as detailed and full as those of Robert Loder, who, in spite of occasional inaccuracies in arithmetic and certain omissions, leaves us what must be a reasonably accurate picture of his earnings, expenses, and annual profits for the period 1612–18. His annual earnings during these years ranged from £319 0s. 9¼d. to £453 3s. 0½d. His expenses, including such items as labor,[228] seed corn, tithes, king's tax, poor rate, etc., were from £120 14s. 7d. to £160 12s. 10½d. per annum. This left annual profits ranging from £181 15s. 7¼d. to £292 10s. 2d., the latter for 1619 being the most profitable year of the eight.[229]

Time and again contemporary records describe an individual as a "wealthy yeoman,"[230] or a woman as a "rich yeoman's widow," until one wonders just what the phrase means. Among contemporary treatises which attempt to deal with the incomes of various classes, three are of note for what they say of the yeomen. Sir Thomas Wilson writing

227. Lindsay Sessions Rolls, 1630–31, in the MSS. at the Shire Hall, Lincoln.

228. From 20 to 25 pounds were paid out in wages. Apparently Loder had no servants by the year but hired both by the day and by the piece.

229. *Loder's Farm Journal, passim.*

230. Somerset Sessions Rolls, 1609; Req. 2, 222/33, 190/16; C. Dep. G. 2/1; St.Ch. 8, 155/29; *Diary of John Manningham,* 1868, Cam. Soc., XCIX, p. 20; W. Kemp, *Nine Daies Wonder,* 1884, p. 20.

in 1600 said, "there are many yeomen in divers Provinces in England which are able yerely to despend betwixt 3 or 5 hundred pound yerely by theire Lands and Leases and some twise and some thrise as much."[231] Robert Chamberlayne in 1669 said of the wealth of the yeomen that £40 or £50 was "very ordinary," £100 and £200 apiece in certain counties "not rare," and that sometimes in Kent they were worth £1,000 and £1,500.[232] And Richard Baxter a few years later, though he left out the "very ordinary" £40-to-£50-a-year men, stated that the "better sort of freeholders" who had "lands of their owne besides their farmes," especially those near London, "had per annum 200, 300, 400, yea 500 pounds of lands of their own."[233]

There are, unfortunately, no figures numerous enough to provide a statistical check on these statements.[234] But the references made in many types of records to the wealth of individual yeomen appear on the whole to accord with the range given in the above estimates.

John Ballyston, a Norfolk yeoman under Elizabeth, was described as "very rich in stocke and offereth to buy the farme he useth at 2,050 pounds."[235] John Austin, a yeoman of Sholden, Kent, purchased a manor of 400 acres for £5,000.[236] John Slocombe, a Somerset yeoman, stood as surety for his brother in the sum of £1,000.[237] It was said of Anthony Strong, Sussex yeoman, that he lent £1,500 to his friends and had money, plate, corn, and other goods and chattels valued at £3,000.[238] William Scarlett, a Shropshire yeoman, paid £2,000 for his lands,[239] and Richard Elmhurst was a Yorkshire yeoman to whom Sir George Ratcliffe was indebted in the sum of £2,200.[240] Only wealthy yeomen dealt in sums as high as these.

231. T. Wilson, *The State of England*, 1600, p. 19.
232. *Angliaie Notitiae*, 3d ed., p. 443.
233. *The Rev. Richard Baxter's Last Treatise* (Powicke), 1926, p. 27.
234. Somerset Sessions Rolls, 1609.
235. *Norfolk Arch.*, XXI, 287–290.   236. St.Ch. 8, 37/4.
237. MSS. at the Shire Hall, Taunton, "Unofficial Collection." See Slocombe.
238. St.Ch. 8, 24/5.   239. *Ibid.*, 263/3.
240. *Royalist Composition Papers*, I, *Y.A.S.*, XV, 227.

An Elizabethan benevolence list of a Norfolk hundred named twelve yeomen among the thirty-two "ablest inhabitants" within that hundred. Most of the twelve are described as having £100 per annum in lands and "rich besides," and were assessed from £20 to £40 each for the benevolence. One of them, Stephen Agas, though a £120-a-year man and "out of debt," was "not Riche besides," and therefore was relieved of any payment on the benevolence.[241] Apparently in Norfolk to be a "wealthy yeoman" one must have store of stock and money, or lands beyond the £100-a-year scale. The term was of course a relative one, and differed according to the general scale of wealth in a given area.

Baxter said there were yeomen near London who had from £200 to £500 per annum in lands, who, "in remote parts would passe for gentlemen of great rank."[242] Symonds, writing in 1644, said that £200 per annum was "a great estate" in Cornwall and that there were many gentlemen in Warwickshire with lands from £100 to £400 per year.[243] Thomas Westcote, in 1630, estimated the income of the Devon yeoman to be from £40 to £100 per annum;[244] and in Cornwall and certain sections of the northern counties it was doubtless considerably smaller. The preponderance of yeomen in many of the knighthood composition lists, made out under Charles I for those who had yearly incomes of £40 or more in lands, offers some key to the wealth of the class. A yeoman paid one of the four highest fines demanded from 139 Hampshire compounders in 1631;[245] and of the 850 to 900 compounders listed in Yorkshire alone, it appears that the majority were yeomen.[246]

Of the three contemporary writers whose estimates of the

241. *Norfolk Arch.*, XXI, 287–290.

242. R. Baxter, *Last Treatise*, p. 27.

243. *Diary of the marches of the royal army during the great Civil War*, kept by Richard Symonds (hereafter cited as *Diary of Richard Symonds*), Cam. Soc., LXXIV, 48, 192.

244. Westcote, *View of Devonshire*, p. 49.

245. Letter book of Sir Richard Norton, Add. MSS. 21922, fols. 181–183.

246. See other knighthood composition lists in Add. MSS. 38139, fol. 77b; S.P. 16, XLVI, 2; *ibid.*, CLXXXIX, 46 (1); *Sussex Arch.*, XVI, 45–51; *H.M.C.*, 5th Report, p. 411a.

wealth of the yeomen for the country as a whole are quoted above, only one, Thomas Wilson, makes any attempt to say what percentage of the group belonged in the higher income brackets which he placed for yeomen in "divers provinces in England" at £300 to £500 per annum "and some twise and some thrise as much." Wilson says that at the time of which he wrote, that is, in 1600, there were about 10,000 in the group of "wealthy yeomen" and about 60,000 of the less wealthy. He states that he used the "freeholders' books," made out to provide the sheriff with the eligible jurymen, as the basis for his status classification. This means that his totals, as a key to yeoman population, are conservative; for there were yeomen of both the wealthy and the less wealthy type who were not freeholders. He does not give his source for the figures upon which the estimate of their wealth was made. It was probably merely an estimate based upon the practical observation of a man who had long interested himself in the social and economic trends of his day. As such it is worth something, for Wilson shows himself in other matters to be a pretty careful observer, but it can make no claim to statistical accuracy.[247]

The next attempt at any such classification appears to have been the population analysis of Gregory King made at the close of the seventeenth century. He placed the number of freeholders "of the better sort" at 40,000, and the smaller ones at 160,000. King's aim was a worthy one; but the science of statistics was not yet born and his methods do not stand the test of modern standards in that field. So again the figures must be taken as suggestive rather than conclusive.[248] In general it may be said that those whose incomes reached a hundred pounds a year or more were of "the better sort." They were by no means rare, but sufficiently above their fellows in wealth to be marked as "wealthy yeomen."

But whether rich or poor according to the standards

247. Wilson, *State of England, 1600,* p. 19.
248. G. King, *Natural and Political Observations and Conclusions upon the State and Condition of England* (Hollander), p. 31.

of their group in various localities, they arrived at such wealth as they had in much the same manner. As the foregoing pages have shown, their profits came by small rather than by large gains. And in their struggle for those gains, their own wit, industry, and initiative counted for much. One of their number, Robert Furse of Devon, said of a kinsman and his wife: "When this John and Marye were fyrste maryed theye hadde but lytell, but God did so prosper theym that before she dyed they hadde cccc bullocks and grette store of monye and other quyche stuffe and were as well furnyshede of all thynges in ther house as anye one man of ther degree was in all ther counterye." Most of his ancestors, he points out, were in the beginning men and women of small possessions, but they had "by lytell and lytel" increased their credit and ability.[249]

It is the method one sees in practice among scores of yeomen whose activities are reflected in wills, leases, and deeds, in market records and court records, and in personal accounts. And the picture they reveal is that of a land-hungry, profit-hungry, and profit-conscious class, a group not willing to rest content with whatever Dame Fortune chose to drop into their laps, but one whose members were somehow vaguely conscious that in the scheme of things about them that lady's gifts would be bestowed not necessarily upon her most deserving, but upon her most aggressive children.

249. *Furse Family Book,* p. 171.

VI

BED, BOARD, AND ROOF-TREE

Talk not of goose and capon, give me good beef and bacon,
  And good bread and cheese now at hand:
With pudding, brawn and souse, all in a farmer's house,
  That is living for the husband-man.

Old Ballad

Some respit to husbands the weather may send,
But huswives affaires have never an end.

T. Tusser, Five Hundred Points of Good Husbandry, 1580

ELIZABETHAN writers frequently described a nobleman's house in detail. They wrote about the
people who lived in it and how they lived. In addition, the papers and correspondence of many county families like the Verneys, the Pettys, and the Oxindens are filled
with allusions to their houses, the purchase of house furnishings, household management, and the like. Thus it is
possible to gain a pretty accurate picture of the homes and
domestic interests of the Elizabethan gentry and nobility.

There are fewer sources which yield similar information
about the yeomen and those of the rank below them. Farmers, small tradesmen, and day laborers were not important
people to the literary folk who wrote chiefly of and for the
upper classes. And writing, either as an art or a pastime,
was as yet little practised by the middle and lower classes.

The situation is not, however, as barren as at first appears. Several contemporary writers like William Harrison, Thomas Gainsford, and Thomas Wilson, actuated by
an honest desire to interpret the social scene about them,
took the trouble to deal somewhat with all classes of society.
The few remaining diaries, account books, and commonplace books kept by the yeomen themselves, though often
provokingly silent on points about which they might have

told so much, are also extremely helpful. And the writings of men like Adam Martindale, John Selden, William Harvey, and Richard Baxter, famous sons from yeomen families whose careers took them out of the class to which they were born, frequently contain reminiscent passages that yield interesting glimpses of their boyhood homes and how things were there.

A still richer source which contains a wealth of concrete information on the subject is the extant wills and household inventories of the yeomen. From these documents in which household furnishings with their appraised value are listed item by item and often room by room, it is frequently possible to reconstruct a picture of the entire house, with each article of furniture assigned to its proper room. In addition one not infrequently sees, particularly in the wills, something of the writer's own feeling for his possessions and often even something of his habits of living and domestic relationships.

Another source of information for the buildings, particularly the family dwelling, is the old farmhouse itself, still a familiar feature in many parts of the English countryside. For in spite of neglect, partial decay, and often cheap and unauthentic restorations, many of these ancient houses have retained something of their original character. Some, indeed, have changed little in their exteriors since Elizabethan and Stuart days when they were the newly built homes of the prosperous rural middle class.

Architecture in England, like many things English, developed along marked local lines. Indeed, the manner in which both architectural style and building materials are part and parcel of the locality that produced them is evident in every English countryside where old houses abound, houses which show as much variety as the topography itself. This is particularly true in respect to the smaller and less pretentious dwellings. Their owners had not the means, nor would they see the need, for importing building materials when there was at hand that which local skill and ingenuity had learned to fashion to their purposes. Local architecture, even when restricted to farmhouses, is too broad a subject to include within the scope of this study. But a few observations regarding regional styles and building materials will serve to suggest the kinds of homes the yeomen occupied.

The southeast, including East Anglia, the Thames Valley, and the southern counties east of Dorset, display perhaps the greatest variety in both style and materials. Closest to the continent and haven of refugees at different periods in the nation's history, it was this region that earliest, and to the greatest degree, felt the imprint of outside influences. Here we see traces of Dutch, Flemish, and French Huguenot patterns in both design and workmanship.[1] That it was also a region subject to the ebb and flow of life from a large urban center, as well as one that produced in its own areas varied materials suitable for buildings, helps further to explain its diversity.

The English under Elizabeth and her successors were already conscious of their decreasing timber supply.[2] But the Kentish weald and the forests of Essex, Surrey, and Sussex still produced magnificent materials for the builder. Indeed, Harrison says that most of the buildings of his day were of wood and that only here and there in the west country were the houses of the commonalty not so built.[3] But Harrison, London born, spent most of his life in Essex, and there were probably few sections in England where wood was used as

1. See D. Morand, *Minor Architecture of Suffolk*, 1929.

2. E. 310, 60/6; St.Ch. 8, 55/23; R. Churton, *An Olde Thrift Newly Revived*, 1612; *S.R.*, 35 Henry VIII and 13 Elizabeth. Industries were still for the most part using wood for fuel. The clothing industry in Kent made great inroads on the local fuel supply, as did the hop gardens there which took annually many small timbers for poles. The Sussex iron foundries likewise depleted the forests. See E. Straker, *Wealden Iron*, 1931, p. 125. John Evelyn in 1664 advocated moving all of the "devouring iron mills" to New England, "for they will else ruin Old-England." It would be better, he said, "to purchase all our iron out of America than thus to exhaust our woods at home," *Sylva*, II, 148, quoted in Straker's *Wealden Iron*, p. 124.

3. *Description of England*, Bk. II, 233.

lavishly as in the southeast. Even the farmhouses and small cottages in this region used oak timbers of tremendous weight and thickness, many of which still remain, sturdy and durable. Oak was considered the best of all timbers for durability, with elm a second, and ash a third choice.[4]

But much of the southeastern region combined its timber with other materials. From the fen country southward, including the Thames Valley and as far west as Hampshire and eastern Dorset, there were large districts of chalk and clay. When brickmaking actually came to England or when it was revived, if its use had ever entirely disappeared after the Romans went, is a matter of dispute.[5] But certainly both brick and tile were in common use by Elizabeth's time. And farmhouses of the period still standing, particularly in Surrey, Sussex, and Kent, show how skillfully both were combined with large timbers to make durable and attractive houses. Many leases and deeds of sales entered into by the yeomen of this region prove the existence of local brick and tileworks.

An indenture of 1577 stated that Edward Newton, yeoman, of Sussex, leased "a tile house with the workehouse belonging" from John Gage, Esq., and was permitted to dig clay and "chauke" for the making of brick tile and lime for building materials. According to the agreement, Newton was to furnish all of the brick, tile, and lime that Gage, his landlord, would need for keeping in repair the houses on his

4. R. Churton, *An Olde Thrift Newly Revived,* p. 6. Mr. Martin Briggs has pointed out that boarded houses, that is, houses with stripped weather boarding or clapboard exteriors so familiar among the early homes of the New England colonists, were numerous at the end of the sixteenth century in East Anglia, particularly in Essex. Being less durable than heavy timbered or stone houses, there are few of them left there. But the examples that Mr. Briggs has discovered give convincing support to his theory that when the colonists, large numbers of whom came from East Anglia, built the first clapboard cottages in their frontier villages on the Atlantic seaboard, they were simply making use of material that was at hand and a type of building already familiar. See Briggs, *The Home of the Pilgrim Fathers in England and America,* 1932.

5. See summary of opinions in A. K. Wickham, *The Villages of England,* 1932, p. 26.

five manors. In return he would receive 8s. a thousand for bricks and tiles, and 6s. a load for the lime.[6] Another yeoman, Jeffry Widger, who leased a manor house and certain demesne lands from the same landlord in 1614 at the high rent of £190 per annum, was to have "20,000 tyle from the tyle oast to be imployed upon the mansion house."[7] Other indentures show that local lime and brick kilns were numerous in Sussex and Kent.

It was natural that builders should make the most of these materials; for little native stone suitable for building purposes was found in the southeast. An exception to this was the flint that existed plentifully in Norfolk and Suffolk where it was cleverly combined with timber to produce houses, many of which still look as if they would last for centuries. Flint, brick, half-timber and plaster, half-timber and tile hangings, and variations of these combinations comprised the chief building materials from which the yeomen living in the southeast constructed their dwellings. And within this range a varied local architecture grew up from district to district. The roofs were mostly of thatch, though tile was beginning to be used in the southernmost parts. Norfolk thatchers still claim a superior skill in their craft which has in some instances been handed down from father to son for generations. The roofs were steeply pitched, which made for durability as well as good drainage.[8]

Moving westward from the southeast the brick-tile-flint country begins to disappear, though along the West Sussex downs, and in the southern chalk hills from the Chilterns to Dorset, there are some stone, clay, and flint.

Few counties of England offer a better opportunity for the study of old houses of the smaller type than Dorset. Whether one sets out from Sherborne or Dorchester or from

6. Sussex MSS., Gage Papers, Box 16, No. 14.
7. *Ibid.*, Box 13, No. 7.
8. The deposition of Robert Cannon, a yeoman of Swaffam Market, Norfolk, taken in 1585, shows how important a matter it was to have drainage that would adequately carry away the water that dripped from the "evesinges," Req. 2, 193/5.

some other center east or west, he cannot go many miles without discovering farmhouses that have changed little in exterior since they were built in the sixteenth and seventeenth centuries. They are made almost entirely of plaster with some timber. Richard Symonds, who traveled with the King's armies in 1644, made interesting observations on the local architecture of the various regions through which he passed. He noted particularly the white chalk quarries of Dorset that furnished material both for local houses and for the fences that divided the lands.[9] The houses in Dorset also had thatched roofs of a type still commonly used in many of the villages there.

Devon yeomen lived chiefly in cob houses. Cob was a mixture of mud with straw, chalk, gravel, broken bits of slate, or whatever the locality afforded that would give substance and strength to the hardened mass. Little wood went into the farmhouses in Devon. It was saved for churches and for the great houses. Little stone also was used except for foundations. The ancient Devon saying that "all cob wants is a hat and a good pair of shoes" referred to the thatched roof and stone foundations that went with the mud-plaster houses. Symonds spoke of some stone around Exeter that was red like the soil, but there, too, he says, "ordinary howses are of soyle mingled with straw, without postes." Of the Plymouth region he wrote: "All the howses be clay without any timber in the wall, except the doores, roofe, and windowes which is the fashion of the Country."[10]

One of the few places in the southwest where native stone was extensively used for small homes was Cornwall. Here one who travels from Land's End around the coast to St. Ives may still see these ancient small houses of granite that look for all the world like outgrowths of the rocky surfaces on which they are built. Here wood was not even used for doorposts and corners, which were chiefly made of a "hard shiny stone like grey marble." Much slate of a bluish color was quarried around Liskard. North of Dorset in Somerset

9. *Diary of Richard Symonds*, p. 151.   10. *Ibid.*, pp. 39, 151.

considerable stone was available and was used for houses as well as for the walls that separated inclosed fields.[11]

Northward in the Cotswold district the sturdy houses for which that locality is still famed were in the building. Since the fifteenth century the farmers in this region, with the exception of brief periods, had done well with their wool, and substantial houses of native stone ranging in color from a cream or yellow to a grayish rose, with mullioned windows and thatched or slate roofs, gave evidence of the prosperity of both yeomen and merchants.[12] Beyond the Cotswolds where the western Midlands reach the Severn Valley, the sandstone district yielded a reddish stone that added warmth and color to churches and great houses, but yeomen and lesser folk did not have their houses made of it, for it was difficult to quarry and hence both troublesome and expensive. They built chiefly of wood and plaster. Black and white timbered farmhouses which date in whole or in part from the late sixteenth and early seventeenth centuries may yet be seen as far north as Chester, and are particularly numerous in parts of Warwick and Worcestershire, and as far west as Herefordshire.

North of an imaginary line drawn from Lincoln to Chester native gray stone was the common building material; and there are still many ancient farmhouses to demonstrate its durability. The Huddersfield district is especially rich in houses built by the yeomen and yeomen clothiers of that region in the early seventeenth century.[13] And a drive along one of the lesser highways such as the Bilsdale road from Stokesley south to Helmsley, and thence across the Hambleton hills, rewards one with glimpses of many farmsteads, a part or the whole of which belong to this period. Even

11. *Ibid.*, pp. 104, 151.

12. See A. Broadbent and A. Minoprio, *Minor Domestic Architecture in Gloucestershire*, 1931; W. Davies and E. G. Dawber, *Old Cottages, Farm Houses and Other Stone Buildings in the Cotswold District*, 1915.

13. W. Crump, *The Yeoman Clothier*. See also L. Ambler, *Old Halls and Manor Houses of Yorkshire*, Plates LX, LXXXVIII, XC, XCVII, XCIX, and pp. 67, 90. The houses shown in these plates have all been identified by Mr. Crump as homes of seventeenth-century yeomen.

those of a later date have in many instances followed the old lines.

Whatever the local differences either of style or materials, there is one respect in which all contemporary writers who dealt with the homes of the commoners agreed, namely, that in regard to both size and comfort the lesser folk of the Elizabethan period had better homes to live in than had their ancestors. It was not only noblemen and prosperous gentry, they note, who were making additions to ancestral dwellings or erecting new ones for themselves and their posterity. Even without this testimony, the recurrence in scores of yeoman wills and inventories of such phrases as "the newe parlour," the "newe chamber," the "parlour I had latelie built," or the "old howse," serves to tell the story in incontrovertible fashion.

Robert Furse of Devon wrote in 1593 that he built "the porch and enterye and seled the hall and glaste all the wyndoes" in his ancestral home.[14] Other prosperous yeomen like the Martindales of Lancashire "pulled downe the old house quite to the ground" and built "that strong and large stone house that now stands in its place."[15] In fact, Adam Martindale's account of the changes in living arrangements that followed each other in comparatively rapid sequence in his father's household is characteristic, we may believe, of what took place in the history of many yeomen families.

Martindale says that his father and mother had first lived in "the old house," apparently a wooden structure. But as the family grew in size and means, the "new house" was built and annexed, as was the practice in some of the northern counties, to the new barn that went up at the same time.[16] This house was the "pretty neat habitation" in which the diarist was born in 1623. In time, with an increase in the corn acreage and the corn yield, the elder Martindale de-

14. *Furse Family Book*, p. 181.

15. *Life of Adam Martindale*, pp. 1–2.

16. This practice of building a dwelling connected with the barn was common on the continent for smaller houses, but in England it was customary only in sections of the north. See Harrison, *Description of England*, Bk. II, 233–238.

cided that the family should move back into the old house in order that the new one could be thrown wholly with the barn "to furnish him with more stowage for his corn." It is significant of the yeoman's scale of values that the family temporarily put up with less good living quarters in order to provide more room for granaries and livestock. But again, "in the process of time," the original "old house" was torn away, the second one continued to be used as an enlargement of the barn, and the new stone house larger and more durable than either of its predecessors was erected as a dwelling for the family.[17]

Many of the wealthy gentry and nobility in the process of erecting spacious and beautiful homes were given to architectural experiment, particularly in matters of ornament and detail: "If ever curious building did flourish in England, it is in these our yeares."[18] But this fashion for the most part did not extend to the yeomen and lesser folk. Their homes were built chiefly for durability. And though bearing the stamp of individuality placed upon them by local differences, they followed in the main the traditional lines of the small English house, a compact rectangular structure of one-and-a-half or two stories.[19]

The size of the house depended largely on the ability and needs of the individual family. Thomas Austin, yeoman, of the parish of Farham, Hampshire, who suffered loss by fire in 1631, had lived in a house of "eight bayes of buildinge," that is of eight rooms. But this included outbuildings;[20] whereas the home of William Cheaney, a wealthy yeoman of Leftwich, Chester, was described as "an ancient large house of tenn bayes of building," not including outhouses of which there were several, and a barn of "five bayes."[21]

Not all of the household inventories name the rooms in which the appraisers found the furnishings they list, but

17. *Life of Adam Martindale*, pp. 1–2.
18. *Description of England*, Bk. II, 238.
19. G. Markham, *The English Husbandman*, pp. 24–25.
20. Order Book, Hants Sessions Records, 1631.
21. Chester Quarter Sessions Records, 1630, No. 102.

fortunately scores of them do. From these it would seem
that the houses of the yeomen ranged from the two- to three-
room dwellings of the poorest members of the group to the
eight or ten rooms, or even more, of the well to do. An examination of several hundred inventories suggests that the
majority fell within a five- to nine-room range including
one or more such appendages as milkhouse, malthouse, and
the like; or a three- to six-room range if these additions
were not considered a part of the dwelling, a less common
practice.[22] Not infrequently, of course, well-to-do yeomen
occupied the "mansion house" or "capitol messuage" of the
familiar Elizabethan type which was often included in their
leases of manors or in their purchases of the demesne lands
of disintegrating manors. Yeomen in very poor sections, on
the other hand, may have been housed less well than the
above range indicates.[23]

In respect to interiors, Elizabethan and Stuart farmhouses still standing offer little aid. For though exteriors
have often changed but little except for porches, entries,
and other details that can easily be identified, it is rare to
find a house that has not been remodeled inside. Often alterations have been made not once but many times, as the
style of living and the taste of housewives in succeeding generations has changed. For the original arrangement of the

22. The largest single collection of inventories that I have used is that
in the Lincoln Probate Registry where there are hundreds belonging to
this period alone. There are, however, good smaller collections such as
those in the Bedford County MSS., and the MSS. of the Ipswich Public Library. They are, of course, also to be found in twos and threes in
almost any collection of family papers, and in many local miscellaneous
collections. Printed inventories are, as a rule, less valuable since they
are usually abstracts which do not give the goods according to the rooms
in which the appraisers found them. One of the largest printed collections
of such abstracts is that entitled *Wills and Inventories,* in the Surtees
Society Publications, XXVI, XXXVIII, CXII, CXLII. Another is the
Lancashire and Cheshire Wills, in the Chetham Society Publications,
XXX, LI, LIV. For the Huddersfield district I have made use of Mr.
Crump's analysis. Wills, like inventories, are scattered everywhere among
local records. But the largest manuscript collections that I have used are
those at Somerset House, and in the probate registries of Lincoln, York,
and Lewes.

23. See D. Tough, *The Last Years of a Frontier,* 1926, pp. 41–42.

rooms, therefore, and their furnishings, the inventories are again our best guide. They do not always tell all that one would like to know, but on certain important points they are both full and exact.

In every yeoman's house, as in more pretentious homes, the main room was the "hall," styled sometimes, "the bodie of the house," or simply "the Howse," eloquent testimony of its prominence in earlier days. Though no longer enjoying a complete monopoly, the hall still remained the living-room for the family. Here they also dined, and here before the open fire on winter evenings their guests were entertained. The furnishings of the hall naturally differed somewhat in quality with the wealth and position of the owner, but certain articles were practically always to be found there: a long table, with perhaps a smaller one; one or two forms or benches with numerous chairs and stools; a cupboard and perhaps a chest; and the fireplace equipment including andirons, tongs, bellows, fire shovel, and warming pan. If the house did not have a kitchen, and a good many of them did not, the cooking was done in the hall, and "pott hangers," "dripping panns," spits, and numerous kettles and pots were included in the fireplace furnishings.

The fireplace or grate with its chimney marks one of the principal innovations in the homes of the commoners of this period. William Harrison quoted old men yet living in his day who pointed to the number of chimneys lately erected as one of the great changes that had come within their memory.[24] Prior to this time all except the wealthy in great houses warmed themselves and cooked their food at a fire built either against the wall, if it were a stone house, or in the middle of the hall on a stone or earthen base,[25] from which the smoke escaped as best it could through the *louvre* in the roof.[26]

24. *The Description of England*, Bk. II, 239.

25. An excellent example may be seen at "The Pedlars," a partly restored house just outside the village of Sundridge, near Sevenoaks, once the home of a Kentish yeoman.

26. See diagrams of various types of chimneys in G. C. Rothery and A. L. Kocher, *English Chimney-pieces*.

Another innovation found in the hall, and sometimes in the other rooms of a yeoman's house, likewise signifying their advance in ability and living standards, was the glass in the windows. Richard Carew in 1602 spoke of the window glass in the homes of private men as a late introduction.[27] And James Aubrey wrote in 1671 that within his remembrance "copyholders and ordinary poor people had none," though such alteration had come that "now the poorest people upon almes have it."[28]

The yeomen looked upon these improvements with pride; and how much they added to the comfort of those who had only recently acquired such advantages can scarcely be realized by an age that takes smokeless, lighted houses for granted. We have already noted how Robert Furse "glaste all the wyndoes" in his Devonshire house at the time that he was enlarging it.[29] Both chimneys and window glass were cherished as personal belongings, and were named in wills along with articles of furniture and other bequests: "and also I give to her the chimney in the house,"[30] says a Lancashire yeoman in his will of 1628. A Yorkshire yeoman in 1607 bequeathed "to Thomas, my sonn, all the glasse in and about my howse."[31] Similar bequests occur again and again in yeoman wills.

In the hall also hung whatever arms or weapons the master of the house possessed. Bows and arrows, the pike, corselet, sword, longsword, billstaff, and daggers are among those items mentioned in inventories, though no individual had all of them. Only along the borders were yeomen still outfitted with armor reminiscent of the medieval period. Here late in Elizabeth's reign "a coate of plaite" and a "Stuffed jacke and a steile cappe" are listed among their

27. Richard Carew, *A Survey of Devon and Cornwall in 1602,* p. 142.

28. John Aubrey, *Natural History of Wiltshire,* 1847, p. 14.

29. *Furse Family Book,* p. 181.

30. *Lancashire and Cheshire Wills,* Chet. Soc., N.S., XXVIII, 37. The word "chimney" was often used, as apparently in this case, to mean the grate or irons, the fireback, etc., which were movable. It was a later development to have the entire fireplace stationary.

31. *Knaresborough Wills,* Sur. Soc., CX, 2.

possessions.[32] But after the accession of James Stuart brought to an end the desultory warfare that had characterized the border region from earliest times, articles of the above type hung in a farmer's hall only as mementoes of other days.

There was little attempt at decoration or ornamentation in any part of the dwelling. An exception is the tapestry or "Painted cloth" that often hung in the hall of even the poorest yeoman's home. Those that were woven, the "carpets," hung either on the wall or were used as coverings for tables and chests. In addition wealthy yeomen, copying the neighboring gentry, frequently had the ceilings and sometimes the walls of their halls and parlors wainscoted. Wainscoting like the window glass and chimney was considered a part of the movable house furnishings: "the wainscott in the hall and in the parlour," and "all the glasse about my house," are bequests mentioned in the will of John Tyther, a Shropshire yeoman.[33] John Butler, yeoman of Surrey, names "all the wainscotte, settles, benches, glasse windowes and paynted cloths" as gifts to his heirs.[34]

The cupboard that stood in the hall held the mugs, bowls, platters, and other dishes on which the food was served at the long table. Wooden trenchers were still in everyday use among the yeomen, but most of them also now had good store of pewter in their cupboards. William Harrison contrasted the old days when "a man should hardlie find four peeces of pewter (of which one was peradventure a salt) in a good farmer's house," with his own time when, in spite of increased rents, every one of them had grown so prosperous that he was not satisfied without "a faire garnish of pewter on his cupboard . . . a silver salt, a bowle for wine (if not a whole neast) and a dozzen of spoones to furnish up the sute."[35]

Even inventories of the poorer members of the group

---

32. *Will and Inventories,* Sur. Soc., XXXVIII, 99.
33. P.C.C., 20 Soame.
34. *Surrey Arch.,* XII, 196. See also P.C.C., 60 Wood, 1 Welden.
35. *Description of England,* Bk. II, 240.

show from half-a-dozen to a dozen pieces of pewter, while
those of the men of average wealth or above often mentioned
from forty to fifty pieces. It is not true that all of them had
the silver salt or silver bowl and a dozen spoons, to which
Harrison refers, though they were no great rarity. It may
even be that in the prosperous country communities near
London which Harrison knew, the majority had them. Of
the dozen-and-a-half silver spoons named in the will of a
Yorkshire yeoman, six were of the popular "apostles" pattern.[36] It is these small amounts of silver that one finds enumerated in scores of wills and inventories of the yeomen: a
silver cup, or maybe two or three, and a dozen or so of
spoons. Sometimes a single spoon, or two or three, are mentioned, and often a set of a dozen or half-dozen spoons was
divided so that each daughter, granddaughter, or god-
daughter might have one or two apiece. Occasionally, to be
sure, yeomen possessed a larger store of silver than this,[37]
but as a rule it was chiefly pewter that filled the cupboards
which stood in their halls.

Next to the hall the most important room in a yeoman's
house was the "parlour" which contained the "best bedd"
and was also used as a semi-living-room. William Harrison's old neighbors who spoke of the increase in chimneys,
and of pewter and silver among farmers, noted also how
many more beds and linens they had now than in former
times: "If it were so that our fathers or the good man of the
house, had within seven years after his marriage purchased
a matteres or flockbed, and thereto a sack of chaffe to rest
his head, he thought himself well lodged," but now, "every
farmer has three or four feather beds so many coverlids and
carpets or tapestrie."[38] Inventories of yeomen amply bear
out this statement. Four or five beds were the rule in the
homes of those of merely ordinary means; eight or ten were
by no means unusual, and some had more. William Streaffe,
a wealthy Kentish yeoman, bequeathed seven feather beds,

36. Wills in York Probate Registry, XXV, 1168.
37. See below, p. 240.
38. *Description of England*, Bk. II, 240–241.

nine flock beds, and one of down to his heirs.[39] Laborers still slept on straw beds and there were some of these still in the houses of yeomen, but feather beds and flock beds predominated.

The numbers of sheets that filled chests and presses cannot fail to impress one who has noted the lack of them among the possessions of the lower classes at an earlier date. "Harden sheets," "canvas sheets," "hempen sheets," "Bockram sheets," "Holland sheets," "flaxen sheets," and "linnen sheets" are named in yeoman wills and inventories. Even the poorest among them often boasted six or eight pairs, while ten, fifteen, and twenty pairs were not at all uncommon. In addition, pillows, bolsters, and "pillow beares," blankets, and coverlids, the latter worked frequently in the popular flower and bird designs, made up the furnishings of the beds. Older people could recall the days when both grownups and children had lain on straw pallets on the floor, without pillows and with but thin and coarse coverings. Certainly Elizabethan yeomen were sleeping in greater comfort than their ancestors had enjoyed.

Their bedsteads were sometimes still the homemade "trestled" type, put together with removable pegs. But "joined" beds were now also familiar articles in the homes of most yeomen, as was joined furniture of all kinds, proof of their ability to patronize the cabinetmakers whose craft was growing apace. Harrison colors the picture a bit when he speaks of the many farmers who had "their beds furnished with silke hangings, and their tables with fine naperie." It is not an overstatement for the homes of the wealthy yeomen, and perhaps it was true of many in the environs of London where additional "fineries" were the natural result of both urban influence and prosperity. But in the ordinary yeoman's home, if one may judge from the contents of wills and inventories drawn from a wider area, there was frequently only one bed, at most two or three, that were curtained; and the "hangings" were rarely of silk.

39. P.C.C., 7 Welden.

The claim of a good store of "fine naperie" for the table is better substantiated. To be sure, the rather heavy linens in common use were perhaps less "fine" than durable; but a sizable supply of tablecloths and napkins of some variety is a common item in most yeoman inventories. In counties like Bedford and Lincoln, where a flax wheel as well as a woolen wheel was in practically every farmer's house, and often also a loom,[40] an amazing amount of linens was hoarded away for the daughters' marriage chests. Often the spinning wheel, or wheels, stood in the parlor, but they were carried from room to room as the housewife or her daughters found convenient.

Aside from the parlor, the other bedrooms frequently had two or three beds to the room, with possibly a chair or two and a chest. This last-named article merits a word of attention because it is to be found in every room in the house. The importance of the chest that stood in the master's bedroom and held the "evidences" of his property, often the sole proof he had of the title of his lands, has already been mentioned. But there were also chests in the other rooms, and sometimes two or three. Chests were the accepted repositories for everything that must be kept free from dust, or out of reach of hungry mice or prying servants' eyes. Chests in bedrooms held extra linens, blankets, and "coverletts." Pewter in general use was usually kept in the cupboard in the hall, but choice pieces and whatever silver the family possessed were packed away in a chest until the parson or the neighboring gentry came to dine, or a wedding or other festivity gave occasion for bringing it out. If the goodman had any money on hand it was usually hidden away in a chest that could be locked. And in the kitchen and storerooms plain chests served as bins to keep seeds and foodstuffs safe. Many of the oak chests in the wealthier homes were carved to match the other furniture.

The kitchen, if the house had one, contained some of the utensils already mentioned in connection with the fireplace furnishings. Here also were extra pots, kettles, vats, and

40. See above, pp. 164–165.

smaller articles like the mortar and pestle, bowls, chopping knives, and various kinds of cutlery.

In addition to the hall, parlor, bedrooms, and kitchen, the other rooms, whether joined to the rest of the house as was customary in many places or set apart, were furnished to meet the needs their names suggest. The dairy house contained "milking bowles," "milke tubbs," a churn, a salting trough, crocks, firkins, and, in regions where dairying was carried on extensively, cheese vats and a cheese press. In the bakehouse or "boulting house" there were the molding trough, molding boards, quernes, "boulting arkes," sacks, bags, and measures of various sizes. The furnishings in the malthouse and the brewhouse depended somewhat on the extent of the activities carried on there. If only a little ale were brewed there might be simple arrangements for it in the buttery or bakehouse, but in many homes a special room, either adjoining the house or standing apart, was designed for this purpose. At the death of Samuel Feake, a gentleman of Norfolk, Thomas Beverly, a neighboring yeoman, bought the equipment of his brewhouse. The purchase included barrels, pipes, firkins, troughs, tubs, "tumeles with brass spouts," a horse mill with two stones and a hopper, a "floor of iron," and an iron door, coolers, a "cistern of lead," one "gild pott," and numerous small articles.[41] In many houses at least one room, perhaps an unfurnished room upstairs, was used as a storeroom with maybe an extra bed in it for emergencies. Here were stored away bags of wheat or rye, flitches of bacon, odd pieces of lumber, old furniture or farm implements in want of repair, and "other hustlement," as such odds and ends were called.

Houses were lighted by candles and the open fire. Most of the candlesticks were of brass and pewter, though many yeomen also owned a pair or more of "latten" candlesticks, made of brass with a slight pewter alloy; and sometimes they boasted one or two silver ones.

Set apart but a little way from the house, or annexed to

41. "Ancient Brewing Tools," *Eastern Counties Collecteana*, 1872, pp. 30–31.

it, as was the practice in some parts of the north, was the barn, called in parts of Yorkshire the "laithe," and in the border counties the "garthe" or "staggarthe." Here the "husbandly furniture" of the farmer was kept: ploughs, harrows, wains, the "horse gear," and "plow gear." These, along with whatever hay, grain, or other crops were garnered into the barn or standing in the field, and the livestock, were usually included in the inventory and were therefore reckoned in the estimate of a personal estate.

The total sum of the personal estate, calculated from the itemized accounts of the inventory, is of little value as a key to the actual wealth of the yeomen; for their chief wealth was in their lands. But it does furnish an interesting index of their scale of living.

Figures taken from contemporary appraisals attached to the wills and inventories of 2,172 yeomen of Berkshire, Lincoln, and Sussex between 1556 and 1650 show an average personal estate of approximately £160. This figure is somewhat lower than the average in any of the three counties would be if complete figures were available; for it was customary for the wills of the wealthiest yeomen to be registered in the Prerogative Court at Canterbury rather than in their local dioceses. Scores of their wills are still available in the Canterbury court records, but unfortunately the estimate of the estate is not attached. Even in the records from which the above averages were taken the estates of certain individuals among the more well to do run as high as seven, eight, and nine hundred pounds, and sometimes higher.[42]

The inventories show, however, that the standard of living, insofar as the quality and variety of house furnishings reveal it, was remarkably similar among the yeomen of greater and less wealth. The difference lay in the number of rooms to be furnished rather than the style, variety, and

42. The figures for the estates of the Berkshire yeomen were drawn from the wills in the MSS. of the Berks Court of the Archdeaconry, in the collection at Somerset House. The estate evaluations of the Lincoln yeomen were taken from the MSS. in the Probate Registry at Lincoln. Those for the Sussex yeomen are from the Administration books in the Lewes Probate Registry.

quality of the furnishings. The estates of four yeomen, chosen at random from several collections of inventories, will illustrate this point. They are evaluated as follows: John Sewall of Suffolk, £75 12s. 4d.;[43] John Goodman of Northamptonshire, £245 13s. 2d.;[44] William Burden of Bedfordshire, £513 3s. 6d.;[45] Richard Clarke of Lincoln, £861 5s. 8d.[46]

In size, the houses of the four men varied from Sewall's five rooms to Clarke's eleven; but their house furnishings show little difference either in variety or in the value ascribed to each item. Each of the four had at least one, but not more than two, posted beds with hangings; each had joined furniture except perhaps for an odd piece or two; all had good store of linens and a good supply of pewter in the cupboard. There are, of course, exceptions to be found at both ends of the scale. There was an occasional yeoman like Thomas Harcock of Suffolk, whose possessions, according to the inventory taken in 1583, show a distinctly lower standard than prevailed in the homes of most yeomen. His dwelling had only three rooms and a dairy house. His "trestled" bed and "bourde bedstede" were of the type found in commoners' homes before joined furniture came into common use. And the generally poor character of his other furniture is suggested by the manner in which it is described as "an ould cheste," "an ould churne," an "ould cubbard," "ould cushiones," and the like. He had but one tablecloth and but a small supply of pewter. In his farmyard ran one sow, one "shote," a gander and two geese, a cock and five hens. He had one mare and colt, three sucking calves, and, this being a dairy section, nine milch cows. His entire personal estate was valued at £27 0s. 2d.[47]

At the other end of the scale we find wealthy members of the group whose homes boasted one or more articles normally found only in the homes of the gentry: a desk, a book-

43. Ipswich MSS., 307/16.   44. Northants MSS., IL, 7.
45. Inventories for 1619, Bedford County MSS.
46. Inventories, Lincoln Probate Registry, By, I, 27.
47. Inventory of T. Harcock, Ipswich MSS., 347/16.

case, a pair of virginals, wicker chairs, needlework stools, upholstered chairs, "Turkey-worke cushions"; and silver cups, bowls, and spoons to the number of thirty or forty pieces rather than the occasional few pieces found in the cupboards of most yeomen.[48] But this standard of living was as much above that of the majority of the group as that of Thomas Harcock was below. Later on, wealthy yeomen were to acquire more adornments and luxuries; but during the period when their wealth was in the making they preferred to live simply, and to invest their money in land and livestock rather than in more elaborately furnished houses.[49]

Young people, newly married, even those from prosperous homes, were expected to set up for themselves very simply at first, and to accumulate as they could by their own efforts. Simon Rider was a Staffordshire yeoman of considerable ability. But when his daughter Joan was married in 1601, she began housekeeping with the following "marriage goods": one joined bedstead, a press, one feather bed and one flock bed, two bolsters, two pillows, a "bed hilling,"[50] two blankets and a "twillye,"[51] five pairs of sheets, and two "pillow beers," one tablecloth and a half-dozen table napkins, two candlesticks, nine pieces of pewter, a salt, one brass pot, and one brass pan. In order that she might by her own industry add to her supply of linens, she received

48. *Cantiana,* XVIII, 223; Lincoln Wills, Lincoln Prob. Reg., By, 15.

49. After the Civil War there was a notable increase in the scale of living among the well-to-do yeomen. This was probably partly due to the growing taste of all of the lower classes for more refinements and luxuries and partly to the fact that many of the gentry who threw in their lot with the Stuarts during the wars were later forced to sell much of what they possessed in order to clear themselves of debt. Plate and furniture thus given up fell frequently into the hands of thrifty yeoman families so that in the last part of the century the inventories of prosperous yeomen more nearly represent those of the gentry of the previous generation. The inventory of the goods of Cornelius Humphrey, a Sussex yeoman who died in 1697, will serve as an illustration: Humphrey lived in a nine-room house (not counting milkhouse, brewhouse, malthouse, and washhouse) furnished with rugs, a desk, mirrors, "18 Turkey chairs," curtained beds, etc. He had twenty-three tablecloths, seven dozen table napkins, and a good store of silver. *Sussex Arch.,* VI, 192–196.

50. A covering or "bed-quilt."   51. A twilled covering.

nine "knitchen" of hemp and five of flax. In addition, she was allowed ten pounds in "readie money" for taking care of other needs as they arose.[52] Simon Rider was an able, upstanding citizen in his community, and there is no reason to believe that his daughter and her husband were not receiving what was considered a good start in life. Their further advance depended on their own efforts.

But if the homes of the yeomen were modest compared with the spacious manor houses of the country gentry, so were they commodious in contrast to the hovels and cottages that housed the thousands of laborers and poorer tenant farmers. They were for their day homes of substantial comfort, and were so regarded.

It was also practicability rather than beauty that determined the location of their houses and the nature of their surroundings. Little thought was given to appearances though already gardens, that happy result of the Englishman's climate and his skill, added beauty and color for a part of the year to the farm and village scene. Large gardens of formal design with a marked Italian influence were the delight of the gentry and nobility of the period. These were beyond the means of farmers and their wives, but smaller gardens set their cottages off to great advantage. The record made by an admiring neighbor of all the flowers that were in bloom in the garden of "Goodwife Cantrey," a Northamptonshire yeoman's wife, on the twenty-eighth of July, 1658, suggests a pleasing picture, and one that has become traditional to the English countryside in midsummer.[53]

There were double and single larkspurs; double and single Sweet Williams; three kinds of spiderwort; lupin in four colors, "the great blew, the little blue, the yellow and the white"; purple and white "scabious"; marigolds; Life Everlasting; London pride; "hollioakes" (hollyhocks); and many other well-known favorites. Like every competent

52. Rider Commonplace Book, p. 122.
53. Northants MSS., FH, 2452. See in same collection the description of the garden of Goodman Hilliard.

housewife, Goodwife Cantrey had planned her garden for usefulness as well as beauty; and in addition to the above, it contained the "double fennell flower," chief ingredient for a brew that was held good for weak eyes; camomile, extensively used as a remedy for headaches; white lilies, "good to break a byle"; goats rue, "to brue in ale against the plague"; and "double fetherfewle" that was "good against a shaking fever."[54] Well might all yeomen say as did the countryman to the citizen in a contemporary dialogue: "You are still sending to the apothecaries and still crying out to 'fetch Master Doctor to me': but our apothecary's shop is our garden full of pot-herbs, and our doctor is a good clove of garlic."[55]

To have the proper garden herbs for the preparation of this or that salve, drink, or other medical concoction was a matter of first importance both to the farmer's own family and to his livestock whose frequent distempers were the cause of much concern. Dried saffron was held effective for diseases of the heart and stomach; aniseed was good for "opening the pipes"; "Elly campane root dryed powdred and druncke" was used "to kill the itches"; while columbine, tansy, stitchwort, and a host of other leaves, roots, seeds, and barks were in constant use.[56] The housewife learned not only what to plant, but also when to garner her herbs to procure the best results. The leaves and flowers of plants were held especially efficacious from Lady Day to midsummer, the stalks and fruits from midsummer to Michaelmas, and the roots from Michaelmas to Lady Day.[57]

Only one flower in the above garden suggests a possible importation, the Indian tuft; and this, like the "French buttons" and the "orange coloured Turk's cap" mentioned in the accounts of other gardens, may refer to the peculiar

54. The uses of these herbs were taken from various cookery and medicine books. See below, p. 248 n.

55. "The Great Frost," *An English Garner, Social England Illustrated* (Lang), p. 167.

56. W. Lawson, *The Country Housewife's Garden,* pp. 9–15; see also G. Markham, *The Country Housewife's Garden,* pp. 88–95.

57. Sloane MSS. 556, fol. 1b.

appearance of the flowers rather than their origin. It was a period, however, when a good many shrubs and flowers from the outside were learning to accommodate themselves to English soil. These, at first, were chiefly in the gardens of the gentry. It was they who read the new books on gardening and brought home seeds and cuttings of new plants and flowers when they traveled in foreign lands. For at heart they were ever a provincial lot, the English gentry; and when a new shrub or blossom caught the eye, whether in the garden of an Italian villa or a French château or in the courtyard of a German castle, they were ready at once to wonder how it would thrive in their own gardens at home or against the walls of their own manor houses. It was an observing playwright who had a shipwrecked Devonshire squire remark as he looked about him on the hills of Spain: "A pleasant country! . . . I would I had a Matter, or a Mannour, indeede, of a 1000 acres of these woodlands and room to set it in Devonshire. I would compare with any prince between Tavistocke and Parridice for an orchard."[58]

But if the gentry were the innovators, they did not maintain exclusive rights over their findings. Seeds and cuttings were passed about the countryside, and plants with strange names came in time to flourish in the gardens of those who had no knowledge or thought of their origins. To what extent those of the yeomen class and below were growing vegetables in their gardens, and in what variety, it is somewhat difficult to say. Harrison says that by his day even the "poore commons" used melons, cucumbers, radishes, skirets, parsnips, carrots, cabbages, turnips, "and all kinds of salad herbes."[59] But again Harrison's picture, drawn from his own knowledge of conditions in the counties near to London, is scarcely to be taken for the country as a whole. Samuel Hartlib, writing as late as the mid-seventeenth century, observed that there were "divers places both in the north and west of England where the name of Gardening is scarcely known." He noted, however, the great improvement that

58. Anon., *Dick of Devonshire*, 1626, act II, sc. 3.
59. *Description of England*, Bk. II, 324.

was in progress, and says that there were farmers near London with flourishing gardens who less than twenty years before "had not so much as a Mess of Pease but what came from London."[60] Probably the fact that there were better markets for their garden produce proved a greater incentive to these farmers than their own desire for a more varied diet. Their taste, on the whole, was for a heavier and what they regarded a more substantial diet. Thomas Fuller wrote of the quantity and quality of their foods as follows: "Still at our Yeomans table you shall have as many joints as dishes; no meat disguis'd with strange sauces; no straggling joynt of a sheep in the midst of a pasture of grasse, beset with sallads on every side, but solid substantiall food; no servitors (more nimble with their hands than the guests with their feet) take away meat before stomachs are taken away. Here you have that which in itself is good, made better by the store of it, and best by the welcome to it."[61]

Much the same impression is given by John Carter, the yeoman character in a play of the period, who says concerning the expected visit of a gentleman's son, a suitor of his daughter: "To-day or to-morrow, when he comes he shall be welcome to bread, beer and beef, yeoman's fare; we have no kickshaws: full dishes, whole bellyfuls."[62]

William Webb said of the farmers of Cheshire in 1656: "They lay out seldome any money for any provision, but have it of their own as Beef, Mutton, Veal, Pork, Capons, Hens, Wild-fowl and Fish. They bake their own bread and brew their own drink."[63]

Many contemporary writers testified to the prevalence of home production, preparation, and preservation of food. The country housewife, said Gervase Markham, "must proceed more from the provision of her own yard than the furniture of the markets." Sugar, if honey would not do, to make puddings and pies a little more tasty, and spices of various kinds, for pickling, preserving and seasoning, com-

60. S. Hartlib, *Legacie*, p. 9.   61. *The Holy State*, p. 106.
62. *The Witch of Edmonton*, act I, sc. 2.
63. *The Vale-Royal*, p. 20.

prised the chief articles of diet that were procured from the outside. With these in her cupboard and the products of her own farmyard, dairy house, and garden at hand, the good housewife might be counted on to do the rest.

The bread that farmer folk ate differed somewhat according to the locality and the standard of living maintained by the individual family. But it is safe to say that by the time of Elizabeth there were few yeomen who did not have enough good wheat flour on hand for cakes and pastry when there were guests, or when the season called for special feasting; and few so poor that they subsisted on rye or barley bread alone.[64] Even the most well to do, however, did not use the best white flour for everyday use. Not only would this seem an unnecessary extravagance when wheat was selling for a good price, but a heavier bread was considered both more nourishing and more satisfying.[65] Bread made of wheat flour which had some of the bran left in was commonly known as "yeoman bread,"[66] a term that crops up frequently in the popular literature of the period. Rye and wheat mixed produced a flour known as *messeldine, messleden,* or *meslin* that was very popular. Sometimes the grains were planted together, sometimes mixed by the miller in the grinding. Tusser thought it better to do the mixing at the mill because the two grains did not always ripen at the same time:

> Some mixeth to miller the rie with the wheat
> Temmes lofe on his table to have for to eate
> But sowe it not mixed, to growe so on land
> least rie tarie wheat, till it shed as it stand.[67]

64. It is significant to note that by 1658 the English commander of the troops whom Cromwell sent to assist in the siege of Dunkirk reported to the authorities at home that he had to buy wheat to mix with the rye for bread, "the soldiers not being able to eat the rye bread without a mixture of wheat in it." Quoted by Sir W. Ashley, *The Bread of Our Forefathers,* p. 47.

65. See Tobias Venner's analyses of the different grades of wheat flour in common use: *Via recta ad Vitam Langam,* 1622.

66. *Ibid.,* pp. 17–18.

67. *Five Hundred Points of Good Husbandry,* p. 39. Mr. Ashley says that "Temmes" bread "seems to be a loaf made of flour from which the coarser bran is taken," *The Bread of Our Forefathers,* p. 62.

The grains could, however, be mixed before sowing if a special variety of white wheat that ripened early were used.

> If such doe desire to have rie with ther wheat
> By growing together for safetie more great,
> Let white wheat be ton, be it deere, be it cheepe,
> The sooner to ripe, for the sickle to reape.[68]

Flour from this mixture was in general use in Henry Best's household in Yorkshire. Best, a member of the minor gentry, says that when they sent *messleden* to be ground for bread for the family, they sent a bushel of the best wheat for their own pies, and "for the folkes puddings a bushel of barley." The "folkes," that is, the workmen, had wheat puddings only at harvest time. "The folkes pye crusts," says Best, "are made of massledine as our bread is."[69] Tobias Venner, an authority on diet and health matters, did not approve of the oatcakes used in Wales and the northern shires, holding them to be unhealthy, but there was many a northern man who would have disagreed with him. And oatcakes were a staple of the diet of the countryfolk of that region.[70]

If bread were a principal staple, meat was a close second; and beef, mutton, and pork had a large place in the diet of the yeoman. At large dinners and on local feast days it was popular to roast a whole animal or several of them. Indeed, if no special occasion were at hand, the roasting itself might serve as one. The deposition of Thomas Barnefield, a Staffordshire yeoman, in a Star Chamber suit describes two "sheep roastings" that took place in his neighborhood on the same Sunday afternoon. At one place the sheep was quartered and roasted, at the other it was "roasted whole with a puddinge in the Bellye." The neighbors went to prayers and then adjourned for the feasting. There was

68. *Five Hundred Points of Good Husbandry*, pp. 39–40.

69. *Best's Farming Book*, p. 104.

70. The table that Mr. Ashley has worked out from the grain returns in the State Papers shows the wide use of rye though probably bread made wholly of rye was seldom used except by laborers. *The Bread of Our Forefathers*, Appendix.

plenty of ale on hand and the guests made merry with music from the fife, and with dancing.[71]

With refrigeration yet in the future, all meat preservatives were welcomed. Pork was cured and smoked for bacon. Mutton was packed away "in salt and pickle."[72] In addition to the meats abovementioned, deer and venison, so popular with the nobility and gentry, sometimes found their way to yeoman tables. This happened when the goodman was able to win at a shooting; or more often, when he crept with some of his neighbors into the deer park of a neighboring nobleman and carried an animal away. It was thought that deer which had been well hunted before the killing was tastier and more digestible, its blood being then "thinner and more subtill."[73] Meat pies, still so popular in England, were highly favored and contemporary cookbooks are filled with receipts for many kinds.

Rabbits and hares were well liked and were raised in abundance. Sometimes yeomen bought or leased cony warrens, hoping in addition to furnishing their own tables to make some profit. But next to beef, pork, and mutton, poultry furnished a main part of the diet. Capons, chickens, turkeys, ducks, geese, and pigeons were baked and roasted and made into luscious pies. Swans also, kept not so much for food as for their feathers, were to be found in the poultry yards of many housewives.[74]

Fish were an important part of the diet of those who lived on rivers or along the coast. Sometimes the lord of a manor through which a river flowed had sole control of the fishing rights. Often these were shared by tenants under such regu-

71. St.Ch. 8, 12/7.
72. Devon Quarter Sessions Depositions, Easter, 1627.
73. T. Venner, *Via Recta*, p. 55.
74. Swan keeping was looked upon as a privilege, being confirmed by statute since 1483 to freeholders who held property of the annual value of five marks. In order that each owner might know his birds that swam upon the river, a special sign or mark was cut into the bird's beak, and every owner during his term of ownership had to compound with the King for his swan mark at six shillings, eight-pence the mark. Add. MSS. 23732, fols. 2–3. See *S.R.*, 32 Edward IV, c. 6. Sometimes ducks that ran on the common were marked in a similar manner.

lations as were defined in the customs of the manor; or fishing rights might be leased. Among the possessions of John Sewells, a Suffolk yeoman who died in 1593, there were thirty-one mackerel nets and twenty-one herring nets. In Sussex well-to-do yeomen had their own fish ponds as did the gentry.

Cheese and other dairy products also figured largely in the diet. Every family made its own butter and cheeses, with usually an additional supply to sell on market day. The country people of Suffolk, Essex, Cheshire, and other dairying districts excelled in the art of cheese making, each region developing its special product. Inventories of yeomen who lived in these areas mention enormous cheeses that were on hand in their dairy houses and storerooms, as well as numerous cheese vats, presses, and other equipment necessary for dairying.

Whatever the food products used, the success of the dishes that finally found their way to a yeoman's table depended largely on the skill of the housewife. Skill in cookery was an object of pride among women of all classes. Cookery receipts and beauty hints have ever had a way of crossing class barriers; and contemporary cookery and household books show that this period was no exception. Lady Dorset's cookbook containing Lady Gore's instructions "How to candye Angelica staulkes," "How to make Briskett bread Mistress White's way," and Mistress Garnett's method of preserving white quinces pays tribute to the culinary skill of the women of the upper classes. But the skill of yeoman housewives did not go unrecognized by the occupants of the great houses; for in the same book there are directions for "Goodwife Wells, her runnet"; "Goodwyfe Rivers her liver cakes"; and "Goody Cleaves receipt for a hogs Cheeke."[75]

Sauces and seasonings were especially important, particularly in the cooking and serving of meats. Spiced and pickled fruits and vegetables were also in high favor, and receipts for pickled "cowcumbers," "quodinack of plum,"

75. Sloane MSS. 556; the MS. is of 1649, a copy of Lady Dorset's book. See also *ibid.*, 2488; and S.P. 16, CCLXXIX, 107.

and other preserves and pickles were handed about the countryside.

The sweets which came at the close of the meal were almost as heavy as the main courses. Pies and tarts held the favored place still accorded them on English tables. Apple pies were a traditional part of harvest fare. And the yeoman who tells in a Star Chamber case of the minced pies that were in his cupboard for the Christmas feasting[76] was merely relating a commonplace. There were probably minced pies in every yeoman's cupboard at Christmas time. Of puddings, made to serve either with the main course, or as sweets, there was no end. Localities were famous for their special varieties. Devonshire whitepot, Gloucestershire bag pudding, Worcestershire black pudding, Salop pan puddings, the hasty pudding of Hampshire, the white pudding of Somerset and, of course, Yorkshire pudding are all mentioned in the literature of the period.

Dinner was the heaviest meal of the day and supper the lightest. The main supper dish that the wife of John Samwayes, a Devonshire yeoman, prepared for her husband and son on a December evening in 1624 was made by bringing milk to a boil in a "skillet" over the open fire, and adding to it several handfuls of raisins. Other records indicate this dish as a favorite supper for countryfolk. After supper Samwayes and his family sat before the fire and drank mead, and ate roasted apples dipped in the mead.[77]

If guests were present, or it was a special time of celebration, the quantities of food and drink prepared for dinners were enormous.[78] The Reverend Mr. Newbury in his sermon to the yeomen of Kent dwelt at length upon the tradition of hospitality that was theirs to maintain. "It has always been," he said, "that at a yeoman's table you might have as good entertainment as at the best Gentlemans, not for variety of messes, but for solid sufficiency and hearty welcome."[79]

Perhaps, therefore, it was not wholly by accident that

76. St.Ch. 8, 123/16.   77. Harl. MSS. 6715, fol. 69b.
78. See below, pp. 304, 306, 312.   79. *The Yeoman's Prerogative*, p. 26.

John Taylor, the Water Poet, adding his stock of "tall tales" to those which passed current among the watermen on the Thames, chose a yeoman for the hero of his story of the most famous eater he had ever known. He was Nicholas Wood, a yeoman of Kent, who, according to Taylor, was famed for his eating as other men were for their piety, wisdom, and learning. He thought nothing, says Taylor, of taking seven dozen good rabbits or a whole sheep at a meal, with three pecks of damsons to finish off with.[80] Like other folklore, the tall tales of any age often bear implications that are not fictitious.

Drink as well as food held an important place in the yeoman's fare. Some kind of drink was held both necessary and healthful; for contemporary hints to health warned especially against the bad effects of drinking water.[81] White wine, Rhenish wine, malmsey, muscatel, and many other wines were highly esteemed, and now and then one encounters yeomen drinking them. But England was not a grape country and wines were usually beyond their purses. They drank chiefly beer, ale, mead, cider, and perry, drinks that were brewed in their own homes or could be bought at the village alehouse.

Beer, unless made "too bitter of the hop," was considered more wholesome than the heavier ale; and beer made of barley mixed with oaten malt was held better than that made of barley malt alone.[82] Mead made of fermented honey and water, similar to the ancient metheglin though not as strong, was still well liked.[83] Rosemary, hyssop, thyme, orgaine, and sage, boiled in water before the honey was added, were thought to improve the flavor of mead.[84] The wives of the gentry as well as those of the yeomen took charge of the home brewing. William Harrison, a member of the minor gentry, says that his wife and her servants brewed once a

---

80. J. Taylor, *The Great Eater of Kent*, 1630, pp. 4, 5, 9.
81. T. Venner, *Via Recta*, p. 22.   82. *Ibid.*, p. 41.
83. Mead was made of four parts of water to one of honey, whereas only two parts of water to one of honey were used in metheglin. See receipts for brewing, Sloane MSS. 3815, fols. 23–25.
84. S.P. 16, 279/107.

month. Few yeomen and gentlemen brewed more than was needed for home consumption. But this was no small amount when one takes into account the extent of country hospitality. Harrison wrote with satisfaction of the economy of home brewing. Figuring his malt at 10s., the wood used for fuel (which he had to buy) at 10s., hops at 20d., the spice at 2d., his servants' wages at 2s. 6d., and 20d. for the wear of his brewing vessels, the entire cost of making 200 gallons in three lots at one brewing came to only 20s.[85]

That the yeomen had an abundance of both food and drink seems apparent. There might be lean years when the profits were small; when perhaps the goodman was hard pressed to find the money for his rents and fines and subsidy rates. But the pinch of hard times was rarely felt at his own table. His situation at such times was very different from that of the townsmen of corresponding wealth and from those of poorer substance in the country who did not produce their own living.

The same was true with clothes as with food and drink. The country housewife, having mastered the problem of feeding her family, "must learne also how out of her own endeavours, she ought to clothe them outwardly and inwardly for defense for the cold and comelinesse to the person."[86] Some linen made from home-grown flax was used for clothing. But wool, grown on the backs of the farmer's own sheep, was the staple. Sheared and washed, it was then either dyed by the housewife herself or sent to a dyer and then carded, greased, and carded again. The spinning was done upon one of the "woolen wheeles" found in every farmer's household, "the action whereof must be got by practice and not by relation."[87] The weaving, and particularly the fulling and dressing of the cloth, were usually not done in the home though they might be.[88] But whether done there or not, one knew the labor and cost that were involved and valued the results. Clothes were patched and mended as long

85. *Description of England*, Bk. II, 156–159.
86. G. Markham, *The Good Housewife*, chap. v.
87. *Ibid.*   88. See above, pp. 154–165.

as they could be used; for the women in yeoman families
were taught to practice frugality as well as industry:

> Good semsters be sowing of fine pretie knackes,
> good huswives be mending and peecing their sackes.

. . . . .

> Though Ladies may rend and buie new evry day,
> good huswives must mend and buie new as they may.[89]

A well-to-do yeoman had his best suit, and sometimes his
wife's best dress, made by a tailor, but the clothes for ordinary wear were made by the housewife herself or under her
supervision.

The sumptuary laws of earlier reigns were repeated under Elizabeth, and according to them no man under the degree of a knight's eldest son could wear velvet in his jerkin,
hose, or doublet, nor any satin, damask, taffeta, or grosgrain
in his "Clokes, Coates, Gownes, or other uppermost gar-
mentes."[90] Nor could women under the degree of a knight's
wife wear velvet or "embrodery with silke or Netherstockes
of silk." But the growing wealth of the middle classes called
for concessions, and in the statute of 1579–80 the above
stipulation was modified to read "except such whose husbands or themselves may dispend cc li. by the yere." In the
same statute the regulations for the dress of those under
the degree of a knight's eldest son's wife were altered to
make room for those whose husbands might dispend one
hundred pounds by the year.[91] Thus was the way opened
for the wives and daughters of prosperous merchants and
well-to-do yeomen to dress according to the family pocket-
book rather than their social station.

This encroachment on traditional preserves did not proceed without opposition. There are those in every age who
feel that the security and maintenance of the highest values
of their civilization depend on keeping the social order in-

89. Tusser, *Five Hundred Points of Good Husbandry*, p. 176.
90. *Egerton Papers*, Cam. Soc., XII, 250.
91. *Ibid.*

tact. A proclamation made in Chancery in 1596 against the excess of apparel now growing among all classes deplored the "confusyon of all degrees" that resulted from ignoring the former divisions and restrictions.[92] Defenders of the status quo grew uneasy. For in externals like these they vaguely read the sign of vaster changes that might ensue if the economic and social forces that were at work in the world about them continued unchecked. Their forebodings were well founded.

There was, however, less disposition among the yeomen and farmers than among the burgher and professional groups to adopt changes of dress and manners readily. Countryfolk are ever a conservative lot; and custom was often a more active agent of social control in rural communities than legislation. Adam Martindale says of his native Lancashire in the reign of James I: "Freeholders daughters were then confined to their felts, petticoates and wastcoates, crosse handkerchiefs about their neckes, and white crosse-clothes upon their heads, with coifes under them wrought with black silk or worsted."[93] Markham's advice to the country housewife was that she avoid "variety of new and fantastic fashions" and dress plainly in garments "comely and strong . . . without toyish garnishes, or the gloss of light colours."[94] But this advice was not always followed. "Our good wife," said Thomas Fuller, "sets up a sail according to the keel of her husband's estate."[95] And even in rural Lancashire with or without the approval of their parents and neighbors, some of the yeomen's daughters, Martindale admitted, were beginning to wear "gold or silver laces (and store of them) about their petticoates, and bone laces or works about their linnens," though as yet, even "the proudest of them below the gentry durst not have offered to weare a hood, or a scarfe . . ., noe, nor so much as a gowne till her wedding day. And if any of them trans-

92. *Les Reportes del cases in Camera Stellata*, 1894, pp. 5-6.
93. *Life of Adam Martindale*, p. 6.
94. Markham, *Cheap and Good Husbandry*, pp. 3-4.
95. *The Holy State*, p. 2.

gressed these bounds, she would have been accounted an ambitious foole." It is interesting to note that Adam Martindale's own sister Jane was one of those who chafed under the restrictions of her class, and significant that when as an old man he wrote the above description, it was of conditions already passed: "Freeholders daughters were *then* confined to their felts. . . ."[96]

The women were probably more receptive to change in dress than the men. Henry Peacham said of the yeoman, "if he does affect to follow the fashion in his cloathes it is long of his wife, some gentleman's daughter who was matched unto him for his wealth."[97] And Thomas Fuller, who declared that the gentry were "more floating after fine fashions" than the yeomanry, pointed to the latter as "the surest landmark whence foreigners may take aim of the ancient English customs."[98]

There were, however, some yeomen who were not averse to a bit of gaiety in their attire. Joseph Foster of Suffolk, who died in 1619, bequeathed to a kinsman his "fustian doublet with silver buttons on it," a green cloak, and a pair of green hose.[99] And there are many bequests in wills to show that, although the term "russet coated yeoman" serves very well as a description of the ordinary garb of the group, there were a good many among them who had for weddings and other special occasions at least one best suit that was similar to that worn by their neighbors among the gentry. "Blue breeches," "blew stockings," "my best red cloake," "my new greene dublit," and "the best yellow jerkyn" are phrases from the wills of yeomen giving evidence that neither taste nor custom prescribed a wholly somber attire for those who had the means and the desire to dress otherwise. The bequest of Thomas Edison, a yeoman of Lancashire in 1607, of "my best jackitt, my best dublit, by best overhoose, and my best netherstockes,"[100] describes the articles of men's

96. *Life of Adam Martindale*, p. 6.
97. *The Truth of Our Times*, pp. 124–125.
98. *The Holy State*, p. 106.　　99. P.C.C., 16 Soame.
100. *Knaresborough Wills*, p. 2.

clothing in vogue among the gentry of the period. Apparently a well-to-do yeoman dressed in his best was turned out in the same fashion.[101]

Whatever the exact character of the family's wardrobe, the fact that the responsibility for planning it, and for making most of it, fell upon the shoulders of the farmer's wife is only another evidence of the wide range of her duties, and her importance.

Contemporary writers were quick to acknowledge this importance, though their readiness to think of the housewife chiefly in terms of a material asset lessens a little, in modern feminine eyes at least, the value of their tribute. "To thrive one must wive," Thomas Tusser advised all husbandmen. For "husbandrie otherwise speedeth not well." He placed special emphasis on this point:

> For husbandrie wéepeth,
> Where huswiferie sléepeth
> And hardly he créepeth,
>   Up ladder to thrift.

Again he wrote:

> Though husbandrie seemeth to bring in the gaines
> Yet huswiferie labours seeme equall in paines.[102]

A well-to-do yeoman, if he were not too parsimonious and had a fairly large household, kept from one to two or three women servants, whereas in the households of those of less substance all of the work was done by the wife and daughters. Servants were not, however, for the most part employed in order that the women of the family might have more ease and leisure, but merely when there was more work than they could possibly do. Certainly the farmer's wife had

101. In addition to the main articles of clothing named above, ruff bands, "shirt bands," and cuffs are among the details frequently mentioned in connection with male attire. Henry Peacham, writing in 1638, said that the preceding three or four decades had witnessed many changes in men's styles in such details as linens, hats, hatbands, and the like. *The Truth of Our Times*, pp. 66, 69.

102. *Five Hundred Points of Good Husbandry*, pp. 152–162.

little rest or leisure. An epitaph carved on the tombstone of
Mabel Mallet, the wife of a Gloucestershire yeoman, in
1647, reads as follows:

> Stand, reader, still, and be amazed awhile,
> Here lyes an Israelite, in whom was no guile.
> From my sad cradle to my sable chest
> Poore pilgrime I did finde fewe months of rest.[103]

A minor note, to be sure, was a mark of excellence in an epitaph and need not be taken too literally; but there was
doubtless many a farmer's wife who could have testified to
the truth of the sentiment expressed in this one.

Standards of what was proper to rank and degree operated in the lower as well as in the upper rungs of the social
ladder, however, and there were some types of work that a
yeoman's wife or daughter might not do. She could work
from dawn till dark in her kitchen, garden, or poultry yard;
but labor in the fields or caring for swine and other livestock, proper work for the wives and daughters of laborers,
was beneath her station. One of the points weighed by the
Star Chamber Court in a case concerning the daughter of
a Berkshire yeoman who had had some unpleasantness with
a stepfather was the charge that he "had given her very
base service to do about the husbandly and household affairs in keeping cattle, swyne and sheep" such as were "un-
comely offices" for a young girl of her degree.[104]

As a rule the work of the women of the yeoman class was
limited to caring for the needs of their own families and
households. If they engaged further in any sort of industry,
as they sometimes did, it was likely still to be carried on
within the limits of their own homes. They sometimes aided
their husbands or fathers in the care and management of an
inn or tavern that was the family's dwelling, or by minding
a shop set up in a part of the house or near by. Certainly the
wives and daughters of the yeomen in localities where a

103. "Rockhampton Inscriptions," *Glouc. Notes and Queries*, III, 538.
104. St.Ch. 8, 259/28.

home textile industry was developed helped with the work of their husbands.[105] It was the period of the putting-out system, and an interesting warrant of 1622, sent to the churchwardens and overseers of certain Suffolk parishes, reports the complaint that "yeomans and farmer's wives of good ability" were procuring for themselves and their children and servants the greater part of the spinning work from the packhouses; "whereby the poor are being deprived of it."[106] Orphaned daughters of yeomen near Bristol were apprenticed to learn the arts of button making, bone-lace making, and "silke knittinge" that flourished there.[107] But, except in rare cases, only those who had no parents to find husbands and provide a dowry for them appear to have been so engaged. And normally the daughters from yeoman families did not leave their homes until they went to establish new ones of their own.[108]

The consciously expressed moral codes of the day demanded much of the housewife by way of exemplary conduct that would make her a worthy pattern for her family. Markham advised that she be godly, constant, and religious, "learning from the worthy Preacher and her husband." She should, he also admonished, be of great modesty and temperance, particularly in her behavior toward her husband, shunning all violence and rage, passion and humor: coveting less to direct than to be directed. If the goodman erred, she should call him home from error with a mild sufferance rather than with the strength of anger.[109]

Thomas Fuller's first admonition to a good wife was that she obey her husband, and his first charge to a good husband that he see that "his love to his wife weakeneth not his ruling her." There were, however, lengths beyond which the

105. W. Crump, *The Yeoman Clothier,* pp. 11–21; also Crump, *History of the Huddersfield Woolen Industry,* 1936, pp. 36–37.

106. A Warrant for parishes of Babergh hundred, Add. MSS. 39245, fol. 65.

107. Apprentice Books, Bristol Corp. MSS., 1626–35, *passim.*

108. See below, pp. 281–283.

109. *The Good Huswife,* 1637, pp. 236, 240; or *Cheap and Good Husbandry,* 1653, pp. 3–4.

husband should not go. Even though the woman were "of a *servile* nature such as may be bettered by beating," it was best to refrain from this method, and "knowing that she is the weaker vessel" to bear with her infirmities. Like Markham, Fuller advised that a good housewife "never crosseth her husband in the spring-tide of his anger, but stays till it be ebbing water."[110]

One duty placed upon a housewife by all contemporary writers who dealt with the subject was that she "be full of good neighbourhood." This obligation implied many things, but particularly that a woman be ready to act in the capacity of nurse and physician if a neighbor were in need. We have already seen that the housewife stocked her garden well with herbs for such occasions:

> Good Huswives Provides ere an sicknes doo come,
> of sundrie good things, in hir house to have some.[111]

And as cookery books testify to the skill of the yeoman's wife in that art, so contemporary medical books show her proficiency in the concoction of home remedies.[112] But the wives and daughters of yeomen did not as a rule learn their medical lore from books, but from their mothers who had learned from their mothers, and they from theirs; and from other women in the neighborhood.

It was the special duty of the housewife to see other women through the trying period of childbirth. For though every neighborhood boasted one or two women experienced in the art of midwifery, their lore was to some degree the common knowledge of all country women, and it was customary for at least five or six neighbors to be present at the

110. *The Holy State,* pp. 1, 7–8.

111. Tusser, *Five Hundred Points of Good Husbandry,* p. 182.

112. "Goody Huntts" receipt for a salve that was an "aproved good meadison for a Burne," declared that "allthough the skinn be broken itt will fetch out fyre and heale it." A favorite cough medicine was made of sage, rue, and cummin, dusted over with pepper and boiled honey. A spoonful was to be taken morning and evening, "and by the helpe of God it shall doe you good." Sloane MSS. 556, fol. 23b. See also *A Closet for Ladies and Gentlewomen,* 1611.

birth of a baby. We shall perhaps know something more about the degree of infant mortality and the death rate of mothers when adequate use has been made of the information available in parish church registers. But the dozens of examples of second, third, and even of fourth and fifth wives whom many husbands survived points all too clearly to the fact that many women often did not live out their time. This was not wholly due to the bearing of too many children or to the circumstances attending childbirth; but often it was. There is little distinction between the women of the upper and lower classes in this regard. Alice Thornton, a gentlewoman of Yorkshire in the mid-seventeenth century, tells of the death of her youngest sister at the birth of her sixteenth child. She was only thirty-two when she died. Six of the babies were stillborn. One can well believe the truth of Mrs. Thornton's comment upon her sister's death: "Although she was married to a good estate, yet did she injoy not much comfort, and I know she receaved her change with much sattisfaction."[113]

Entries in the diary of James Fretwell, a Yorkshire yeoman who lived in the first half of the next century, tell the familiar story of infant mortality, still common then:

May 1733. My sister Mary was married to Thomas Routh.

Jan. 1734 was my sister Routh brought to bed of a son; it lived until the following Thursday, and then dyed.

Mar. 1735. I heard that sister Routh was brought to bed of a son. This child lived longest of any they have yet had. [He died in June 1737.]

June 1737. Sister Routh was brought to bed of a son—lived but a few days.

Jan. 1739. My sister was delivered of a daughter—but she also dyed.

Dec. 1739. My sister Routh was brought to bed of a son which is called Thomas.

Jan. 1742 Sister Routh was brought to bed of a daughter—very ill.

113. *Life of Alice Thornton*, Surtees Soc., LXII, 49.

Feb. 1745. Brother Routh had a daughter born.

Jan. 1753. This day it pleased Almighty God to deliver my
  dear sister from all her troubles, which she had so pa-
  tiently borne for several years.[114]

The melancholy and brief biography of Wealthean Snelling after her marriage to the son of Robert Furse is recorded in the latter's diary as follows: "She had issue Elizabeth, and one that was borne too sune, a woman childe, and
Robert and Francis and John and Fardinand, and then
died."[115]

It would, however, be a mistake to picture the women of
the yeoman class as a mournful lot who grieved over their
condition or rebelled against it. Not at all! The situation
probably looks much worse to us than it did to them. They
accepted it as a matter of course, and divine dispensation.
If, at the birth of a baby, fortune smiled on both mother and
child, all was well. The good gossips of the neighborhood
crowded in to admire the infant and proffer their advice
and good wishes to the mother, while the goodman passed
around the ale among his friends at the tavern. If, on the
other hand, fatal infection or other mishap claimed the life
of the mother or child, or both, it was looked upon as an in-
tervention of divine providence for reasons known only to
the Almighty and not to be questioned. Relatives and
friends rallied around to make what arrangements they
could for the bereaved family, and then awaited such time
as it would please God to settle the choice of the goodman
upon another helpmeet who would take up the duties of the
departed.

Many country women of hardy stock lived to rear their
families and were on the whole a hearty, happy group. Robert Furse wrote of his maternal grandmother: "She levyd
untyll she was nere c yeres of yage and yeven at her laste
tyme was a lustye woman."[116] Women often took part in the

114. "Diary of James Fretwell," reprinted in *Yorkshire Diaries*, Surtees Soc., LXV, *passim*.

115. *Furse Family Book*, p. 183.   116. *Ibid.*, p. 180.

activities of the countryside with vigor and enjoyment as
did their menfolk. One wishes some of them had written diaries; but most of them could not write, and those who could
appear to have had neither time nor inclination for it.
But we catch glimpses of them in court records and other
documents: riding on the pillion seat behind their husbands
to fairs and markets; engaging in neighborhood bicker-
ings; and taking part in friendly social gatherings at each
other's houses or at the village tavern. As individuals, they
exhibited all the varied traits of women of every class and
age. Adam Eyre's high-spirited, nagging wife was better at
driving a bargain than he was, and little inclined to be too
easy on a husband who sometimes wasted his time at bowls
and drink. Adam Martindale's mother, on the other hand,
was a saint on earth whose humility and virtue left an enduring imprint upon the minds of her children.

Measured by the standards of their age, English women
were held, in general, better off than their sex elsewhere.
Hentzner, a German traveling in England in 1598, declared they were fortunate above all women in the world.
Other foreign travelers expressed similar views,[117] as did
contemporary English writers. It was probably true; and
as the yeomen in England enjoyed a position superior to
that of the non-noble classes on the continent, it is likely that
a yeoman's wife was, in many respects, better off than a
commoner's wife elsewhere. Her home was the center of her
life. She liked to see her children do well in the world and
shared with her husband the duty of rearing them according to the dictates and standards of their class and age.
What that involved in the way of training and education is
the subject to which we shall now turn.

117. See extracts from the writings of S. Kiechel (1585), Jacob Rathgeb (1602), and E. Meteren (1614), in *England as seen by Foreigners*
(Rye), 1865.

VII

SCHOOLING AND PLACEMENT

All the whetting in the world can never set a razor's edge on that which hath no steel in it.

T. Fuller, The Holy State, 1642

Better make a poor match in the country than a worse one in London.

Old Proverb

ENGLAND'S intellectual climate in the early seventeenth century was vastly affected by the religious controversy that shaped daily the thoughts and actions of men of all classes. Parents felt that their children must be trained from earliest youth if they were to be prepared to meet the strength of the opposition. Even when girded with the armor of righteousness, one was not wholly out of danger. The Devil was a wily fellow.

Reared in this atmosphere, the children of yeoman families received what religious instruction could be carried forward both in the home and in the parish church. It was chiefly oral and consisted largely of familiarity with the Scriptures, and a knowledge of the prayer book or catechism, according to the religious complexion of the household or the community. Nonconformist groups paid much attention to memorizing passages of Scripture, and it was a mark either of mental deficiency or moral laziness for one in such a group not to have attained a reasonable amount of this kind of learning. William Giles, a Sussex yeoman, called into court as a witness against an eighteen-year-old youth who faced indictment, based his testimony of the boy's "shallow capacity and understanding" on the fact that he was not able to repeat the Ten Commandments.[1]

1. MSS. of the Court of Delegates in the Public Record Office, 3/2, fol. 800.

Bible stories were familiar fare for the young: "I had a singular affection to the historyes in the bible," wrote Ralph Josselyn, the son of an Essex yeoman, "being acquainted with all those historyes in very yong dayes."[2]

How much education yeomen received, beyond this oral or semioral religious instruction of home and church, is not an altogether easy question to answer. The signatures of some 2,500 to 3,000 yeomen, attached to wills, leases, bonds, and the like, show that between 60 per cent and 70 per cent of those involved could write their own names. The remaining number made their marks, usually a small cross, though not infrequently a more elaborate symbol was consistently used by an individual as his signature. What percentage of the above number who could write their names were able to do more than that one cannot even hazard a guess. But there is considerable evidence from various sources which throws light on the attitude of members of the class toward education, and the amount of training they thought desirable. The countryman in Nicholas Breton's dialogue (1618) must have spoken the mind of many of them when he said: "We can learn to plow and harrow, sow and reape, and prune, thrash and fanne, winnow and grinde, brue and bake, and all without booke; and these are our chiefe businesse in the Country, except we be jury-men to hang a theefe, or speak truth in a man's right, which conscience and experience will teach us with a little learning."[3]

It was no disgrace in the eyes of one's fellows not to be able to read or write. If such knowledge were required for the handling of everyday affairs, farmers without it did exactly as Breton's countryman says: "Now if we cannot write, we have the Clerke of the church, or the schoolmaster of the towne to helpe us, who for our plaine matters will serve our turnes well enough."[4] It will be remembered that in the struggle between the tenants of Westmoreland and their landlords over tenant-right it was the vicar who drew

2. *Ralph Josselyn's Diary,* 1616–83, Cam. Soc. 1908, XV, 2.
3. *The Courtier and the Countryman* (Hazlitt), p. 193.
4. *Ibid.,* p. 198.

up the resolutions for the group, and the village school-master who put the tenants' protest in the form of a play.[5] Scores of documents touching the activities of yeomen show how often these two individuals served as the scribes in rural communities.

But there is also evidence of a growing feeling among farmers that a little education might not be a bad thing. Men were farming for profit now and they needed to be able to cast up their own accounts and to keep track of their yearly gains and losses. We have observed the care with which Robert Loder set down each small item in his farm accounts, pondering over his records at the end of the year in order to see how he might make the next year a more profitable one.[6]

William Bilson, a yeoman of Drayton, Berkshire, who, under Elizabeth, was bailiff in husbandry to two neighboring gentlemen, once had his accounts brought into question. Being unable to keep them himself, he had secured the services of the local schoolmaster; and now that they were under fire, he was unable to explain the contents of the record or to help himself out of a bad predicament.[7]

Moreover, a written indenture was by Elizabeth's time the accepted form of evidence for land conveyances, including leases, bonds, and all manner of agreements; and precedence was given to written evidence in all suits at court.[8] This being true, it behooved a man, as in the case above, not only to be able to sign his name to a document but to know exactly what he was signing. Thomas Bradbery of Milton, Kent, was another yeoman who learned this to his sorrow. In the Court of Requests in 1593 he stated that because he was unable to read or write he had permitted the man to whom he was selling wheat to make out the indenture covering the bargain. It was not until later that he realized he had entered into an agreement detrimental to his own inter-

5. See above, p. 152. 6. *Farm Journal,* p. liii.
7. Req. 2, 180/12.
8. See Holdsworth's account of the development of the deed and other forms of land conveyance, *History of English Law,* II, 221, and *passim.*

ests, not being fully aware of the content of the document he signed.[9]

Instances like these proved to yeomen that at least a knowledge of the rudiments of learning had practical value. Whereupon many of them determined that their children should receive more education than they themselves had. When they stipulated in their wills, as scores of them did, that their sons should be given such education as was "proper to their degree and calling," they apparently had in mind chiefly such practical training as would help them to forestall troubles of the above type. Again Breton's countryman, willing to concede that a little learning is not amiss, summed up the matter in a way that was probably acceptable to the majority of yeomen: "Now for learning, what your neede is thereof I know not, but with us, this is all we go to school for: to read common Prayers at church, and set downe common prises at Markets; write a letter and make a Bond; set downe the day of our Births, our Marriage day, and make our Wills when we are sicke for the disposing of our goods when we are dead; these are the chief matters that we meddle with."[10]

One occasionally finds yeomen, however, who had a better education than that; men who could not only cast up accounts and read and write well enough to attend to such matters as those enumerated above, but who were able as well to serve their neighbors or themselves when clerical aid was needed, and could for their own pleasure and instruction read the Bible and such other books as their day found interesting.

Simon Rider's commonplace book includes not only the record of actions pertaining to his own affairs but many indentures and other documents which he drew up for his neighbors.[11] Robert Furse was likewise a yeoman of some education. The majority of his forebears had remained yeomen, but apparently from early Tudor times various ones

9. Req. 2, 179/59.
10. N. Breton, *The Courtier and the Countryman*, p. 191.
11. Rider Commonplace Book, *passim*.

among them had sent their bright sons to the Inns of Court or the universities where they made records the family was proud of. Of one of these ancestors Robert wrote: "This Roberte was greatly to be commended for that he trayned uppe his son John Furse to be a lernede man for by that menes our credyt and livings is grettly incresed."[12] He considered it belittling and shameful for a man "to be ignorant of that whyche he ofte to knowe," which included, he thought, an ability to read, at least sufficiently to read the Scriptures. A note of regret concerning his own limitations occurs in his introduction to the family record, wherein he laments that "hyt be but sympellye and rudely sette fforthe . . . but I cane nott sowe better sedes than I have repen."[13]

Furse wrote in 1593. Adam Eyre's diary of 1646–49 shows a yeoman with a somewhat better education. Eyre, like Simon Rider, speaks of the letters that he wrote for his neighbors and the indentures and petitions he drew up for them. He also makes it evident that his small library was used freely by other yeomen in the Penistone community who could read, and who too had a few books which they lent back and forth. No complete list of the volumes that stood on the new shelves Eyre had built for his books is extant. But the careful record that he kept of those which his neighbors borrowed and returned serves to acquaint us somewhat with his library and with the reading tastes of a Yorkshire farming community.[14]

Of the fourteen titles mentioned by Eyre, nine were of a religious or semireligious nature. They included Foxe's *Book of the Martyrs*, one of the best sellers of the period,[15] and various books of sermons and religious commentaries.[16]

---

12. *Furse Family Book*, p. 173.   13. *Ibid.*, p. 170.

14. *Diary of Adam Eyre, passim.*

15. John Foxe's *Actes and Monuments,* called commonly the *Book of the Martyrs,* was first issued in 1563. By the time Eyre wrote of it in his diary eight editions had been published, the eighth in 1641.

16. Among these were *Sermons* by Tobias Crisp, John Saltmarsh, William Dell, and John Archer, all noted Puritan divines and controversialists.

There were two historical works: Raleigh's *History of the World*, and *The State of Europe*.[17] Also in the list were Michael Dalton's *Country Justice*, a practical manual concerning the duties of county and parish officials that was much in demand among Eyre's neighbors;[18] Erasmus' *In Praise of Folly;* and three works on astrology by William Lilly, then at the height of his popularity.[19] The fact that several of the religious books were purchased by Eyre within the year of their publication or soon afterward shows the interest that he and his friends had in the contemporary religious struggle.

An entry in William Honiwell's diary for 1602 mentions the lending of a book entitled *The Passions of the Mind*.[20] He also spoke of owning other books, but does not tell what they were. The Bible was, as one might expect, the book most mentioned in yeoman wills. Next to it the two books oftenest chained to the pulpits of parish churches for community use were the abovementioned *Book of the Martyrs*, and Bishop Jewell's *Works*.[21] A Lincoln yeoman mentioned Lyttleton's *Tenures*, and *Canterbury Tales* among "Certen Inglysh bokes" in his possession.[22] A yeoman of Tewkes-

17. This may have been *The History and Present State of Europe in xiv books* published in 1628, the authorship of which is uncertain.

18. Dalton's book was not the first of its kind, for it was preceded by the much earlier work of Fitzherbert (1514), and by William Lambard's *Eirenarcha* in 1581, a book that went through seven editions by 1610. But *The Country Justice* quickly gained popularity. The first edition, 1618, was followed by six others in the seventeenth century.

19. *The World's Catastrophe*, 1644; *England's Propheticall Merlin*, 1647; and *The Starry Messenger*, 1647.

20. *The Honiwell Diary*, 1602. This was very likely *The Passions of a Discontented Mind*, often attributed to Nicholas Breton; or possibly Thomas Easts' (Este) *The Passions of the Spirit*, 1594.

21. John Jewell, famous bishop of Salisbury, wrote the first systematized statement of the Anglican position as opposed to the Roman position set forth at the Council of Trent, *Apologia pro Ecclesia Anglicana* (1562). It was later ordered by Archbishop Bancroft to be placed in all parish churches, and one frequently finds references in church wardens' accounts to money "laid out for a newe chaine for Bishop Jewell's Works." A copy can still be seen chained to the lectern at Cirencester.

22. *Lincoln Diocesan Archæological Society*, XVII, 23.

bury named, among bequests in 1607, "a book of printed sermons" and "my book called *Resolution*."[23] Edward Ford, a yeoman of Ottery St. Mary, bequeathed to his cousin all of his "schoolbooks in Greek and Latin and a great many in English."[24] And a Kentish yeoman who died in 1596 left a sum of money to buy Calvin's *Institutes* in English, and a chain with which to fasten it to a desk at the lower end of the parish church at Maidstone "for the better instruction of the poor and simple therein."[25]

But these instances represent wide gleanings, and though they suggest that it was no extraordinary thing for yeomen to possess some books and to be able to read them, it should be noted that there are many more wills and inventories which do not mention any books among the personal possessions of the yeomen than there are those which do. And the yeomen who had more education than was required for their minimum needs, as set forth above by Breton's countrymen, were in all likelihood in the minority.

When bright boys of yeoman families showed an aptitude for learning and a desire for a career or occupation other than that of their fathers, their ambitions met with varying responses from their parents and neighborhood advisers. Adam Martindale tells how the neighbors tried to persuade his father to discourage his leanings toward scholarly pursuits, "alledging too many instances of such as made no advantage of their learning though they had been brought up so long to it as to be fit for nothing else."[26]

But in scores of cases parents did all they could to further the ambitions of their book-minded sons. To have a son in the church or in medicine or the law raised the position of the family in the community and made available more land for the others who remained at home.

A yeoman's son who planned to enter one of the universities or the Inns of Court joined the sons of the gentry at the

23. "Old Wills," *Glouc. Notes and Queries*, VI, 6–7.
24. MSS. of Mrs. Frances Rose-Troupe, Ottery St. Mary, Devon.
25. Streatfield Collection, Add. MSS. 33916, fol. 156.
26. *Life of Adam Martindale*, p. 24.

nearest grammar school deemed qualified to give the necessary preparation. He might first have learned the rudiments of reading and writing at the village dame school, with the vicar, or at home if there were some one there to teach him.

Adam Martindale, one of those bright sons of a yeoman family, has left an excellent picture of the preuniversity education he received in his native Lancashire, and there is no reason to believe that it differed greatly in character and method from the preparatory education offered to boys in other sections. He says that he learned to read at the age of six from an "A.B.C." that had been the gift of his sponsor at baptism. His first teachers were his older brothers and sisters, and "the youth that came to court my sister"; so the ability to read must have been an accepted thing among the young people of this family, and their friends. At the age of seven the lad began his formal instruction in the free school of St. Hellens. Here he was under five different teachers during his first five years at school. The first was a "young ingenious sparker having a good full schoole, but so bad a husbande that he quickly spoiled all and left us"; and the second "an old humdrum curate, that had almost no scholars, nor deserved any, for he was both a simpleton and a tippler." The third, it is interesting to note, was a woman, daughter to a famous schoolmaster. Adam says she had a smattering of Latin, and "could teach us to construe the Latine examples of the English rules called the *Parvular* . . . and the *Quimihi* and Lillies rules . . . and put us sometimes to read English; so with her I did something better than quite lose my time, but not much."

After some time with this teacher, the boy's father, listening to the advice of Adam's older brother and relatives, took him out of school and set him to work to learn the carpenter's trade. But soon seeing the way the lad's mind was bent, and as Adam said, "thinking it a pittie I should lose all I had got, he frankely put it to my choice, whether I would go on as I did at present, or returne to schoole againe." As there was no question in the boy's mind what he wanted to do, he was returned to school and to his fourth teacher, a man trained at Winwick, the famous ecclesiastical foundation in Lancashire. Of this teacher his pupil later wrote: "He had the Winwicke method right enough, and was scholar sufficient for me then; but he was a very silly and unconstant man, always making new laws, in so much that if a boy had beene absent a day or two he knew not how to behave himself for feare of transgressing some new order or other." According to his pupil he also showed partiality among his students, and at the request of a gentleman scholar who had more money than the yeoman's son, placed Adam at the bottom of the class. Yeomen accorded deference to their superiors in social matters but the elder Martindale apparently considered that his son had been mistreated in this instance and removed him to another school, though it meant higher fees.

It proved a good move for the boy. Here he had his fifth and best teacher, a man who, though he gave way to capricious moods and beat the boys for small faults, yet was to be endured because he "was of good parts, both natural and acquired." At fourteen Adam was studying Latin prose, Greek grammar, together with a Greek catechism and Greek Testament; Latin poetry including Terence, Ovid, Virgil, and Horace; and rhetoric. And in two more years of training in similar subjects he was ready for Oxford.[27]

Ralph Josselyn of Essex was another bright son of a yeoman family who wished to prepare for the ministry. He says that he had a "nimble head and a strong memory," and early exhibited a desire to be "a scholler," a course "from which nothing would divert me." Again a sympathetic parent did all he could to forward his son's ambitions: "God putt it into my father's heart to listen to mee." Josselyn apparently received all of his preparation from a local schoolmaster until he was ready to enter Jesus College, Cambridge, at not quite sixteen. Then because of an unfortunate land deal, the elder Josselyn lost money and could

27. *Ibid.* See also "Wills of the Taske family," Fenland *Notes and Queries*, XV, 45.

not meet his son's university expenses: "I was forced to come from Cambridge many times for want of meanes & loose my time in the country." In spite of this young Ralph managed to keep up with his fellows and received his Bachelor of Arts in 1636.[28]

How many sons of yeomen like these two desired and received a university education, it is difficult to say. Early registers of schools and universities give less full information than one could wish concerning the status of their students. But those whose records are complete in this regard show a fair number of sons of yeomen among the scholars. The register of the pupils of the famous Merchant Taylors' School in London shows that the sons of yeomen from counties scattered all about England were being entered there.[29]

The registers of the University of Oxford from 1567 to 1622 reveal this classification:[30]

Sons of Noblemen (Earls, Lords, and Barons)	84
Sons of Knights	590
Sons of Esquires	902
Sons of Gentlemen	3615
Sons of plebeians	6635
Sons of the clergy	985
Those whose status is not given	758

How many of the 6,635 plebeians were sons of yeomen, one cannot say, but it is evident that England's upper classes were being recruited plentifully from below. A yeoman's son had no family tradition to prescribe his choice of university, and could choose indifferently. Thomas Hockett of Hertfordshire died in 1611 leaving money for the education of his two sons at "either of the universities."[31]

Other yeomen who themselves had no desire or ambition

28. *Ralph Josselyn's Diary*, pp. 3–4.
29. C. Robinson, *Register of Scholars of Merchant Taylors' School, 1562–1874*, 1882, I, 48, 69, and *passim*.
30. *Register of the University of Oxford* (Clark), II, Oxf. Hist. Soc., 1887, XI, 414.
31. P.C.C., 60 Wood.

for learning, and who had no sons as bright or as much inclined toward letters as young Adam Martindale and Ralph Josselyn, showed their interest in education in yet another way, namely, by bequeathing money for the building and repair of schoolhouses or for the aid of poor scholars. The most famous philanthropy of this kind, though unusual for its extent and later development rather than for its nature, was that of John Lyon of Harrow. Without children of his own, this yeoman designed the wealth that he had accumulated for educational purposes, and "by instinct of charity . . . purposed in his mind a certain grammar schoole and one schoolemaster and usher within the village of Harrow-on-the-Hill."[32] Lyon himself had some education and a great deal of shrewd common sense. The *Five Articles* appended to the *Statutes* of the school which he wrote were read to every parent who presented his children for entrance. They show the shrewdness and practical nature which Lyon possessed and are in many respects characteristic of the class to which he belonged. Each child was instructed to bring his own supply of paper, ink, pens, books, and "candles for the winter." Required archery practice, with each child furnishing his own bowshafts, bowstrings, and a bracer, was designed to foster physical exercise and at the same time contribute a service to the state. No tardiness at school in the morning would be tolerated. Lyon closed his articles with the wise advice that any child who at the end of the year showed himself "inapt to the learning of grammar" should be withdrawn and put to a profitable occupation.[33]

The curriculum of Lyon's school like that of other grammar schools of the day was chiefly classical, and like that of the school in which Martindale studied, provided a course

32. Royal grant to Lyon, Harl. MSS. 2211, fol. 6.

33. *Ibid.* See also W. Druett, *Harrow through the Ages,* 1935, pp. 120–121. It was a phrase in the *Statutes,* permitting the master to accept "foreigners" as students in case there were vacancies after the local youth were accommodated, that brought the first students from beyond the village and parish to this school that was by the future turns of fortune to become one of England's famous Public Schools.

of study that would make no appeal to boys in a rural community save the bookish-minded ones. For the rest, they might go for a year or two or gain a smattering of reading and writing at one of the schools set up casually from time to time in the village by anyone who felt inclined to seek this means of picking up a meager livelihood.

The last-named type of village school, the "dame-school," was frequently taught by a woman. Sometimes it was the work of an itinerant schoolmaster who stopped for a time in a community and offered his services. One even sometimes finds a yeoman or a yeoman's son turning schoolmaster, resolving, as did Thomas Woodwerde of Belford, "according to his enablement and education to Keep a school and teach children to read and write the English tongue and to cast accompts."[34]

It is less easy to say specifically what education, if any, the daughters of yeomen could or did receive. There were many intelligent and some highly trained women among the upper classes of Elizabethan and Stuart England whose accomplishments are a challenge to members of their sex in a generation that takes women's education for granted.[35] And

34. St.Ch. 8, 303/26. A presentment was made to the Hertford sessions in 1677 that "William Barefoote of Chesthunt, yeoman, kept a school and was a schoolmaster, outside any university or college of the Kingdom, and in no public or free grammar school, nor in the service of any nobleman or noblewoman, or gentleman or gentlewoman not being recusants and not licensed by the Diocese of Lincoln under whose jurisdiction, Chesthunt lies," *Hertford Sessions Records*, VI, 302.

35. The precocious Lady Jane Grey and Elizabeth Tudor were by no means alone in their accomplishments. Ann Conway was the friend and confidante of the Cambridge Platonists and other intellectuals of her age. Lady Ann Fanshawe, though the mother of twenty-two children, found time to write a diary that furnishes a mirror for her class and her times. The Verney women and those who married into that family, though not especially literary, were intelligent level-headed women, capable of carrying on the business of country estates when their husbands were away from home and of keeping them informed by letter of all that went on in their absence. Alice Thornton was a high-minded gentlewoman of sound intellect and fortitude of spirit as her *Journal* shows. Her contemporary, Brilliana Lady Harley, was a woman whose spirit and initiative would make her outstanding in any age. And to Lucy Hutchinson's voluminous memoirs of her husband we are indebted for one of the best pictures left us of seventeenth-century Puritanism.

if a woman of this group had the inclination to train and exercise her brains, she might do so, though under a tutor, for there were no institutions of higher learning open to her. Practically all of the authorized free schools were also expressly closed to girls. A few, however, admitted them, and gradually a small number of schools for girls were founded.[36]

But in the lower classes there was less opportunity as well as less inclination among women for even a small degree of education. It has been pointed out that there were many men in the yeoman class who could neither read nor write. There were considerably more women of the group who could not. Time and again one notes on leases, deeds, and other documents, requiring the signatures of both man and wife, that the husband has written his name and his wife has made her mark, though in exceptional instances the situation is reversed.[37] One or two wives of yeomen in Adam Eyre's community were reading the same books their husbands did; and Catherine Culling, the daughter and heiress of James Culling, a wealthy Kentish yeoman, went four years to a boarding school for girls along with the daughters of her father's friends among the gentry.[38] But this was unusual, and there were certainly many like the wife of Edward Duffield, a yeoman of Suffolk, who testified that she "could not write or reade a written hande."[39] A yeoman's will frequently states that a daughter shall have "such breeding and education as is fit and necessary for one of her degree and calling." This suggests a certain standard. The question is to determine what it was.

Robert Furneis, a yeoman of Northamptonshire, stipulated in his will that the guardian of his daughter should provide her with food and clothing, "and such further education for books and needle and other qualitys fitt for her

36. D. Mead, *Education of Women and Girls in England in the Time of the Tudors,* a MS. thesis of the University of London, 1928, pp. 372–399.
37. Sussex MSS. 1610. PN. 12.
38. *Oxinden Letters* (Gardiner), 1933, pp. xxix, xxxi, 278.
39. St.Ch. 8, 10/3.

degree and calling," until she reached the age of eighteen.[40] And a Star Chamber Court record tells of the daughter of a Berkshire yeoman who was sent to live with a kinsman that she might be put to school and taught to sew.[41] From these and similar instances it seems apparent that proficiency in needlework was held desirable for the daughters of yeomen as for the gentry. Other training given at home in the management of domestic affairs and, for those who had the inclination, a smattering of reading and writing learned at the village school appear to be the qualities which fulfilled the standard of those who talked of the training and education that was fit for the degree and calling of a yeoman's daughter.

One fact is very evident, namely, that when parents in yeoman families planned for the training and education of their children, either for sons or daughters, they thought in terms of future security rather than of cultural development. Even the education of the bright sons who entered the universities was chiefly spoken of in utilitarian terms, as affecting their social advancement and economic security.

Where primogeniture was the common practice, the bulk of the land passing to the eldest son made his future more or less secure. Often substantial sums of money were given to younger sons that they might buy or lease land for themselves; and to daughters for their marriage portions. Often, as we have seen, a shop or small business that the farmer owned or controlled an interest in became the means of providing for younger sons. But if family circumstances did not permit this, other means of placement must be found. Many youths who could not expect an adequate inheritance for setting up independently hired themselves as tenant farmers to their fathers and elder brothers or to neighboring yeomen and gentry, in the hope that they would in time be able to get ahead sufficiently to acquire land for themselves. Still others, lacking these means of assistance, or from inclination, found it desirable to quit the land altogether and seek their fortunes in the active and rapidly growing fields of trade and industry. The customary route by which a young man gained a place for himself in mercantile or industrial activities was apprenticeship. And many an Elizabethan and Stuart yeoman sought this training for his sons. Probably circumstance and necessity were the chief factors in this type of parental planning; but there is evidence that some parents, at least, attempted to act in accord with the natural aptitudes and abilities of their children.

Thomas Hockett, a Hertfordshire yeoman who would have liked to see both his sons attend the university and had the means to send them, was aware of the possible ineptitude of John, the younger of them, for training of this kind. Hence in his will an alternative plan was prescribed by which the boy might be apprenticed to some "religious and honest tradesman," as appeared "most meete and convenyent and the child most apt and fitted."[42] Adam Martindale's father recognized his son's unfitness for the carpenter's trade though his neighbors advised it.[43] There are other examples of wise fathers, but it was probably convenience rather than aptitude or ability that determined most choices.

Often parents sought masters for their sons in near-by towns where home ties could be more or less maintained throughout the period of their service. Others went to more distant cities, many of them to London, to join the great army of apprentices who played a colorful part in the life of the metropolis. Those who were successful there would in time gain membership in one or another of the great London companies. Some who grew rich would buy land and move again to the country whence they or their ancestors came. The following lines from the speech of Old Barnacle, a rich citizen in James Shirley's play, *The Gamester*, illustrates a familiar cycle in the history of England's social classes:

42. P.C.C., 60 Wood.   43. *Life of Adam Martindale*, p. 24.

> We that had
> Our breeding from a trade, cits, as you call us,
> Though we hate gentlemen ourselves, yet are
> Ambitious to make all our children gentlemen:
> In three generations they return again.
> We for our children purchase land: they brave it
> I' the country; beget children, and they sell,
> Grow poor, and send their sons up to be prentices.
> There is a whirl in fate.[44]

The normal term for an apprenticeship was seven years, but it might run as high as twelve or as low as four, depending on the age of the boy and the character of the business or trade. An indenture that sealed the covenant between the lad's father and his new master stated the terms of obligation on both sides.

Apprentice books show that the sons of yeomen were well represented in practically all trades. Yorkshire lads who left their fathers' farms went in large numbers into the silk-weaving trade that flourished in York. Many also from that district were apprenticed to joiners, and the craft of haberdashers was popular. In Chester the ironmongers attracted many yeomen's sons and were popular also with gentlemen's sons of that region who were apprenticed. Many of the sons of Gloucestershire yeomen and those from other parts of the west country, as might be expected, threw in their lot with the Bristol merchants and mariners whose far-flung interests made that port second in importance to London in the early seventeenth century. In East Anglia, where mercantile and colonial ventures were likewise deeply rooted, more yeomen's sons were apprenticed to mariners than to all other trades together. Country boys came from as far away as Cumberland and Northumberland to enroll as apprentices with the Ipswich mariners.[45] Mr. Mendenhall's interesting study of the Drapers' Company in

44. *The Gamester,* 1633, act I, sc. 1.
45. See Appendix II, for table showing the distribution of yeomen's sons in the various trades at York, Chester, Bristol, and Ipswich.

Shrewsbury shows that between the years of 1608 and 1659, 17 per cent of the new freemen who entered the company were sons of yeomen and approximately 13 per cent of the apprentices enrolled came from yeoman homes.[46]

Many apprentices fared well upon completing their term of service. Some became wealthy and founded famous families. But competition was keen in the mercantile and industrial world as in the agrarian. There were years of depression and uncertainty in which one venture succeeded and another failed. For those sons of yeoman families who met with ill success, or who felt for one reason or another that there was no future for them at home, either in the trades and the professional world, or on the land, there was from the early seventeenth century on, one other alternative: a long ocean voyage, and at its end a new home in an English colony beyond the seas.

By many contemporaries the colonies were regarded primarily as a sinkhole into which Britain's undesirables and her excess population could be drained. And the sessions records of a populous county like Middlesex show that many legal offenders saved their heads or a long term of imprisonment on condition that they go to Virginia, New England, or the West Indies.[47] This was particularly the case if it could be shown that the felon was of the carpenter's art, or had skill in any craft that would make him useful to the colonial venture; for often the J.P.'s who sat in the quorum had interests in colonial enterprises.

But many promoters of colonial projects came to realize that the success of their undertakings depended as much on the type of colonist they secured as upon the financial backing their venture received, perhaps more. And a pamphlet by Richard Eburne, *A Plaine Path-way to Plantations*, published in 1624, shows how highly the yeomen were regarded as prospective material for the colonies.[48] It was nec-

46. T. C. Mendenhall, The Shrewsbury Drapers and the Welsh Cloth Trade, MS. in preparation, p. 131.

47. *Middlesex Quarter Sessions Records*, II, 225, 226, 305; III, 283, 292, 335, 337.

48. R. Eburne, *A Plaine Path-way to Plantations*, London, 1624.

essary, Eburne contended, to secure people of good breeding, experience, and ability, for settling the colonies, many
members of the gentry, if possible. But if, as would probably always be the case, there could not be enough of the
gentry prevailed upon to venture the undertaking, then
"those of a degree next unto Gentlemen, that is Yeomen
and Yeoman-like men," would be the best choice. Not only
would the colonies be aided thereby, but men of this class,
"that have in them some good knowledge and courage,"
themselves stood to profit much by the opportunities they
would have there. The very fact that there would be among
them a relatively small number of men of higher degree
would in itself mean that the yeomen who went might expect in time "to be advanced to places of preferment and
government there."[49]

In the New World, moreover, Eburne pointed out, a yeoman might not only receive free fifty acres of land for himself, but he could be assured that it would go to his children "in perpetium forever"; for socage was the accepted
tenure for land in the colonies.[50] That these and similar
arguments did not fall on deaf ears is attested by family
records, and by the records of towns and villages, in both
England and America. Many of these migrations were effected through means of the apprentice system; and hundreds of "indentured servants" sought their fortunes in
the New World.

The relatively recent discovery in the Bristol archives of
two large manuscript books bearing the names and in many
cases the status of those who embarked as "Servants to the
Foreign Plantations" from the port of Bristol 1654–85
provides us with some definite statistical data concerning
the classes from which the colonial recruits came.[51] Alone in
the years from 1654 to 1661,[52] not, according to historians,
one of the most active periods in colonial migration, 4,136

49. *Ibid.,* I, 224.
50. Money rather than land was given in some colonies.
51. Bristol Corp. MSS.
52. The reason for selecting these years only is that the status of the applicant is less frequently given as the record is carried forward.

men and women sailed from the port of Bristol to Virginia, New England, and the West Indies. Of the 1,600 men whose status can be ascertained, approximately 63 per cent were from the agricultural classes, and of this number approximately 45 per cent were yeomen or sons of yeomen.

Those who went to Virginia received fifty acres of land at the end of their term. Usually also an axe and hoe, a year's provisions, and one or two suits of apparel were a part of the recompense. The normal award for the men and women apprenticed to Barbados, St. Nevis, St. Christopher, or others of the West Indian islands was ten pounds sterling, though the amount differed slightly, and was sometimes given in tobacco, indigo, or cotton. If the apprentice were young, the term was usually seven years or more, but for many adults it was as low as three or four years. This, together with the fact that all apprentices had their passage paid, accounts no doubt for the fair representation of the sons of merchants and gentlemen one finds among those who went over as indentured servants.[53]

Some of the yeomen who migrated from Bristol and other parts did indeed push forward in the New World, as Eburne had prophesied, to positions of trust and influence. Henry Dunster, the son of a Lancashire yeoman, became the first president of Harvard College.[54] Henry Adams, of Somerset yeoman stock, founded a family dynasty in New England that has furnished the republic with a long line of educators and statesmen. Thomas Jefferson's father was of yeoman stock transplanted to Virginia and married into the colonial gentry. Many did not achieve vast wealth or become famous, but in their new location, as at home, furnished the brawn and brain of a sturdy middle class that greatly strengthened the New World fabric.[55]

53. Servants to the Foreign Plantations, Bristol Corp. MSS.

54. Nathaniel Eaton was the first head of Harvard College, but Dunster, who took charge following Eaton's brief term and dismissal, was the first "president," and the first to furnish the New England College with real leadership. See S. E. Morison, *The Founding of Harvard College*, 1935, pp. 242–262.

55. It may well be argued that in so doing they helped to seal the

Unfortunately the records of the indentured servants from Bristol do not, in most cases, include the status of the women apprentices. It is therefore impossible to tell how many daughters of yeomen were among them. Both boys and girls were sometimes sent to the colonies against their will.[56] One of the charges made against a man sentenced to execution in 1618 was that he had, under counterfeit of the Royal Seal, taken up "rich yeomans daughters . . . to serve his Majesty for breeders in Virginia."[57] But most of the kidnapings took place in urban centers among the waifs that ran the city streets. And it is doubtful if many daughters of yeoman families were subject to the abuse, or indeed if many of this station who were unmarried, except they be orphaned daughters, were among the indentured servants. Orphaned daughters of yeomen were probably well represented for they were frequently apprenticed for service and sometimes for other work at home. But there were certainly many yeomen's daughters among the brides and young wives who braved the hardships of the long sea voyage to set up new homes with their husbands across the seas.

It was a matter of pride and of obligation with parents of the yeoman class to secure marriages for their daughters, and to that end to provide marriage portions that would attract as good a catch as possible. This was the future that a yeoman's daughter planned for and normally expected.

Only now and then does one encounter a farmer's daughter who wished to spread her wings farther afield unless in

future doom of their class at home. The time-honored explanation of the inclosures and the industrial development must still be given some weight as a reason for the decline of yeomanry. The colonies certainly acted as a great drain. A limited amount of investigation in the records of the eighteenth century leads to a question in my own mind whether or not the class did actually disappear to the extent often believed, or whether with the triumph of landlordism in the eighteenth century it merely ceased to exert so great an influence in rural communities, and suffered thereby a psychological "disappearance" rather than wholly a numerical one. It is a question outside the scope of this study, but one which calls for more investigation.

56. *Middlesex Quarter Sessions Records,* III, 239, 253, and *passim.*
57. Quoted in T. Birch, *The Court and Times of James I,* 1849, p. 108.

company with a husband to look after her; but there were a few. Anne Atwood, the daughter of a Somerset yeoman, got her father's consent to go to Bristol in the service of a mariner's wife there. Her mistress was to teach her "silk knitting," provide her with both woolen and linen clothing, and in all things to see that she was "well brought up according to her estate and degree."[58]

Adam Martindale's sister Jane was another yeoman's daughter who got foolish notions in her head of leaving home before a marriage had been planned for her. The girl had lived all her life in her native Lancashire, but when some city folk who had fled London in 1625 to escape the plague wished her to accompany them upon their return, she was eager for it. Her parents and the neighbors were against her going, nor did they understand why she wished to go: "She wanted nothing at home nor was likely to lack anything"; and her father was "in a good capacity to preferre her" when she had a mind to get married. The city was probably not yet clear of the plague, and even in healthful times they doubted if the city air would agree with one who was country bred, Jane being "of a fresh complexion and not very hardly." But the girl's mind was made up, and having "her father's spirit and her mother's beauty, no persuasion would serve, but up she would to serve a ladie as she hoped to doe, being ingenious at her needle."[59] Unhappily in this case, the misgivings of the family proved to be justified; for though Jane early made what appeared to be a good marriage with a young innkeeper, she sickened and died a few years later without ever seeing her family or Lancashire again.

Her story was no doubt told to other girls as an example of what befell a girl who left home against her parents' wishes. But probably not many were so tempted. It is plain to see that Adam Martindale considered his sister unlike the average girl of her community and station. For the most part the daughter of a yeoman asked nothing better than to

58. See cases in Bristol Apprentice Books, Bristol Corp. MSS.
59. *Life of Adam Martindale*, pp. 6–7.

marry the son of a neighboring farmer, or perchance a
gentleman's son if her portion were fair enough, and like
the girl in Massinger's play she was content, and never

> Look'd further than her father's farm, nor knew more
> Than the price of corn in the market or at what rate
> Beef went a stone? that would survey your dairy
> And bring in mutton out of cheese and butter.
> That could give directions at what time of the moon
> To cut her cocks for capons against Christmas,
> Or when to raise up goslings.[60]

Both the common law and the civil law stipulated twelve
years as the minimum marriage age for a girl and fourteen
for a boy, but contemporary opinion held that each should
be older.[61] A case in the Court of Requests which tells of the
marriage of a yeoman's daughter at slightly under twelve
indicates clearly that the match was concluded against the
will of her guardian, and that the disapproval which it
merited from the girl's friends and neighbors rested largely
on the basis of the child's age.[62]

To provide suitable matches for their children was one of
the solemn duties that God laid upon parents.[63] It was likewise held to be the duty of sons and daughters to accept
their parents' arrangements in such matters. But while this
course was approved in theory, and partially in practice,
there is considerable evidence to show that the young people
of the yeoman class often had a good deal to say about the
matter themselves. Sometimes, indeed, they took things
wholly in their own hands though they went against accepted conventions in so doing. John Stockwood in 1589 expressed the conventional opinion when he deplored the tendency of the younger generation to "whollie follow their own
will and let out the raines unto their owne unbrideled &
unsettled lusts, making matches according to their own
fickle fantasies, and choosing unto themselves, yoke-fel-

---

60. Philip Massinger, *The City Madam,* act II, sc. 2.
61. W. Gouge, *Of Domesticall Duties,* 1634, p. 180.
62. Req. 2, 196/64.   63. Gouge, *Of Domesticall Duties,* p. 571.

lowes after the outward deceivable directions of the eie." He begged such graceless sons and daughters not to offend further in this fashion, but to assist in stamping out what was "neither the least nor the last" among those vices "wherewith the worlde at this day is full fraughted."[64]

But voices were also raised on the other side. George Whetstone wrote in 1582: "I crye out uppon forcement in Marriage, as the extreamest bondage that is: . . . the father thinkes he hath a happy purchase, if he get a riche young Warde to match with his daughter: but God he knowes, and the unfortunate couple often feele that he byeth sorrow to his Childe, slaunder to himselfe and perchaunce the ruine of an auncient gentleman's house by the riot of the sonne in Lawe not loving his wife."[65]

And even many of the writers who felt that it was the children's duty to obey their parents in the matter of marriage urged the latter to refrain from forcing the match if all manner of fair means to persuade the child to accept their choice proved unsuccessful.[66] For "Tis to be feared," said Thomas Fuller, that "they that marry where they do not love, will love where they do not marry."[67]

It was advice that went unheeded, however, in many cases. Yeoman wills frequently named bequests that were to go to daughters provided they did not marry without the consent of parents or guardians, or named parts of the patrimony that were to be withheld from them if they did. But there were also parents like John Carter, the wealthy Hertfordshire yeoman we meet in the play, who showed a genuine concern for the feelings of their daughters in the matter. Carter says of the gentleman's son who is asking for his daughter's hand:

I like young Frank well, so does my Susan too; the girl has a fancy to him, which makes me ready in my purse. There be

64. J. Stockwood, *A Bartholomew Fairing for Parents*, 1589, pp. 11–12, 16.

65. G. Whetstone, *An Heptameron*, 1582, F 1.

66. Gouge, *Of Domesticall Duties*, p. 572.

67. *The Holy State*, p. 13.

other suitors within, that make much noise to little purpose. If Frank loves Sue, Sue shall have none but Frank.[68]

It is, of course, significant that the speech was made to young Frank's father, who had come to see how ready in his purse the yeoman was; but it is equally apparent that the girl's desire in the matter figured in her father's mind. Later in the play, he says of both his daughters: "they shall choose for themselves by my consent." The nurse in an anonymous play of the period, begging that her young mistress be allowed to choose her own husband, said: "These made marriages prove not well."[69] And there were parents who took that position.

A Derbyshire indenture of 1601 between two yeomen, John Parker and Thomas Bright, states that "John Parker, eldest son of him the said John Parker, shall and will marry and take to his wife Dyonise, daughter of the said Thomas, *if she will thereunto consent*."[70] Likewise James Culling, Kentish yeoman, in designating his choice of a husband for his daughter Catherine to whom he was leaving the bulk of his estate, says, "if it may so bee withoute hurte or discouragement to herselfe."[71]

It was usually the question of the money or property involved in the marriage contract which caused pressure to be brought to bear on the contracting parties: "Wealth is ever a strong Agent for enforc'd marriages,"[72] and where parents were not willing to show consideration beyond the material advantages involved, the young people sometimes took things in their own hands. Elizabeth Denny, the daughter of a Suffolk yeoman, brought herself into great disfavor because she married against her father's will. For a time he swore that he would never give her a pennyworth of her inheritance, though later he relented.[73] Other cases in

---

68. *The Witch of Edmonton,* act I, sc. 2.
69. Anon., *Wily Beguiled,* Tudor fac. text, 1912, p. 31.
70. *Derbyshire Arch. Soc.,* V, 36. The italics are mine.
71. Will of James Culling, Add. MSS. 28008, fol. 35.
72. R. Brathwaite, *The Two Lancashire Lovers,* 1640, p. 24.
73. Req. 2, 189/35.

the court records give instances of the daughters of yeomen marrying without the consent of their parents.[74] At least three of the young people in the Martindale family married as they chose, and against the wishes of their parents. Their father wished to see his eldest son marry a neighbor's daughter who had seven-score pounds for her portion. But when most of the arrangements had been completed, Thomas forsook his father's choice for "a young wild airy girle" of fifteen or sixteen who had but forty pounds as a portion, and was beside, "a frequenter of wakes, greenes, and merrie nights where musick and dancing abounded." As if that were not a bitter enough pill for this Puritan family, Hugh, the second son, "did to all our griefes marrie a papist, and went with her into Ireland."[75] And the daughter Jane, as we know, went to London against the wishes of the family and married there.

Even in matches arranged by the suitors themselves, the business angle often figured largely. As young Thomas Coppin said to his uncle, "you know the manner of this age is first to know what shee is worth."[76] A man of the lowest classes who had little and demanded little might marry as he would or could. But the yeomen were an ambitious lot, eager to get ahead, and even when the young farmer married the girl of his choice, it is pretty evident that his choice was often made, partly at least, with the material end in view. The country suitor's love letter in Nicholas Breton's *Dialogue* is true to the spirit revealed in many an indenture containing the terms of a yeoman's marriage contract:

Sweet hearte, I commend me unto you, and have beene as good as my promise, and I have sent you a paire of gloves by Meg your brothers best beloved, and upon Friday (God willing) I will meete you at the Market, and wee will be merry and talke further of the matter, and if you be as I am, say and hold, I know my portion, and when yours is put to it wee shall live the

74. See especially St.Ch. 8, 42/7; Req. 2, 201/62.
75. *Life of Adam Martindale,* pp. 16, 21.
76. Quoted in the *Oxinden Letters,* p. xxxi.

better. And so, keeping your Handkerchiffe neere my heart:
till I see you, I rest

Yours during life in true love
W.T.[77]

Many found it possible to combine love with business; but
often the business angle was uppermost. A Star Chamber
case for the reign of James I relates the story of Thomas
Milles, a yeoman of Gloucestershire, who lent two hundred
pounds to two gentlemen of Warwick, Mr. Brode and Mr.
Badger. According to Milles, they tried to evade the debt
by effecting a marriage between him and one of Badger's
daughters. For a time it appears that the yeoman was agreeable to the plan, settling his choice upon Rose, the youngest daughter. He promised her a jointure of lands worth
fifty pounds per annum, in return for which the two hundred pounds was to be paid as Rose's dowry. It was not
long, however, before Milles grew skeptical of the good
faith of his future bride's family and friends, and under
pretext of testing the girl's love, whether or not her "show
of affection to him did not proceed from the persuasion of
her friends and not of herself," he suggested that the wedding be postponed a year. He was, thereupon, accused of
being a "cold wooer," especially since he had sent no gift to
his betrothed during their courtship. This defect Milles
tried to correct by the belated present of a twenty-shilling
gold piece, but his own fears grew; and finally on the very
morning of their wedding day, after the minister and all of
the friends had assembled to go to the church, Milles refused to go through with the ceremony unless he were then
and there presented with a bond in the sum of five hundred
pounds as assurance that the two hundred pounds would be
paid him.[78]

The financial side of the arrangement was probably not
often thrust into the foreground at so inopportune a time.
But it was usually there, nor was it considered bad form

77. *The Courtier and the Countryman,* p. 198.
78. St.Ch. 8, 208/4.

that it should be. On the contrary, it is quite certain that a yeoman would prefer marrying his daughter to one whose family, or himself, looked well to these considerations. A girl's future would be more secure if she were married to a "painfull" husband.

VIII

PARISH CHURCH AND VILLAGE GREEN

He allowes of honest pastime, and thinks not the bones of the dead
any thing brused, or the worse for it, though the Country Lasses
daunce in the Church-yard after Even-song. . . . Rocke Monday,
and the Wake in Summer, shrovings, the wakeful ketches on Christmas Eve, the Hoky, or Seed Cake, these he yearely keepes; yet
holdes them no reliques of Popery.

Sir Thomas Overbury, "A Franklin," *New Characters*, 1615

In Merry Mansfield on a Market day
Wrestling there was, and yeomen came to play.

A. Munday, *The Downfall of Robert Earl of Huntington*, act I, sc. 2

RELIGION," said John Selden, himself a yeoman's
son, "is like the fashion; one man wears his doublett
slashed, another lac'd, a third plaine, but every man
has a doublett."[1] Every man had a doublet indeed in Selden's day. An individual might not approve of this or that
religious group; but it would not occur to him to be indifferent to religion itself. Not only did everyone have a religious
affiliation, but he was ready to defend it with all of the
warmth and vehemence that an age of religious controversy
breeds in its people. The Elizabethan settlement was probably as successful as any that could have been devised at the
time. But there was much that it did not settle. And in its
wake came a century of turmoil in which divers motives, religious and otherwise, operated in the name of religion to
engender conflicts that spread among all classes of people.

Religious talk was the talk of the day. It was news in the
current newsletters and broadsides, as scientific matters
and sports items are news in today's press. Religious discussion was in the very air the seventeenth century breathed.

1. *Table Talk of John Selden* (Pollock), 1927, p. 117.

The yeomen were not as a group highly enough educated, nor of a sufficiently speculative turn of mind, to grasp the fine points of dialectic that troubled the theologian. But like everyone else, they held tenaciously to their religious loyalties and were ready upon any pretext to fight for them.

Records that tell of everyday talk and activities are replete with examples of their concern for and with religious and semireligious matters. William Honiwell of Devon wrote in his diary (1602) of a dinner with his neighbors: "there was little talk to any effect, but of arguments of scriptures, and somewhat of Mr. Gee and Clampitt his adversary."[2] William Cooke, an Essex farmer, told the sessions in 1577 of George and William Binkes, two local tailors whom he found "reasoning very earnestly with his servant" on the question of transubstantiation. Impressed by the arguments of one of them in favor of the Roman contention, Cooke exclaimed, "Whye, then we are wronge taught!" "Marye, soe you are," the tailor replied, "and that I will prove by good authors, for the true religion is at Rome . . . but what maner of religion we have here in England I knowe not, for the preachers now doe preache theare owne inventions and phantazies and therefore I will not believe any of them."[3]

John Howard, another Essex man, reported a conversation that took place at dinner among the servants of Mr. Wentworth of Bocking, who were "reasoning upon" the sermon they had listened to the preceding Sunday. Howard, apparently of the old faith, was moved to say that "it was never mery in Ingland sithens the scriptures were so comonly preched and talked upon among suche personnes

2. *The Honiwell Diary,* June, 1602. The Gee family was well represented in the annals of the Elizabethan and Stuart clergy. This reference is probably to the Rev. Edward Gee (1565–1618) who became rector of Tedburn St. Mary, Devonshire, in 1599. His sermons were edited and published shortly after his death by his two brothers, also members of the clergy. A nephew, John Gee, was famous for his anti-papal writings. Clampitt was probably, likewise, a local divine, but he seems less well known.

3. Essex Sessions Rolls, 65/61.

as they weare"; whereupon one named King retorted that he "hoped he should live to see no other time but when the Gospel should be preached here in England."[4]

So went the talk at dinner tables, in servants' quarters, in the fields, and at the village tavern. It was a period when many shades of faith were developing and yeomen were to be found among the followers of practically every group. Two of the three Roman Catholic priests hanged in Derbyshire in 1594 were sons of yeomen.[5] Practically all of the lists of recusants examined for the period 1580–1650 include the names of some yeomen among the adherents of the old religion. One indictment book containing a list of recusants arrested in the first decade of the reign of James I, in certain southern and western counties, shows that slightly more than 32 per cent of a group of 439 men were yeomen.[6] Most of these lists, however, where status terms are given, show a preponderance of gentlemen, husbandmen, and laborers, an indication that in the main it was the larger landlord and his faithful undertenants who held by the old faith. As John Earle said of the latter, "his religion is part of his copyhold which he takes from his landlord, and refers it wholly to his discretion."[7] But in certain sections of Lancashire,[8] and in parts of Hampshire[9] and Cheshire,[10] the yeomen were still predominantly Roman Catholic in the early seventeenth century.

There were also many yeomen who were content to accept the Anglican settlement and happy to worship in peace in the places where their fathers had worshiped without troubling their heads too much about the parson's surplice, the position of the communion table, or the method of baptism

4. *Ibid.*, 64/44.

5. J. Cox, *Three Centuries of Derbyshire Annals,* I, 261–262.

6. El. MSS. Hn. 2178. The status of the women on the list is not given. The gentlemen ranked slightly above the yeomen in numbers.

7. *Micro-Cosmographie,* 1650, pp. 50–51.

8. English MSS., Rylands Lib. 737.

9. Indictment Book, 1646, Midsummer, Hants Quarter Sessions Records.

10. Recusants lists, 1641, Grosvenor MSS., Chester; Presentments and Indictments, 1640–54, Chester Castle MSS.

favored by the vicar. In the main, however, they leaned toward some form of Puritanism, whether the milder form that grew within a moderate Anglicanism or a more vigorous brand that drew them into the various nonconformist sects. This fact is not surprising; for there was much in the reformed doctrine and practice that accorded well with the basic tenets of thought and action in which the yeomen had been reared. Simplicity in religious practices found a ready sympathy among those who had been bred to a simplicity of manner and living. And the virtues of thrift, economy, and independence, extolled in Puritan circles, found quick acceptance in a class whose ambitions as well as their training had already taught them to set great store by these traits.

Bright sons of yeoman families were willing and desirable recruits for the Puritan clergy and such of their writings as we have, particularly those of a personal nature, show how well their early training fitted into the pattern of their later thinking. The autobiographies of Richard Baxter, one of the ablest religious leaders of the seventeenth century, and of Adam Martindale, sought after by nonconformist churches far beyond his native Lancashire, are stamped in many places with the philosophy of the class from which they came.

Ralph Josselyn, vicar of Earles Colne, Essex, for forty-three years, was a yeoman's son whose diary furnishes an excellent example of the farmer-parson; for not only, as in the case of Baxter and Martindale, did he show in character and habits the impress of his early background but, unlike them, continued throughout his life to carry on the activities of his family and class in connection with his acquired profession. Never, apparently, did Josselyn neglect his church or clerical duties. He preached hundreds of sermons, and after the fashion of his day they were long ones. Burials, baptisms, and arguments with Anabaptists found a large place in his diary; but so also did the price of hay and corn, the rate of excise duty on hops, and leases, rentals, and land deals. The following entry, not meant to be amusing, is only one among many which demonstrate his two major interests: "April 3—Cow calved; administered the sacrament, only 14 present."

Josselyn was thrifty and a good hand at creating opportunities for turning an extra penny: "Halfe I have gained hath not been from Colne [his living] but on other occasions." In spite of his Master of Arts from Cambridge and a social and professional standing strengthened through a long and active pastorate, there was always much of the yeoman in Ralph Josselyn. He settled his daughters well in money and lands and died possessed of what, for one of his position, was a good estate. The last legible entry in his diary was made in late July: "Wee begun harvest. . . ."[11]

Presbyterianism attracted a good many yeomen, and along with the minor gentry they furnished many of the elders and other lay leaders in the *Classis*, focal training point for early Presbyterian doctrine.[12] So with other nonconformist groups. Yeomen and husbandmen were predominant in the little group that left Scrooby for Holland in 1609, and eleven years later, strengthened by new recruits, made its way across the Atlantic to found the Plymouth Colony in New England. There were many East Anglian yeomen among the Puritan emigrants in the decades of the 'thirties and 'forties. And later in the seventeenth century they fill the annals of early Quakerism. Thirty of those early Friends, who came later to be known as "The Seventy," or the "First Publishers of the Truth" to spread the doctrines of George Fox, were described either as "yeoman" or "husbandman."[13] "Within the Craven dales of Yorkshire," says a historian of the Friends' movement, "the message of the early pioneers of the society of Friends found ready acceptance particularly amongst the yeoman stock and resulted·in settling may groups in that area."[14]

11. *Ralph Josselyn's Diary*, p. 182, and *passim*.
12. *Bury Classis*, Chet. Soc., 2d Series, XXXVI. For character of the *Classis*, see *The Presbyterian Movement, 1582–1589*, Cam. Soc., 3d Series, VIII.
13. There were actually only sixty-seven. See *Journal of the Friends Historical Society*, XIX (1922), pp. 66–69.
14. H. Hodgson, "Quaker Sketches," *The Bradford Antiquary*, June,

Families as well as communities were often split by differences of religious opinion. The tense situations resulting from such divisions became acute as the period of the Civil Wars heightened religious and political feeling. The Seddon family of ancient yeoman stock in Lancashire illustrate a situation that must often have existed where brother differed from brother, or the younger generation cut itself adrift from parental moorings during those troublous times. Peter Seddon was a strong Puritan. His eldest son, Peter, followed in his footsteps. But John, a younger son, was drawn toward the Laudian wing and the causes with which it was affiliated. Hence he followed his king when the wars began, and later won a commission in the royalist army. His family did what they could in the earlier years to persuade him to correct the error of his ways but to no avail. The following postscript, appended to a long letter of argument and persuasion which the elder son wrote to his brother in 1642, suggests something of the spirit of seventeenth-century Puritanism as well as something of the heartache that attended such family ruptures:

Jan: 15th 1642.

Dear John, I charge you as you expect the prayers or blessing of your mother and me be advised by us your Dearest friends and welwishers peruse diligently what is above written and the Lord Direct you to walke in the Right way so praeth

Your ould father

PETER SEDDON.

Your mother with tears saluteth you.[15]

Had John Seddon been the eldest son and his father's heir, the prospect of being cut off from his father's blessing might have held material implications as well as sentimental

1932. See also the account of the preaching of Thomas Goodayear, Yeoman-Quaker in "Reports of First Publishers," *Friends Historical Journal Supplement*, 1907, pp. 124–126.

15. Letter of Peter Seddon, in "Nathan Walworth's Correspondence," Chet. Soc., Ser. I, CIX, 83.

ones. Certainly economic considerations often had a good deal to do with the transfer of religious loyalties. Yeoman recusants in Nottingham who debated in their minds whether or not to take the oath of conformity were not unaware and perhaps not unaffected by the order of the quarter sessions court that for those who had taken the oath voluntarily, "the several sums by them heretofore forfeited for absence from church are recondoned and not extracted."[16]

Among the records of the sequestration of estates of recusants to meet expenses in the Civil Wars, the testimony of William Blackburne, a Lancashire yeoman of Walton-in-the-dale, is significant. In his request for the return of an estate Blackburne declared: "God, by his marvellous light, hath discovered unto your petitioner the darke and erronious wayes of the popish religion wherein he was bredd; out of a sence thereof, in testimony of his conformity to the protestant religion, your petitioner doth frequent the church and doth partake of the ordinances of God there, and hath solemnly and sincerely taken the oath of Abjuracon before your commissioners in the county of Lancaster."[17] The change of heart in this case may have been wholly sincere, but the thought of losing his lands no doubt sometimes made it easier for a man to discover the error of his way.

Certainly it is true that in the quarrels which religious loyalties engendered other motives came often to be linked with the religious, to the end that a dispute might easily grow into the means of outwitting an enemy, befriending an ally, or satisfying personal or economic ambition: "religion is made a Jugler's paper, now 'tis a horse, now 'tis a Lanthorne, now 'tis a Boate, now 'tis a man. To serve ends religion is turn'd into all shapes."[18] An unconscionable number of local disputes arose from the minutiae of religious detail whether of doctrine, organization, or ceremony.

16. Nottingham Quarter Sessions Records, I, 132.
17. *Royalist Composition Papers*, Lanc. and Ches. Rec. Soc., XXIX, I, 191.
18. *Table Talk of John Selden*, p. 117.

The proprietorship of a church pew, the form of baptism for a new-born baby, how the surplice should be worn, or how to get rid of an unpopular parson, were all subjects that could set a whole parish on its ear and furnish controversy for months. Frequently the dispute ended in litigation either in the ecclesiastical or secular courts. The theological tenet involved, if there were one, was often but vaguely understood by the participants, perhaps not at all, but that detracted nothing from the liveliness of the quarrel.

Often local politics were injected into the conflict. Adam Eyre's diary for the year 1647 shows an entire country community in a fluster over the attempt to eject the minister. Traditionally the appointment of the vicar was in the hands of the local lord of the manor who held the right of presentation among his ancient customary privileges.[19] But as the seventeenth century progressed and many livings became vacant through ejection or voluntary resignation, this rule was not always maintained. In 1644 Parliament authorized Lord Fairfax to fill the vacant pulpits in York, including that of Penistone, Eyre's community. Whether Fairfax consulted the wishes of the principal parishioners is not clear; but it is obvious that by 1647 they considered his choice a bad one, and held the matter of the vicar's ejection and the choice of his successor their own affair.

Penistone was a rural community in which the leading citizens were yeoman families of parliamentary persuasion: Adam Eyre, the Riches, Wordsworths, Micklethwaites, and others. The charges they brought against Mr. Dickinson, the vicar, included such matters as the fact that he had been a chaplain on the royalist side in the recent fighting, that he had too much preached other men's words rather than his own, and too often repeated the same sermon. He was further charged with being a frequenter of alehouses and with

19. In Elizabeth's reign, it was estimated that in Norfolk 688 out of 864 parishes had the granting of their livings from lay patrons, and in Suffolk, 471 out of 554 parishes followed that practice. Tanner MSS., 178, fol. 45, cited in *The Presbyterian Movement, 1582–1589*, Cam. Soc., 3d Ser., VIII, xxv.

having been several times drunk, so drunk on one feast day as to be incapable of executing his offices. He was accused also of being a quarreler and stirrer up of dissension.

After weighing these and other charges, Eyre and his friends decided to allow the vicar forty pounds in money and the benefit of the vicarage during a reasonable time while he searched for another post; but to consider the Penistone living vacated. Eyre himself and one or two others took their own horses and rode about the parish to collect the shillings and pence for the payment of the forty pounds. It was not an easy task. The farmers of the moorland parish had little money and did not part with it easily. The collectors had reason to feel gratified when the sum was finally in hand.

But the vicar was not a man to give in easily. He refused to move from his post. Thereupon Adam Eyre was dispatched to London with a petition to the Committee for Plundered Ministers, set up by Parliament to deal with such matters, to gain an official sanction for Dickinson's dismissal. The vicar, in the meantime, had rallied some supporters to his cause, and local differences on other matters were injected into the quarrel. It was not until the matter dragged on some months past the time when the post was declared vacant that Eyre and his neighbors gained their point and Penistone was rid of its tippling parson.[20] There was no objection to the vicar taking a glass of ale or wine. It was expected that members of the clergy should drink with their friends, in moderation, when abroad with them; nor was it taken amiss if they served a glass of wine or other beverage to callers who came to the vicarage. But Puritan consciences drew the line at drunkenness, particularly when it was accompanied by royalist sentiments.

Neighborhood squabbles like the above were extremely common in country communities and matters affecting churchgoing and church practices often led to bitterness and resulted in costly lawsuits involving both **clergy** and

20. *Diary of Adam Eyre,* pp. 20–21.

parishioners.[21] Despite this fact, the church as the center of community life afforded also means of expression for the best elements of community spirit and enterprise.

An English rural church still serves its community in a variety of ways. But many of the functions earlier performed by it have now passed into the hands of other agencies. The church in smaller towns and communities in Elizabeth's time was often a center for local administration where parish officials met to hear reports, select officers, and sometimes to administer judgments. In most rural villages the church was the headquarters for the village fire department, housing the great hooks, ladders, and long array of buckets, chief fire-fighting equipment of seventeenth-century rural centers.[22] It also often served as the armory where in time of war, or threat of war, such firearms and ammunition as the community wished to have on hand could be stored. Men made the churchyard the scene of their business deals and exchanges. Bargains sealed at the church door, on the church steps, or under a designated yew tree in the churchyard held a special sanctity and acted as a binding force to which even a court of law paid some deference. Records are filled with instances of money paid and bargains sealed at the church door or in the churchyard. Finally, of course, the church was the accepted center for the social life of the neighborhood and much that was finest and best in community relationships found expression here.

Indeed, it was the church of pre-Reformation days that had created most of the feast days and *holy days,* and the Elizabethan settlement had wisely retained many of them on its calendar. So firm a hold did these have on the affections of rural England that even the frowns of a militant Puritanism were in most places insufficient to check their observance.[23] Whitsuntide was invariably a time for feast-

21. See quarrels over church pews, St.Ch. 8, 37/5, 140/29.
22. See examples of such equipment in the *Dorchester Records* (Mayo), 1908, p. 540; see also J. Cox, *Churchwardens' Accounts,* 1913.
23. *The Mirror of Character,* 1869, p. 69.

ing and merriment. Poor folk tried to get a little money on hand "to spend against Whitsuntide." Farmers went out or sent their men to watch the sheep for a night or two previous to this holiday, "for feare of stealinge now against Whitsuntide."[24]

When Puritan communities made efforts to curb the observance of holidays considered either pagan or papist in origin, the local officers upon whose shoulders rested the obligation of apprehending the merrymakers frequently had a sorry time of it. A Star Chamber case for 1604 tells how a group in the country parish of Alton, Southants, procured a minstrel and danced on Whitsunday. When the constable and church wardens tried to arrest the musician, they were overpowered by his supporters who moved him to another part of the village, locked him in a house and, posting one of their own number on the roof to keep watch, continued to dance merrily on the lawn to the strains of the music that came out through the open window.[25]

The Christmas celebration, best loved perhaps of all holidays, was observed both in the church and at home. John Taylor has left a delightful picture of Christmas evening in a farmer's house. After the bountiful dinner there were services at the village church, and after services more feasting. In the evening "some went to cards, some sung Carrols, many mery songs, some to waste the long night would tell Winter-tales. . . . Then came maids with Wassell, jolly Wassell, cakes, white loafe and cheese, mince pies & other meat. These being gone, the jolly youths and plaine dealing Plow swaines being weary of cards fell to dancing to shew mee some Gambols, some ventured the breaking of their shins to make me sport—some the scalding of their lippes to catch at Apples tyed at the end of a stick having a lighted candle at the other—some shod the wild mare; some at hotcockles and the like."[26] It is a scene that must have been du-

24. Somerset Sessions Rolls, 1610, 9, leaf 32.
25. St.Ch. 8, 262/11.
26. J. Taylor, *Complaint of Christmas,* 1631, p. 23.

plicated at many a yeoman's fireside, for references to "keeping Christmas" are many and occur in a variety of documents.

As the period of the Civil Wars drew all questions of religious practice into sharp dispute, attempts were made under the leadership of the Independents to remove all earmarks of secular gaiety from the Christmas season, an effort that reached its height in the Ordinance of 1647, by which the Christmas celebration was legally abolished along with "all festivals or Holy-Dayes" that had been "heretofore superstitiously used and observed."[27] But the habit of making merry at Yuletide was deeply rooted in English soil and the extent to which the reform ever became effective even in Puritan communities is debatable.

May Day, of pagan origin, but commonly classed among the popish superstitions, was especially obnoxious to Puritans. Again their ban met with much defiance. The dispute in which Martyn Jackson, a Lincolnshire yeoman, in 1593, contested the ownership of a house in the village of Scapwick is no longer of particular significance to us. But the records of the quarrel afford an interesting glimpse of a country merrymaking led by Jackson's daughter and her friends who chose the unoccupied house for a morris dance in honor of May Day. The empty dwelling proved an ideal place for games and dancing and the young people set about to enjoy themselves with great hilarity. Trouble arose only when one of the guests whose father claimed a right in the house decided to remain in occupancy after the party was over. The affair ended in a riot, as typical of the raucous character of the village life of the period as was the morris dance that preceded it.[28]

Country folk often sought a near-by town for the May Day celebration. Oliver Baptist, a Devon yeoman of Cheriton Fitzpane, tells of going to Plymouth on May Day in 1600. He took his fife along and together with an old man

27. "An ordinance for Abolishing Festivals," *Arts and Ordinances of the Interregnum*, I, 954.

28. St.Ch. 5, J. 22/16.

who "sounded the drum" played an accompaniment for the
company that "went about with May games."[29] Another
yeoman who was the constable of Brinkloe in Warwickshire
describes his efforts to keep order on May Day in 1621. The
holiday fell on Sunday that year and after prayers a group
of young people met to set up a maypole, having hired a
wandering minstrel and his son "to make them melody"
while they carried forward their task. When it was time for
afternoon prayers they repaired to the church but again returned after prayers to the maypole and to dancing along
the street. Wandering minstrels were the particular target
for Puritan attack; and it was the constable's unpleasant
duty to apprehend the father and son as vagabonds.
Whether the official in this case lacked proper zeal for the
task is not clear; but his efforts were apparently fruitless,
and the merrymakers continued their celebration.[30]

Church ales in some places were a favorite form of entertainment and provided means for raising money to take
care of parish needs. The parishioners of a Devon parish in
1573 "made an ale and gathering & brought in redie monye"
to the sum of forty shillings. Entertainment was furnished
by one of their number acting the part of Robin Hood, and
another in the role of "Lytle John."[31] But parts of Puritan
Devon later became so opposed to this sort of frivolity that
the Devon J.P.'s in the reign of Charles I ordered the sup-
pression of all "church ales, bridal ales, and clerk ales."[32]

No festivity of the countryside was welcomed with
greater zest than a wedding. Custom dictated that the bride
and groom make it an occasion for neighborhood merrymaking. Their parents, if it were a match to their liking,
regarded the occasion as the successful consummation of
their parental obligations and an opportunity for making
a creditable showing among their neighbors. Everybody,
young or old, liked a wedding.

29. Devon Sessions Rolls, Depositions, 1601.
30. St.Ch. 8, 245/27.
31. Accounts of Woodbury Parish, 1573, Exeter MSS.
32. S.P. 16, CCLV, 39.

The period of courtship which preceded the event appears rarely to have lasted longer than six months, or at most a year. If there were a betrothal, or "contracting before marriage," it took place in the presence of witnesses. Current opinion favored this step though it was not always taken.[33] The records of a Star Chamber case describe the betrothal of John Eppes, the son of a well-to-do Kentish yeoman, and Anne Heywarde, the daughter of a knight. In a room in the Eppes home each pledged the other's troth in the presence of their friends as witnesses. As tokens of their faith, young John gave Anne a piece of gold and she gave him a gold ring.[34] A pledge thus formally taken was accepted as binding on both parties.

A case in the Chancery records which throws light on courtship customs tells of the jilted love of Edward Bynd, a husbandman who courted a yeoman's daughter. Young Bynd declared in his charge that he had carried on a suit for the hand of Elizabeth Marwicke for three quarters of a year "to his great charges and expense and loss of time." She had professed to return his affection, and as a token of his love and good will had accepted a gold ring valued at forty shillings, which he says he intended, "if she at any time afterward did refuse to marye with him, she should hand it again." But the fickle Elizabeth, so her suitor claimed, not only later refused to become his wife but also refused to give up the ring. Whereupon he brought suit for its recovery.[35] Another case in the Court of Requests tells of the efforts of Adam Hicke to recover gifts he had given to Marie Heyfould, the daughter of a Kentish yeoman, during their courtship. The girl's father declared that the match had been broken off by Hicke when he heard where he might have a widow of more wealth and had "made meanes to obtain her."[36]

It is evident that gifts of various kinds marked the suc-

---

33. W. Gouge, *Of Domesticall Duties,* pp. 200–204.
34. St.Ch. 8, 268/22.
35. Abstract of case given in *Sussex Arch.,* 1892, XXXVIII, 195.
36. Req. 2, 215/35.

cessive stages of the courtship. Timothy Dannett, a Lincolnshire yeoman, tells of his courtship with Ellen Lambert, whom he met one evening while she was milking the cows in her father's close. Some of their match-making friends had been busy, so the encounter was probably not entirely accidental. She being "an inheritrixe by dicent from her father to the said lands was a fitt match for him," they had said, and "upon sight and liking of her" he made suit to her. A purse, a silver ring, a pair of gloves, and a girdle were among the gifts he gave her as the courtship proceeded.[37] John Eppes gave his sweetheart a pair of garters prior to their betrothal.[38] These and gloves were among the gifts most commonly exchanged.

Henry Best, who had attended many weddings among the yeomen and minor gentry of Yorkshire says that when a marriage project was pending it was held proper that either the young man or his father should broach the matter to the father of the girl to see how the suit would be regarded. If the youth were assured upon this point he then called once or twice to see how "the mayde standeth affected," an indication that the girl herself had something to do with forwarding or frustrating the match. If she encouraged the suit the young man felt justified in presenting her with a ten-shilling piece or a ring of equal value on his next visit, or perhaps even with a twenty-shilling ring or coin. At the next visit, or the next, the gift would be a pair of gloves worth six, eight, or ten shillings a pair; and after that as the prize grew more sure, "some conceited toy or novelty of less value."

Following a courtship of six months or so the parents of the young people met to treat of the dower and jointure, after which the wedding day was set and plans for the wedding and wedding dinner went forward.[39] Best omits to say anything about the bride's clothes; but we know from other sources that this was an important matter both to the girl and to her father who must see that his daughter was turned

37. St.Ch. 8, 195/20.   38. *Ibid.*, 268/22.
39. *Best's Farming Book,* pp. 116-117.

out in a fashion suited to her station. The covenant of the marriage settlement made in 1563 between Isabel Gibson and Robert Hemingway, both of Yorkshire yeoman stock, stated that Isabel's father should apparel her on her wedding day, "with all maner of wedding apparel, as shall be seemly and comely for his and her calling."[40]

Simon Rider gives some indication of the standard in this matter among the yeomen of Staffordshire in his record of the cost of the wedding finery of his daughter Joan, who was married in 1601. The cloth for the wedding gown cost 31 shillings. An additional 7s. 6d. went "for bones to line it"; and the "trimming" came to 16s. Her hat cost 8s. 6d. The cloth itself came within a sixpence of costing the same as had the material of her mother's wedding dress twenty-two years before; but the expensive trimming made the daughter's dress half again as costly.[41]

New gloves, gifts of the bride and groom, were usually in evidence among the young men and girls of the neighborhood who were in attendance at the church on the day of the wedding. Following the marriage ceremony a wedding dinner was served at the home of the bride, where the young man and his wife would reside for a month. At the end of that time the dowry was paid and they departed to the home of the groom, where another period of feasting began. There is some evidence that in certain regions the expense of the bridal dinner was shared by both families, though this may have differed in localities. Whatever the arrangement, there was no lack of food. A bullock and seven sheep supplied the meat course served at the wedding dinner of a young Suffolk yeoman and his bride in 1589. In this instance the bullock and the "breadcorne" were provided by the groom's father and the remainder of the provisions by the family of the bride. Sometimes it appears that the guests shared in the expense, at least of the drink.[42]

40. J. Lester, "History of Shibden Mill," *Halifax Antiq. Soc.*, 1911, p. 228.

41. Rider Commonplace Book, pp. 122, 128.

42. Req. 2, 199/66. A remark of the bride's sister in regard to this wedding is of interest. She says that her father "procured his friends to

Almost as popular as church holidays and wedding celebrations were the festivities kept in connection with certain seasons or seasonal activities on the farm. Some of these no doubt had once had religious significance; for pagan cults often connected religious observances with seedtime and harvest. But now they were for the most part merely excuses for a holiday and merrymaking, as Thomas Tusser indicates in his advice to farmers' wives:

> Good huswives whom God hath enriched enough
> forget not the feasts that belong to the plough.
> The meaning is onely to joy and be glad
> for comfort with labour should sometimes be had.[43]

Plough Monday that fell on the first Monday after Epiphany stood for the inauguration of the new season's labors. It was celebrated particularly in the northern and eastern counties. Another festival observed in localities where fruit was grown had to do with invoking a blessing on the forthcoming crop. Tradition held that good spirits would be ever near if these rites were carried out. They too were performed with local variations. In parts of Sussex groups of boys went about on New Year's Eve from orchard to orchard, wassailing the apple trees and singing this and other chants:

> Stand fast root, bear well top,
> Pray the God send us a good howling crop,
> Every twig, apples big;
> Every bough, apples enou;
> Hats full, caps full,
> Full quarter sacks full.[44]

the marriage dynner & they spent their money there." The only additional evidence I have found to throw light on this custom is in an Elizabethan court roll of Holesowen, in Shropshire, which states that any person "that shall brewe any Weddyn ale to sell, shall not brewe above twelve strike of mault at the most" and that the person being married shall "before his Bridal daye . . . keep no unlawful games in hys House nor out of hys House on pain of 20 shillings," Stowe MSS. 1055, fol. 25.

43. *Five Hundred Points of Good Husbandry*, 1580, p. 180.

44. "Extracts from the Journal and Account Book of the Rev. Giles Moore," *Sussex Arch.*, 1848, I, 110.

One of the happiest occasions of an occupational nature was the sheep shearing. In addition to the regular workmen who helped about the farm, shearing time in sections where sheep were the mainstay of husbandry meant the hiring of expert shearers and their helpers. Food and drink were plentiful throughout the shearing season, but at its close a special supper did honor to the skill and industry of the workmen and furnished a general excuse for a good time for everyone. Harvest suppers to mark the successful garnering of the grain were also everywhere common, and like sheep shearings, were known for their special dishes, for plenty of drink, and for ballads and songs suited to the occasion.[45]

Fairs and market days had a social as well as an economic significance for the farmer and his family. One catches fleeting glimpses in records not written for that purpose of country folk on their way to fairs and markets. Sometimes it is a wain packed with laborers and driven by the farmer's son; sometimes a yeoman on horseback with his wife on the pillion seat behind him; and again a group of men and boys

---

45. The following stanzas belong to a sheep-shearing song that was sung for generations among the Sussex downs:

"Come all my jolly boys, and we'll together go
Abroad with our masters, to shear the lamb and ewe
All in the merry month of June, of all times in the year,
It always comes in season the ewes and lambs to shear.

  . . . .

Our master he comes round to see our work is doing well,
And he cries, "Shear them close, men, for there is but little wool"
"O yes good master," we reply, "We'll do well as we can"
When our captain calls, "Shear close, boys!" to each and every man.

  . . . .

And then our noble captain doth unto our master say,
"Come, let us have one bucket of your good ale, I pray!"
Then out with the bucket pretty Betsy she doth come,
And Master says, "Maid, mind and see that every man has some"

This is some of our pastime while we the sheep do shear,
And though we are such merry boys, we work hard, I declare;
And when 'tis night and we have done, our master is more free
And stores us well with good strong beer, and pipes, and tobacy.

Sussex Arch., II, 251.

walking together toward the market town. The speech of Henry Peacham's countryman in a contemporary play rings true to the spirit observed in the evidence of such activities:

And now and then, on Faire and market-dayes I walk with a neighbour or two to the Faire or the Market to buy or sell, and having drunke a dozen of Ale amongst us, wee come home the same night, scarce feeling the ground we tread on.[46]

It was a good place to see a cross section of rural society. The following picture of Stourbridge Fair taken from a contemporary play depicts a scene that one might have come upon at almost any fair or on market day:

Here should you meete a Nor-folk yeoman, ful-but; with his head able to over-turne you; and his pretty wife, that followed him, ready to excuse the ignorant hardnesse of her husband's forhead; . . . here two gentlemen making a marriage betweene their heires over a wool-pack; there a Minister's wife that could speake false lattine very lispingly; here two in one corner of a shop. . . . I could make an excellent description of it in a comedy.[47]

Business was attended to first. But most of the buying and selling took place in the morning, and the afternoon was largely given over to amusement. There was dancing in the streets or on the village green if Puritan consciences were not set against it, and athletic contests for the young men. Strolling players were often on hand to furnish amusement. If it were a large fair, or a market to which many strangers came, pickpockets and other rogues would be about, and country folk, fit victims for such tricksters, learned to look well to their money wallets.[48]

Strolling players made their way not only to fairs and

46. *Coach and Sedan,* 1636, C 3 v.
47. T. Dekker and J. Webster, *North-ward Hoe* (Tudor fac. text), 1914, act I, sc. 1.
48. MSS. of the Assize Courts in the P.R.O., 45/2; Harl. MSS. 6715, fol. 98.

markets but in groups about the country. Puritan legislators, who held that all theatrical activities smacked of the
devil, attempted to ban their wanderings. But actors and
musicians continued to find their way about the countryside;[49] and it was hard for parents to keep their boys and
girls from the enticing strains of music and laughter that
echoed from the audiences they were sure to gain. Richard
Baxter, son of a Puritan freeholder of Shropshire, remembered in later life how the Scripture reading and family
prayers of his childhood days were often interrupted by the
strains of the tabor and the pipe, and the echoes of jollity
that came from the strolling dancers where "all the town
did meet together to hear them." It was sometimes more
than even a Puritan boy could bear, and this one admits
that he now and then "broke loose from conscience" and
joined the merrymakers, though in his heart he did not
question the belief that "father's exercise of reading the
Scripture was better than theirs, and would surely be better
thought on by all men at the last."[50]

The instinct for play acting among the common folk of
Shakespeare's day is no myth. One meets with it often in
records not meant for that purpose. The play of the Kendall
schoolmaster written in connection with the tenant-right
dispute under James I, and acted by local players, has been
mentioned.[51] The records of another Star Chamber case of
the same period show William Pratt, a yeoman of Claverly,
Shropshire, and John Ridge, the clerk, bringing charges
against a local group whom they accused of having written
and acted a play that brought discredit upon Elizabeth,
Ridge's daughter and wife of the yeoman.[52] Whether or not
the libel charges were justified it is difficult to say, but the
play and the conditions under which it was acted are of considerably more interest to us now than the original point at
issue.

It was performed at Claverly on a Sunday afternoon

49. S.P. 16, CCXXXVIII, 32.
50. *Autobiography of Richard Baxter,* 1925, p. 6.
51. See above, p. 152.   52. St.Ch. 8, 250/31.

after prayers which the parson closed "sooner than usual of purpose that there might be time for the acting of the play for the recreacon of the spectators." The local nailor and cooper and their friends who took the parts give evidence that Nick Bottom, Snug the joiner, and the rest of that "crew of patches, rude mechanicks" who "met together to rehearse a play" in a much more famous production than the one given at Claverly, were not the artificial creation of the poet's imagination but the type of villagers who actually did that sort of thing. The text of the play is crude and filled with rather coarse humor, but it is a good example of the folk literature of the period and thoroughly in keeping with the taste of the age and the group that produced it.

The tavern or village ordinary was always a social center in the country community. Games and dicing in public houses often led to disorder; and alehouse keepers were warned to keep things under control on pain of losing their licenses. But there is abundant evidence that moderate indulgence was permitted. Adam Eyre and William Honiwell both tell in their diaries of afternoons and evenings spent at bowls and cards. Only when done to excess was this exercise frowned upon. Money in small sums was usually the stake of the game:

July 11—I went to Trusham to fornoon prayer, I dined at Tuckett's, in the afternoon I bowled and won xvi d.[53]

Card tricks were popular. Shuffleboard, or "shovelborde" as it was called, was also a favorite game. This too fell under criticism if it were used as an excuse for gambling, that caused "poore neighbors to loose theire money at vs. a game whilest theire wieves & children lye at home and want."[54] But talking, singing, and the drinking of ale, principal amusements of the pubs, were the pastimes that the countryside never tired of.

Drinking parties were always popular. Mention has been

53. *The Honiwell Diary,* 1602.
54. Indictment Book, 1626, Sussex Sessions Rolls.

made of "church ales." Another type of semisocial, semi-charitable function was known as a "help-ale." These, according to Adam Eyre's diary, flourished in his Yorkshire community and they were doubtless common elsewhere:

George Bray . . . requested mee to be a meanes to help him to some money by an ale or some other course.

.   .   .   .   .

This morne I went to Shore-hall and so through the nether part of the towne to bid guests to an ale to Catchaw for Anthony Crosland the next Tuesday.

.   .   .   .   .

Sent Jo. Wordsworth for my shott to an ale he had for Christopher Batty, 1s. 6d.[55]

Presumably the ale on such an occasion was furnished by one or more of the neighbors, probably from their own home supply, and sold for the benefit of some unfortunate person who had fallen on hard circumstances. Even without an ale as an excuse, it was easy for the yeomen and their friends in this Penistone community to plan a little drinking party. They were largely nonconformist in their religious sympathies, but Puritan ideas of a strict brand did not flourish among them. Eyre often mentions neighborhood drinking parties to which the men took their wives: "Borrowed Christofer Marsden's meare this day, to cary my wife and my-selfe to Jo. Shawe's of Swindenwalls."[56] John Shawe's was a public house, but a respectable one. John and Richard Wainwright, Edward Hinchcliffe, and other yeomen were there with their wives. It was February and the fog hung heavy on the Yorkshire moors; so they whiled away the long February day: "Wee stayd til night, and then came home. . . . Wee met this day only to be merry." Sometimes they met at each other's homes for the same type of frolic. Drunkenness was frowned upon among all self-respecting people

55. *Diary of Adam Eyre,* pp. 40, 42, 63.
56. *Ibid.,* p. 12.

in country communities; but not the moderate drinking which both men and women indulged in.

Football was a favorite out-of-door game, and there were frequent matches played between villages and parishes. It was a rough and tumble game, but perhaps no more so than some of the forms it takes today.

Hunting and fishing were popular pastimes, as one would expect. Fishing rights varied. Some yeomen in Sussex, Norfolk, and perhaps elsewhere, had ponds of their own like those of the gentry, well stored with tench, roach, and other fish. Others like John Denys of Littleham in Devon compounded with their local landlords for fishing rights in certain waters. Denys secured privileges in the Denshe where he could get bass, mullets, and roach.[57] In some waters the fishing rights were free to everyone. Fly casting was not unknown. It was called "dibbling" and considerable interest was being shown in it,[58] but fishing with hook, line, sinker, and bait was the usual method. Adam Eyre often fastened his line to the bank in the "rocher pitt," an abandoned stone quarry in the bend of the Don that flowed by his homestead. The place can still be seen.

Shooting at butts, it will be remembered, was encouraged among the country boys who attended John Lyon's school. Tudor and Stuart writers continually deplored the decay of archery. But efforts of public-minded subjects to keep alive this dying art were not encouraging. Bows and arrows were giving way to the new handgun.

The game laws of the period were designed to keep hunting privileges pretty much in the hands of the upper classes. But a good many yeomen were sufficiently well-to-do to be free of them; and if one can judge from the number of recognizances that appear in the sessions records in connection with the breaking of the game laws, hunting regulations were but poorly kept by any one. Some yeomen

57. St.Ch. 8, 126/9. There was a controversy in this case over the fishing rights, whether the lord held all of them or if a part of them belonged to the tenant whose lands touched the river's edge.

58. Sloane MSS. 1160, fols. 2–17.

ran their own hounds, as did their neighbors among the gentry. Robert Furze says that his grandfather "was lustye and geven to all plesure as to hunte, dyse, cards and all other pastyme but spessyallye to shottynge."[59] Probably all of them took the small game that frequented their woods and fields. Adam Eyre tells of taking his fowling piece when he went out to look over his crop, hoping to come upon a lapwing or a cony. And the morning he went on an errand for his neighbor Greaves he took the latter's greyhound along so that he could hunt on his way over the moors. Hunting with a greyhound was forbidden to any yeoman who was not a ten-pound freeholder or a thirty-pound leaseholder.[60]

Adam Eyre's errand for his neighbor Greaves was to the Wordsworth home to tell them of the death of Greaves's wife Ellen, and "to invite them to the buryall." Funerals must take their place among the social events of the countryside; for though a funeral was an occasion for mourning, it also furnished an excuse for dispensing hospitality and entertainment; and provided a meeting place for neighbors.

Scores of yeoman wills contain bequests of sums of money for the provision of food and drink at the funeral of the testator. John Goodgreene, a Kentish yeoman, left ten pounds to be used "for a drinking att my house to such friends as shall accompanie my corpse to the earth."[61] Nicholas Parker, a yeoman of Staffordshire, provided similarly for a dinner for which twenty pounds were set aside.[62] Robert Robinson, yeoman, left thirty pounds "to be spent uppon a dynner, at John Field's house against the church in Soringfield amongst my good neighbours that accompany my body to the buryall."[63] Some of these occasions must have equaled a wedding feast in the amount of food and drink consumed. In addition to the above bequest, Robinson, who was a wealthy yeoman, left six pounds of cheese and four barrels of "double beare" to be given to the poor

---

59. *Furse Family Book,* p. 179.
61. P.C.C., 48 Pile.
63. *Ibid.,* 30 Soame.

60. *S.R.,* 1 Jac. c. 27.
62. *Ibid.,* 77 Skynner.

on the same occasion. John Beacham, a yeoman of Somerset, tells how two fat sheep were sent home out of his fields in preparation for his mother-in-law's funeral, for which beef and other provisions were also provided.[64]

The yeomen never countenanced a life of frivolity as such. That would smack too much of idleness which was not a part of their code. But when weddings, or funerals, or holidays, or slack seasons of the working year provided an opportunity for neighbors to come together to eat, drink, and be merry, they made the most of it. They were lively exponents of the robust age they lived in, an age that laughed heartily, ate and drank heartily, called a spade a spade, and was little troubled with prudery or overconventionality.

Such good living was not indulged in by all classes. There were those in "Merry England" at this time, hundreds of them, who never went to sleep on full stomachs save as the largess of their betters was thrown their way on feast days and social occasions. But few yeomen can have fared badly in this regard. Theirs it was to keep alive the tradition of good living and jollity in the countryside; and when on the eve of the Civil Wars it appeared that this tradition was dying out, there were among those who mourned its passing some who held that "when hospitality died in England, she gave her last groan amongst the yeomen of Kent."[65]

64. Sessions Rolls, 1630, 64, leaf 3.
65. Fuller, *The Holy State,* p. 106.

IX

FOR THE COMMON WEAL

What spruce fellow's this?
    He is an hundred and fifty pounds a year in *potentia*, a yeoman's son, and a justice of peace's clerk.

James Shirley, *Love Tricks*, 1631

The Justices of the peace doe meete foure times in the yeare . . . at which daies the Sherife or his under-sherife with his Bayliffes be there to attend upon him, who must prepare foure enquests of four and twenty yeomen a peece.

Thomas Smyth, *The Commonwealth of England*, 1583

O NE of the marked features of the political framework of Tudor and Stuart times is the tremendous amount of regulation and supervision extended by the government to the smallest particulars of local life. This regulation called for an administrative program requiring the services of hundreds of men. And it was only through the labors of a large corps of public servants that the wheels of an unwieldy machinery were kept moving with even a semblance of success. It was an unpaid and, for the most part, a thankless job that brought no end of inconvenience to those individuals who were asked to perform it. Not infrequently it called for personal sacrifice of both time and means, and for losses that were but poorly compensated, if at all.

Cheyney and others have spoken up for the local nobility and gentry, emphasizing the vast number of obligations that fell upon their shoulders in this scheme of things. It is an emphasis well deserved. It was the sheriffs and the lord lieutenants and especially the justices of the peace of each shire whom the Parliament and Privy Council held responsible for the execution of their orders. Indeed, the importance of the J.P. in English local history, and at points where local matters touched national ones, can scarcely be overestimated. He merits all the attention he gets from the historians. But below the J.P.'s who acted for the body of the county were the numerous officers of the parish, the smaller unit of local administration within the shire. Upon them the final execution of countless public duties rested. And though local records are filled with their activities, these men have yet to receive the attention they deserve.[1]

Their work comes to the fore in this study because in country parishes, and England was largely made up of country parishes, it was chiefly from the yeoman class that they were drawn. In fact, an account of the contribution of the yeomen to local government almost resolves itself into a chapter on parish administration. For if, as has frequently been said, the gentry were the backbone of the shire administration, certainly it is true that the yeomen were both bone and sinew of rural parish government.

It was the duty of the justice of the peace to charge the constable with freeing the town of vagrants, and to see that he was presented at the next meeting of the sessions court if he failed to comply. But it was the duty of the constable actually to apprehend the vagrants, to whip them or have them whipped, and to see that they were sent out of the parish toward the place of their birth. It was the justices, assembled in quorum, who issued orders to recalcitrant communities to mend their highways and repair decayed bridges. But it was the bridgewardens and the surveyors of the highways who had to see that the countryfolk came out

1. The place of the parish officials in the later period has been ably handled in the various volumes of Sidney and Beatrice Webb, *English Local Government from the Revolution to the Municipal Corporations Act*, 1906–22, I–IV. But for the period in question no adequate study has yet been made, though good chapters may be found in the works of E. P. Cheyney, David Ogg, Godfrey Davies, G. N. Clark, and other writers who deal with the sixteenth and seventeenth centuries. I am inclined to think that the fullest treatment of the work of the various parish officials is that given in the critical analysis inserted in the Introduction to certain sets of local records, especially by the editors of the various quarter sessions records which have been published. See Bibliographical Note on the quarter sessions records.

on the appointed days with their wains and horses to do the work, and who must keep account of the money expended on materials and be responsible for its collection and disbursement.

It was the J.P.'s who charged the father of a bastard with his child's upkeep, and ordered the orphans of the parish to be placed in apprenticeships. But it was the overseers of the poor who had to collect the weekly stipend from the father, send the mother to the house of correction if that were her sentence, and see to finding a suitable home for the child as soon as he was old enough to be apprenticed. Again it was the J.P.'s who in dear years conveyed the orders from the Council demanding that all markets be watched for forestallers and regrators, that the poor have the first chance to buy, and that surveys be made of the county's grain supply. But it was the parish officials who must actually make the surveys of their neighbors' barns, and be on hand on market day to inform against all offenders. It was usually the duty of the justices to fix the rates for this or that local obligation, but often they were fixed by the constables, churchwardens, and overseers of the poor themselves and in any case, it was they who had to collect from the unwilling hands of farmers, butchers, bakers, and candlestickmakers the pence and shillings that made up the parish stock.

No claim is made that these duties were done with a high degree of speed, willingness, or efficiency. In fact the contrary was often true. But to understand something of the extent and nature of the tasks and the time they required is to wonder that they were accomplished at all.

A word concerning the parish itself is perhaps a prerequisite for dealing with its activities. Ecclesiastical in nature in its earlier period, the parish had by Elizabeth's time drawn within its compass elements and survivals of a number of other local units.[2] "Vill," "township," "town," "tith-

---

2. For the character of the parish see S. and B. Webb, *The Parish and the County*, 1906, Introduction and Pt. I; and Cheyney, *History of England from the Defeat of the Spanish Armada to the Death of Elizabeth*, 1926, II, chap. XLI.

ing," and sometimes even "manor" are words used with a bewildering lack of discrimination in contemporary documents. And at least two of them, town and township, are frequently used interchangeably with the word "parish," though I think rarely or never in the northern counties where townships were distinctly subdivisions of the large parishes common to that region.

Despite this confusion of local terms, the word parish was by Elizabeth's time pretty generally used to designate the central unit of local administration within the county, though the "hundred" or "wapentake," a larger division than the parish, was still recognized for certain purposes. Some localities, it is true, still held to peculiar local units for the performance of certain duties; but the parish was common to every English shire. It was, moreover, the unit recognized by parliament, king, and privy council as the subdivision of the shire through which their rulings could best be administered throughout the realm.

It is a curious fact that the parish, though thus recognized officially, had no legal existence; that is, in the sense that it had no surveyed or legal boundaries. Its boundaries were merely traditional ones, kept alive from generation to generation by a yearly "perambulation" such as that described in the Essex Sessions Rolls for 1578, in which David Simpson, the clerk, Thomas Church, gentleman, Richard Clarke, yeoman, Thomas Shorye, yeoman, and other principal inhabitants of the parish met together "according to custom, to go round the bounds of the parish of Runwell in procession."[3] The processions stopped at certain stones, hilltops, and brooksides, for psalm singing and commemorative services, the better to fix them in the minds of all present. Small boys walked at the side of their elders to absorb the information which they would one day pass on to other lads following in their footsteps. If less exact than the results attained by modern surveying instruments and blue-

3. Essex Sessions Rolls, 70/4. Simon Rider painstakingly wrote down in his Commonplace Book the landmarks of the parish of West Bromwich, "as old men said" who had often gone on the perambulation, p. 109.

prints, it was a method long in use and wholly acceptable to
an age that asked no better authority for any custom than
that it had existed "time out of mind, to which the memory
of no man is to the contrary."[4]

Next to his own farmstead, the parish in which he lived
was the center of a yeoman's existence. A well-to-do yeoman
might own land in several parishes, but the one in which he
made his home and where he went to church held the chief
place in his affections. It was bound up usually with his earliest memories and only a little less well than he knew his
own lands, he knew its every road and footpath.

Perhaps the most important of the four or five major offices in which the yeomen served their parish was that of
constable. What Daniel Defoe said of this office in Queen
Anne's day was equally true in Elizabeth's: "The imposi-
tion of the office is an insupportable hardship; it takes up
so much of a man's time that his own affairs are frequently
wholly neglected . . . yet there is neither profit or pleasure
therein, but an inconceivable fatigue."[5] David Ogg, one of
the few recent historians to pay his respects to the parish
officials in the seventeenth century, says: "Parliament was
a wonderful institution; but the unpaid parish constable
was much more remarkable."[6]

The office was not filled exclusively by yeomen. Town records show that shopkeepers, innkeepers, and tradesmen
were also sometimes constables. But in country towns and
parishes the yeomen in the office so far outnumber those of
any other class as to make it appear almost a status obligation. It was no accident that Michael Dalton's manual, *The
Country Justice* (1618), long an authority on the duties of

4. The Norfolk Sessions Rolls, 1618, tells how the inhabitants of a
certain town which included parts of the two parishes of Hockwals and
Wilton "retorned home from walkinge the circuite and bounds of the
parishes, and in friendlye and neighbourlike sorte mett together." See also
"The Perambulation of Cuckfield, 1629," *Sussex Arch.*, LXI, 40; and the
small volume of directions for the perambulation of a parish in the Bristol
Corp. MSS. 04253.

5. D. Defoe, *Parochial Tyranny*, 1727 (?), p. 17.

6. *England in the Reign of Charles II*, 1934, II, 494.

local officers, gave the formula for the official charge to the constable at his induction in this manner: "To our loving Friend, A. B. of W., *yeoman*. . . ."[7] A constable, according to Dalton, should have "Honesty, to execute his office truly, without malice, affection or partiality; Knowledge to understand what he ought to do . . . ; Ability, as well in Substance or Estate, as in Body, that so he may intend and execute his office diligently. . . ."[8] It is clear from the records that not all yeomen who became constables lived up to these standards. But the plea made by contemporaries that the office not be allowed to go into the hands of those of less substance and ability than the yeomen would seem to indicate that as a group they were considered more desirable for it than any others who were available. Now and then a gentleman is listed among the parish constables, but rarely. Gentlemen did not find its duties to their liking, nor did they hold it fitting to their station; so they usually escaped it. Yeomen did not enjoy it either; but custom and current opinion had made it a public obligation of men of their station just as the office of justice devolved upon their neighbors of the gentry.

In earlier days it had been customary for the court leet to choose the constable, and this was still done in some places,[9] though by no means in all, as court leets no longer existed everywhere. In Lewes, Sussex, they were chosen by *The Twelve*, a group of the wealthier and more influential men of the town (and never exactly twelve in number, as a contemporary explains).[10] Robert Brooker, a yeoman of Eaton Bridge, Kent, was named constable in 1644 by two of the justices, acting under order of the sessions,[11] a practice followed in many places. Two constables in a Hertfordshire village were appointed by Thomas Coningsby, Esq.,

7. *The Country Justice,* chap. 174. See above, p. 267 n.
8. *Ibid.,* p. 85.
9. *Manchester Constables' Accounts,* 1891, I, viii.
10. *The Book of John Rowe,* p. 120.
11. Order Book, 1644, in the MSS. of the Kent Quarter Sessions Records at Maidstone.

the lord of the manor.[12] It seems likely that as the court leet had disappeared in various places, its duties in regard to this office as in other spheres were taken over by whatever person or group seemed the logical and expedient agent for exercising the choice. An order of the Nottingham sessions for 1642 states that the constables of Lowdham "shall be chosen by the Court Leete to be held for the manor of Lowdham next after Michaelmas (if any such be)," or else by the townsmen at about that same time, "without any regard to such former usage."[13]

In his oath the constable swore to arrest all rioters or persons breaking the king's peace; to apprehend all felons and barrators, or pursue them with hue and cry if they tried to escape to another parish; to apprehend all rogues, vagabonds, nightwalkers, and other suspects; to keep an eye on the people who managed alehouses, ordinaries, and inns, for the curbing of unlawful games and inordinate drinking; and to present all offenders to the proper court, according to the nature of their misdemeanor.

Furthermore, the oath stated that the constable should arrest all popish recusants with their children and servants who did not attend church regularly; have a care for the maintenance of archery; assist in finding laborers to help save the crops at harvest time; see to it that the parishioners choose the surveyors of the highways each Easter week; test the quality and amount of malt made and sold in the community to see that it meet statute requirements; and execute all precepts and warrants given him by the J.P.'s or other superiors in the county. In case anything were omitted in the foregoing list, the concluding stipulation of his oath prescribed that "he must do all other things belonging to the office of constable."[14]

Constables' accounts give some idea of what those "other things" sometimes were. They usually arose from emergencies that grew out of the special circumstances of time or

12. *Hertford Sessions Records*, I, 75.
13. Nottingham Sessions Papers, 1642.
14. Dalton, *The Country Justice*, pp. 608–609.

place. Hence, after periods of warfare, constables were required to collect and sometimes to levy relief money for maimed soldiers. In years when there was a dearth of grain they were required to execute market regulations. And always at the calling of the musters, either for a review or for the impressment of troops, it was the constable's duty to issue the summons for all the "able men" to appear on the delegated day. They frequently were called upon to levy lays for special repair work on bridges or to supplement the poor stock. Sometimes it fell to their lot to hold petty sessions. And often a multitude of smaller details, from the mending of the village stocks to assisting unfortunates who came through the parish with a permit to beg, fell within the range of their duties.[15]

It is no wonder that busy farmers dreaded taking their turn at the office. If, however, the above duties indicate something of its onerous character, they likewise show its importance to the rural community. John Selden, who never forgot the impressions gained in his early youth among the countryfolk of Sussex, once said: "The parish makes the Constable, and when the Constable is made, hee governes the parish."[16] This does not mean that the office carried with it any acclaim or honor. Quite the contrary! Constables were often the victims of slander and abuse and sometimes

15. The foregoing paragraphs on the duties of constables are based on three contemporary manuals, those of Dalton and Lambard, hitherto cited, and that of W. Sheppard, *The Offices of Constables, Churchwardens, Overseers of the Poor, Supervisors of the Highways,* etc., 1652, as well as upon dozens of instances in the various records that touch the activities of yeoman constables; e.g. S.P. 14, CXL, 19; Devon Minute Books, 1631; S.P. 16, D 11, 41; St.Ch. 5, W, 63/10. There are many such examples. There are also many excellent constables' accounts and presentments. A few of those consulted are here listed: Essex Sessions Rolls, 1580–1640; Norfolk Sessions Rolls, 1556–1647; "Account Books of Stephen Fox, yeoman," *Old Yorkshire,* 2d Ser., III, 59–61; *Manchester Constables' Accounts,* 1891–92; Constables' Presentments from Cornwall, S.P. 16, CCCXCV, 7; Reports of Hertford Constables, S.P. 16, CCCXLVII, 67; Reports from constables in various counties, *ibid.,* CCCLXXXVIII, 7; Accounts of Prescott constables, 1617, Prescott Manor Rolls; Constables' accounts, Add. MSS. 36981; Reports of Hunts. constables, *ibid.,* 34400. Practically all of the sessions rolls contain some constables' returns.

16. J. Selden, *Table Talk* (Pollock), p. 93.

actually feared bodily danger in the performance of their duties among those who resented the interference it entailed.

When Penrose Butler, an Essex yeoman, was constable at Codham, a theft occurred in the village. It became his duty to spread the news for everyone to keep a lookout for the stolen property. Yarn of the type stolen was later found in the house of one John Sadler, a weaver, who was brought before a justice for questioning. The latter, unable to prove anything against Sadler, reprimanded him and let him go, but Sadler at once presented Butler for having entered his house and brought him under suspicion. In time the case reached the Court of Requests. Here Butler argued with feeling that if the king's subjects were to have action brought against them for activities done in the performance of their duties, the effect would be to discourage officials from performing those duties faithfully, thereby frustrating the only existing means for maintaining the king's peace.[17]

James Syffon, the constable of a Surrey parish in the reign of Charles I, took to ballad making to express the difficulties that went with the office. One stanza of his complaint stated:

> The Justices will set us by the heels,
> If we do not as we should;
> Which if we perform, the townsmen will storm
> Some of them hang's if they could.[18]

Evidence is not wanting to show that the courts and higher officials made considerable effort to enforce respect for the office and to protect the person who held it. How effective this effort was we cannot be sure, though there are frequently records of fines for abusing or assaulting the constable. The assize records of the Western Circuit bear an order to one Anthony Downes of Devonshire to make a public confession in the parish church of Woodford Wor-

17. Rep. 2, 181/73.
18. Reprinted in A. Judges, *The Elizabethan Underworld*, 1930.

thy for wrongs done to Richard Hangar, the constable there.[19] And in 1609 it was ordered that Robert Batte of Middlesex should be set in the stocks for three hours on the next market day "for his contempte in refusinge to ayde the Constables apprehendinge a number of Rogues in a Barne at Hillingdon."[20] To aid the constable in the execution of a duty when he asked for such assistance was a legal obligation.

But even when due respect and aid were given the office, it carried with it more drudgery than prestige, and nobody performed its duties for love of the tasks involved. Often, too, the yeomen who served as constables were out of pocket temporarily and sometimes permanently as a result of their expenditures. The sessions records are filled with reports of constables seeking to reimburse themselves for money expended in connection with their duties. Usually the sums involved were small, often not more than a few shillings, but sometimes they ran as high as fifty pounds.[21] The retiring officer often had to wait months, sometimes years, to collect the money that he had spent for the parish.

That constables often did not perform their duties well is evident. John Pakeman, yeoman, constable of an Essex parish, was presented to the sessions for suffering rogues and vagabonds to pass through his hands without punishment.[22] Anthony Carter, yeoman, also a constable in Essex, was indicted in 1567 for not executing four warrants of arrest passed on to him from the justices.[23] Robert Knapp, yeoman, a constable of Nedham, Suffolk, in 1604, was accused of having connived at the escape of some thieves.[24] Robert Metcalf, yeoman, a constable in the North Riding of Yorkshire, was presented for not seeing the day watch kept in his parish.[25] And William Fownes, yeoman, the con-

19. Ass. 24/20.

20. *Middlesex Sessions Records,* II, 52.

21. See Lindsay Quarter Sessions Records, 1637, A 8; Prescott Court Records, 1625; Norfolk Sessions Rolls, 1623–24; Somerset Sessions Records, Chas. I, 24/21.

22. Essex Sessions Rolls, 1622. 23. *Ibid.,* 1567.

24. St.Ch. 8, 4/15.

25. *North Riding Sessions Records,* II, 2.

stable in a Worcestershire parish, was presented for "letting Mr. Apleton, a recusant, escape his hands."[26]

But were one to read only the court records of any age, he would have a distorted picture of the situation. And though these instances of neglect are numerous enough to take account of, they must not overshadow the work of scores of men who not once but many times took their turn at a thankless task and fulfilled it in an acceptable manner. "That he should have functioned at all," says Mr. Ogg of the constable, "is a tribute to the sense of order and discipline inherent in the humblest of Englishmen."[27]

In order that the burden might not fall too heavily on the same people, there came in some places to be an almost automatic schedule whereby all who were eligible in the community took their turn.[28] But such a distribution of duties was not made everywhere; probably not in most places. Information presented to the Nottingham sessions in 1642 stated that the constable's office in Lowdham had for years fallen wholly on the shoulders of seven farmers who now begged that others in the community take their turn. Now and then one presented an excuse that he hoped would free him from obligation. A Wiltshire constable in 1616 begged to be relieved from the office, "forasmuch as I am unlearned & by reason thereof am constrayned to goe two miles from my howse to have the help of a scrivener to reade such warrants as are sent me and am a poore man."[29]

John Royle, a yeoman of Leftwich in Cheshire, tried to claim exemption on the grounds that he dwelt on the glebe land of the parsonage of Davenham which did not fall under the ordinary jurisdiction of Leftwich.[30] But the J.P.'s

26. *Worcestershire Sessions Papers,* I, 237. For other examples of neglect of the office, see St.Ch. 8, 304/30; S.P. 16, CXCIII, 33; Chester Sessions Records, File I, No. 47; Devon Minute Books, 1630. *Notts. Sessions Papers,* IV, 10, and *passim.*

27. D. Ogg, *England in the Seventeenth Century,* p. 494.

28. *Warwick Quarter Sessions Records,* I, 167, 184. Notts Sessions Records, 1642; *Book of John Rowe,* p. 139.

29. *Wiltshire Quarter Sessions Records of the Seventeenth Century* (Cunningham), 1932, p. 54.

30. Cheshire Quarter Sessions Records, 1631, 4, 19.

found the excuse insufficient. It was held that he was *Idoneus homo*, as the statute said a constable should be; that he had served as surveyor of the highways and in other parish offices; that he was of sufficient substance to qualify for the office; and that his father and stepfather had both in their time, while living on the same land, served as constable, as now he also must do. Devon records show that constables there were discharged of further service because of their great age and long term in office, and these were probably the only reasons looked upon as legitimate grounds for relief from the duty. An entry of 1625 in the memorandum book of Robert Roberts, a Devonshire yeoman, states that his brother Thomas had been "Cunstabell" of his parish for twenty-three years,[31] and it is clear from the Journal of Simon Rider of Staffordshire that both he and his father served term after term.[32]

The overlapping of duties among parish officials made for much trouble and inefficiency. Often the same duty was laid upon two or even three offices. What is everybody's business is nobody's business, was as true then as it is today. When a constable left it to the churchwarden to apprehend the beggar who loitered at the tavern door, and the churchwarden left it to the overseer of the poor, and he in turn thought one or the other of them would do it, the lucky beggar might go free; yet constable, churchwarden, and overseer could, according to the law, be presented at the sessions for neglect of duty if anyone were disposed to make the charge.

The office of churchwarden, like that of constable, drew hundreds of yeomen into the service of their communities, and it would be difficult to say which of these two officials was the busier man in a country parish. Their duties were closely related and, as stated above, frequently overlapped. Just as the parish itself had developed from an ecclesiastical unit to one of civil administration, so the churchwarden had come to be a civil as well as an ecclesiastical servant. The

31. Diary and Household Book of Robert Roberts, 1622–46, p. 13.
32. Rider Commonplace Book, *passim*.

office, like that of the constable, was not legally restricted to
the yeoman class and in larger towns tradesmen and minor
gentry took their turn at it. But the yeomen, by virtue of
their qualifications and availability, supplied the rural parishes with most of their wardens.

Already we have noted the wide range of activities connected with the parish church which was the integrating
center of community life. It is doubtful if anyone, even the
vicar himself, knew more about these activities than the
churchwardens. Ordinarily there were two wardens in a
rural parish, whose election or appointment, like that of the
constable, varied somewhat with locality and circumstance.
Records of a Star Chamber case show that Thomas Serle,
an Essex yeoman, was chosen warden at Elmsden "by the
minister and most substantiall part of the inhabitants."[33]
And this appears to have been a practice followed in many
places. Sometimes the vicar selected one of the wardens and
the parishioners the other. And sometimes both were elected
by the vestry.[34] The parish records of Burford for 1613
show that there were four wardens there, "one for the rector, one for the vicar, and two for the township."[35] But this
was not the usual practice. The term of office was one year
or two, according to local practice, and often individuals
served many terms.

I have met with no formula for a warden's oath or charge.
Perhaps each parish used its own method for inducting the
incumbent into his office and charging him with his duties.
Certainly the following charge from the records of a Berkshire parish of the early Tudor period is individual in character and sufficiently plain to have put the warden-elect on
his good behavior: "Cherchye Wardenys thise shal be your
Charge to be tru to God and to the Churche for love nor
favore off no man wythe in thyse parish to withold ani

33. St.Ch. 8, 265/28.
34. March *Reports* (1639–1642), 1675, p. 5; Harden *Reports,* p. 379;
J. C. Cox, *Churchwardens' Accounts,* pp. 4–6; Add. MSS. 19081, fols. 380–
381.
35. R. Gretton, *The Burford Records,* 1922, pp. 40–41.

Righyte to the Churche but to Reserve the Dettes to hyt belongeth or else to go to ye Devell."[36]

Some of the duties of the office required a good deal of business skill and experience. The administration of bequests made to the parish church was usually in the wardens' hands. These ranged all the way from a few pence to mend the bell ropes or a silver plate for the communion bread to sizable amounts of land and money. Frequently donors left the entire disposal of these bequests to the discretion of the churchwardens; sometimes it was to be exercised through the combined judgment of the wardens and the overseers of the poor.

It was also the duty of the wardens to allocate church funds for repairs, furnishings, and the like, and to collect the rates that had been levied by the community on itself for such purposes; often a tedious and sometimes a wellnigh impossible task.[37] Like the constables, they frequently had to supply money from their own pockets for expenses. Ultimately they would be reimbursed from the public stock, but this often took a long time. Two wardens of Fettleworth, Sussex, made a claim in 1637 for a debt of £12 3s. incurred in connection with their official duties. It was twelve years later that the sessions finally ordered repayment.[38] These collections and expenditures called for the keeping of detailed accounts. At the close of a warden's term of office these account books or rolls were placed in the parish-church chest for safekeeping and here many of them have been preserved with a completeness and continuity almost unequaled by any class of local documents. The items listed there serve well to show the type of work done by the yeomen who filled the office, and much also about the life of the country community. The following, chosen at random from the accounts of a Devonshire warden in the reign of Charles I, may be taken as an example. They could be aug-

36. "An Ultimatum," *Berks, Bucks and Oxon Archæological Journal,* 1895, I, 30.
37. See S.P. 16, CCCXVI, 71.
38. Sussex Sessions Records, Order Book. 1649.

mented and duplicated from similar records of scores of
parishes throughout the realm:[39]

paid for our Diners and the Counstables	7 *s.*
paid to Mr. Francklin for washing the surplesses and writing out the regester booke	11 *s.*
paid for mendinge of the locke of the Churche dore	1 *s.*
paid for bread and drincke when wee went to viewe the bonds of the parishe	7 *s.*
paid to Longaller for makeing cleane the church against WhitSundaye	1 *s.*
paid for ringers the 5th of November	6 *s.* 6 *d.*
paid to 2 men which came out of turkey by con- sent of the parishe	7 *d.*
paid to Thomas Gyles for making of a new wheele for the little bell	3 *s.* 5 *d.*

In items from the December accounts of a Gloucestershire warden we see the country parish preparing for the
Christmas season:[40]

For holly ageyne Crystmas	1 *d.*
To the clarks for the syngyng of the carrolls	xvi *d.*
On Christymose day at nyght to ye clarke for syngying of ye carolls	viii *d.*
For hollye and Ivie	ii *d.*
Payde the Clarke for strewings at Christmas	1 *s.*

An item from the accounts of a Somerset warden shows
the scarcity of books:[41]

39. Plymstock Rate-book, 1638, Exeter MSS., pp. 230–231. See biblog-
raphy of published churchwardens' accounts by Miss E. Philips, *The
English Historical Review,* XV, 335–341.
40. "Payments at All Saints Bristol," *Glouc. Notes and Queries,* I, 252.
41. *Somerset Arch.,* 2d Ser., XV, 60.

sants;[48] and the collection of fines from those who broke the
Sabbath by bearbaiting, bullbaiting, the giving of plays,
interludes, and the like.[49] In 1609 three Worcestershire yeomen, the constable, and the two churchwardens of the parish of Curewyadd were presented at the sessions for their
failure to elect the surveyors of the highways at the appointed time and to set the days for road repair,[50] another
duty belonging to both offices.

Other duties the wardens shared with a third group of
parish officials, the overseers of the poor, who likewise in
country parishes were chosen largely from the yeoman class.
The municipal records of Shrewsbury for 1635 show that
the overseers there were yeomen in ten out of the fifteen parishes.[51] In smaller villages the percentage was larger. The
work of the overseers is perhaps somewhat better known
than that of other parish officers; for the problem of the
Elizabethan poor and the laws that were enacted toward its
solution have received considerable attention.

The acts of 1597 and 1601, although modified and enlarged by later statutes, became the groundwork for English poor relief for more than two centuries. To aid the already overworked parish officials in the execution of the new
duties these laws entailed, the justices were instructed to
nominate two, three, or four men, as the circumstances required, who should have the main responsibility for the
poor-law administration.[52] The laws dealt chiefly with the
care of the sick, disabled, aged, and impotent persons of the
parish; the provision of work for the able-bodied unemployed; and the apprenticing of orphans and the children
of poor families to suitable masters: in short, with the general problem of ridding the parish of all beggars, vagabonds, drifters, or unfortunates of any nature who were
likely to become a public charge.

48. *Worcestershire Sessions Papers*, I, 236, 244.
49. *S.R.*, 1 Car. I, c. 1.
50. *Worcestershire Sessions Papers*, I, 130. See also W. Lambard, *The
Duties of Constables, Borsholders, Tythingmen*, etc., p. 62.
51. Overseers of the Poor, 1635. Shrewsbury MSS.
52. *S.R.*, 39 Eliz., c. 3, and 43 Eliz., c. 2.

Paupers who could prove that they were in the parish of their birth had a right to work or support from that parish. But if they were merely wandering through the country, as many were doing, the statute declared it the duty of the overseers, in conjunction with the constables, to free the town of them. An offender, according to the statute, should be taken to the public square, stripped to the waist, whipped until he bled, and then sent along in the direction of the parish of his birth. An entry in the diary of Robert Roberts, yeoman of Devon, for 1622, shows how the statute operated:

Giles Roles a vaggorant Begger was the fourth day of February . . . openly whipped in Upton Hellings for a wandering Roge according to the lawe and is assigned to pass forthwith from tything to tything the next sennight way to Ashton within the county of Heryford whereat as hee confesseth he dwelleth . . . and is limited to be there within twelve days where he is to be delivered to the churchwardens and overseers of the poor . . . and there by them to be set on work . . . as the law biddeth.[53]

The overseers met monthly with other officers and responsible citizens of the parish and went over plans for the ensuing month. They had to keep accounts and to justify the expenditure of all funds in their control. Charges brought against John Waters, a Norfolk yeoman, who was one of the overseers at Torrington in 1630, accused him of giving to the poor when it was not necessary, and of withholding help when it was needed.[54] Dispensing the public relief money to everybody's satisfaction is not an easy task in any age.

If suitable employment for the able-bodied were not

53. Diary and Household Book, 1622–46, p. 5. It was not always easy to discover the culprit's birthplace, if indeed the unfortunate himself knew. Beggars often make good liars, and the records frequently show the parish officers much in doubt on this point. Often the poor victims, both men and women, were sent long distances, being whipped from parish to parish. Add. MSS. 34400, fol. 276.

54. Norfolk Sessions Book, 1630.

available, it was the duty of the overseers to provide materials and set them to work. In 1634 five yeomen, overseers of the poor in a Worcestershire parish, were indicted for not providing hemp, flax, iron, and wool, and setting the paupers of that locality to work with them.[55] The work provided was usually spinning or weaving. If a parish were excessively poor and unable to take care of all of its paupers and unemployed, the overseers might appeal to the justices for aid. If they deemed the request reasonable, they could demand that the wealthier parishes of the shire help with the burden, an obligation that the latter never fulfilled without reluctance and one not often asked of them. In years like 1630–31 when the dearth of grain, high prices, and the employment of fewer laborers on the farms increased the number of beggars and idle folk, the problem often became acute. Overseers in such years were held to a stricter account.

The desire to keep down the numbers of those whom the parish must care for was in large part responsible for the attention paid to the illegitimate children born in the parish. Orders regarding the care of bastards fill the pages of the sessions records. The execution of these orders fell almost entirely in the hands of the overseers.

Local officials felt a tremendous concern over keeping down the list of those who might become a charge on the town. A Star Chamber record tells how the report came to Edward Terrill, yeoman, one of the constables of Dunster, and to one of the overseers of the poor that a man named Aldrich Lewes and his wife, the parents of a family of eight, were about to depart for Ireland, leaving two of their small children behind. Fearing that the children would become a charge on the town, the above officers went "speedily" to Robert Poore, yeoman, the other constable, and to the rest of the overseers; and together they "hurried" to one of the J.P.'s, George Luttrell, Esq., to demand that he send for Lewes before he got away. Lewes later claimed that he had

55. *Worcestershire Quarter Sessions Papers,* II, 556.

made arrangements for the children's upkeep and that he intended to come back for them, but the parish officials were suspicious, a suspicion doubtless based on former experiences.[56] They were constantly under pressure to prevent additional demands being made upon the funds that were already insufficient for all the needs they had to meet.

As the churchwardens looked after the expenditure of gifts left to the church, so the overseers of the poor were responsible for the handling of many bequests made for charity. Since practically everyone made some gift of this kind even if it were a very small one, this was no small task.

The existence of many overseers' accounts throws light on the detailed and tedious nature of their labors; and sessions records show that they, like the other parish officials, were often out of pocket because of expenditures made about their parish work. Men sometimes tried to get out of serving in the office, but usually their efforts were fruitless. Walter Collins, a yeoman of Fareham, Hampshire, begged to be relieved from serving as overseer in his parish in 1649. But his request was refused on the grounds that the poor would be wronged thereby and that it would be a bad example to set to others in the office.[57] Only age and illness were held to be valid excuses for not serving. The men who were elected to the office knew this and for the most part accepted their obligation as a necessary part of the civic duty that the age demanded of men of their station.

Another major piece of work falling to the lot of the parish official was the care of bridges and highways, a responsibility delegated to the surveyors of the highways and the bridgewardens. Now and then one finds a member of the minor gentry in these offices, particularly if an important bridge were under construction; but in nine cases out of ten they were filled by yeomen. Practically never did a tradesman or any townsman serve as surveyor of the highway or bridgewarden.

The choice of the surveyors, supervisors, or waywardens,

56. St.Ch. 8, 194/26.   57. Hants Order Book, I, fol. 283.

as they were labeled in different localities, was made by the constables and churchwardens on Tuesday or Wednesday of Easter Week. At this time also they set aside six days as a period for voluntary work on the highways under the direction of the supervisor. Every able-bodied man in the parish except hired servants had to give his labor on these days or else pay someone to take his place. Landholders had also to furnish carts, horses, and workmen, according to the size of their holdings.

The statutes and orders regarding highways, and the presentments made at the sessions courts concerning roads that were in decay give us some idea of the Elizabethan conception of good roads.[58] Certainly the standard falls far short of our modern notion of wide, hard-surfaced highways. If the roadway were kept clear of outcropping hedges and overhanging tree boughs; if weeds, logs, stones, and impedimenta were cleared from the main surface and drainage ditches at either side kept scoured, it was held to be satisfactory. All large streams running across the road had to be bridged with structures sufficiently well-built to carry the loads that should be taken over them, and the deepest mudholes, particularly any deep enough that "a man and his horse should mire fast therein," must be filled with stone and gravel.[59] The rules for road maintenance contained in the acts of 1555, 1563, and 1576 remained in use for more than a hundred years.

It was a difficult task for the supervisor to get men out to do their road work. To present the defaulters who were his friends and neighbors was likely to invoke their enmity. On the other hand failure to get the work done meant that the supervisor himself was open to presentment for neglect of duty. Nor did the voluntary road work prove very effective.

58. *S.R.,* 5 Eliz., c. 13; *ibid.,* 2 & 3 Philip and Mary, c. 8; Sussex Order Book, I; Devonshire Minutes Books, III; Ass. 24/21; S.P. 16, LIV (1–2), CXCI, 63, CXCVIII, 64, CCXXXVII, 54; Essex Sessions Rolls, 1571, 1630; T. Proctor, *A Profitable Work to this Whole Kingdom concerning the mending of all highways,* 1610.

59. *Worcestershire Quarter Sessions Papers,* II, 528.

"The rich," said William Harrison, "doo so cancell their portions, and the poor so loiter in their labours, that of all the six, scarcelie twoo good days work are well performed."[60]

Supervisors learned to welcome the payment of fines by those who preferred to meet their obligation that way. As the surveyors of a Lindsay parish said in 1642: "Experience has taught that the work will be much better done with the money than if the carriage and labourers had come in to do the same."[61]

Harrison tells us that surveyors were at times accused of being interested only in the improvement of the highways from which they would benefit personally: "Sometimes, also, these daies works are not imploied upon those waies that lead from market to market, but each surveyor amendeth such by-plots & lanes as seeme best for his own commoditie and more easye passage unto his fields and pastures."[62] One can scarcely withhold a partial sympathy from the farmers who thus sought to gain some compensation for the labor of an office that demanded so much.

The upkeep of bridges was clearly a large part of the highway problem. Small bridges were in many cases under the care of the highway supervisor. A special bridgewarden was appointed for the larger bridges, and a relatively large amount of money was spent for the building and mending of bridges. A good deal of this work was done by paid labor,

60. *Description of England,* Bk. II, 148.
61. Lindsay Sessions Papers, 1642, 10A. E. Mather, writing in 1696, said, "one hired labourer will do as much at the highways in one day as is done by six or seven others," quoted in B. & S. Webb, *The Story of the King's Highway,* p. 28. By this time road labor had largely been put on a paid basis. Ordinances of 1654, 1662, 1670, 1691, and 1697 dealt with highways and brought considerable improvement though the question continued through the next century to remain a major local problem. See *The Story of the King's Highway,* pp. 20–23, and *passim.*
62. *The Description of England,* Bk. II, 149. The law gave surveyors the right to enter any quarry and take loose stone and gravel for highway repair. If there were no such quarry or pit, they had the privilege of entering private property that fronted the roadway and taking therefrom what was needed, provided certain precautions in the care of the land were followed. See case of William Butcher, yeoman, and Christopher Gooday, gentleman, in Essex Sessions Rolls, 1630.

since much of it required somewhat more skill than the ordinary road work.[63]

The bridgewarden continually faced disputes between individuals and parishes, and sometimes between counties over the question of whose duty it was to pay for the upkeep of bridges that crossed boundary lines. It was not always an easy matter to settle. There was great variety in the local practices regarding bridge repairs, even within a single shire. One presentment from Essex stated that a certain bridge should be repaired by the inhabitants of the parish. The repair of another bridge in the same region was said to be the duty of two of the local gentry, "because they are the lords of the manor there." In another instance it was left to James Bretton and Reginald Payne, two yeomen, who "were wont to repaire it by reason of the tenure of their lands there." And in still another case the record states that the bridge was in need of repair, "but who shoulde make it, we know not."[64]

The following account of the labors of William Ripon, a Yorkshire yeoman who occupied the position of bridgewarden in his locality, shows something of the demands of the office. In this instance it was an intershire dispute over repair obligations that caused the trouble.

The question was whether the responsibility for repairing the bridge that linked the two counties of York and Durham across the river Tees, at Yarm, belonged to the Yorkshiremen or to those who lived in Durham. When Ripon became the warden in 1621, the bridge was already known to be in great decay. According to the statute, a case of this kind required that both counties share the expenses of repair equally unless it could be proved that the entire cost rightly belonged to one of them. The Yorkshire men took the initiative and offered to pay their share. But Durham representatives, citing the exception clause of the statute, held that they could prove that the responsibility lay

63. *S.R.*, 23 Henry VIII, c. 2.
64. These illustrations are taken from the Essex Sessions Rolls of 1571–72.

alone with Yorkshire. Among other reasons, they stated the
fact that for years the lords of the town of Yarm on the
Yorkshire side had exacted toll from all passers who crossed
the bridge. This fee, they claimed, was in the nature of
"pontage" and should be applied to the maintenance of the
bridge. Furthermore, they declared the chief reason the
bridge had decayed was the hard usage it had received from
the Yorkshire men who hauled coals over it from Durham.
They were confident in their position and declared themselves ready to go to trial to prove their case. But aware of
the slowness of legal machinery and knowing that bridges
can wear out while lawyers quibble, the Durham men offered
to levy two hundred pounds for immediate use provided
Yorkshire would raise a like amount, and pledge, in addition, to return the sum Durham had paid in the event the
decision went in the latter's favor. The case required four
years for settlement. The details are not all clear; but
enough of them stand out in Ripon's record of accounts to
show what disheartening business it was for the bridgewarden, and probably for everyone else concerned.

In the course of the four years Ripon made trip after
trip with messages to and from the justices of the North
Riding and those of Durham. The expenses of each trip
were from twelve to fifteen shillings which he paid out and
got back when he could. Often upon his arrival with such a
message not enough justices could be got together for action, whereupon Ripon writes: "they putt me off until another time." Twice he was sent to London, a long journey
from Yorkshire when one made it on horseback. The first
time he carried a petition to the King from the local justices, and on the second trip he conveyed a request of the
assize judges into whose hands the matter was finally placed.
On both trips he was compelled to pay out a good many fees
for the purpose of expediting his business, and the second
trip kept him six weeks. By the beginning of the fourth
year, it appears that the judges of the assize, whom Ripon
had followed about from meeting to meeting at Thirske,
Leathley, Durham, Newcastle, and York, were ready to

hand down a decision at the latter place, when the justices of the North Riding, getting wind of the fact that matters were likely to go against them, ordered Ripon to come away before the decision was given him. Their next move was to gain the ear of a privy councilor to whom they paid several fees, evidently with the desired effect; for the final decision was given in favor of Yorkshire and the two counties bore the charges equally.

Perhaps someone else could have handled the matter more efficiently than Ripon, perhaps not. The point is that nobody with greater skill or ability wanted the job, and apparently his superiors were content with his services; for they kept him in the office throughout the period covered by the dispute. That it was disheartening business to Ripon himself, as his records plainly show it to have been, did not matter. To serve his community in this fashion was the normal expectation and obligation of a man of his station.

In addition to the services given by the yeomen in the above parish offices as constables, churchwardens, overseers, and highway and bridgewardens, there was another duty designated especially to their class: service on the jury.

The manor courts still functioned in a good many places. Even the old hundred court, now probably in private jurisdiction, was still in existence here and there as late as Elizabeth's time. And the shire court or county court by virtue of its being the place of election for the knights of the shire seemed assured of its place in local life, though its work was largely relegated to that function. Much business was handled at the assizes under the supervision of royal judges, as the above story of the bridgewarden shows. But the court which had by Elizabeth's time come to overshadow all of these in the amount and variety of local business within its jurisdiction was the quarter sessions court, frequently called simply the sessions. It was in this court that the yeomen gave their greatest, though by no means their only, service as jurors.

Theoretically, as its name would imply, the quarter ses-

sions court met four times a year, immediately following
Michaelmas, Epiphany, Easter, and St. Thomas's Day, ap-
proximating the autumn, midwinter, spring, and summer
seasons. In practice, however, the number and time of the
meetings were largely determined by expediency. It was not
uncommon for it to meet seven or eight times annually, and
sometimes oftener, with the justices of the peace sitting in
quorum.

The panels from which the trial juries were chosen were
taken from the Sheriff's Book that contained the names of
all the freeholders of the county eligible for jury duty. According to the statute of 1584 which supplanted an earlier
one dealing with the subject, these lists were to include all
men with an income of four pounds per annum in land, or
forty pounds per annum in goods. Gentlemen of ability
were urged to consider it an honor to serve; and sheriffs and
their bailiffs were roundly scored for omitting gentlemen
of larger substance from the freeholders' lists.[65] But the attempts to make jury service attractive and to have it regarded as a privilege and an honor were never successful. It
passed for what it was, an onerous duty, and the gentry continued in the main to free themselves from it. Hence, since it
was a service traditionally held to be the duty of landholders, it fell chiefly to the lot of the yeomen. Wherever the
status term is given in jury panels for the sessions, they
show practically 100 per cent return of yeomen.

These were the trial or petty juries. The grand jury or
presenting jury, drawn from the body of the county, was
held more properly the province of the gentry, though
again, as we have noted with other offices, where there were
not enough gentlemen available, or willing, yeomen were
substituted. In Cheshire and Lancashire, with their many
resident gentry, no yeomen appear on the lists of the grand
juries. In Devon the gentry predominated, but yeomen also
served, as they did in Hampshire and Norfolk. On the Essex
panels there was a large representation of yeomen and the

65. S.P. 14, XXVIII, 67.

same was true in Staffordshire.[66] This evidence accords well with Cowell's statement (1607) that a grand jury was a body made up of "twenty-four grave and substantiall gentlemen or some of them yeomen."[67]

The hundred jury was still a part of the local administration of a good many counties.[68] This too was a presenting jury, but unlike the grand jury did not speak for the body of the county.[69] Gentlemen might serve on these juries, but in places they were manned entirely by yeomen.[70] The most widespread service of the yeomen, however, was on the trial juries, where year after year they faced the unwelcome duty of passing verdicts upon recalcitrant neighbors and friends. It was this jury to which Thomas Fuller referred when he said of the yeoman: "In his own country he is a main man in juries. Where if the judge please to open his eyes in matters of law, he needs not to be led by the nose in matters of fact . . . he cares not whom he displeaseth so he pleaseth his own conscience."[71]

66. The material for this paragraph is based on the sessions records of the counties mentioned.

67. J. Cowell, *The Interpreter, J U.*

68. Derbyshire, Dorset, Essex, Kent, Norfolk, Northants, Somerset, Wilts, and Yorkshire, had active hundred juries as late as the period under discussion and there may have been others. The entire subject of the hundred jury is badly in need of investigation. It often is not mentioned at all in secondary accounts which treat of juries. It is frequently difficult to distinguish between the hundred jury and the grand jury in the sessions records.

69. Another difference can usually be detected in the form of the presentment, that of the grand jury being usually drawn up in the technical formula of an indictment, whereas the presentments of the hundred jurors are made in their own words in the presence of the sessions. See W. Lambard, *Eirenarcha,* 1602, p. 381.

70. The *Sessions Records* of the North Riding of Yorkshire covering a long period of years show many lists of hundred juries. Only in rare instances is a gentleman included among them though scores of yeomen appear again and again. In Northamptonshire, on the other hand, the hundred juries were predominantly drawn from the gentry. If the western division of Northants were like the eastern division, there were relatively few yeoman freeholders in that county which may account for the above situation. See Muster Roll for the Eastern Division, S.P. 16. Case E, No. 15.

71. *The Holy State,* pp. 106–107.

It is only too evident from the many suits in which the integrity of jurors was attacked that the yeoman jurors did not always possess the independence of mind and lofty character that Fuller attributed to them. There are many charges of packed juries, and a clerk of the peace in South-ants in the reign of James I declared that of all the offices and misdemeanors that were committed against right and justice, that of "jury procurement and subornacon" were the most wicked.[72]

But the charges against packed juries, true though many of them undoubtedly were, must not make one forget the hundreds of unrecorded instances in which jurors carried out their duties as best they could, giving to England's rank and file a type of justice which, though admittedly imperfect, was vastly superior to that of an earlier age when blind chance rather than a neighbor's opinion determined one's guilt. Tristram Risdon said of the Devon yeomen on the juries: "such of them as have Free-hold, be returned in Tryals of Matters of Fact in Causes Criminal and Civil, and, upon their Oath, be to give in the Truth, as near as they can, of the matter given them in charge."[73] There must have been many who did just that.

It is not easy to determine to what extent the requirement that a juror be a freeholder was adhered to. Early statutes carried this qualification in the hope that it would raise the character of the service and keep men of the "meaner sort" from being jurors.[74] Apparently the regulation was still observed in certain regions: Risdon recognized it as a qualification for Devon jurors, and the Devon sessions records bear him out. At least, we find a juror there in 1597 who was able to make good his claim to be relieved of jury service because he had no freehold.[75] On the other hand, it is significant that the statute of 1584, designed to take into account the change in the value of currency by making a four-

72. St.Ch. 8, 40/6.
73. Risdon, *Survey of Devonshire,* pp. 106–107.
74. *S.R.,* 13 Edward I, c. 38.
75. Devon Sessions Rolls, Minutes, I, 193.

pound-per-annum income the qualification, rather than forty shillings, does not stipulate that this income must be from freehold.[76] An order, moreover, from the high sheriff of Lincoln to his bailiff in 1630 for making out the jury panels, specified that every juror should have freehold to the value of twenty shillings, or copyhold to the annual value of four nobles.[77]

Evidence on the subject is not plentiful. But it seems likely that the same practice held in this as in other provinces of local activity: namely, that in a community where most of the yeomen had freehold the restriction was adhered to, but that where this was not the case substantial copyholders of yeoman status were considered sufficient, with possibly some such differentiation in income requirement as in the above Lincoln case. Otherwise, gentlemen would have to serve on the trial juries and that they were very loath to do. In an earlier chapter we have had an example of a group of the gentry determining to serve as jurors for the purpose of an immediate class interest,[78] but in the main they preferred to leave this onerous task to the *boni et legales homines* in the class below them.

The yeomen did not like the duty either. The evidence is clear on that. But it had come to be regarded as an obligation of men of their station, and most of them, accepting that fact, did not try to escape it. Jurymen who attempted evasion were likely to find themselves presented at the next meeting of the sessions. A Hertford juror was ordered to jail until he should pay a ten-shilling fine for attempting to evade his jury duty.[79] In the North Riding of Yorkshire in 1610 the sessions demanded that all freeholders refusing to appear at the sessions upon summons were to be fined from thirty to forty shillings apiece. Two years earlier the same sessions had fined a jury twenty shillings apiece for departing without license of the court before all of their duties had been attended to. And in 1620 William Metcalf, a yeoman

---

76. *S.R.*, 27 Eliz., c. 6.
77. Lindsay Sessions Rolls, A 8.
78. See above, p. 153.
79. *Hertford Sessions Records,* II, 284.

of Askrigg, was fined ten shillings for leaving his fellow jurors before their verdict on certain items was given.[80] There was, however, some attempt made to see that the duty did not fall too continuously on the same individuals. The following item appears in the orders of the North Riding Sessions: "Those men who were summoned as jurors at this Session on showing that they gave their services at the Sessions holden for the Liberty of St. Peter's at York, are excused."[81]

To be sure, a juror was held disqualified for the service if he were proved guilty of concealing and suppressing indictments and presentments that had been preferred to him. But few would wish to take this method of escape. A man's standing among his neighbors was important to him. Frequently in lawsuits or elsewhere a yeoman who wished to prove his credit and reputation offered for the record the fact that he was a man of long service on the juries of his county. The yeomen had little or no knowledge of the law to bring to their aid in this service, and little or no formal education. But they possessed a good deal of native intelligence, a close knowledge of the customs and standards of their neighborhoods, and, unless some personal issue were involved, had a wholesome desire to see the king's peace preserved.

Though jury service and the work of the parish offices already dealt with comprised the major civic duties prescribed by statute and custom to the yeomen, their contribution in a variety of other capacities merits a word of attention.

There was, for instance, the office of the high constable, or constable of the hundred, which, though generally considered the province of the gentry, was often filled by yeomen. This officer, representing an administrative unit that had lost much of its old importance, acted somewhat as a coördinating agent between shire and parish: assisting the justices on the one hand to convey their order to parish offi-

---

80. *North Riding Sessions Records,* I, 124, 193; II, 253.
81. *Ibid.,* IV, 124.

cials, and on the other submitting to them the reports of the lesser officials.

Cheyney chides Francis Bacon for including yeomen among the freeholders who filled the chief constable's office,[82] setting it down as evidence of Bacon's ignorance of the local institutions of his time. "As a matter of fact," Cheyney says, "to the names of all high constables actually mentioned in the accessible records, the name *gentleman* is attached or suggested."[83] But there is much evidence in the local records to uphold the contention of the earlier writer. Gentlemen were in the majority among the high constables, but the statute held either "substanciall gentlemen or yeomen" eligible for the office,[84] and there are many instances of yeomen who held it.

Philip Cullyer, yeoman, of Norfolk, was described in an Elizabethan benevolence list as "cheefe cunstable."[85] Walter Horne, yeoman, who complained in 1609 of the onerous duties that he and his fellow officers had to perform, was the constable of the hundred of Carhampton in Somerset.[86] William Hill, yeoman, of Norton, Leicestershire, was the high constable of his hundred in 1624.[87] Nicholas Brice, yeoman, was the high constable in the hundred of Cookham in 1633.[88] Thomas Pecock, a Devon yeoman, was for eight years the constable of the hundred of Crediton.[89] John Moreshead, another Devon yeoman, was, according to his grandson's account, "cunstabell" in the hundred of Stanbury for twenty years.[90] And the sessions book of Devon contains the names of many yeomen who were recommended for the office. Thomas Emery, a yeoman of Danbury, Essex, petitioned the sessions in 1572 for relief from the office of high constable of the hundred of Chelmsford, which he had held for ten years. It is significant that among his argu-

---

82. F. Bacon, *Works* (Spedding), VII, 751.
83. *History of England from the Defeat of the Armada to the Death of Elizabeth,* II, 390.
84. *S.R.,* 34–35 Henry VIII, c. 26.   85. *Norfolk Arch.,* XXI, 287.
86. Somerset Sessions Rolls, 1609.
87. Leicestershire Papers, Hn., 1624.   88. S.P. 16, CCXXXVII, 12.
89. St.Ch. 8, 231/28.   90. *Furse Family Book,* p. 179.

ments for release is his claim that he was "muche inferyor to a great nomber of honeste and substancyall yeomen within this hundred in habytinge . . . farre neter and muche better hable in all respects" to execute the office.[91]

The office of high collector of the subsidy, though filled in the majority of cases by gentlemen, fell likewise fairly frequently on the shoulders of yeomen. The subsidy was ratable on either lands or goods. The collector's task was no pleasant one for people grumbled over assessments and payments of taxes as they do in every place and age. But it was a position of trust and responsibility. I have encountered yeomen among the high collectors of the subsidy in the records of Bucks, Cambridgeshire, Cornwall, Derby, Devon, Hertford, Hampshire, Hunts, Kent, Lincoln, Norfolk, Sussex, and Wiltshire.[92] Further search would probably disclose them in the records of other counties.

Yeomen performed still other public or semipublic duties of a miscellaneous nature. Almost everywhere they served as sheriffs' bailiffs, the men whose duty it was to make out the freeholders' lists from which the jury panels were drawn, to execute warrants for the sheriff, and in general to make themselves useful to that official or his deputy. Another type of bailiff was the officer of a franchise or corporation, a man who, according to Cowell, served with the magistrates in the municipal organization. It was in this capacity that William Davenport, a Gloucester yeoman, served the town of Chipping Camden in 1605. The borough's new charter gave the powers of making laws, and the right of punishing those who broke them, into the hands of the bailiffs and capital burgesses. John Price, gentleman, and William Davenport, yeoman, were the first bailiffs.[93]

91. Essex Sessions Rolls, 40/3, 45/47. See also St.Ch. 5, G..12/18; St.Ch. 8, 40/22, 193/25, 282/7; Ass. 24/21; *North Riding Sessions Records*, I, 167; *Royalist Comp. Papers*, II, *Y.A.S.*, XV, 299; *Hertford Sessions Rolls*, V, 88.

92. E. 179, Subsidy Rolls, 79/239, 92/182, 121/228, 122/204, 127/567, 139/628, 153/622, 174/193, 191/359, 199/403; *Cambridgeshire Subsidy Rolls*, 1912, pp. 45, 57; Exeter Sub. Rolls, Sec. II, no. 17; St.Ch. 8, 233/10.

93. *Bristol and Gloucestershire Arch. Soc.*, IX, 180. Yeomen are also frequently described as bailiffs of the hundred: Essex Sessions Rolls,

Yeomen were frequently named among the purveyors for the king's household, men who were required to collect animals and other food for royal maintenance or else composition money for the same. Christopher Walton, yeoman, "purveyor of Beefs and Muttons" for Devon in 1593, was requested to "provide for the royal household . . . forty fatt oxen, and three hundred fatt muttons" from his shire.[94]

The instructions given by Sir Henry Jernegan, lord lieutenant of Kent, for setting up beacons on the coast stated that "honest yeomen" along with gentlemen should be chosen to search the watch daily in an effort to discover defaults among the workers.[95] Thomas Bagshawe, yeoman, in the reign of James I was made forester in the High Peak in Derbyshire.[96] Yeomen were appointed jailers, and masters or governors of houses of correction in various shires.[97] A good many counties, especially in the south and southwest, still had headboroughs, third-boroughs, tithing men, borseholders, sidesmen, and like officials as assistants to the regular parish officers hitherto discussed. Yeomen also sometimes served in these offices, though as a rule they were filled by men of lower status, husbandmen, and sometimes even laborers.

Whatever the nature or variety of the yeoman's services, they were, it will be observed, all local, identified primarily with the parish, his special domain, and secondarily with the hundred or shire, where he assisted the gentry. In only two fields of activity were the yeomen asked to participate in service or potential service of a national character. One of these, political in nature, was participation in the election

47/50; Somerset Sessions Rolls, no. 2, 79; St.Ch. 8, 61/61; C. Jac. I, Hil. 20/8. According to Cowell, this is merely another term for the constable of the hundred, *The Interpreter, BA*. There are, of course, scores of instances of yeomen who were bailiffs in husbandry to gentlemen, but this was wholly a private employment, not public service.

94. Devon Sessions Books, 1592–1600, p. 47; also Add. MSS. 39245, fol. 30; Essex Sessions Rolls, 53/30; Calendar of Wynn Papers, p. 61.

95. Robert Hassal's Commonplace Book, MSS. of *Y.A.S.* at Leeds, fol. 42.

96. St.Ch. 8, 35/6.

97. Northampton MSS., Brudenell jxxxiv, 2; St.Ch. 8, 12/17, 290/1, 304/18.

of the knight of the shire for parliament; the other, a military duty, demanded enrolment in the trained bands of militia which gave England such permanent national defense as she possessed. Military duty had figured largely with their ancestors, and the vote was to figure largely with their descendants; but not until the period of the Civil Wars brought Englishmen of all classes into active military service and current issues began to whet their political consciousness, did either of these obligations weigh heavily upon the yeomen.

From the accession of Elizabeth to the Civil Wars, England took part in no great conflict as a principal, except for her engagement with the Spanish Armada. But throughout this period she attempted to maintain a certain amount of national preparedness through her trained bands. By statute order every able-bodied Englishman was subject to military service if and when needed, and each was required to furnish himself with arms according to his station and degree.[98] The trained bands were under the supervision of the lord lieutenant of the shire, an appointee of the Crown, and his assistants. It was their duty to see that the musters were called on an appointed day, that everyone was properly armed, and theoretically that a certain amount of training was carried forward.

The Gloucestershire muster roll for 1608, which is unique in that it gives the status of the majority of the members, shows a total of 19,402 names. Of the 17,046 whose status or occupation is given, 1,037 were yeomen, with an additional 144 listed as sons or brothers of yeomen. There were 457 from the gentry, 3,774 husbandmen, and 1,831 laborers. The remainder were chiefly clothiers, merchants, and smaller craftsmen and tradesmen.[99] To fail to be pres-

98. *S.R.*, 4–5 Philip and Mary, c. 2.

99. *Men and Armour in Gloucestershire*, 1608, London, 1902. The above figures from this list are taken from A. & R. Tawney, "An Occupational Census of the Seventeenth Century," *The Economic History Review*, October, 1934, V, 25–64. The Muster Roll for the Eastern Division of Northamptonshire, which like the Gloucester roll is exceptional in that it gives the status terms of those enrolled, shows a far larger percentage of husbandmen, and many fewer yeomen than the Gloucester roll.

ent at the musters made one liable to presentment and fine
at the quarter sessions court. Thomas Dade, a yeoman of
Norfolk, who was described as a sixty-pound-a-year man
in lands, and "rich in money" besides, and Henry Dewinge,
yeoman, a two-hundred-pound-a-year man, were among the
eight defaulters at a muster held in that shire in 1619.[100]
The remaining six were gentlemen and esquires. Yeomen
and gentlemen were also in the majority among the defaulters in Bucks when the musters were taken there in 1626.[101]
But on the whole these defaulters' lists were relatively
small.

Attendance at the musters, however, more or less a per-
functory duty, did not mean enthusiasm for military activity. Efforts were continually made to enlist the interest
of the upper classes in such activity, to encourage the practice of archery among the middle groups, and in general to
keep alive the military spirit. A letter to the Earl of Huntingdon, lord lieutenant for Leicestershire and Rutland in
1614, urged that ordinary vacancies in the trained bands
be filled "as well of those of the better quallitye as of such
other freeholders, farmers, owners of land or housholders as
shalbe fitt for the same." It denounced all attempts at evasion: "from the which duty and service noe person is to excuse himselfe of what degree or quallitye soever," except
servants in the royal household, and in the households of
noblemen.[102]

There were many expressions of this kind, but in spite of
all such efforts it is notably apparent that both gentlemen
and yeomen had lost their taste for fighting. As a rule they
furnished themselves with the proper armor and appeared
for the taking of the musters on the appointed days; but
they had no desire to be called into service. Nothing is more
significant of the change that had come over England since

---

100. S.P. 14, CVIII, 92. 101. S.P. 16, XXXVI, 55.
102. Hastings MSS. Hn. Leicestershire papers, 1614, fol. 1. See Matthew Sutcliffe, *The Practice, Proceedings, and Lawes of Arms,* 1593, and
T. Smith, *Briefe Treatise to Prove the Necessitie and Excellence of Archerie,* 1596, two of many such books that were written in the late sixteenth
and early seventeenth centuries.

the days when fighting had been both the occupation and pastime of all but the lowest classes. Knights, whose very existence as a group harked back to the time when military service marked their right to that status, preferred now to spend their energies in the management of their estates and to take their sport in following the hounds with their neighbors in the countryside.

It is true that younger sons of the gentry and nobility frequently still found satisfactory careers as officers in His Majesty's army and navy; but even to them a future in other fields was often more alluring. As for the yeomen whose first appearance on the pages of English history was in connection with Crécy, Poitiers, and Agincourt, they were now a settled farming class who found an outlet for their energies in the cultivation of their lands, the performance of their parish duties, and in hours spent with neighbors at the village tavern. Those whose ancestry went back to the freemen who fought in the above battles and in the wars with the Scots were proud of the family heritage, but they showed no desire or disposition to emulate it. Englishmen would not be found wanting when a major crisis came. They had proved that fact. They would prove it again. But already the nation of shopkeepers, of landholders who would grow rich in supplying their wants, and of people addicted to enjoying the fruits of peace was in the making.

It was not, to be sure, wholly a period of peace. Sporadic aid was given to the Protestants of Germany and the Low Countries. Irish troubles flared up now and then as they have had a way of doing throughout English history. Pirates and freebooters, rivals of England's own buccaneers, had to be dealt with. And until Mary Stuart's son united the English and Scottish crowns, border skirmishes might at any time prove troublesome.

To cope with these dangers England resorted to her levies of impressed soldiers, asking for fifty or a hundred or two hundred from each shire when the demand arose. In general, officialdom concurred with the accepted view of the countryside that it was the people who were of least sub-

stance and worth in the community who could best be spared
for this service. Perhaps they knew that if gentlemen and
yeomen were called they would seek release. At any rate the
lists of impressments show a preponderance of men from
the groups below the yeomen. Among all those pressed from
Derby, Gloucester, Leicester, Rutland, Somerset, Stafford,
and Warwick in 1627, there were only one gentleman and
one yeoman. The majority were styled "laborer," next in
number were the "husbandman," and the remainder were
small craftsmen and tradesmen.[103] Other lists for other
years are similar.[104]

In cases where yeomen were pricked for the impressment
they apparently lost no time in paying a fine for their release or hiring a substitute. Thomas Allen of Staffordshire,
in 1596, gave five pounds to one Captain Norton "for his
releasement for not serving her majesty on her last voyage
in her wars."[105] The Roberts Memorandum Book shows that
two members of this family of Devon yeomen were pricked
for service in Scotland in March, 1639, along with three of
their neighbors. But another entry states that "William
Marshall and Robert Roberts were injoined by Capting
Norcot to pay thirty shillings a peece and the others were
to get spared so God Cheepe as they could."[106]

The general low level of the membership of the levies resulted in a poor service and there was considerable criticism
of the practice. A letter from the Privy Council to the lord
lieutenant of Northants in 1596 advised "that there be speciall choice made of hable and likelye menn knowne to be of

103. S.P. 16, LXXII, 11; LXXV, 49, 67; LXXVII, 31; LXXVIII, 13;
LXXXI, 4.
104. S.P. 14, CLXXIX, 883, 886; Lieutenant's Book, Uncatalogued Hastings Papers, Hn., Add. MSS. 34217; 39245, fol. 179b. I have found but
one exception. In the impressment of Northumberland men in 1627, the
entire list of 102 was made up of *yeomen*, S.P. 16, CCCCXVIII, 82.
Whether this means that the yeomen of that region were not of sufficient
substance to be able to secure their release, or that a dearth of laborers
and husbandmen made it necessary for yeomen to go; or whether it was a
careless recording of status by the Newcastle scribe who made the list,
one cannot even guess. It is unique among many lists examined.
105. *Staffordshire Sessions Records,* III, 170.
106. Diary and Household Book of Roberts Family, p. 323.

good behavior and not vagrant and of the bassar sorte . . . who so soone as they cann finde the meanes to escape do runne awaye from theire captaines."[107] And Matthew Sutcliffe, in a book published in 1593, deplored the fact that local officers used the impressment lists as an opportunity "to disburthen the parish of rogues, loyters, drunkards, and such as no other way can live." If any of the better sort of men were chosen, he declared, "it is for some private grudge and of those that are chosen if they have either friends, favor or money, most of them are dismissed."[108] George Plowright, a yeoman of Northants, claimed to have fallen victim to such a grudge. In the execution of his duties as constable of Burton he had presented one Thomas Bacon to the court; whereupon Bacon connived with one of the local justices to have Plowright included in the impressment.[109] But certainly, in the main, the yeomen escaped active duty in the press until their interest in the Civil Wars drew both them and the gentry into action.

In regard to their participation in the parliamentary elections, the attitude of the yeomen was rather one of indifference than aversion. Parliamentary representation in the House of Commons had in its earlier days been regarded by everyone as an obligation rather than a privilege.[110] By the close of the sixteenth century, however, there was a growing awareness among the gentry of the importance of their position in that body and a disposition to strengthen their role there. But the yeomen who made up the bulk of the voters could not themselves stand for parliament, and had not yet come to regard the voice they gave in the elections as a tool that might be wielded to serve their own interests. Only near the end of the period in question, when the issue of the Civil Wars brought a rift between yeomen and gentry in many

107. *Musters, Sessions, Subsidies, etc., in the County of Northampton, 1586–1623.* Northants Rec. Soc., III, 32.

108. M. Sutcliffe, *The Practice, Proceedings, and Lawes of Arms,* 1593, p. 63.

109. S.P. 16, CCCCXVIII, 82.

110. See excuses given by members for sending proxies in answer to the summons to attend parliaments in the fourteenth century, *Parliamentary Writs* (Palgrave), II, Pt. 2, pp. 139, 293–299, and *passim.*

localities, is there evidence that here and there the free-holders were showing some consciousness of their strength as a body, in a manner that now appears significant as one looks back upon it. Prior to that time they appear to have been either wholly indifferent to the suffrage obligation which their status placed upon them, or else at most the willing accomplices of their friends among the gentry who invoked their aid at election time.

The very absence of any mention of the suffrage in most of the records touching the activities and interests of yeomen is a commentary on the insignificant place it held in their thoughts. Only one of the half-dozen diaries and commonplace books of yeomen used in this study even speaks of the matter. This exception is an entry in the commonplace book of the Roberts family of Devon for 1625: "the 26 day of Aprel were chosen at the Castel of Exeter to be Knights of the sheere for Parlament Ser Frances Fulford & Ser Frances Courtney." There follow the "names of those that bee of our Parish that were to the chousing of the Sheere Knights," a list which included Roberts himself, and four or five others.[111] That was all. It was an obligation to be fulfilled, but there is no indication that it was a matter of interest or concern to the yeomen who were voting.

Where the records of elections show yeomen actively engaged in election activities, it is chiefly in the role of assistants or accomplices to their friends among the gentry. The elections could be lively affairs if we may judge by the account of the one held on the castle green at Worcester where the members of one of the early parliaments of James I were chosen. The chief local issue was a religious one. It was only two years after the Gunpowder Plot and antipapist feeling ran high. Sir William Ligon, egged on by the Bishop of Worcester because he knew he could count on him "to be sound in religion," and Sir Henry Bromley stood for the Protestants. Sir Edmund Harwell and Sir John Packington were the choice of a strong Catholic contingent. The keeper of the castle was apparently a Protestant, and under

111. Diary and Household Book of Roberts Family, p. 318.

color of guarding against the escape of some prisoners that were housed there he permitted one of Bromley's kinsmen and young William Addis, a yeoman, son of Sir William Ligon's bailiff, to be the gatekeepers. They were to open only to "all who could give the pass word," that is, to Bromley and Ligon supporters. These, upon arrival, gathered about a big fire in the courtyard and ate head cheese and drank ale, furnished them free, while they warmed themselves and talked about the election.

There was a moment of excitement when George French and some of the Harwell henchmen who were refused admittance at the gate succeeded in crawling through the pale, and showed a bold spirit by shouting as loudly as they could: "A Harewell, a Harewell." Upon hearing it, one of the anti-papists replied, "And whie not a Bromley, a Bromley," and struck French into the ditch. At length the vote was taken, all those present crying out in unison for their candidate when his name was presented. Bromley and Ligon were declared to have received "the greater voice," having, as it was later claimed, the voice of the J.P.'s and all the "better sort" present. The verdict was disputed, but one of the Protestant squires declared that he had made a previous person-to-person survey of the county's voters which showed that the election would certainly give "the greater voice" to Ligon and Bromley.

According to the statute requirement, a voter must hold free land to the annual value of forty shillings, but the accusations made by both sides in the above case suggest infringement on this point. A yeoman on the Protestant side, William Addis the elder, had gone the rounds prior to the election to persuade people to be present on election day. And from the testimony given later by some of those who had been approached, it is clear that he had not been too careful to inquire into qualifications. A local tailor who was "neither freeholder nor copyholder" said he had been urged to come anyway. One John Lynton who protested that he shouldn't come because he held his land only by indenture for years was told that that was no matter. And Edward

Hurford, a husbandman who had no freehold and apparently only held his copyhold by right of his wife's indenture, said that he was present and "gave voice." The Harwell and Packington side was similarly charged with having voters present who had "neyther copyhold, freehould, nor Indenturehould to the value of xl *s* a peece by the yeere"; and it was said that "the poorest that could be got were got to the end that they would make a great cry for Harwell." Whether any attempt was made to check this matter at the time of the election is not clear, but it appears likely that no strict account was taken of the voters' eligibility.

Another report in a Star Chamber case regarding an election held in Hunts, also in the reign of James I, accused the sheriff of accepting "sundry such persons as were but meane coppieholders and customary tenants and had no freehold at all . . . nor ought to have or to give any voice in the said election, to yet give their voyces . . . for Sir Sydney Montague."[112]

Cornwall landholders "that have forty shillings yearly of inheritance or for terme of there owne lives or for anothers life" were asked to be present to vote in the election of 1627–28.[113] Feeling ran high throughout England that year and elections were doubtless hard fought in many places. A report from Essex states that "Dyverse Riche men that are freehoulders hath sould some twoe Dayes, some three or foure dayes to poore men that hath noe freehould lands nor coppiehould at all, 40 s. a year, some 5 li. a year that they may come in and take thear oathe if thear shoold be opposition that they ar ffreehoulders, and soe soone as this ellecton is over then to returne backe againe the sayde estates."[114]

It is an example of the way in which the growing parliamentary struggle made elections a matter of greater import than they had ever been before to the county men; and new methods of pressure or persuasion are in evidence. A letter

112. St.Ch. 8, 47/7. For Worcestershire election described above, see St.Ch. 8, 201/17.

113. S.P. 16, XCVI, 48.   114. S.P. 16, XCV, 35.

to Edward Nicholas, secretary to the Duke of Buckingham, concerning the above Essex election, states: "Wee have strange things which some of our justices hathe done uppon Satterday last." The action to which he referred was the sending out of warrants to the high constables of every division bidding them to instruct the freeholders to come to Chelmsford on election day and "give thear voyses on that side which most of the justices of the peace doe," which, says the writer, "is a thing that never was Done before."[115] Pressure to that degree was apparently going too far even for the seventeenth century, though it was everywhere regarded as natural and proper that men should influence their friends and landlords their tenants. In the October elections for Kent in 1640 when members for the Long Parliament were chosen, John Craige wrote to Sir Edward Dering, one of the candidates, as follows: "Sir Georg Sands shewed me your letter and told me that he knew nothing to the contrary but that you might have his assystance at least in his friends and tennants." In an earlier letter Craige said, "I spoke with Mr. Green who promises to labour the towne. I find the yeomen about us wonderfully desirous to choose you."[116]

The next two years, however, were to do much to educate the yeomen on national issues, and the following protestation of 1642 from Yorkshire, made when the royal party at York acted upon important current issues without consulting the freeholders below the gentry, indicates the manner in which the approaching struggle was sharpening the consciousness of their position. It is worth quoting in full; for it displays the spirit of the men from whom Cromwell was soon to choose his "russet-coated captains":

Whereas his Majestie hath beene pleased to give summons to the Gentrie of this County to Attend Him at his Court at York the 12th of May instant, to advise with him in some particulars concerning the honour and safetie of His Majesties person and the well being and peace of this our countrie, and in the

115. *Ibid.*
116. Stowe MSS., 743, fols. 153–155.

same summons was pleased to omitt the Free holders of this
county, out of a tender respect of putting them to any ex-
traordinarie charge, yet we conscious of our sincere Loyaltie
to his Majestie our Gratious Soveraigne, and conceiving ourselves according to the proportions of our estates equally interested in the common good of the country did take boldness
to come in person to York and were ready to attend his Majesties pleasure there. And whereas his Majestie was pleased
there to propound severall things to the purpose aforesaid, at
the meeting of the Countrie, to consider a fit answer to returne
to his Majestie thereupon, the doores of the meeting house
were shut, we utterly excluded, and in our absence a Referee of
Knights and Gentlemen chosen without our Knowledge or consent to draw up the said answer: we the Freeholders who petitioned his Majestie, the day above said conceiving our selves
abundantly injured in the election (not knowing any warrant
by writ or otherwise for the same) of the said Referee, and that
we ought not however to bee concluded by any resolution of
theirs without our assent in their election doe absolutely protest and declare against the said election: and as farre as con-
cernes us disavowe whatsoever shall bee the result of their consultation thereupon, and doe desire, a new and faire election
of a Referee be made, we admitted to our free votes in the same,
and some one or more to be nominated by us, allowed to deliver
our sence for us at another meeting. And that wee shall not
make good in the least respect anything whatsoever which
shall otherwise be concluded upon.[117]

More than two hundred years were to pass before political democracy became a reality in England; but the in-
gredients from which it was made had long been brewing.

This chapter has thus far dealt chiefly with the contribution of the yeomen to the commonwealth by means of public
service. They were likewise a pillar of the state financially.
Most of the financing of the local government was taken
care of through the lays and assessments ordered from
above, but actually, as has been shown, many were made by

117. *The Protestation of the Freeholders of Yorkshire,* London, 1642.

local men, sometimes the shire officials, sometimes the parish officials, and frequently the two working together.

Presumably assessments were made according to the relative wealth of the inhabitants. To what extent they were fairly made, honestly collected, and fairly dispensed depended on the honesty and sense of public duty of those in charge, in many cases the yeomen themselves. Some communities had a reputation for order and peaceful living; some were known as quarrelsome, disorderly spots where neighbor suspected neighbor, and a deal of injustice flourished. Everyone grumbled at having to pay his rates, but usually in the end he paid them; for there was no way out.

The chief tax for national expenses was the subsidy, successor to the old tenth and fifteenth though not yet wholly superseding them. The subsidy was periodically granted the king by parliament, and collected from the several divisions of each shire according to assessments made by two local men appointed for that purpose.

Fuller said of the yeoman: "He makes a whole line in the subsidy book." He spoke truly. Not that the yeoman's property was assessed at anything like its real value; nobody's was. But the amount of the subsidy contributed by the agricultural classes below the gentry, that is the yeomen and well-to-do husbandmen, indicates that a large part of the burden of state support rested on the shoulders of the common folk. The Bedfordshire subsidy roll covering the assessment for the grant made by parliament in 1593 offers an excellent illustration. The names of 1,721 ratepayers are listed in this subsidy roll. Of this number, 1,427 belonged to the agricultural groups. The following table indicates the yearly property valuation on which the assessment was made, and shows the distribution of the tax between the gentry and those of the ranks below who were of sufficient value to be listed in the subsidy.[118]

118. E. 179, 72/212–215. This subsidy roll is particularly interesting as it gives the status of practically all of the ratepayers. A critical analysis including data concerning all classes and occupations listed is in preparation. The minimum limits of wealth brought within the scope of the subsidy were 20s. in land and £3 in goods. An individual was as-

Rates Paid by Agricultural Classes in Bedford, 35 and 36 Elizabeth

Status	*Number of rate-payers*	*Annual valuation of property on which assessment was made* £	*Average annual valua-tion per person* £	*Total amount of tax paid* £	*Average tax per person* s.
Knights, es-quires, and gentlemen	250	1797	7.15	206.62	16.53
Yeomen and husbandmen	1177	3773	3.21	531.55	9.03
TOTAL	1427	5570		738.17	

As is frequently the case, figures based on averages leave out some of the most interesting features of the picture; for they cannot show the great differences among individuals within the various groups. It is interesting, for instance, to note that, although the large amounts paid by certain knights, esquires, and gentlemen of great wealth bring the average tax of that group to 16.53 shillings, by actual count 119 of the 250 members of the gentry listed paid lower than 12.17 shillings, the average amount contributed by the yeomen,[119] whereas many individuals in the latter group paid as high as 20 to 30 shillings, far above the average shown for the gentry.[120]

From time to time "benevolences" were used to supplement the subsidies. The pill was no easier to swallow for being sugar-coated. And the collection of this kind of tax be-

sessed either on the income from his land, or that of his personal property, whichever was the more valuable. The rate of the assessment for the above subsidy was 4s. in the pound of the annual value of land, or 2s. 8d. in the pound of the value of goods. This was the normal rate for most subsidies. See F. Dietz, *English Public Finance, 1558–1641*, 1932, pp. 382–383.

119. The average paid by the husbandmen was 8.15s. as compared to the 12.17 paid by the yeomen. The average for the two groups together was 9.03s., the figure used in the above table.

120. One yeoman from the parish of Stoppesley in Flitt paid a tax of £2 8s., three times the average amount paid by the gentry.

came increasingly difficult as the ingenious methods of Stuart kings in the realm of finance caused their subjects to be more and more touchy on the matter. These gifts or loans were presumably exacted only from the abler inhabitants in the community. That the yeomen are freely numbered among those so assessed is both a tribute to their wealth and further recognition of the fact that they stood little chance of escaping any of the tax levies. Of the 179 persons assessed for three such loans in the counties of Bedford (1588), Cambridge (1605?), and Rutland (1625), the gentry with 45 donors had the highest representation; the yeomen came next with 40 donors. The average assessment for the gentlemen was 17.31 pounds each, and that of the yeomen, 17.01 pounds each.[121] Mention has already been made of the yeomen in the knighthood composition lists.[122] Ship money was another of King Charles's experiments that brought to them as well as to the larger landholders more cause for grumbling, and their voices were added to the protests made against irregular taxation.

Whatever the nature of the obligation, whether in the financial field or that of public service, it is apparent that the conditions determining the contribution of the yeomen were much the same. Too low in the social and economic scale to gain the privileges and immunities that birth and wealth can sometimes buy, and too high to be freed from the obligations that the poor, by virtue of their circumstances, escape, they fulfilled the function of a "middle people." It is perhaps most of all in this connection and at this period that they deserve the epithet which the textbook writers have been pleased to ascribe to them. They were indeed on several counts *the backbone of the English nation.*

121. Returns for Bedford, Titus MSS. B. IV, pp. 176–177. Returns for Cambridge, S.P. 14, XVII, 86. (The date is uncertain here, but 1605 is the one given greatest credence by the editors of the *S.P.D.*) Returns for Rutland, Local Papers *re* Leicestershire, Hn. See Appendix IV for analysis of these loans. See also the account of an Elizabethan benevolence from the point of view of class distribution, *Norfolk Archæology,* XXI, 287.

122. See above, p. 218.

X

THE MEASURE OF THE MAN

Be not an negard; nor yt too lyberall.

The Diary and Family Book of Robert Furse, yeoman, 1593

Yea, a seasonable industry can turn stones into bread, and make barrenness itself fruitful.

The Yeoman's Prerogative, 1652

WHEN Jane Martindale wished to go up to London where she could have a livelier time and prettier clothes than were thought fitting for a yeoman's daughter in Lancashire, both her family and the neighbors disapproved, deploring the fact that she did not "measure by the same mete-wand" that they did.

Something of importance will have been left out of this study if no effort is made to discover the nature of the "mete-wand" by which the Martindales and their neighbors, and yeomen everywhere, measured and were measured by the society of which they were a part. It is not an easy task. Much that reveals the character of any social group is too subtle to be readily understood and often too elusive to be captured by the written word. It takes time, moreover, to find the two and two that make four in matters of this kind. And it is often not until one has encountered a phrase again and again or returned to the same record many times, armed with related evidence picked up elsewhere, that its significance becomes apparent.

But certainly to discover insofar as it can be done what code of morals and manners shapes the pattern of behavior and determines the outlook of a group, what standards define its scale of values, and what traits are its identification marks, is an obligation that the student of a social class cannot well shun. Nor would he wish to. A fuller knowledge of such matters is the reward—a kind of by-product—that comes from the laborious perusal of many documents until one is able to read what is between the lines of records as well as their actual wording. Not all of the answers to the above questions are difficult to come by. The reader has already observed in the foregoing pages certain features of the code under which the yeomen lived. A fuller acquaintance with the records but enhances the range and basis for conclusions.

Externals like speech and dress are not the most fundamental characteristics of a social group, but in real life they are usually the labels first noted, and are sometimes the only ones that attract the casual observer. Somewhat has been said earlier of the dress of the yeomen; their speech also deserves a word of attention. It was the homely robust speech of Chaucer's pilgrims enriched by two centuries of growth, the same that Shakespeare heard and used as a boy on the village streets of Stratford.

Words and phrases filled with imagery occupied a large place in everyday conversation. Yeomen of the north country scorned to speak of the "decease" of a relative or friend, or of his "dying," but clung rather to the older and more imaginative word "forthfarren." A burial was frequently spoken of; but as often they called it the "homebringen," or told how one was "brought home handsomely." The word "dusk" is of early English origin, but many countryfolk found more picturesque ways of referring to that part of the day. In the north they drove their sheep home "betwixt sunsett and day goeing"; and to Devon and other west-country yeomen it was the time "between the lights."

Idiom, proverbs, and figures of speech, rich heritage of the common folk of all ages, flavored their talk at every turn. The wife of a Cheshire yeoman said of one of her neighboring gossips that "shee could take a tale out of the ground to shame or undo anyone." A north-country yeoman expressed his feeling about a neighborhood matter by declaring that he "wold never sturr his foot in his shoe about the business further." Robert Furse advised his children not to trouble themselves about the affairs of others but to "lett everye man shutt his own bowe."

Nouns and adjectives were frequently made to serve as verbs, a hangover from an earlier usage. The badgers at the Malton market had "to buy soone" that they might "be goinge betimes for fear of being 'nighted.' " Gentlemen let their land to yeomen because it "gladded" them to have ready money in hand. Chaucer's form of "hit" for "it" was commonly used; and double negatives abounded. Michael Bull of Northamptonshire confided to a neighbor that he was "not able noe longer to conteyne and bridle within him the secrett and cruell hatred, splene, and rancour" that he bore certain people. And parish officials reporting on specific local expenditures often complained that they could "not get noe money for the same."

The following entry from the diary and account book of the Roberts family of Devon is an interesting example of a yeoman's everyday speech:

The xiiith day of March John Pleace had bine at Cheriton in the forenoon and the afternoone he came at Stockley Church and he had dronke so hard at Cheriton that he sleept part of the time that Master Tamson reade the Cannons and all the while the Salme was a-singing and part of the time that the beeleefe was a-saying untill Geore Matthew gut him twise before he did awake and after prayer he went out of the church ramling.[1]

Speech among the unlettered changes slowly; and many expressions common to the Elizabethan yeomen may still be heard where communities of English folk or their descendants have escaped the main ebb and flow of outside influences. Countrymen in Lincolnshire still speak of having "cutten" their grass. A farmer in the Wye Valley will stop his labors to direct a stranger along the right "paff" across the downs. And the mountaineers of the American Appalachians still carry their meat in a "poke"; believe that

1. Roberts Diary and Household Book, p. 52.

"hit's better to rise soon in the morning"; and are "mightily holpen up" by religious exhortation. With the growth of Puritanism, scriptural phraseology characterized much of the common speech.

There were many ways of expressing approval or disapproval. Those who enjoyed the esteem of their neighbors were described as "peaceful," "full of good neighborhood," "of good estimation and creditt." But a man who lost the respect and "well liking" of his neighbors was labeled a "crafty noddy," "shifting knave," "scurrilous rogue," "quarrelling parson," or "knavish coxcomb"; sometimes it took all of them to express one's feelings.

The Elizabethan yeomen were no self-controlled, submissive lot. Rural communities had standards of respect and decency which they attempted to uphold, but living was still a rough and ready matter and by no means free from physical danger. Country roads and village streets after dark were probably safer than they had ever been in England, for time was bringing a higher conception of public law and order. But nobody trusted too much to this. And a yeoman riding to and from fairs and markets, or on other business, usually carried a pike, staff, or other weapon, particularly if he were alone. The preservation of the king's peace was a fairly well-established ideal, but life was held rather cheap and quarrels and brawls that resulted in bloodshed were a commonplace. There were laws, and courts where wrongs might be righted, and where a man could be held to his bargain if it were in writing. But the way of the law was a long way, and countryfolk who had been wronged, or thought they had, did not always take it.

It was no unusual thing for men to assemble with their servants and womenfolk, and armed with pikes, bills, staves, pitchforks, bows and arrows, or any other weapons that came handy, to enter into the lands and houses of a person against whom their ire was raised, carrying off his goods or his stock in restitution of wrongs real or imagined. Physical injuries, and not infrequently loss of life, were the toll of neighborhood quarrels and local drinking bouts. The description of a drinking party at the local inn or tavern mentions casually that someone's "head was broken," but except sometimes to say that they "sent for a barber to dresse his head," no attention is paid the incident.

A Staffordshire yeoman named Bradley had some trouble with the curate of the local church who finally forbade his appearance at church again; whereupon Bradley seized the curate by force and put him in the village stocks.[2] Disputes like theirs did not always proceed to such lengths, but more than one court record tells of seizures at the communion table, and of quarrels that brought the Sunday church services to an end.

A good deal of the feud element was still present in neighborhood relationships. Country memories are long, and grudges carefully nursed were handed down from father to son. Alexander Wretham, a wealthy Cambridgeshire yeoman, was charged with tearing down windmills, cutting up fishing nets, defacing family tombstones, and doing all sorts of devilment to members of the Pedley family, "such was his malice against the name and blood of the Pedleys." And the Pedleys were quick at retaliation.[3]

This kind of feud flourished particularly along the borders where, at least until King James's time, men went always armed. Philip Green, yeoman, of Morpeth, mortally wounded in a neighborhood fight in 1583, lived long enough to beg his friend, Francis Dacre, to avenge his murder which he declared to be the work of members of the Ogle family "haven no cawsse agaynst me, but that I compared the Dacres bloude to be as goodd as the Ogles."[4]

The following account from the diary of the Roberts family is characteristic of many entries that describe their relations with their neighbors, the Gibbs's:

The xxth day of November being Saynt Andrewes day John Gib the younger came to me in John Vesie's meddow and came

2. Req. 2, 180/25.   3. St.Ch. 8, 236/8.
4. "Will of Philip Green," *Wills and Inventories*, II, Surtees Soc., XXXVIII, 82.

and gut me 2 or 3 times then he strake me and his father rann to me and caught me about the neck and did draw me at the ground. So the oulde Gib and Gib sunn and his man were at me all at one time and did beat me.[5]

But in spite of many examples of direct action it was a litigious age, and no group did more to make it so than the yeomen. To the point of monotony one reads in the court records of this one who had "a very troublesome disposition given altogether to vexatious and multiplycitie of suites against his neighbours," and of that one who was a man "no less able than willing to continue suits." A Berkshire yeoman accused a neighbor of harboring malice against him, "upon no grounds or cause at all only to weary your said subject with multiplicity of causes and frivolous suits in law."

Some contemporary writers blamed grasping lawyers for inciting this prodigious amount of litigation. George Whetstone, writing in 1586 of the tendency of the yeomanry toward so much lawing, urged them to leave off spending their money on costly suits. He declared that it was "of the spoyles of these good men, a great number of Attourneyes and petifoggers live."[6] In 1627 attorneys on the Isle of Wight were charged with having "stirred up sutes between the farmers and the yeomanrie until almost the whole communaltie were undone."[7] And in the same period John Norden deplored the activities of greedy lawyers among the yeomen, merchants, and husbandmen of Cornwall, though he admitted that it was not all the lawyers' fault. These men were themselves, Norden says, "verie litigious" and "muche inclined to lawe quarrels for small causes."[8]

Their plain speaking no doubt accounted for some of the quarrels the yeomen brought upon themselves. They never minced words. But this characteristic had good effects as well as bad. It was part and parcel of their independent

5. Roberts Diary and Household Book, p. 14.
6. Whetstone, *The English Myrrour*, 1586, pp. 234–239.
7. *Oglander Memoirs* (Long), 1888, p. 21.
8. Harl. MSS. 6252, fol. 28.

spirit, which, on the whole, exercised a healthy influence in the community and made for an upstanding, self-reliant group that strengthened the fiber of the English nation. Yeomen respected their betters, but did not fear them. In social matters they gave them deference, for that was the code they lived under; but they upheld their own rights with fearlessness and evident satisfaction when they felt they were being trampled on.

When George Elsham, yeoman, in 1615, put his horses and sheep to grass on lands recently inclosed by Richard Rossiter, Esq., thereby bringing a suit upon himself, he frankly admitted that he did it "of purpose to try the title thereof."[9] The poorer copyholders had neither the means nor the position to carry a case of this kind through the courts. There were many yeomen with both means and inclination for just such test cases.

Edward Lawman, a gentleman from London who moved into the country in the reign of James I, began to inclose a roadway and bits of the common that had been used by the neighborhood as a recreation center. William Nicoll, a local yeoman, presented him at the court baron. When he continued to encroach by planting trees in the common way, Nicoll and his neighbors on their own authority pulled down the trees. Nor did they bring any opprobrium upon themselves for the act: "the lord of the manor coming by said if he had come sooner, he would have done it himself."[10]

Their independence of action toward those above them showed itself in other ways. Tribute has already been paid the local gentry who as justices of the peace were the chief arbiters of local affairs. Many of them, perhaps the majority, executed the office with a commendable degree of fairness and judgment. When some yielded to the temptation to use it for the furtherance of their own ends, they were often challenged. The challenge might come from above or from their own group. But it might also come from below.

Paul and Thomas Taylor, two Nottingham yeomen,

9. St.Ch. 8, 128/5.   10. St.Ch. 8, 12/10.

brought such charges against Gervase Markham, Esq., declaring that he had used his authority as a justice unfairly and to forward his own ends. Their grievances were embodied in a petition to the Lord Chancellor, who in turn put the matter to the judges of the assize, directing them on their next visit to Notts to inquire and examine Markham's fitness for the office. This inquiry was made. The charges of the two yeomen were substantiated, and at the Chancellor's direction a new commission for the peace was sent down with Markham's name omitted.[11]

The same spirit was displayed in other directions. It was a group of yeomen who led the people of the parish of Enfield, in Middlesex, to frame a petition to the Privy Council in 1638 against what they considered an unfair levy of ship money. The petitioners stated that in response to a warrant sent by the Council to the sheriffs, they had assessed themselves in proportion to their abilities, and returned this report to the sheriffs. But these officers had "in a private way" and without their knowledge altered the assessments so as to ease the burden on the wealthy landholders in the county, forcing it to fall more heavily on the yeomen and farmers. They therefore requested that the first assessment be accepted, and that in the future they be assured the right to enjoy their traditional privilege of assessing themselves.[12] It boded well for the future growth of democracy in England that there was a group among the nation's lesser folk with a knowledge and conviction of their rights, and the wit and courage to make them known.

Elizabethan and Stuart yeomen shared with other classes many attitudes characteristic of the mental climate of their age. This is particularly evident in their conception of the material universe and man's relation to it. The sixteenth and particularly the seventeenth century saw the frontiers of human knowledge pushed far forward; but years were to elapse before the discoveries of the great natural philoso-

11. St.Ch. 8, 208/31.
12. S.P. 16, CCCCVII, 43. For other cases showing similar display of spirit, see St.Ch. 8, 43/3, 228/21, 242/26, 252/1, and 2, 296/4.

phers affected greatly the knowledge of the rank and file of the nation. It was for most of them still an age when natural phenomena were regarded with a good deal of wonderment and the supernatural accepted with credulity.

This belief in the supernatural extended into many fields. One sought to find out from almanacs, astrologers, or wise old women of the neighborhood what were the best days for buying and selling, when to begin a new house, or when undertake a journey. The dependence of the farmer on the weather has already been noted. There were weather portents without end. If the crow wet her beak at the water's brim, if the raven croaked in a hollow voice, if the pigeons came home late to the dovehouse, if bees flew not far from their hives and fleas bit sharply, if bells seemed to sound louder than was their wont, if soot fell much from the chimney, if a cat washed behind her ears, or oxen ate more greedily and "with a more earnest stomacke than their usual custom"; then one might surely expect rain. But if the sun rose gray and clear in the morning, if the evening sky were "ruddy and not fierie," if the dew fell in great abundance, if bats flew after sunset and water fowl made their haunts far off from the water, if the owl did "whup much and not scrytch," and the cranes flew high, fair weather was certain to follow. If the oak were laden with acorns, if the breastbone of the mallard looked red when it was killed, if hornets were seen after the end of October, a long sharp winter would likely come. A snowfall in February, great store of blossoms on the broom, and more blossoms than leaves on the walnut trees would bring a fruitful year. But if comets or meteors were seen, if the sun were in an eclipse, or if the wood birds flew "to the planes" and refused to covert, a barren year was ahead. The bridge between the natural and the supernatural was a narrow one.

Skeptics were increasing among the more intelligent who assailed the ancient belief in demons and witches, but it was not wholly taboo in sophisticated circles, as the lamentable record of witch hunting in the period shows, and certainly it still flourished in the countryside. Nicholas Stockdale, a

Norfolk yeoman, was accused of being a witch and bringing a languishing sickness on the wife of an enemy. Agnes Godfrey, the wife of a Middlesex yeoman, was indicted at the sessions in 1610 for exercising a witch's power, by which she caused the death of three people in the neighborhood and brought a severe illness upon another. Richard Weare, a yeoman of Clist Honiton, Devon, was charged with advice of impostors and witches concerning things that were lost. Advice from those claiming supernatural powers was frequently sought in matters of love, and many believed in the efficacy of love potions. John Sauell, a yeoman of Kidderminster, claimed in 1611 that his twelve-year-old daughter had been given drugs and drinks that would lead her to be enamored of a certain suitor. Another yeoman in the same period confessed that he had paid a sum of money for love powders whereby to win the love of a rich widow, though it is somewhat significant that he had concealed the fact for fear of ridicule and jest. Frequently the accusations against those who practiced sorcery were merely an excuse for satisfying a personal grudge. But often they were genuine enough, and country women themselves sometimes confessed to being "able to witch a little."[13]

Any variations in the manifestations of natural phenomena were almost sure to be regarded as portents from the Almighty. Providence, it was thought, constantly took a hand in the commonplace affairs of man's life with results that were manifest if often incomprehensible. Typical of many accounts published in broadsides or passed by word of mouth is the following from the west country: *The Wonderful Recompence of Faith; or Strange News from Dursley in Gloucestershire; being a True and Perfect Relation of how a Godly farmer had his barn full of corn burn down, and bore his loss in extraordinary patience.*[14]

William Pate, a Cambridgeshire yeoman within the Isle

13. For examples in this paragraph and others that are similar, see St.Ch. 8, 203/28, 260/12, 276/25; *Middlesex Sessions Records,* II, 57–58; Devon Minute Books, 1604.

14. *Glouc. Notes and Queries,* III, 97–98.

of Ely, believed that God had withheld a high wind in order
to foil the schemes of some of his wicked neighbors who
wished the destruction of his windmill. Members of a yeoman community in Heptenstall, York, were persuaded that
salt and some old iron laid under a cow that was ailing would
effect a cure if accompanied by prayers to God for its recovery. Thomas Dawson, a Lincoln yeoman, told how he
and his wife accepted cheerfully and with a kind of content-
ment the gracious visitations and merciful corrections of
sickness and infirmities that came upon them because they
knew the cross was sent by God to test them.[15]

At one point in his diary Adam Eyre reflects a mind out
of sorts with life, an irritable disposition, the inclination to
quarrel with his wife over little things, and an inability to
face the practical problems of the day. But it did not occur
to him to attribute this state of things to his poor health, the
financial worries that harassed him, or to the natural rest-
lessness of a returned soldier. If things went wrong and a
man's equilibrium were upset, the seventeenth century had
but one way of explaining it. Either the victim was in the
clutches of the Devil who had laid ghoulish snares to entrap
him or else the Almighty in his infinite wisdom was punishing him for wrong-doing or was testing him in order to take
the measure of his spiritual strength. That this was the
proper diagnosis Adam Eyre did not question. He likewise
accepted the treatment that his century prescribed. He read
some good counsel from a contemporary commentator "concerning the assistence of the Angell, and the Devill, and our
own wills provoking to him," and some selections from
Foxe's *Book of the Martyrs*, and prayed God that his
"present dull and indisposedness" would not permanently
divest him of divine favor.[16]

Medical practices were shot through with a hocus-pocus
that even a child of today would question. William Harvey,

15. For examples in this paragraph, see St.Ch. 8, 114/14, 238/15; Ass.
45/1, 1646.
16. *Diary of Adam Eyre,* pp. 53, 78, 84, and *passim.*

the son of a Kentish yeoman, led the innovators of his age
to a new knowledge of the human body and its functioning;
but his old neighbors among the countryfolk of Kent and
their ilk elsewhere still held to traditional notions concerning the nature of the blood and other "humours." Long
after he had left the home of his boyhood and could match
wits with the eminent divines of his day, Richard Baxter
tells how he was moved to swallow a gold bullet for an in-
ternal disorder, having read in Dr. Gerhard of the admirable effect of that treatment.[17] A rate was made upon an
entire parish in Surrey to pay for taking the children of
one Widow Hilles up to London that they might receive the
royal touch thought to be a cure for the scrofulous ailment
known as the King's Evil.[18] These beliefs and practices were
also held and practiced by the gentry, as their diaries and
the medical books in their libraries amply show.

Another significant trait common to both gentry and
yeomen, perhaps to the long-settled of every age and place,
may be described for want of better terms as a sense of the
continuity of things and a love of the familiar which found
expression in family pride and sentiment and in a devotion
to personal possessions.

The yeomen, it has been noted, were of two groups: those
of ancient lineage sprung from old free-tenant families long
settled on the lands of their fathers, and those who had risen
from a lower estate. Those of the first group valued their
ancient name as did old families among the gentry. It was a
fact to be recorded on tombstones, to be mentioned in deeds
and other legal documents, to be given in testimonies at
court in proof of the worth of a man's word. James Culling
of Kent expressed a desire that his daughter and heiress,
Catherine, marry with a Culling, "and for that my desire is
that my lands and tenements shall if it may be, remaine and
continue in the name of the Cullings."[19] In like manner,

17. R. Baxter, *Autobiography*, p. 76.
18. "Churchwarden's Accounts," *Surrey Arch.*, II, 42.
19. Will of James Culling, Add. MSS. 28,008, fol. 47.

Thomas Newton, of ancient Northamptonshire yeoman stock, stated that in case of the death of Arthur his son and heir, his land should go to his sister Jane Newton, on condition "that shee marry with a Newton to keep it in the name."[20]

But equally interesting and significant was the attitude of the newly prosperous yeoman who, having no such heritage of his own to look back upon, wished to create one for his children. A new dignity had come with his acquired lands and increased wealth. His was a position largely of his own creation. He was eager to have his gains established and made permanent. Hence material things that are the outward symbols of stability and an enduring well-being must be preserved. No heirlooms had been handed down to him, but he would create heirlooms that could be passed on to his children, and God willing, to his children's children, and to theirs. Time and again yeomen named in their wills a special chest, or table, or carved press, or certain articles of silver and brass which were to "remaine unto this house as heire loomes." They were rarely, outwardly at least, persons of sentiment. But a fondness for that which was familiar and intimately bound up with their everyday lives was marked. Women treasured the sheets, often "wrought" and of superior quality, that were used on their beds at childbirth. They were kept for that occasion only and passed down to their daughters for similar use.

There is something curiously touching in the request of a Yorkshire yeoman to be buried in his parish church "in the place there near to my deske or pewe wher I do sitt." It is as if he hoped to retain some claim to that place that had been his for years; and felt that his bones would be more at home there. A Warwickshire yeoman asked to be buried in the middle aisle of his parish church "nere unto the seate Dore where my wife usuallie doth sitt." Requests like these were a commonplace.

One is persuaded, moreover, that a farmer's reference to

20. *Wills and Inventories,* Surtees Soc., CXLII, 63.

"my cow called Blossom," "the best cow called Ladie," or "one brown nagge with a white star on his forehead that is a good nagge," carried with it something more than mere identification. He felt for them the same friendliness and sense of ownership that he held for the familiar haunts about him. To be sure, he believed in the joys of paradise which the parson described on Sunday. He hoped one day to enter into them. But he had never seen pearly gates nor walked on golden streets, whereas hedges white with may, new-ploughed fields, faithful animals, and the companionship of friends and neighbors were dear homely pleasures that could not be relinquished without a pang.

Two sketches of the yeomen written by contemporaries, from which items have already been quoted, deserve further scrutiny for the light they throw on the yeoman's scale of values. The fact that one is wholly laudatory and the other gives only blame to the type it portrays by no means renders either of them without value. Both Thomas Fuller and John Taylor knew yeomen in flesh and blood; besides, one meets in the records many of the type that each wrote about.

Fuller was their champion. To him every yeoman was "the wax capable of a genteel impression when the prince shall stamp it"; and he spoke with pity of France and Italy, whose walls "though high, must needs be hollow, wanting filling stones" which the yeomen supplied the English structure. The yeoman wore "russet clothes," says Fuller, but could always make "golden payment." He seldom went far abroad, but "his credit stretcheth further than his travels." In his house he was "bountiful both to strangers and poor people." He only went to London when returned on a jury but "seeing the King once, he prays for him ever afterwards." He improved the land to double its value by his good husbandry. He served his country both financially and through public service. And in times of famine he was the Joseph of the country who kept the poor from starving.[21]

21. *The Holy State*, pp. 106–109.

If Fuller idealized his yeomen, Taylor supplies a corrective in the other direction. A yeoman was among his "Brood of Cormorants" in company with a Jesuit, a lawyer, a usurer, and other companions of dubious reputation, and his rhyming sketch is full of barbs:

The Country Yeoman

The Romane Histories doe true relate
How Dioclesian chang'd his Emp'rors state,
To live in quiet in a Country Farme,
Out of the reach of treasons dangerous arme,
Then was a Farmer like a lab'ring Ant
And not a Land devouring Cormorant.
For if a Gentleman hath land to let,
He'll have it, at what price so 'ere 'tis set,
And bids, and over-bids, and will give more,
Than any man could make of it before:
Offers the landlord more than he would crave,
And buyes it, though he neither get nor save.
And whereas Gentlemen their land would let
At rates that tennants might both save and get,
This Cormorant will give his landlord more,
Than he woulde aske, in hope that from the poore
He may extort it double by the rate,
Which he will sell his corn and cattle at.
At pining famine he will ne're repine,
'Tis plenty makes this *Cormorant* to whine,
To hoard up corne with many a bitter ban,
From Widowes, Orphanes, and the lab'ring man,
He prayes for raine in harvest, night and day,
To rot and to consume the graine and hay:
That so he mowes and reeks, and stacks that mould,
At his owne price he may translate to gold.
But if a plenty come, this ravening thiefe
Torments & sometimes hangs himselfe with griefe.
And all this raking toyle and carke and care,
Is for the clownish first borne sonne and heyre,

Who must be *gentled* by his ill got pelfe,
Though he to get it, got the divell himselfe.

.   .   .   .   .

For almes he never read the word relieve,
He knows to get, but never knows to give.[22]

Actually we find upon close scrutiny that Fuller and Taylor are not as contradictory as they at first appear and that most of their differences are of degree rather than quality. Industry and ambition can easily lead to greed and selfishness, and the line between thrift and a grudging stinginess often wears very thin.

Certainly in the yeoman's scale of values industry and thrift stood close to the top, as the foregoing chapters have amply testified. Nor were they requirements that the times demanded from every class. Indeed it was the mark of a gentleman's son that he be able "to live idlely" and spend with a prodigal hand. But a yeoman's son who would measure up to what was expected of him by his family, the neighbors, and society in general must not be indolent. Industry was the very prop on which his status often depended. Without it he would not only lose his own and his neighbors' respect, but his very economic independence might be jeopardized. The road from yeoman rank to that of small tenant farmer or landless laborer was an open road for an indolent yeoman.

The Reverend Nathaniel Newbury, in a special sermon prepared for the yeomen of Kent in 1652, made industry the first prerequisite of success. *If any man will not work neither shall he eat,* he read to them from the second book of Thessalonians. They may have doubted that. There were plenty of beggars about who seemed to keep going at the expense of those who did labor. But his next injunction, *He becometh poor that dealeth with a slack hand, but the hand of the diligent maketh rich,* would carry weight. *He that gathereth in summer is a wise son, but he that sleepeth in*

22. "A Brood of Cormorants," *Works* of John Taylor, 1630, p. 12.

harvest is a son that causeth shame were also words that they understood, and the truth of which some of them had experienced. "Lazy" or "slothful" he declared to be words of the same importance, whereas "diligence" and "riches" were "Foster Sisters."[23] Parents did not consider a young man who was not industrious a proper suitor for their daughters; nor could he command credit from his neighbors.

Thrift was held in the same high regard. Waste and extravagance would ruin the reputation of a yeoman almost more quickly than anything else. *Did you ever know any lavish expenses or unthriftie disposition in the complainant as did manifest him to be likely to waste or consume his estate?* This was the type of question asked in scores of interrogatories in which a yeoman's failure or success in living up to the standards of his community and his station was weighed as important evidence in a case at court.

Only by being frugal and thrifty could yeomen honor their "calling," said the Reverend Mr. Newbury. He warned against squandering "by loose and luxurious courses" what they had gathered with pains. If they took care to save what God sent, their families would be provided for and they would be able with ease and cheerfulness to discharge all public taxes and assessments: *Consider that thou sowest thy Furrow by the handful not by the sack. . . . Be frugal while you have it; it will be too late to put two fingersful in the purse when you have thrown all away by handfuls.*[24]

The thrift extolled among them was that which set a watchful eye on expenditures, whether of money or materials, that which held a penny saved a penny earned. Let gentlemen go gallant and spend if they must, shillings would never burn holes in a yeoman's pocket. A good yeoman, however, never kept money long in his pocket, but tried to increase it. Inventories almost invariably show that even the most well-to-do members of the group rarely had

23. *The Yeoman's Prerogative*, 1652, pp. 6–9.
24. *Ibid.*, pp. 25–26.

much of their riches in the form of money. Richard Baxter said he had known frugal freeholders who were pretty well off that "had much ado to raise as much as ten shillings which they might be in dire need of." As soon as money was acquired it was invested. As Thomas Byng, a Hertfordshire yeoman, said of his father in 1592, "he was a man that alwaies loved money well and disposed to great thrifte, and was alwaies carefull to encrease that porcion which he had." It was likewise said of Anthony Strong, a Sussex yeoman who had £750 at interest: "He did not use to keepe mony lyinge Idlely by hym but as soone as he had gathered together any some of value he eyther bought land therewith or put the same out to Interest."[25]

Often executors and overseers of wills were enjoined to see that bequests made to wives and children were withdrawn if they did not avoid wasting or wilfully spending what was left them. The Furse family were yeomen of considerable estate by the time Robert wrote the family history; but prosperity had not changed their scale of values. It was "by lytell and lytell" that their forebears had gathered their wealth. And it was because they had by "ther wysdom and good governanse so runne ther corse . . . and alwayse kepte themselves wytheyn ther own boundes" that they had grown in credit and ability. "Be not ashamed to rede or here of them," he counseled his own children who enjoyed the fruits of this past economy; "for of ther small porsyones they did increase and that was to them a grette credett," and "yf you do the lyke you shall have the like commendacyon of your sequele and increse your on credett and the credett of your house."[26] That is yeoman philosophy in a nutshell, the *credo* that they held both safe and admirable.

His practice of thrift and frugality may have helped to develop another quality recognizable in the yeoman's scale of values, namely, a liking for unostentatiousness and sim-

25. For examples in this paragraph, see *Richard Baxter's Last Treatise*, p. 29; Req. 2, 176/81; St.Ch. 8, 24/25.

26. *The Furse Family Book*, p. 171, and *passim*.

plicity in habit and manner. A yeoman, to put it in his own words, should be a "plaine honest man." To be *honest*, as the Elizabethans commonly used the word, meant not so much truthfulness as simplicity, genuineness, and lack of display. This sort of honesty was in the yeoman's mind applicable not only to food, clothes, and personal possessions, but also to manners and morals. "A plain honest good man," a "plain honest man," and "a very honest good man" are the terms which they applied with pride to their ancestors. They spoke of each other and were spoken of by men of other classes as "plain honest countrymen," "honest yeomen of the country," one who "liveth in playne and ordinary fashion." Scores of yeomen directed that their burials be "in simple manner" in accord with their station and degree. The gentleman's code called for a certain amount of elegance in manner and speech as well as dress; but a yeoman's manner and speech should be of homespun variety as were the clothes he wore.

Living simply and within one's own bounds did not necessarily mean niggardliness. One might spend as one had it, on occasion even rather lavishly, but never wastefully. Adam Martindale says that at his father's death, "considering how well he had always lived among his neighbors," and as a filial tribute, the family decided to "bring him home handsomely" befitting his position in the parish. The description of the funeral shows how successfully their aim was achieved: "All that came to the house to fetch his corpse thence (beggars not excepted) were entertained with good meat, piping hote, and strong ale in great plentie." Also, a great dinner was prepared at the tavern after the funeral sermon for the kindred and as many friends as the large room would hold. Wine was served as well as ale, and enough food and drink were left over to provide amply for the "rag and tag" that waited on such occasions outside the door. Certainly there is no sign of niggardliness here. But it is significant that Martindale, writing of the event years later, said: "And the matter was so discreetly ordered by such as were employed about it . . . that I am verily persuaded that some funerals have cost twice as much that have not been so creditable to the costmakers."[27]

That thrift did lead in some cases to niggardliness and penuriousness is to be expected. There were Taylor-yeomen as well as Fuller-yeomen. A Norfolk list containing the names of a number of yeomen considered wealthy enough to contribute a "gift" to the King in 1621 mention Thomas Hobbs who was "riche in money, gathereth wealth very much . . . and liveth at a meane rate," and George Fynderne who was "an usurer and lyveth at a meane rate and gathereth much wealth." Two others were described as "great and griping usurers." Robert Teasdale of Westmoreland was described as "a yeoman that liveth by usurie . . . and love of money and by gripinge of poore men by usurious contracts and bargains." John Collet, a Devonshire yeoman, who lent money to a Totnes merchant against the time when his ships should return from Newfoundland, was charged with being so greedy that he would not be content with making less than twenty in the hundred on his loan.[28]

The fact that economy carried too far might become a vice rather than a virtue was well recognized among them. John Cambridge, a yeoman of Gloucester, tells of reproving a neighbor "for his close handedness." The Kentish yeomen who were urged by their parson to be economical were likewise warned to make a distinction between "care" and "niggardliness." And charity as well as industry and thrift was set forth as a means whereby they could honor their calling. *Does he keep good hospitality?* and *Is he good to the poor?* were questions asked of yeomen in scores of court interrogatories; and their standing in the community was gauged by the answer.

The custom of bequeathing alms to the poor took many forms. Robert Furse tells of an ancestor of the fifteenth cen-

27. *Life of Adam Martindale,* pp. 119–120.
28. For examples in this paragraph, see "Assessment of the Hundred of Frehol, 1621," *Norfolk Arch.,* XXI, 287–290; Req. 2, 201/57; St.Ch. 8, 236/8.

tury who bequeathed a cow to his heir with the instructions that the value of every calf that she bore should be "bestowed in some good deed of charity." His descendants were requested to continue this custom which they must have done at least more or less regularly; for instances of its observance from the fifteenth century to the end of Elizabeth's reign are found in the family record.

Bequests of the yeomen varied greatly in nature and amount, ranging from a few shillings or a strike of barley to substantial gifts and annuities in perpetuation. But everyone gave something. John Truelove, a yeoman of Kent, willed ten pounds for the use of two poor scholars at Cambridge, twenty pounds outright to the poor of the parish and an additional tenement and garden, the returns of which were to go to the poor. Thomas Leeman of Sutton, Lincolnshire, left ten acres of land with the yearly revenues to the poor. Robert Robinson, a wealthy yeoman of Essex, left money to twenty parishes where he had lived, or had friends living. Scores gave to the repairs of churches, both of parish and diocese. Many gave to schoolhouses. A Yorkshire yeoman left money for the repair of the stools that were in decay at the local schoolhouse. Money was frequently left for bridges and highway repairs, particularly highways leading to and from the church. John Spier, a yeoman of Warwick, left fifty pounds toward the making of a stone bridge and causeway in his parish.

Peter Bartoe, a yeoman of Ottery St. Mary, Devon, left money "for the relief and succour of poor Husbandmen, labourers and handicraftsmen" of his community. Bennett Broadmead, another Devon yeoman, left money to five poor tradesmen, and four "househoulders weavers." And Nicholas Parker, a public-spirited yeoman of Staffordshire, left the town of Walsall a hundred pounds to be used "for the good of the said towne." The charitable bequests in a set of thirty-seven Somerset and Dorset wills of yeomen and gentlemen totaled £1065 10s. Of this amount the twenty-one gentlemen contributed £567 10s., or slightly more than an average of £27 per capita, and the fifteen yeomen gave

£496 40s., or slightly more than an average of £33 per capita. Other lists might well show the reverse in relative amounts, but none would show the yeomen as nongivers.[29]

A final quality, the importance of which was recognized in a score of ways in the yeoman's standard of values, can perhaps best be expressed in the Elizabethan term "good neighborhood." It is a quality that touched their lives on many sides. The word neighbor still exists in our vocabulary and is well loved by those who use it often. But the literature of the Tudor and Stuart periods suggests a much wider meaning and usage for it than it has in our day. Other words and expressions that have found their way into present-day vocabularies carry the implications that Elizabethan yeomen conveyed in the one word "neighborhood."

As we speak of the good citizens of a town who have met to look after this or that, Adam Eyre, in exactly the same meaning, wrote of the "good neighbours of the towne" meeting together to select the parish officers or attend to other community business. Functions that are today performed by nurses, physicians, social workers, secretaries, real estate agents, and lawyers were among the countryfolk of Elizabethan and Stuart days performed by neighbors for each other. Neighborliness stands perhaps first in the criteria by which the social and ethical standing of an individual in a country community was measured. And the man or woman who fell short in its practice soon suffered a damaged reputation. *Is he well-accounted among his neighbors?* was another question asked of yeomen in court interrogatories. One who was a poor neighbor, or who detracted from the spirit of neighborliness in a community, sinned against the community itself. Thomas Keyes, an Essex yeoman, was bitterly arraigned before the sessions for causing false clamors and quarrels among his neighbors. Margaret Rye,

29. For examples in this and the preceding paragraph, see Add. MSS. 33916, fol. 155; Req. 2, 174/55; P.C.C., 58 Cobham, 23 Soame, 60 and 77 Skynner; York Wills, XXV, 1160; Will of Philip Bartoe in the MSS. of Mrs. Frances Rose-Troupe; "Bequests to Dorset Parishes, Schools, etc.," *Somerset and Dorset N. and Q.*, 1897, V, 197–201.

the wife of a Norfolk yeoman, was presented by the hundred jury of North Erpingham in 1612 because she was lacking in good neighborhood and "doeth make discord betweene neybour and neybour." And other sessions records show many instances of those who were called to account because they were "common sowers of debates and discords amongst neighbours."

The quality of neighborliness in a country community was not based wholly upon a social or beneficent impulse. It was partly grounded in hard-headed, practical, common sense. In a turbulent age where life was held cheap and comforts and conveniences were few, there was actual need for maintaining harmony between neighbors if the community were to be a safe and agreeable place to live in. This note of self-interest that furthered the advocacy of neighborliness among countryfolk was frankly admitted by them, and approved. Nobody made any bones about the fact that it was good business to be a good neighbor. Experience had taught them the truth of the old adage: "As you measure to your neighbour he will measure back to you."

Nicholas Breton's countryman emphasizes well this practical aspect of neighborliness: "It is enough for us to give a Cake for a Pudding, and a pinte of wine for a Pottle of beere: and when we kill hogs to send our children to our neighbours with these messages: My Father and my mother have sent you a Pudding and a Chine, and desires you when you kill your Hogges, you will send him as good again."[30]

One of the first steps in the *Ladder of Thrift* which Thomas Tusser recommended to all husbandmen was this:

> To love thy neighbour neighbourly,
> And show him no discourtesy.

For, as he frankly stated later,

> Lending to neighbour, in time of his need
> Wins love of thy neighbour, and credit doth breed.[31]

30. *Dialogue between a Courtier and a Countryman*, p. 199.
31. *Five Hundred Points of Good Husbandry*, p. 19.

His advice to the good housewife was in the same vein: "Thy love of thy neighbour shall stand thee in stead." If a man lent his plough, the unwritten code of neighborliness prescribed to him the right in turn to borrow his neighbor's cradle, or scythe, or flail when he had need of them. A yeoman's wife would scarcely have dared, from a selfish standpoint alone, fail a neighbor who was ill or in trouble. Who could tell when her own time might come?

Neighbors needed each other's aid in business deals. By Elizabeth's time it was customary, in fact necessary, to have written indentures for almost all kinds of bargainings. Thousands of these indentures were made; and oftener than not it was a neighbor, one with somewhat more education and experience than his fellows, who drew them up. Other neighbors acted as witnesses who signed or made their marks. Often such deals required bonds as assurances that the terms would be met. In this event it was a mark of good neighborhood for a man to stand as surety for his friend. In transactions where there was no written evidence it was equally important that a man have a neighbor or two along whose word as a witness would be trusted.

One of the most important services that yeomen rendered their neighbors was the semijudicial one of acting as arbiter in the settlement of quarrels and difficulties. When George Whetstone, in 1586, urged the yeomanry to end their troubles at home by the judgment of their neighbors and kinsfolk instead of spending their money on sharp lawyers, he was merely advocating a practice already followed by scores of them. For many of them had discovered that it was cheaper, more expeditious, and often just as satisfactory to "let neighbours make an end of it."

On such occasions the disputant on each side selected one or more neighbors who came together, weighed the evidence presented by both contenders, and rendered a decision which each side had previously agreed to accept. In case no agreement could be reached, they chose a third person or persons believed to be disinterested in the matter to act as umpire. A settlement made in this fashion between neigh-

bors had the same sanction in the community as if it had
been issued by a court of law. And a man who failed to abide
by it stood to lose as much through the disapproval of an
adverse public opinion as he might hope to gain any other
way.

Adam Eyre reports a trip to Silkston on such a mission
for Nicholas Greaves, where, with the aid of William
Wordsworth, the arbiter for the other disputant, an end
was made to a controversy between Greaves and a fuller
named Hutchinson. When Eyre himself had difficulties
with his tenant Edward Mitchell, Ralph Wordsworth and
William Rich, his nearest neighbors, served in like capacity
for him.[32]

Simon Rider served in dozens of arbitration cases. He
says of an adjustment between two quarreling neighbors
in 1592 that it settled "all matters whatsoever betweene
them depending or being from the beginning of the world
till that date." In another, the settlement provided that "all
suits controversies, debts and demands between them . . .
should ceasse and be void & so to be lovers and friends without any money geving eyther to other." Sometimes a part
of the settlement required that the contending parties be
made to drink each other's health and to shake hands.[33]

Neighbors were asked to assist in all kinds of settlements.
John Mather and Thomas Ballim, two Devonshire yeomen,
held certain lands in joint ownership, each with a right to
an equal share. Formerly they had grazed their cattle on
the land in common and shared it in other ways. But in keeping with the trend toward individual ownership they decided
in 1641 that a permanent division would be an advantage
to both. No lawyers, surveyors, or other official agents had
a hand in the matter. But two other yeomen, Robert Bennett and Giles More, their neighbors, were called upon to
make the division. They measured the land, listed the build-

---

32. *Diary of Adam Eyre*, pp. 9, 80. For other examples see Req. 2,
180/25, 181/30, 177/5, 206/64; Chester Sessions, 1638, File I, f. 98; Dorset Sessions Book, 1633; Chancery Dep. A 1/5; Ass. 24/1.

33. Rider Commonplace Book, pp. 52, 57, and *passim*.

ings and appurtenances, accorded each man what seemed to them his fair share, and set down the terms of the agreement in an indenture that was regarded as binding as if it had been the work of experts and stamped with an official seal.[34]

Yeomen who could read and write with ease were in special demand for such services, as sample entries from Adam Eyre's diary show:

When Thomas Marsden, Henry Swinden, and Robert Sandern met me I drew them a petition.

. . . . .

at the Weet's yate I mett with two lynleys, who came to request mee to be a commissioner for them and I directed them to Mr. Eyre of Bramley for another.

. . . . .

In the afternoone I went to Jo. Shawe's and drew a pair of indentures for his sonne John to be a prentice to one Taylor of Tintwisle a blacksmith.[35]

Neighborliness was thus to some extent merely a projection of the yeoman's shrewd, thrifty, and provident nature. It paid good returns. But this was far from being the only important aspect of it. The spirit of good fellowship which neighborliness bred permeated and helped to shape the most colorful and attractive features of social relationships. It pervaded the atmosphere of community gatherings. It was present when men sang songs and drank ale at the village tavern. It caused groups to linger on the steps of the parish church on Sunday morning while women exchanged receipts for marchpane and quodinack of plums, and men talked of their crops and the weather. It set the tone of country weddings where each man and woman present felt a personal interest in the bride and groom because they were neighbors' children. Gifts were often the outward manifestation of neighborliness as they are today. Gifts of food were the most popular. A leg of veal, a flitch of bacon,

34. Exeter Deeds and Documents, 2131.
35. *Diary of Adam Eyre*, pp. 2, 31, and *passim*.

a pint of honey, and a sucking pig were among the gifts that yeoman families carried to each other.

Neighborliness, moreover, in many instances was the trait through which the yeomen found expression for their finest impulses. They were loyal with a steadfast loyalty to whatever brand of religion happened to have their allegiance. But the religious loyalties of the seventeenth century with their highly controversial character often led to bigotry and bitterness among friends and neighbors and were often, inadvertently, a disruptive rather than a unifying force in country communities. Not so the gospel of good neighborhood to which the countryfolk of all sects adhered. Whatever was warm and kind and fine in their natures found hearty expression here.

Adam Eyre, as his diary shows, was none too amiable in disposition; but he never refused to perform a service for a neighbor when he could. Harassed with financial and other problems of his own, he was yet always willing to take time to organize or assist at a help-ale for one of the unfortunates of the neighborhood, or to proffer his services to neighbors who were in trouble: ". . . thence to Birchworth, where I called at John Miclethwait's who had a daughter sick. . . . Thence I went to Shephouse to see Ellen. Nicholas Greaves, his daughter, who was sick and dyed that night."[36]

A man could, and would, be forgiven much if he were known to be a good neighbor. The love that neighbors felt for each other was one of the happiest and most vital influences in the life of the countryside. And if one can judge from chance phrases that turn up in scores of documents, it was his neighbors, along with his family and his lands, that made life in this world sweet to the average yeoman; and they from whom he was most loath to part when death approached. Funeral feasts have been mentioned earlier. A Lancashire yeoman's will contains this statement: "And I doe give sixe pounds in mony to be bestowed in a dinner to

36. *Ibid.*, pp. 8–9.

make my honest good neighbours welcome for my last faire well to them." Once more, by virtue of his good six pounds, he would be able to perform the office of genial host and neighbor. Richard Meade, an Essex yeoman, extended the idea by instructing his executors to have his former neighbors come together once every year for a dinner for which he left a small annuity.

An item in the church registers of Shrowardine, a small parish in Shropshire, for the year 1659, reads as follows:

June 8. Richard Typton, *yeoman*, aged about four score; an *honest* man, and a loving *Neighbour* was buried.

It is a simple statement of a plain man written by one of his own kind. But in the language and code of his group, as measured by its own "mete wand," it expressed the approval with which an English yeoman might well rest content.

APPENDIX I

EARLY USAGE OF THE WORD YEOMAN

As stated in Chapter I, the word yeoman from the thirteenth to the fifteenth century was in general usage as a term of service. The attendant or servitor thus described was not a menial, but one giving honorable service. Hence this was designated the primary usage of the word. It occurs in the French as *vadlet, vallet,* or *varlet;* in Latin documents as *valettus* or *valectus;* and in the vernacular as *ȝoman, zeman, yogman, yoman,* and the like; and is to be found in official and semiofficial writings as well as in the popular literature of the period.

In 1292 an order of safe conduct was issued for "Peter de Weston, yeoman of Otto de Grandisono, whom some friends of Otto are sending to the land of Cyprus to him, with a horse laden with cloths and other things."[1] In 1312 Ralph le Forester, receiver in the ward of Penreth in the forest of Ingelwode, was ordered "to deliver to the King's yeoman, John de Harttla all the money that he has received . . . from the issues of the forest."[2] In 1332 a pardon was issued to Richard Calware "the King's yeoman and butler."[3] Over and over in these and similar records one meets with the king's yeomen or yeomen of other lords who are sent hither and yon on varied missions.[4]

Now and then, in calendars and other translations of these documents, the original *valetto* or *valecto* is placed in parentheses beside the word "yeoman" as if the translators were uncertain in their use of the latter term as the proper English equivalent.[5] But the nineteenth-century scholars who prepared the calendars of the Close Rolls and Patent Rolls from which the above examples are taken express no such doubt and their position appears to me wholly justified, since Chaucer and other writers of the fourteenth century whose works are in the vernacular continually used the

1. *Calendar of Patent Rolls, Edward I, 1281–1292,* p. 465. There are similar examples throughout this volume.

2. *Calendar of Close Rolls, Edward II, 1307–1313,* p. 464, and *passim.*

3. *Calendar of Patent Rolls, Edward III, 1330–1334,* p. 376, and *passim.*

4. Charter Rolls, No. 4, m 7; *Close Rolls,* No. 104, m 3; *Calendar of Inquisitions, Edward II,* VI, 52, and *passim.*

5. See *Calendar of Inquisitions,* VI, 52.

word "yoman" as it is used in the above passages. Chaucer says of the Squire in the *Prologue*:

> A Yeman hadde he, and seruantz namo
> At that tyme, for him liste ryde so

And it will be remembered that it was the Canon's yeoman, "full of courtesy," and

> wont to be right fressh and gay
> Of Clothyng and of oother good array

who told one of the last of the pilgrims' tales.[6]

Whether or not the word yeoman should be employed as the English equivalent of *vadlet* or *valettus* in documents of the thirteenth and fourteenth centuries when those words are used to designate the rank or status of a social class or group, is, I think, more debatable. For it seems evident that at that time "franklin," not "yoman," was the term employed by writers of the vernacular to convey that meaning. Only later did the term "yeoman" come also to be generally used as a status term.

An example of *valettus* used in this fashion occurs in a group of early statutes of uncertain date, but held by scholars to fall within the period 1287–1313.[7] Mention is made here of certain *valetti* who have paid sums of money to sheriffs or their bailiffs that they might not be compelled to become knights as by recent legislation they were supposed to do, being holders of twenty librates of lands.[8] Again, in the parliamentary writs of the same period, one finds certain counties returning *valetti* to parliament instead of knights as was the accepted practice. In 1311 Rutland sent two members designated simply as *homines*. In 1322 Worcestershire and Devon sent one *valettus* each; and Middlesex, Hereford, and Leicestershire sent two *valetti* each. In the returns for 1324 it is expressly stated that the men returned were not knights but *valetti*.[9] We know that in France young men of free birth who had not become knights, and some who never became knights, were designated as *vadletz* or *varlets*.[10] But in England, if we are to judge from the contemporary

6. *Canterbury Tales* (Manly and Rickert), III, lines 100–101; IV, 724–725.

7. *S.R.*, I, 234.

8. *Ibid.*, p. 229. See also Bolland, *Eyre of Kent*, Selden Soc., XXIV, 31.

9. W. Palgrave, *Parliamentary Writs*, II, Pt. I, 51, 277–278, 317.

10. For examples from medieval literature see *Garin le Lorrain*, 1862, pp. 100, 396; *Lays of Marie de France*, pp. 6, 8, 10, and *passim*. See also

literature written in the vernacular, the upstanding freemen of creditable position and substance who ranked next below the knights and esquires were known in this period as "franklins." Examples from the *Chronicle of Robert of Gloucester* (1298), the *Cursor Mundi* (*ca.* 1320), the *Chronicle of Robert of Brunne* (*ca.* 1327), *Piers Plowman,* and Chaucer have been given in Chapter I.[11]

It was not until the early part of the fifteenth century that "franklin" began to give way to two new status terms: "gentleman" and "yeoman." Neither was in itself a new term; but neither had heretofore been used generally to denote status. Some attention has been given to the development of the word "gentleman" in this usage.[12] Suffice it here to say that from the early fifteenth century forward one finds that term used increasingly to designate the group next below the knights and esquires, comprising often their sons or other younger sons of the nobility as well as many scions of old "franklin" families who could claim a coat of arms and otherwise maintain themselves as a more or less leisured rural class. The remainder of the franklins whose ranks were now being recruited generously from below as well as from above, those smaller landholders who supervised and tilled their lands, who were either not eligible to coat armor or did not wish to press their claims for it, but who maintained a position of worth and independence in the countryside, came more and more as the fifteenth century progressed to be known as "yeomen."

But the period is obviously a formative one in respect to status terms as to many other developments, and they are frequently used loosely and often interchangeably. Old terms maintained their hold in some places while elsewhere new ones took root and flourished. Sir George Sitwell has found the record of one William Smith of Caldwell Hall, Eckington, who was described as "gentleman" in 1443, "ffrankleyne" in 1446, and "yoman" in 1465 although there is no evident change in his circumstances.[13] And Fortescue (*ca.* 1463) spoke of those next to the esquires and knights as "Frankeleynes," "Freeholders," and "Yeomen."[14] In fact, one even finds an

---

Medieval Latin Word-List (Baxter and Johnson), 1934; and the discussion by Sir George Sitwell in *The Hurts of Haldworth,* p. xxxiii.

11. See above, pp. 13–14.

12. See Sir George Sitwell, *The Ancestor,* I, 73 ff. and *The Hurts of Haldworth,* p. xlvi.

13. *The Hurts of Haldworth,* p. xlvi.

14. Sir J. Fortescue, *The Laws of England* (Grigor), 1917, p. 48.

occasional writer as late as the reign of Elizabeth or James I employing the older term franklin,[15] though in general yeoman had by that time definitely replaced it as a status term.

Whether this newer usage of the word yeoman originated independently of the earlier meaning in circumstances long since lost sight of, or whether it is a natural and logical offshoot of the old, is a nice question. There may have been no connection between the two usages. None, I believe, has ever been pointed out and there is not enough evidence to prove that any existed. There is, however, in a series of examples that occur in the *Rolls of Parliament* and in certain statutes of the latter part of the fourteenth and the fifteenth centuries the suggestion of a connection that seems worth noting. The following observations make no claim to offer anything more than a hypothesis or, as I should prefer to call it, a common-sense guess concerning the possible relationship between the two usages. Whether further evidence, if found, shows it to have been a poor approach or develops it into a tenable theory, a point of attack will at least have been made.

The clue to the connection between the two usages occurs first in relation to a petition in the *Rolls of Parliament* for 1363. The petition is in the form of a request that measures be taken against extravagance of apparel throughout the kingdom. It declares that "servants use the apparel of people of trade, people of trade the apparel of Valletz, Valletz the apparel of Esquires, and Esquires the apparel of Knights."[16] Here and in succeeding petitions and statutes for three quarters of a century *vadlets* or *valletz* refer unmistakably to a rank between the knight and esquire on the one hand and the tradesmen and other rural people of a lower sort, just as the word *valettus* is used in the parliamentary writs quoted above. The first connection with the word yeoman as an English equivalent occurs in the king's *reponsio* to the above petition of 1363. In this document the word *valletz* is omitted in the restrictions regarding dress, and for it is substituted the phrase, "those of the office called Yomen" (*de office appelez Yomen*).[17] And in the same year the order went into statute form as follows: *item, qe gentz de meistere, d'artifice, & de office appele Yomen, ne ne preignent ne usent drappe de plus haut pris. . . .*[18]

In the petitions and statutes that appear at intervals throughout the remainder of the century and during the first part of the next,

15. See above, p. 13 n.
16. *Rotuli Parliamentorum*, 1777, II, 278–281.
17. *Ibid.*, p. 281.　　　　　　　　18. *S.R.*, 37 Edward III, c. 9.

the phrases "Vadlets appele Yomen," or "Vadletz de office appele Yomen," sometimes translated in the statutes as "officers called Yomen," appear again and again.[19] The first petition and statute of 1363 apparently had to do with extravagance of dress in general throughout the kingdom, but practically all of the subsequent instances are concerned with the question of "livery and maintenance." Livery and maintenance grew out of a practice common to the late medieval period whereby those freemen who could not afford to become knights and to give the military service required of knights, attached themselves to a knight or lord of higher rank and fought under his banner. These men were identified with the knights or lords whom they served by certain insignia of dress or decoration. Followers of the great lords were outfitted with complete liveries, but those of the lesser lords or knights were known only by a "badge" or "sign of company." Such bands or companies of men served as an essential part of local and national defense and were "maintained" by their lords.

The king depended upon the support of these groups for aid in his wars and during the earlier period of the wars with the French and the Scots their services were demanded and welcomed. But as the monarchy grew in power, paid troops were more generally used. Furthermore, it became apparent that in times of peace the presence of armed bands could be, and often was, a menace to the community and a temptation to turbulent nobles to use force for the furtherance of their own ends. Hence throughout the fifteenth century there was a growing tendency on the part of sovereigns to whom such armed bands now often boded no good, and also on the part of many of their subjects who suffered from the use of violence in neighborhood disputes, to urge restriction of the system of "livery and maintenance." The petitions and statutes mentioned above were the result of this tendency. They served first to restrict, and finally to do away entirely with the practice, except as it affected the retainers whom the lord kept permanently in his household and those who belonged to the household of the king.

It may be that this system had nothing to do with the development of the word yeoman as a status term. But the following connection suggests itself.

When a freeman followed his lord to war, according to the practice outlined above, wearing his livery or "badge" or "sign of company," and subject to attend or serve him, he was, according to the

19. *Rotuli Parliamentorum*, III, 307a, 339a, 345b, 428b, 478a. *S.R.*, II, 84, 93, 113, 130.

primary usage of the term, his "yeoman." Men of this type would be the "vadlets of the office of yomen" mentioned in the statutes against liveries and maintenance. If this were the case, the next question is how the term came, as we know it did, to be identified will all *vadlets,* as that term is used to designate a social group and not merely with those "of the office of yomen."

The plausible answer would seem to lie in the fact that the wars of the fourteenth and fifteenth centuries, whether with the French or the Scots or at home under the standard of the white or red rose, were practically all of an intermittent nature. A considerable number, therefore, perhaps the greater part of able-bodied "franklins" or "vadlets" were from time to time engaged in the service of some lord, and were according to the early usage of the term, his yeomen. During the periods of peace, sometimes brief, sometimes of greater length, these "yeomen," except the ones who remained as personal retainers in the lord's household, returned to their lands. Many of them, in fact, held lands from the same lord to whom they gave military service, preserving thereby through their tenurial services something of the old relationship. If they were styled "yeoman" while they were with their lords, and if their periods of service were intermittent, it seems plausible to believe, or so it does to me, that the name stayed with them during the periods when they were not actually in the lord's service, and that they continued to be designated as "yeoman." When at length this type of warfare grew less frequent, and the strengthening of the national monarchy led to the prohibition of bands and companies except such as the lord kept as retainers in his household, most of the group of small landholders, as did most of their lords, left off military service to devote their energies to their lands and neighborhood pursuits. A man in this position was no longer a "yeoman," in the restricted sense of that word. But the term remained with the group, from whom the majority of such servants had once been drawn, and came gradually to replace the older term "franklin." This, at least, is the possibility suggested by a careful reading of the above petitions and statutes and by the fifteenth-century usage of the term.

APPENDIX II

TABLE SHOWING TRADES AND INDUSTRIES TO WHICH SONS OF YEOMEN WERE APPRENTICED IN BRISTOL, CHESTER, IPSWICH, AND YORK, 1550–1651

Trades and Industries	Bristol 1566–1590 1607–1618	Chester 1550–1642	Ipswich 1596–1651	York 1591–1650	Totals
Apothecary	....	1	1	1	3
Armorer	....	....	....	1	1
Baker	7	1	....	6	14
Barber	1	3	1	....	5
Barber-surgeon	3	....	....	12	15
Blacksmith	2	....	....	1	3
Brewer	6	8	....	....	14
Butcher	....	....	....	6	6
Cardboard maker	1	....	....	....	1
Carpenter	1	....	1	4	6
Carrier	1	....	....	....	1
Chirurgeon	2	....	....	1	3
Clothmaker	8	....	....	2	10
Cooper	11	2	....	6	19
Cordwainer	....	....	....	11	11
Cutler	1	1	....	....	2
Draper	10	12	....	....	22
Dyer	7	2	....	....	9
Embroiderer	....	....	....	1	1
Feltmaker	6	....	....	6	12
Fisherman	....	....	1	....	1
Fishmonger	....	....	....	1	1
Glazier	....	....	....	1	1
Glover	3	6	....	11	20
Goldsmith	....	2	1	....	3
Grocer	19	....	3	....	22
Haberdasher	6	....	....	16	22
Hatter	1	....	....	....	1
Hooper	2	....	....	....	2

APPENDIX II (*continued*)

Trades and Industries	Bristol 1566–1590 1607–1618	Chester 1550–1642	Ipswich 1596–1651	York 1591–1650	Total
Hosier	1	....	....	....	1
Innkeeper	....	2	....	....	2
Ironmonger	3	.... 21	....	....	24
Joiner	10	....	....	20	30
Linen draper	1	....	....	....	1
Maltmaker	....	....	....	1	1
Mariner	1	....	.... 22	....	23
Mercer	16	.... 14	....	....	30
Merchant	20	.... 8	1	3	32
Miller	....	....	....	5	5
Navigator	1	....	....	....	1
Notary public	3	....	....	....	3
Painter	....	....	....	1	1
Pewterer	....	....	....	4	4
Saddler	3	.... 1	....	11	15
Sailmaker	1	....	....	....	1
Shearman	6	....	....	....	6
Shipwright	2	....	....	....	2
Shoemaker	14	.... 11	5	....	30
Silkweaver	....	....	....	19	19
Skinner	1	.... 1	....	3	5
Soapmaker and chandler	12	....	....	3	15
Spurrier	....	....	....	1	1
Stationer	....	....	....	1	1
Tailor	18	....	.... 3	1	22
Tanner	4	....	....	15	19
Tucker	2	....	....	....	2
Turner	4	....	....	....	4
Upholsterer	1	....	....	1	2
Vintner	7	....	....	....	7
Weaver	2	....	....	11	13
Whittawer	7	....	....	....	7
Wiredrawer	1	....	....	3	4
Woolen draper	2	....	....	....	2
Totals	241	.... 96	39	190	566

The materials for the above table were taken from the Apprentice books in the Bristol Corp. MSS.; the Apprentice books in the Chester Corp. MSS.; a MS. transcript of apprentice indentures in the MSS. of the Ipswich Free Library; and the Register of Apprentices (D, XII) in the MSS. at the Guildhall in York. They cannot be taken as a complete record; for there were a good many names for which no status was given and certain years for which the records were not complete. But they are of interest as an indication of the representative trades and industries which the sons of the yeomen were entering, and to show the popularity of certain trades in different regions.

APPENDIX III

SERVANTS' WAGES BY THE YEAR, 1592–1635

	1592 Herts	1593 E. Riding of York	1594 Devon	1610 Rutland	1612-18 Essex	1630 Suffolk	1635 Dorset
	s. d.	s. d.	s. d.	s. d.	s. d.	s. d.	s. d.
A bailiff or servant of the best sort capable of directing the work of others — With apparel	40 0	33 4	60 4	*52 0	*66 8	60 0	80 0
— Without apparel	46 8	40 0	73 8			80 0	100 0
A man servant of the second-best sort, chief hind or chief ploughman — With apparel	33 4	26 8		*50 0	*60 0		60 10
— Without apparel	40 0	33 4				80 0	70 10
A man servant of the third-best sort, or second hind or plain laborer in husbandry — With apparel	26 8	23 4	*40 0	*40 0	*16 8		46 8
— Without apparel	33 4	30 0				40 0	53 4
A woman servant of the best sort; able to take charge of malting, brewing, and baking — With apparel	21 0	13 0	16 8	*26 8	*33 4	*40 0	30 0
— Without apparel	26 8	17 0	23 4				35 0
A woman servant of the second-best sort; but not to take charge — With apparel	18 0	13 4		*23 4	*26 8	*30 0	
— Without apparel	23 0	16 8					
A woman servant to do "out work and drudgery" — With apparel				*16 10			
— Without apparel							

* The schedule does not designate in this instance whether the wage was with or without apparel. As it seems to have been the usual practice for the master to provide apparel, I have placed it in this column.

These figures were compiled from the schedules of wages set down in the following records: Devon Quarter Sessions Records, 1594; Dorset Quarter Sessions Records, 1635; Essex Quarter Sessions Papers, 1612 ff.; *Hertford Quarter Sessions Records*, I, 11–12. Those for Rutland, *Archæologia*, XI, 201; those for Suffolk, the MSS. of the

ASSESSMENTS FOR PRIVY SEAL IN THE COUNTIES OF BEDFORD, CAMBRIDGE, AND RUTLAND

Status of persons assessed	Bedfordshire 1588		Cambridgeshire 1605(?)		Rutland 1625		Total number assessed from each group
	Number of persons from each group	Average amount per person £	Number of persons from each group	Average amount per person £	Number of persons from each group	Average amount per person £	
Baronets					2	10.0	2
Knights					5	11.0	10
Gentlemen	15	27.0	5	26.40	17	8.24	45
Esquires	8	38.12	13	16.69	13	10.38	31
Yeomen	11	25.0	10	19.70	12	7.91	40
Tradesmen	1	25.0	17	18.12			1
Widows			1	20.0	2	7.50	3
Clerks and D.D.'s			9	14.88			9
Status not given			37	14.82	1	5.0	38
Total	35		92		52		179

The returns for Bedford are in the Titus MSS. in the British Museum B–IV, 176–177. The Cambridge returns are in the State Papers, S.P. 14, XVII, 86. Their date is uncertain, but 1605 is the date suggested by the editors of the calendared State Papers (*S.P.D.*, 1603–1610, XVII, 86), though they indicate its uncertainty with a question mark. The returns for Rutland are in a set of local records chiefly pertaining to Leicestershire in the Hastings MSS. at the Huntington Library.

BIBLIOGRAPHICAL NOTE

MATERIALS for the study of a social class must almost inevitably be drawn from a variety of sources. This is especially true if the group in question is an inarticulate one as were the Elizabethan yeomen. There is no body of "yeoman material" as such; yet there are few kinds of contemporary writing in which some pertinent evidence may not turn up. The findings, however, oftener than not, are fragmentary and taken singly have relatively little significance. Hence an exhaustive list of the separate items used in this study would not only be unwieldy, but of somewhat doubtful value. The purpose here is rather to suggest the principal types of material that have proved most valuable, with representative illustrations. Additional particulars are listed throughout in the footnotes.

MANUSCRIPT SOURCES

The available manuscript material, varied, and for some aspects of the subject, abundant, falls into two general categories: certain large and well-known collections in the central archives in London, and the smaller, but nonetheless significant local collections. Of the former, those in the Public Record Office (P.R.O.) and the British Museum (B.M.) are the most important.

Especially useful among the collections in the P.R.O. are the State Papers for the reigns of Elizabeth (S.P. 12), James I (S.P. 14), and Charles I (S.P. 16), with their wealth of reports from local officials concerning conditions and activities in rural shires and parishes. Records of the Court of Star Chamber for the reign of James I (St.Ch. 8), and those of the Court of Requests under Elizabeth (Req. 2), are also extremely rewarding, their usefulness for these particular reigns being enhanced by excellent indexes that give the status of the principals in each case, and something of the nature of the subject matter. It is the lack of this information, particularly of the status term whereby material relating to a single class can be identified without a prohibitive expenditure of time, that renders several similar collections less useful. The typescript index of the Star Chamber records for James I, especially full and descriptive, is now also available in film at the Yale Library.

Other collections in the P.R.O. used less extensively, but in some instances for important items, are the records of the Chancery (C.) and the Exchequer (E.), including depositions, affidavits, and orders of the Court of Chancery and the Court of the Exchequer. Some use was also made of the records of the Duchy of Lancaster (D.L.) and the Court of Delegates (C. of Del.) ; and of the records of the clerks of the Assize (Ass.), particularly those of the southwestern and northeastern circuits.

Unlike the manuscripts in the Record Office which are chiefly official, those in the British Museum are largely collections of family papers. They are by no means, however, all of a private nature but contain many official and semiofficial papers describing local matters which the J.P.'s, chief local administrators, permitted to accumulate in the muniment rooms of their country houses among their own private correspondence, manor rolls, and other family papers. Hence the variety of the collections is often but slightly suggested, if at all, in the printed indexes. Those proving most useful for this study were the Additional Manuscripts (Add. MSS.) including the Egerton manuscripts (Eg. MSS.) and Additional Charters (Add. Ch.), and the Lansdowne (Lansd.) and Harleian (Harl.) collections. The Sloane and Stowe collections were also used, but less widely.

Another of the London archives indispensable to a student of the social classes is the large collection of early wills at Somerset House. Again because of the descriptive indexes, wills proved in the Prerogative Court of Canterbury (P.C.C.) are the most useful. Significant also is the smaller collection of those proved in the court of the Archdeaconry for Berkshire, the unique value of which lies in the fact that the amount of each personal estate is affixed to the will, now an accepted practice, but one rarely followed in the Tudor and Stuart period.

Volumes of English history have been, and may still be, written from the central archives alone; for they contain material pertaining to every English county—I daresay, to every parish. But the student of social and economic history can no longer afford to neglect the smaller manuscript collections that are the rich heritage of many English localities. Not only do they contain certain types of material not represented at all, or but incidentally, in the London archives; but even where there is duplication some advantage is to be gained from using a document in the vicinity of which it is a record. This is particularly true in the case of records describing lands, though the added stimulus given the imagination by the use of local collections is not limited to a certain type of document. A sense of reality for the past is a coveted possession. Nothing in one's experience, I believe, can come as near creating it as the use of local records in their own habitat.

Despite fundamental changes in the character of local government, many records formerly kept by officers of county, town, and parish remain in the custody of those who carry on with similar work or its equivalent today. Others, varied in nature, have been collected and preserved through the zeal of antiquarians and public-spirited citizens. Whatever their character, practically all local collections benefited either directly or indirectly from the establishment of official local repositories, subsidiaries as it were, of the Public Record Office. This was done in connection with the Law of Property Amendment Act of 1924, a measure designed to encourage the preservation of manorial court rolls, which, with the abolition of copyhold tenure for which they had served as title deeds, now became legally worthless. But the focusing of attention on these particular manuscripts and the provision for proper housing facilities furnished the incentive for many additional loans and gifts of family papers and other manuscript materials to the official local collection, of which every county now has at least one. Many of the wealthier shires provided funds for trained archivists to repair, classify, and in many cases to index and calendar thousands of documents that had hitherto been inaccessible to the student.

Significant for notable progress in this work as well as for their content are the Devonshire manuscripts housed in the public library at Exeter; the manuscripts relating to Norfolk and other parts of East Anglia in the public library at Norwich; the well-catalogued records relating to Warwick, Worcestershire, and other counties in the Midlands in the public library at Birmingham; the manuscripts of the Yorkshire Archæological Society at Leeds; and those of Gloucestershire and the surrounding country in the public library at Gloucester. There is an excellent printed bibliography of the Gloucester collection: R. Austin, *Catalogue of the Gloucestershire Collections, Books, Pamphlets, and Documents in the Gloucester Public Library*, etc. Gloucester, 1928; and a similar one for the manuscripts at Leeds: W. Lancaster, *Catalogue of MSS. in the Library of the Yorkshire Archæological Society*, Leeds, 1912. Recent acquisitions in both cases are covered by hand lists which are also available for the other above collections.

Good collections for which somewhat less elaborate aids to research have been completed, but where some kind of hand lists are available and where calendaring and indexing are making progress, are the Stafford manuscripts at the William Salt Library, Stafford; the large collection of Sussex manuscripts in the custody of the Sussex Archæological Society, Lewes; the Bedfordshire county records at the county offices in Bedford; the manuscripts of the Northamptonshire Record Society in the shire hall at Northampton; the Somerset county records in the shire hall at Taunton; and the county records of Essex in the shire hall at Chelmsford. Excellent records for the period in question, but badly in need of better classification, are the Lincolnshire records in the new shire hall at Lincoln, and the Norfolk county records in the shire hall at Norwich. This list by no means covers all of the worthwhile collections of this type, not even all of those used in this study; but it will serve to suggest something of the richness of the local manuscript field.

For the most part, municipal records were of less value for this study than were those of shire and parish; but in many instances material relating to the surrounding country is included in corporation manuscripts. I found especially useful items in the corporation manuscripts of Bristol, Chester, Coventry, Shrewsbury, and York. The apprentice books of Bristol, Chester, and York throw light on the occupations of those localities, and indicate the contribution of agricultural classes to the ranks of trade and industry. The record of the indentured servants who took passage from the port of Bristol between 1654 and 1685, contained in two large manuscript volumes that were unknown even to the custodians of the Bristol MSS. until a few years ago, is a unique source not only for the history of English social classes but also for American colonial history.

In addition to the central and local archives above-mentioned, some use was made of the Additional MSS. in the University Library at Cambridge; the "English MSS." in the John Rylands Library at Manchester; and the archives of the Huntington Library at San Marino, California. It is early printed books, however, rather than the manuscripts that make the Huntington Library valuable for a study of this kind, though certain items from the Hastings-Huntingdon papers, and from the Stowe and Ellesmere manuscripts, will be found in the classified list below.

The collections hitherto described proved so voluminous that little effort was made to utilize private libraries. Occasionally, however, my attention was called to specific manuscripts in private hands. A number of these are listed below. The manuscripts of the Cruwys family in the muniment room at Cruwys Morchard, near Tiverton, Devon, are rich in Elizabethan material. A good many small libraries of private clubs or organizations such as that of the Plymouth Institution at the Athenæum, Plymouth, contain interesting small collections of manuscripts that are open to students through the courtesy of the members. Mention should also be made of the excellent card catalogue of Devonshire materials compiled by Mr. Burnet Morris and housed in the library of his home at Teignmouth, also available to students through the courtesy of the owner.

PRINTED SOURCES

Collections of sources from the central archives which have been published in full or in abstract help to supply the groundwork for any period with which they deal. Chief among these are the official publications of the Public Record Office: the famous Rolls Series issued under the supervision of the Master of the Rolls from 1856 to 1886 and the later publications of the *Calendars* of famous documents including the State Papers and many others which have enriched the sources available, and greatly facilitated the work of research. Particulars from these records will be found in the classified lists below, and in the footnotes.

Another collection of printed sources rich in material for the Tudor and Stuart period is the publications of the Camden Society, now carried on under the direction of the Royal Historical Society. The 232 volumes of this collection vary in usefulness for this type of subject; but as a series they have maintained increasingly high standards, and particular volumes listed below have been of inestimable value for this study. Among the printed sources drawn from local collections, largely from the collections of private libraries, should be mentioned the mass of material, usually in the form of digests and abstracts, published in the *Reports of the Historical Manuscripts Commissions* (H.M.C.), London, 1879–1934, though it must be admitted that this material, great in volume, proved singularly disappointing in respect to materials relating to the yeomen. This was true partly because the indexes, deficient at best except for proper names, are practically useless for a study of this kind; and page by page searching proved more time-consuming than rewarding.

Another type of collection, more miscellaneous and thoroughly local in character, deserves more detailed attention; namely, the publications of the various local and antiquarian societies. Though they vary tremendously, both in content and in the character of the editing and publication, no student of social and economic history, particularly one concerned with rural society and local differences, can afford to neglect these publications, even the most unpromising appearing ones. They are not, properly speaking, collections of sources only; for they include accounts of the proceedings of the various organizations which sponsor them, and many articles, chiefly by local historians and antiquarians, on a variety of subjects. But imbedded in this miscellany, or occupying the space of an entire volume, or more than one, is a large body of source material that is available in no other place. An almost complete list of the societies at present active, with their current publications, is available in *The Official Year-Book of the Scientific and Learned Societies of Great Britain and Ireland* (C. Griffin, London). Many of the older files of societies now defunct are also well worth consultation. These are pretty well covered in the sections on local history in Gross, Read, Davies, and other standard bibliographies. Among the outstanding collections of the local societies may be mentioned:

Archæologia Cantiana, Kent Archæological Society Publications, London, 1858–1942.

Historical and Literary Remains of Lancaster and Chester, Chetham Society Publications, London and Manchester, 1844–1942.

Norfolk Archæology, Norfolk Archæological Society Publications, Norwich, 1847–1942.

Publications of the Northamptonshire Record Society, Kettering and Lincoln, 1924–42.

Publications of the Surtees Society, Durham, 1835–1942.

Publications of the Sussex Record Society, Lewes and Cambridge, 1902–42.

Reports and Transactions of the Devonshire Association for the Advancement of Science, Literature and Art, Plymouth and Exeter, 1862–1942.

Staffordshire Historical Collections, Staffordshire Record Society Publications (formerly known as William Salt Archæological Society), Birmingham and London, 1880–1942.

Sussex Archæological Collections, Sussex Archæological Society Publications, Lewes, 1846–1942.

Yorkshire Archæological Collections, Yorkshire Archæological Society Publications, York, 1885–1942.

But many others have proved valuable as the footnotes and the following classified lists will show.

CLASSIFIED ANALYSIS OF SOURCES

None of the above collections either general or local deals exclusively with the yeoman. Pertinent matter has been found in all of them; but certain classes of documents which have proved much richer than others may be singled out as basic material for this and kindred subjects. The following classification is based on this distinction, the items selected for illustration being drawn from both the manuscript and printed collections above and from independent manuscript or printed works.

Works of Contemporary Historians and Chorographers

Writings of this type usually serve two purposes: to describe the topography of the country with the principal occupational pursuits of the people, including the industries and products of each region; and to furnish some kind of analysis of the social structure, offering sometimes meager, sometimes full and illuminating passages on the various classes of society. Significant among the books which deal with the country as a whole are:

William Camden, *Britannia or a Chorographical Description of the Flourishing Kingdoms of England, Scotland and Wales and the Islands Adjacent,* London, 1695.

Edward Chamberlayne, *Angliae Notitia; or The Present State of England,* London, 1669.

Michael Drayton, *Poly-Olbion: a Chorographical Description of All the Tracts, Rivers, Mountains, Forests, and Other Parts of This Renowned Isle of Great Britain,* in *Works of Michael Drayton,* IV, J. Hebel, Oxford, 1933.

Thomas Gainsford, *The Glory of England,* London, 1618.

William Harrison, *An Historical Description of the Iland of Britaine,* New Shakspere Society, London, 1908.

Gregory King, *Natural and Political Observations and Conclusions upon the State and Condition of England,* G. Barnett, Baltimore, 1936.

Sir William Petty, *Political Arithmetick or a Discourse Concerning the Extent and Value of Lands, People, Buildings, Husbandry, &c.,* C. Hull, Cambridge, 1899.

Sir Thomas Smyth, *De republica Anglorum, or a Discourse on the Commonwealth of England,* London, 1589, 1906.

Thomas Wilson, *The State of England Anno Dom. 1600.* State

Papers, F. J. Fisher, ed., Camden Society Publications, LII, London, 1936.

Of even greater value in many instances than the above general works are those of local chorographers and historians. Written by members of the local gentry whose pride in their class and county is apparent throughout, these works are often discursive and chatty to a discouraging degree. But their authors knew the regions of which they wrote, and some of them were not only actuated by a genuine desire to give as complete a picture as possible of their respective localities but had considerable skill with which to execute the task.

Devon was particularly blessed with native sons ready to make their county known to the rest of England and perchance to the outside world. In Thomas Westcote, *A View of Devonshire in 1630,* Exeter, 1845, we have perhaps the best description of the county and its social classes. But another book written in the same year by Tristram Risdon, *A Survey of the County of Devon, 1630,* London, 1714, is well worth consulting. Thomas Hooker, "Synopsis Chronographical of Devonshire in 1599," has never been published in full, but valuable extracts are reprinted in the *Devonshire Transactions,* XLVII, W. J. Blake, ed., Exeter, 1915. Kent was not as prolific of local historians as Devon, but no book of its kind excels the work of William Lambard, *The Perambulation of Kent,* London, 1656, first published in 1576. Agrarian conditions and social classes in East Anglia in the reign of James I are dealt with in Robert Reyce, *Breviary of Suffolk,* London, 1902. A brief report on the state of Northamptonshire in 1614 is in the Manuscripts of the Duke of Buccleuch, *H.M.C.,* III, 1926; and William Webb's *Description of Cheshire,* in 1621, was published in the work of D. King, *The Vale Royal,* London, 1656. Valuable also on the topography of the country and for manorial relationships and agricultural conditions are John Norden's descriptions of certain counties. Though an Essex man, Norden's work as surveyor took him into various localities where keen powers of observation were used to advantage. His following "Descriptions," given in the order in which they were written, are well worth consulting:

A Delineation of Northampton in the Year 1610, London, 1720.
The Description of Hertfordshire, London, 1598.
A Description of Middlesex, London, 1593.
An Historical and Chorographical Description of Essex, Camden Society Publications, London, 1840.

A Topographical and Historical Description of Cornwall, London, 1728.

Sometimes foreigners traveling to another country make pertinent observations that are omitted by native writers because they concern facts or practices taken for granted. Visitors to England often commented especially on the position of the commoners. A valuable work of this type is Thomas Platter's *Travels in England,* C. Williams, London, 1937. Extracts from the works of various foreign visitors are to be found in *England As Seen by Foreigners in the Days of Elizabeth and James the First,* W. B. Rye, London, 1865. Other extracts are reprinted in Harrison's *Description of England,* Appendix II.

Tenurial Treatises, Manorial Records, Rentals, etc.

Although Tudor and Stuart landholders were becoming more independent of manorial control, the manorial organization was still an active factor in agrarian life. Variations in manorial practice were rather the rule than the exception, but contemporary manuals containing general theories, principles, and practices held proper in manorial management are worth consideration. Among the best of these are three printed by the Manorial Society:

Anonymous, *A Fac-Simile Reproduction of the Order of Keeping a Court Leet,* London, 1914.
Anonymous, *A Mannor and Court Baron,* N. Howe, London, 1909.
Sir Charles Calthorpe, *The Relation betweene the Lord of a Mannor and the Coppy-Holder His Tenant,* London, 1917.

The standard legal contemporary authority on tenure was Sir Edward Coke whose work is important, particularly *The Institutes,* II, London, 1797; and *The Compleat Copyholder,* London, 1719. But legal suits show that many practices were outrunning the legal formulae that defined them; hence the needed corrective for Coke and the form manuals are the court records themselves and such cases as were written down in the *Law Reports* by judges and students of the law. Since this material is also a valuable source for much that is not connected with the land or tenure, it is treated below in a separate classification.

Indispensable are the books of certain men whose own experience as trained surveyors, or legal and semilegal advisers, equipped them to discuss tenurial problems. Best among these works is that of John Norden, *The Surveyors Dialogue,* London, 1618. Though usually the employee of the landlord, Norden saw things also from the tenant's point of view, and along with a good deal of preachment and pious advice has given a wealth of information about existing conditions. Less good, but of some use, is the earlier work of John Fitzherbert, *Surveying*, London, 1539, still quoted as an authority in the seventeenth century; and the work of Aaron Rathborne, *The Surveyor, in foure bookes*, London, 1616.

The fact that manorial rolls list tenants in terms of their tenure rather than by status restricts their usefulness because of the difficulty of isolating evidence for a particular class. Surveys, extents, and customs, however, reveal much that is of importance to the yeomen, and records of this type abound. Important among those in the P.R.O. are the "Miscellaneous Books," Series I, XXXVII–LII; and "Rentals and Surveys," CCVII–CCCCXXXV, both in the records of the Exchequer. Many collections in the B.M. are rich in manorial records. Among those dealing with manors of specific localities may be mentioned the following: Bedfordshire, Add. MSS. 38065; Berks and Oxford, Lansd. MSS. 105; Chester, Harl. MSS. 2010; Durham and Notts, Add. MSS. 36981; Somerset, Eg. MSS. 2223; Sussex, Add. MSS. 497; and Warwick, Add. MSS. 36909. "Views and Surveys" of manors in Cornwall, Devon, Dorset, Somerset, Stafford, and Wiltshire are in the Harl. MSS. 71. And particularly interesting are Norden's surveys of Prince Charles's manors in the year 1617, Add. MSS. 6027.

Local collections notable for their manorial records are the Exeter MSS.; the Bedford county records; the MSS. of the Northampton Record Society; and those of the York Archæological Society. But practically all of the local collections, both manuscript and printed, contain some, often a great many, manorial records. Unique in some of its information and interesting for the comments of the author who was for twenty-five years steward of the manors he describes, is the *Book of John Rowe*, W. Godfrey, ed., Sussex Record Society Publications, XXXIV, Lewes, 1928. Another illuminating record, including material on fifteen Sussex manors and reproductions of contemporary manorial maps, is *The Buckhurst Terrier, 1597–1598*, E. Straker, ed., Sussex Record Society Publications, XXXIX, Lewes, 1933. The manors of the hundred of Berkeley in Gloucestershire at the time of James I are described in the inimitable style of John Smyth of Nibley, for forty years steward of the hundred, in *Lives of the Berkeleys*, III, J. Maclean, Gloucester, 1885. Documentary material for a large group of Suffolk manors is printed in W. A. Copinger, *Manors of*

Suffolk, I–VII, London, 1905–1912. And similar material for manors in the border country is in the *History of Northumberland,* I–XIII, M. Dodds, Newcastle, 1893–1933. Scores of works containing manorial records up to 1660 are listed in M. F. Moore, *Two Select Bibliographies of Medieval Historical Study,* London, 1912; and many are included in other standard bibliographies. References to manorial records that have been reprinted in the local historical publications will be found in the footnotes of this study.

Deeds, leases, and other documents pertaining to land conveyance are also rich in information concerning land values, the nature of holdings, rents, and the like. There are thousands of these documents in existence, but their cumbersome form and lengthy legal phraseology make their use in large numbers a slow process. Better than most materials, however, they can be reduced to abstracts and digests without loss of the essentials. And the process of calendaring and abstracting is going on apace in many English archives. The excellent typescript calendar of the large collection in the Exeter library, known as "Exeter Deeds and Documents," is a good example. Staffordshire deeds calendared as the "Salt Charters" are in the MSS. of the William Salt Library at Stafford. Work of a similar kind is being done with the large collection in the Bedford county records; and to some extent it is being carried forward in practically every locality. The local historical society publications contain many reprints of such abstracts. Representative collections of these, including bonds, leases, etc., are in the following publications:

Bradford Historical and Antiquarian Society *Publications,* Series II, Pts. 1–3, W. Robertshaw, Bradford, 1931–36.
Gloucestershire Notes and Queries, VI, Gloucester, 1899.
Kent Records, VII, London, 1922.
Somerset and Dorset Notes and Queries, IX, Sherborne, 1905.
Sussex Record Society *Publications,* XXIX, W. Budgen, Lewes, 1925.
Transactions of the Cumberland and Westmoreland Antiquarian Society, New Series, XIV, XXXVIII, Kendal, 1914, 1938.
Yorkshire Archæological Society *Publications,* L, LXIII, LXV, LXIX, CII, York.

Another class of document which employs the status term, thereby enabling one to identify the lands of yeomen, is the Post-Mortem Inquisitions (P.M.I.) that were taken on all lands held of the Crown by knight service. As a key to land values they are wholly untrustworthy like the records of real estate assessments in our own age, and the acreages given are also open to question. But there is still information to be had from them regarding land measures in different localities, the nature of holdings, the character of nominal rents, etc. Abstracts of Gloucester and Wiltshire inquisitions for the period are in *The Index Library*, XXI, XXIII, London, 1893, 1897. And P.M.I. manuscripts for all counties are in the records of the Chancery in the Record Office (C. 142).

Books on Husbandry, and Other Treatises Relating to the Care of the Land and Its Cultivation

The late Elizabethan period, and particularly the age of the Stuarts, witnessed a vast amount of interest in improved husbandry and produced a great number of treatises from the pens of the "improvers," forerunners of the agrarian developments of the next century. These writers indulged in a great deal of plagiarizing; whole sections being the same in various books with rarely any indication that it is borrowed material. Some of their suggestions are practical; many are fantastic in the light of modern scientific knowledge. Their chief value lies in the fact that contemporary conditions and farming practices were often discussed in relation to the innovations which the authors wished to introduce. The British Museum, the Huntington Library, the Goldsmiths' Library in London, and the small but well-selected library of the Royal Agricultural Society in London have rich collections of early editions. But most of the works went through many editions and are not rare. Best known in their own day and perhaps still, are the works of Thomas Tusser, Barnabie Googe, Gervase Markham, and Samuel Hartlib. These are listed in Read, Davies, and other standard bibliographies. Examples of additional works used for this study are the following:

Walter Blith, *The English Improver Improved,* or *The Survey of Husbandry Surveyed,* London, 1649.

Thomas Hill, *The proffitable Arte of Gardeninge, etc., to which is annexed three treatises: The marveilous gouernmente . . . of the Bees . . . ., the yearly conjectures meete for husbandmen to knowe, and Arte of Graffing and planting of Trees,* London, 1572.

William Lawson, *A New Orchard and Garden,* London, 1618.

Leonard Mascall, *The Government of Cattell,* London, 1627.

Gabriel Plattes, *Practical Husbandry Improv'd,* London, 1639.

Other titles will be noted in the footnotes. Special bibliographies of the works on husbandry are the "Chronological List of Agricultural Writers Down to 1700," in Lord Ernle, *English Farming, Past and Present,* Appendix I, London, 1927, and D. MacDonald, *Agricultural Writers from Sir Walter Henley to Arthur Young,* London, 1908.

Contemporary opinion on the inclosure movement is included in most of the above books on husbandry, though a considerable literature grew up about that subject alone (consult Read and Davies). The tendency as the seventeenth century progressed was toward approval rather than disapproval, particularly among the writers on husbandry; but diatribes against the movement continued to be published at intervals. Examples are:

J. Moore, *The Crying Sin of England of Not Caring for the Poor, Wherein Inclosures . . . is Arraigned,* etc., London, 1653.

R. Powell, *Depopulation Arraigned, and Condemned by the Lawes of God and Man,* etc., London, 1636.

F. Trigge, *The Humble Petition of Two Sisters: the Church and Commonwealth,* London, 1868.

Typical of the treatises in favor of inclosures are:

Joseph Lee, *Vindication of a Regulated Enclosure,* etc., London, 1656.

Adam Moore, *Bread for the Poor . . . Promised by Enclosure of the Wastes and Common Grounds of England,* London, 1653.

S. Taylor, *Common Good: or the Improvement of Commons, Forests and Chases by Inclosure,* London, 1652.

Two books in particular should be mentioned for their treatment of farming activities in particular localities: Henry Best's *Farming Book* or *Rural Economy in Yorkshire in 1641,* Surtees Society Publications, XXXIII, Durham, 1857, a detailed description of farming methods and interests among the minor gentry and yeomen of the East Riding of Yorkshire; and *Robert Loder's Farm Accounts, 1610–1620,* Camden Society Publications, 3d Series, LIII, London, 1936, an itemized account of the yearly expenditures, profits, and losses of a Berkshire farmer. Interspersed among Loder's accounts are his own shrewd comments on his progress and failures— a rich source, with an excellent critical introduction by G. E. Fussell, himself a specialist in agrarian history.

Excellent among the sources for grain prices are the reports in the State Papers, submitted by local officials to the Privy Council when years of dearth made the corn supply a matter of national concern, or bountiful harvests brought petitions for a lessening of export regulations. Examples are S.P. 14, XL, CXXX, CXXXI, CXXXVIII, CXLII, CXLIII, and S.P. 16, XLV, CXII, CLXXVI, CLXXXIV, CCIII. Consult indexes of the *Calendars of State Papers* for the reigns of Elizabeth, James I, and Charles I. The fluctuation of prices in the period is best shown by a continuous file of records. Excellent for this purpose in the field of livestock prices are the records of the horse and cattle sales at Shrewsbury Fair in the manuscripts at the town hall in Shrewsbury. They span the period from the mid-sixteenth to mid-seventeenth century and give the status and locality of the buyer as well as the prices he paid. The Beveridge Committee of the International Price Commission has data on other such files, including prices of both livestock and farm produce. Some of this is published in their first volume: *Prices and Wages in England from the Twelfth to the Nineteenth Centuries,* London, 1939. Their unpublished files are available to students upon request.

Court Records, Local and National, and Law Reports

Basic material for any study of rural society in the Elizabethan and Stuart period are the records of the court of quarter sessions. They have contributed in some way to practically every chapter of this book. They include presentments, indictments, orders of court, reports of parish officials, jury panels, minutes of court meetings, and examinations of witnesses on every conceivable aspect of life in the rural community. Their publication, therefore, on a fairly large scale, is a boon to the student of social and economic history as well as to the historian of local administration, and marks one of the most laudable achievements of the local historical societies who have sponsored most of the publications of the sessions records. Some records for the Elizabethan and early Stuart period, either in full or in abstract, have been published from the sessions records of fifteen counties; but the publications differ in the quantity of material published, and to some extent in the quality of the editing. The following are examples of some of the better publications:

Calendar of Quarter Sessions Papers, 1591–1643, in *Worcestershire County Records,* Pts. I–II, J. Willis Bund, Worcester, 1899–1900.

Middlesex Sessions Rolls, 1550–1689, in *Middlesex County Records,* I–IV, J. Jeaffreson, London, 1886–92.

Notes and Extracts from the Sessions Rolls, 1581–1698, in *Hertford County Records*, I, W. Hardy, Hertford, 1905.

Quarter Sessions Records of the County of Northampton, 1630, 1657–58, J. Wake, ed., Northamptonshire Record Society Publications, I, Hertford, 1924.

Quarter Sessions Records of the North Riding of Yorkshire, J. Atkinson, ed., North Riding Record Society Publications.

Staffordshire Quarter Sessions Rolls, S. Burne, ed., William Salt Archæological Society Publications, I–III, Kendal, 1931–36.

At least four large manuscript collections of sessions records, rich in material for the Elizabethan and early Stuart period, merit mention: the Chester sessions records at the Castle, Chester, dating from 1559, including many volumes of "Quarter Sessions Books," with the usual indictments, orders, etc., and a large collection of "Quarter Sessions Files" relating to the administrative work of the sessions; the Devon sessions records at the Castle, Exeter, with beautifully preserved Minute Books dating from 1592, and dozens of bundles of depositions covering the late sixteenth and early seventeenth centuries; the rich Essex sessions records at the shire hall, Chelmsford, dating from 1556, which include, in addition to the splendid series of Sessions Rolls that have recently been calendared, a large body of Sessions Papers, as yet only roughly classified; and the large collection of Norfolk sessions papers at the shire hall, Norwich, second to none in interest and value but woefully in need of attention and of adequate indexing or other classification. Scattering selected excerpts from the Chester and Devon records have been published, but the greater part of the ore there is yet unmined, as is wholly the case for the Essex and Norfolk collections.

A well-preserved series of Minute Books dating from 1603, of which only a few excerpts have been published, is in the Nottingham sessions records at the shire hall, Nottingham. And a smaller but interesting collection of the Lindsay sessions records are at the shire hall, Lincoln, especially good for showing the plight of the agricultural laborer in the reign of Charles I. Wage schedules, not unique but rare enough to merit notice and not included in most of the printed lists of wage schedules, are in the Essex sessions papers; and in a single manuscript volume at the shire hall in Dorchester, all that remains of the Dorset sessions papers prior to the eighteenth century. There is a large collection of Wiltshire sessions records for the period extant, but their usefulness is curtailed by the fact that the county offices in whose custody they remain are now at Trowbridge while the sessions records are still housed at Devizes with no provision made for opening them to the researcher. A considerable number of the Hunts sessions papers for the reign of James I and Charles I are in the British Museum, Add. MSS. 34399–34400. But for the most part the sessions records have not strayed from their original habitat.

The sessions records are important to this study not only because the yeomen often figured as culprits in the matters described therein, but because they cover also the record of their work as parish officials. Many records of that work exist also outside the sessions papers, especially in the form of the accounts kept by churchwardens, constables, overseers of the poor, and surveyors of the highways; accounts that are replete with information concerning the problems and activities of the men who set them down. Perhaps no records of this type are extant in such large quantities as are the accounts of churchwardens, many of which have been published in part or in full. E. Philips' "Bibliography of Churchwardens' Accounts Printed Prior to 1900" was published in the *English Historical Review*, XV, London, 1900. And a good survey with extracts drawn from the accounts of many parishes is the work of J. C. Cox, *Churchwardens' Accounts*, London, 1913. Excerpts abound in the county society publications, as many references in the footnotes will indicate (see especially chap. ix).

Accounts of constables, overseers of the poor, and road or bridge-wardens have been published less often than those of churchwardens, but are also fairly abundant, particularly in extracts in the local society publications and histories of particular parishes and regions. Excellent examples of records of parish officials are in the British Museum, Add. MSS. 10457, 34400, and 36981; and in the State Papers at the P.R.O., particularly S.P. 16, CXCVIII, CCCXCV, and CCCLXXXVIII. There are a good many bridge-wardens' reports in the Essex MSS. at the shire hall, Chelmsford; and some are scattered through practically all the sessions papers.

Contemporary manuals defining and elaborating the duties of parish officials were popular, and constitute one of our best sources for the principles and practice of local administration. Those most useful in this study were:

Michael Dalton, *The Country Justice*, London, 1622.
William Lambard, *The Duties of Constables, Borsholders, Tythingmen*, etc., London, 1602.

William Sheppard, *Offices and Duties of Constables,* etc., London, 1641.

Valuable as are the above records for portraying the public duties of the yeomen, their personal interests and activities are less well portrayed there than in the full and detailed records of the national courts. The records of the Court of Star Chamber and the Court of Requests were mentioned in the above collections. A further word of their specific nature is pertinent, for they constitute a field that the social and economic historian is only beginning to work; yet one almost unexcelled in richness and variety. Yeomen figured in large numbers both as principals and witnesses in the *bill,* the *reponsio,* and the *depositions* of these cases. Since it was customary to record testimony as nearly verbatim as possible, the depositions provide one of the few sources where they and their kind talk in their own way concerning things that affect them and their neighbors. Many records in the Court of Chancery, the Court of the Exchequer, etc., contain similar material, but as stated above, their usefulness is curtailed by the lack of a status index.

The *Law Reports,* brief digests of court cases and of precedents set by them, though of less value because they rarely describe a person by his status term, are nevertheless worth consulting, particularly in tenurial matters and for disputes involving parish officials. The following are good examples of those which have been printed:

Edward Bulstrode, *Reports of Cases in the Court of King's Bench in the reigns of James I and Charles I,* London, 1688.
John Godbolt, *Reports of Cases arising in the severall courts in the raignes of Q. Elizabeth, K. James and the late King Charles,* London, 1653.
John March, *Reports on new cases in the King's Bench and the Court of Common Pleas,* London, 1675.

Diaries, Journals, and Commonplace Books

Unique in this class of material is the *Diary and Family Book of Robert Furse, yeoman,* 1593, published in part in *Devonshire Transactions,* XXVI, H. Carpenter, Plymouth, 1894. Written primarily to provide an exact record of the family lands in Devon, it reveals more of the author and his outlook on life than do most of the personal narratives left by yeomen. Another record kept by a

Devon yeoman, or rather by several, for it is more in the nature of a family commonplace book, is the Diary and Household Account Book of the Roberts family of Stockleigh Pomeroy, 1622–46. The manuscript is at present in the ownership of Maj. Edward Chanter of Barnstaple. Obviously the work of unlettered men, the Roberts diary is filled with accounts of the daily small concerns of country-folk. Another unpublished journal or commonplace book of an Elizabethan yeoman with considerably more education is the *"Hypomnema"* of Simon Rider of Staffordshire, the original of which is in the William Salt Library, Stafford. In addition to much personal data, it contains copies of petitions, bonds, and contracts of various kinds that Rider drew up for his neighbors. Likewise the work of a yeoman with a fair degree of education is the diary of Adam Eyre: *A Dyurnall, or Catalogue of all my Accions and Expenses,* etc., in *Yorkshire Diaries,* Surtees Society Publications, LXV, Durham, 1877. Eyre was a yeoman of the West Riding who rose to a captaincy under Fairfax. The diary depicts his activities and those of his neighbors after his return from the army, 1646–48. Other personal accounts of yeomen of somewhat less value are:

"Account Book of Richard Bax, a Surrey Yeoman, 1648–1662," *Gleanings After Time,* G. L. Apperson, London, 1907.

An Anglesey Farmer's Diary, 1629–1636, anonymous MS. in the national library of Wales.

"Book of Accompts and Remembrances by William Honiwell, yeoman, 1596–1614," *The Western Times,* Exeter, October, 1832— February, 1833.

In addition to the above accounts, at least three other narratives written by sons of yeomen who were university-trained and later entered the church, should be mentioned for the light they throw on the early home life of the authors:

Autobiography of Richard Baxter, J. Thomas, London, 1925.

Life of Adam Martindale, R. Parkinson, ed., Chetham Society Publications, 1st Series, IV, London, 1845.

Ralph Josselyn's Diary, 1616–83, E. Hockliffe, ed., Camden Society Publications, 3d Series, XV, London, 1908.

Only the early part of the works of Baxter and Martindale is relevant. But Josselyn was throughout his life half-yeoman, half-parson, and his diary is a storehouse of information on the life of both.

Wills and Inventories

Like the diaries and other personal accounts listed above, the wills of yeomen, and inventories of their household possessions, give clues to the personal side of their lives, their homes, possessions, and standard of living. In addition to the large collection at Somerset House, hundreds of wills covering the Elizabethan and Stuart period are housed in district probate registries. Many of these are restricted in use for a study of this kind because there is no status index. Such an index is available however for the excellent collections in the probate registries at Lewes, Lincoln, and York. Inventories for the period are by no means as numerous as wills, but there is a large manuscript collection in the Lincoln probate registry, and useful smaller collections are in the Bedford county manuscripts, and in the Suffolk manuscripts at the public library, Ipswich. Individual wills and inventories have been printed in full in many family papers in the publications of the local societies and elsewhere; and series of abstracts of both types of documents have been frequently published. A good deal is usually lost in the abstracting, but some are full digests with the contents carefully selected. Examples are: *Lincolnshire Wills,* I–II, A. Maddison, Lincoln, 1888–91, with good critical introduction; four volumes of Lancashire and Cheshire wills in the Chetham Society Publications, XXVIII, XXXIII, LI, LIV, Manchester, 1857–61; and eight volumes of wills and inventories of the northern counties in the Surtees Society Publications, II, XXVI, XXXVIII, CIV, CX, CXII, CXXI, CXLII, Durham, 1835–1929.

Subsidy Rolls, Muster Rolls, and Impressments

The bulk of both muster and subsidy rolls gives but limited aid to the student of social classes because they do not give the status term of persons appearing on the rolls. Exceptions in both cases, however, merit attention. The muster roll for Gloucestershire in 1608, published as *Men and Armour for Gloucestershire in 1608,* London, 1902, and an unpublished roll for the eastern division of Northamptonshire in the reign of Charles I, in the State Papers (S.P. 16, Case E 15), give the status terms for the majority of those enrolled. The same is true of the subsidy rolls of Bedfordshire for 36 Elizabeth (E. 179, 72/212–215). Though of little value for determining the wealth of the yeomen, since tax assessments are rarely made according to full value of property, the subsidy rolls nevertheless furnish a key to the relative support given the state by the various classes. And all three of the above rolls offer interesting information regarding the occupational character of the respective counties. An analysis of the Bedfordshire rolls is in preparation. See articles listed below for Mr. Tawney's analysis of the Gloucestershire muster roll.

The returns for military impressments of fifty or a hundred men each from the various counties, as their services were required in army or navy, unlike the muster rolls, usually give the status or occupation of the persons impressed. Interesting lists for the reigns of James I and Charles I are in the State Papers (see S.P. 14, CLXXIX, and S.P. 16, LXXII, LXXV, LXXVII, LXXVIII, LXXXI, CCCCXVIII). For additional information regarding musters, trained bands, etc., consult Add. MSS. 34217, 39245; also, *Papers Relating to Musters, Beacons, Subsidies,* etc., in Northampton Record Society Publications, III, Northampton, 1926. The names of those subject to benevolences and forced loans often appear in the State Papers with the status of the person and the amount for which he is assessed given (consult indexes in the *Calendars of the State Papers Domestic*). Additional references to this material are in the footnotes.

Plays, Sermons, and Other Literary Sources

No student of the history of social classes can afford to ignore the popular literature of his period. The writing of "Characters" was popular among the Elizabethans and if their portrayals of the social types about them need often the corrective of other data, they are not without value. Interesting sketches of the yeoman are in the following works:

John Earle, *Micro-Cosmographie,* Westminster, 1895.

Thomas Fuller, *The Holy State and the Profane State,* M. Walten, New York, 1938.

Sir Thomas Overbury, *The Mirror of Character,* Percy Reprints, XIII, Oxford, 1936.

John Taylor, *A Brood of Cormorants,* in *Works of John Taylor, the Water Poet, to 1630,* London, 1872.

See also Gwendolyn Murphy, *Bibliography of English Character-Books, 1608–1700,* London, 1925.

Sermons of the period are well worth consulting for contemporary attitudes on social and economic questions. Of special use in this study were the Rev. Nathaniel Newbury's *The Yeoman's Prerogative,* London, 1652, preached to "the yeomen and farmers of

Kent"; and three sermons preached by the Rev. Charles Fitz-Geffrie before the general sessions in Cornwall, and later published as *The Curse of Corn-horders with the Blessing of Seasonable Selling,* London, 1631.

Few among the literary sources are more rewarding than the plays. Frequently those works that are poorest in literary merit prove the richest for social history. Typical of plays helpful for this study are the following:

Anonymous, *George A'Greene, The Pinner of Wakefield,* Malone Society Reprints, London, 1911.

Anonymous, *A Knack to Know a Knave,* Tudor Facsimile Texts, LXII, London, 1911.

Anonymous, *Two Wise Men and All the Rest Fools,* Tudor Facsimile Texts, CXXXIII, London, 1913.

Anonymous, *Wily Beguiled,* Tudor Facsimile Texts, CXLV, London, 1912.

John Day (sometimes attributed to Chettle and Day), *The Blind Beggar of Bednal Green with the merry humor of Tom Strowd the Norfolk Yeoman,* Tudor Facsimile Texts, VII, London, 1914.

T. Dekker, J. Ford, W. Rowley, *The Witch of Edmonton,* Mermaid Series, London, 1894.

Thomas Tompkis, *Albumazar,* London, 1634.

Other titles will be found in the footnotes. Ballads are worth reading. Ballads relating to Kentish yeomen are printed in *A Kentish Garland,* Devayne, London, 1881. Standard collections should also be consulted. Literary works of a general nature that throw light on economic and social conditions are too numerous to mention. But the student of social classes will do well to consult such works as those of Nicholas Breton, Robert Crowley, Henry Peacham, and John Taylor. Many miscellaneous works of a literary or semi-literary nature by less well-known authors contribute a variety of information concerning attitudes and activities of the times. They deal with everything from practical matters like food, diet, and health, to manners and morals and the state of the nation. Only a few titles can be given to show the wealth of this type of literature (unless otherwise indicated they were published in London):

Anonymous, *The Institution of a Gentleman,* 1586.

Andrew Borde, *The Boke for to Lerne a Man to be Wyse in Buildyng of his Howse for the Helth of his Body,* 1540(?).

Richard Brathwaite, *The English Gentleman: Containing Sundry Excellent Rules*, 1630.

—— *The English Gentlewoman Drawne out to the Full Body*, 1631.

Walter Cary, *The Present State of England*, 1627.

Sir Robert Cotton, *Danger Wherein the Kingdom Now Standeth*, 1628.

T. Dawson, *The Good Huswife's Jewell*, 1610.

Richard Eburne, *A Plain Pathway to Plantations*, 1624.

Sir John Ferne, *The Blazon of Gentrie*, 1586.

J. Ferrarius, *Touchinge the Good Orderynge of a Common Weale*, 1559.

Sir J. Fortescue, *The Governance of England*, 1885.

—— *The Laws of England*, 1616.

Thomas Gataker, *A Good Wife God's Gift*, 1623.

William Gouge, *Domesticall Duties*, 1634.

Maurice Kyffin, *The Blessedness of Brytaine*, 1587.

Francis Markham, *The Booke of Honour*, 1625.

Oxinden Letters, ed., D. Gardiner, 1933.

Sir Hugh Platt, *Delightes for Ladies*, 1609.

C. Pyrrye, *The Praise and Dispraise of Women*, 1569(?).

Barnabie Rich, *The Excellency of Good Women*, 1613.

—— *Roome for a Gentleman*, 1608.

Thomas Smith, *The Art of Gunnerie*, 1600.

—— *Briefe Treatise to Prove the Necessitie and Excellence of Archerie*, 1596.

John Stockwood, *A Bartholomew Fairing for Parents*, 1589.

E. Tilney, *A Brief and Pleasant Discourse of Duties in Mariage*, 1568.

George Whetstone, *The English Myrrour*, 1586.

SECONDARY WORKS

Although it has stemmed chiefly from the sources, this task could scarcely have been undertaken without the aid of numerous scholars whose works have helped in the interpretation of the sources and furnished necessary groundwork for an understanding of the period. On the legal side two works, the well-known classic of Sir Frederick Pollock and Frederic W. Maitland, *The History of English Law*, I–II, Cambridge, 1911; and Sir William Holdsworth, *A History of English Law*, III–V, London, 1922–24, are indispensable. Pollock and Maitland deal with the medieval structure on which Tudor and Stuart land law still rested; and Holdsworth is particularly valuable because he takes account of the effect of contemporary agrarian changes on legal practices. The best analysis of those changes is the work of R. H. Tawney, *The Agrarian Problem in the Sixteenth Century,* London, 1912. Though less concerned with the yeomen than the smaller copyholder, it is an admirable presentation of the changing agrarian pattern that affected all landholders. The best account, though a brief one, of local government for the period is Edward P. Cheyney, *A History of England from the Defeat of the Armada to the Death of Elizabeth; with an Account of English Institutions during the Later Sixteenth and Early Seventeenth Centuries,* II, New York, 1926. Though its emphasis is on the period after 1689, the splendid work on local government by Sidney and Beatrice Webb has also much for the earlier period: *English Local Government from the Revolution to the Municipal Corporations Act, 1689–1835,* I–V, London, 1926–29. Both Cheyney and the Webbs are dealing with the broader aspects of local government, and with the country as a whole. The best analyses of its operation in specific localities are the critical introductions to the published quarter-sessions records listed above.

Farming methods, animal husbandry, and the like are best dealt with in the work of R. Prothero (Lord Ernle), *English Farming Past and Present,* London, 1922, 1927; and in the articles of G. E. Fussell noted below. The classic discussions of Edwin F. Gay and I. S. Leadam are still basic material for the inclosure movement. Their works and those of other writers on that subject are well noted in the standard bibliographies. Significant for its approach from the point of view of practical farming and the physical features of the land rather than from the conventional constitutional and legal side, is the work of C. S. and C. S. Orwin, *The Open Fields,* Oxford, 1938. Useful also for the general problem of the small landowner is A. H. Johnson, *The Disappearance of the Small Landowner,* Oxford, 1909.

Authorities in many fields have been valuable for certain aspects of the subject. Examples of such works are:

Sir William Ashley, *The Bread of Our Forefathers,* Oxford, 1928.
W. Crump and G. Ghorbal, *History of the Huddersfield Woollen Industry,* Huddersfield, 1925.
F. C. Dietz, *English Public Finance, 1558–1641,* New York, 1932.
H. L. Gray, *English Field Systems,* Harvard Historical Studies, XII, Cambridge, 1915.

Herbert Heaton, *Yorkshire Woollen and Worsted Industries,* Oxford Historical and Literary Studies, X, Oxford, 1920.

J. U. Nef, *The Rise of the British Coal Industry,* I–II, London, 1932.

Bertha Putnam, *The Enforcement of the Statute of Labourers,* in Columbia Studies in History, Economics and Public Law, XXXII, New York, 1908.

E. Straker, *Wealden Iron,* London, 1931.

R. G. Usher, *The Presbyterian Movement in the Reign of Queen Elizabeth,* etc., Camden Society Publications, London, 1905.

George Wiebe, *Zur Geschichte der Preisrevolution des XVI und XVII Jahrhunderts,* Leipsic, 1895.

Adequate material on the sixteenth- and seventeenth-century farmhouse is not plentiful. Best, on the whole, are the works in the *Minor Domestic Architecture of England Series,* edited by D. Morand. The work of L. Ambler, *Old Halls and Manor Houses of Yorkshire,* London, 1913, contains a number of excellent plates of houses built by seventeenth-century yeomen. Also worth consulting is M. Briggs, *Homes of the Pilgrim Fathers in England and America,* Oxford, 1932.

Histories of families who rose from yeoman status are pertinent. Many of these are still in unwritten form in family papers, and scattered documents in the county society publications. Examples of some that have been published are:

P. W. Adams, *A History of the Adams Family of North Stafford,* London, 1914.

D. S. Boutflower, *The Boutflower Book, a History of an English Middle Class Family from 1303–1930,* Newcastle-upon-Tyne, 1930.

Sir George Sitwell, *The Hurts of Haldworth,* Oxford, 1930.

A. C. Wood, *Memorials of the Holles Family,* Camden Society Publications, 3d Series, LV, London, 1937.

Mary Frear, "Personnel of the Long Parliament" (MS. in preparation), supplied helpful information concerning several yeoman families.

The histories of special regions, parishes, and villages are also of value. Many of these are noted in the footnotes; others are listed in standard bibliographies. Good examples are the following:

N. S. B. Gras, *The Economic and Social History of an English Village,* Cambridge, Mass., 1930.

R. Hine, *The History of Hitchin*, I–II, London, 1927–29.

C. M. Hoare, *The History of an East Anglian Soke*, Bedford, 1918.

R. Lennard, *Rural Northamptonshire under the Commonwealth,* in Oxford Studies in Legal and Social History, IV, Oxford, 1916.

A. Ruston and D. Whitney, *Hooton Pagnell, the Agricultural Evolution of a Yorkshire Village,* London, 1934.

G. H. Tupling, *The Economic History of Rossendale,* Manchester, 1927.

W. Willcox, *Gloucestershire in the Seventeenth Century,* New Haven, 1940.

Four unpublished theses have contributed to my study:

T. C. Caldwell, "Devonshire from the Accession of Queen Elizabeth until the Civil Wars," MS. in the Yale University Library.

D. Mead, "Education of Women and Girls in England in the Time of the Tudors," MS. in the Library of the University of London.

T. C. Mendenhall, "The Shrewsbury Drapers and the Welsh Cloth Trade," in process of publication by the Yale University Press.

J. Spratt, "Agrarian Conditions in Suffolk and Norfolk, 1600–1650," MS. in Library of the University of London.

Articles and other periodical material have often proved valuable. Special mention should be made of the admirable brief study of W. Crump, "The Yeoman Clothier in the Seventeenth Century," *The Bradford Antiquary,* New Series, V, Bradford, 1932 (since published also in booklet form); A. and R. Tawney, "An Occupational Census of the Seventeenth Century," *Economic History Review,* V, 1934, admirable statistical analysis of the Gloucestershire muster roll of 1608 (see above); and the articles of G. E. Fussell which have appeared in various historical and agricultural publications. Most helpful for this study is Fussell's "Farming Methods in the Early Stuart Period," *Journal of Modern History,* VI, 1935. An extremely able treatment of the market situation in the London area is that of F. J. Fisher, "Development of the London Food Market, 1540–1640," *Economic History Review,* V, 1935. References to other articles will be found in the footnotes.

Additional Notes on Some More Recent Publications

Local and national societies continue to print valuable sources. Wills, deeds, inventories, manorial records and other such documentary materials are listed in the excellent *Texts and Calendars, An Analytical Guide to Serial Publications*, edited by E. L. C. Mullins for the Royal Historical Society (London, 1958). The resumption of the publication of the Victoria County Histories under the general editorship of R. B. Pugh has already added much local material, and more is forthcoming. Wallace Notestein's *The English People on the Eve of Colonization* (New York, 1954), is a good analysis of the general social structure in the early seventeenth century, particularly of the relation of classes to each other, and their participation in public administration. A good deal of interesting material concerning the part of the yeomen and husbandmen in charitable activities is to be had from W. K. Jordan's admirable studies, the first volume of which is now in print, *Philanthropy in England, 1480–1660* (London, 1959).

The Agricultural History Society with its journal, the *Agricultural History Review*, begun in 1953, has greatly stimulated work in that field, and readers interested in land usages, farming methods and the like, will do well to consult it.

Almost everything that W. G. Hoskins has written has a bearing in some way on the theme of this book. Particularly pertinent are: *The Leicestershire Farmer in the Sixteenth Century* (Leicester, 1942), reprinted from the *Transactions* of the Leicestershire Archaeological Society, 1941–42; and published also in *Essays in Leicestershire History* (Liverpool, 1950). See also certain of the essays in W. G. Hoskins and H. P. R. Finberg, *Devonshire Studies* (London, 1952). Particularly notable also are Joan Thirsk's *Fenland Farming in the Sixteenth Century* (University of Leicester Publications, 1953); and by the same author, *English Peasant Farming: The Agrarian History of Lincolnshire* (London, 1957). The following books of G. E. Fussell, a prolific and knowledgeable writer on many aspects of the history of farming, contain pertinent chapters: *The Old English Farming Books: From Fitzherbert to Tull, 1523–1730* (London, 1947); *The English Rural Laborer* (London, 1949); *The Farmer's Tools, 1500–1900* (London, 1952); and *The English Countrywoman: A Farmhouse Social History* (in collaboration, with R. K. Fussell (London, 1953). Articles by Dr. Hoskins, Dr. Thirsk, and Mr. Fussell are to be found in *The Agricultural History Review*, and other standard historical journals.

Additional books and articles:

Barley, M. W., "Farmhouses and Cottages, 1550–1725" *Economic History Review*, Second Series, VII, 291–306 (1954–55).

Cook, Olive, and Smith, Edwin, *English Cottages and Farmhouses*, London, 1954. Many excellent photographs, and quite superior to the usual romanticized treatment of the subject.

Hole, Christina, *The English Housewife in the Seventeenth Century*, Chatto and Windus, 1953.

Habakkuk, H. J., "The Market for Monastic Property, 1539–1603", *Economic History Review*, Second Series, X, 362–380 (1958).

Kerridge, Eric, "The Movement of Rent, 1540–1640", *Ibid.* VI, 16–34 (1953).

————, "Ridge and Furrow and Agrarian History", *Ibid.* IV, 15–36 (1951).

Raglan and Fox, "Monmouthshire Houses: a study of building techniques and smaller house plans in the 15th–17th Centuries", Nat. Mus. Wales (1951).

Rich, E. E., "The Population of Elizabethan England", *Economic History Review*, II, 247–265 (1950).

INDEX